FOREWORD

ALF RAMSEY may have disliked most journalists, but this book stands on their broad shoulders. In Alf's lifetime, Fleet Street's prestige, and the enviable contact lists of football reporters, eased their access to his players and team-mates. Most of those have now died but invaluable biographies by Bowler, published just before Alf's death in 1999, and especially McKinstry from seven years later, are rich in the important interviews and gossip those players gave. So are other brilliant, broader books by Glanville (2007), Hayward (2022) and Hamilton (2023). Wherever this work draws on interviews, whether via books or newspapers, references are provided.

In contrast, this new biography of Alf Ramsey is written by an historian and researcher who, given the passage of time, has had to draw on new sources and different types of historical evidence. They have prompted some radical reinterpretations, and to make clear for readers what those are, and the arguments underpinning them, any significant evidence in each chapter is briefly referenced via endnotes. Those endnotes then tie into a comprehensive 'references' section at the back of the book. That starts by explaining the main types of historical evidence used, briefly explains how those appear as abbreviations in the endnotes, then lists all the books, articles, archive collections, websites and broadcast material upon which this biography rests.

Equally and whatever the biographical approach, or the decade it was written in, Alf's deep distrust of the media, and obsessive attitudes to privacy, make him a serious and mysterious challenge. After his 1974 England sacking and despite being short of money, he spurned lucrative publishing opportunities for an authorised biography, or autobiography. Either could have catalogued his remarkable career and would have sold in large numbers. In 1952, a brief autobiography had been published, whilst Alf was still playing, but nearly 20 years elapsed before anything else vaguely autobiographical appeared: two sets of four interviews each, in short newspaper articles. Even there he was painted as 'always reserved, reticent, thoughtful', someone who believed 'his other life is simply no one else's business' (*Sunday Mirror* 18 January 1970). Consequently, his serial interviewer admitted, Alf was known by insiders 'as the silent knight' (*Daily Mirror* 6 November 1972).

Making sense of Ramsey's silence suffuses this new biography. Despite new snippets occasionally emerging, because Alf has been dead over 25 years no secret diaries, or overlooked personal letters, now seem likely to surface. Picking up from where journalists have left off, historians therefore need to rework the existing evidence or find new sources. This book pursues both. Every chapter unearths documents previously buried in archives, places them alongside under-used historical sources, and uses the combination to question long-accepted stories surrounding Alf Ramsey and 1966. Readers are warned that this often entails citing, albeit using asterisks, the discriminatory language that 20th-century Alf grew up with and never totally escaped.

Such evidence is then analysed using modern ideas and perspectives, in ways that would have been unrecognisable in Alf's lifetime. Yet the results revolutionise our understanding. Pivotal aspects of England men's first football World Cup-winning manager have long lain unseen or unheeded. Sir Alf Ramsey, this book suggests, was a different kind of hero; not just in the past but for the present, too.

THE UNSEEN
SIR ALF
A Different Kind of Hero

GRANT BAGE

First published by Pitch Publishing, 2025

1

Pitch Publishing
9 Donnington Park,
85 Birdham Road,
Chichester, West Sussex,
PO20 7AJ
www.pitchpublishing.co.uk
info@pitchpublishing.co.uk

A CIP catalogue record is available for this book
from the British Library.

ISBN 978 1 80150 958 9

Typesetting and origination by Pitch Publishing

Printed and bound in the UK on FSC® certified paper in line
with our continuing commitment to ethical business practices,
sustainability and the environment.

Printed and bound by CPI Group (UK) Ltd, Croydon, CR0 4YY

CONTENTS

Dedication

To my wife Jane, who reads me like a book,
and without whom none of this would have
been possible.

INTRODUCTION

THANK YOU for reading this. You have picked up my book and I'm grateful. Once Alf was sure neither of us were journalists, he might feel the same and perhaps nod that wide forehead, or let a faint smile crease his lips. After years in the biographical twilight, he might even feel flattered by our interest, albeit uninvited. For, throughout his extraordinary career, he presented as unfailingly modest, painfully shy, often difficult and always hardworking. To team-mates, journalists and even friends, he seemed elusive and hard to connect with. So why re-examine such a reticent life after all these years?

Sir Alfred Ernest Ramsey (1920–99) achieved football greatness against daunting odds all whilst, for reasons this book unpicks, fiercely protecting his privacy. In stilted 1960s TV clips, Alf appears stereotypically male, ethnically pale and, compared to the youthful social revolutions breaking around him, deeply middle-aged. In the 1970s, as his professional world crashed, he grew increasingly tetchy and apparently outdated, stranded in panic under glaring studio lights. It has been claimed Alf 'hated the bloody Scottish' and that he labelled Argentinian footballers as 'animals'. His victory in 1966 became beloved by jingoists not just for England winning the World Cup, but for beating 'The Germans' to do so. This is the tabloid Sir Alf, a clichéd patron saint of suburban Little England. Should liberal modernity loathe him?

Genuinely, 'No.' Years of research have revealed an Alf Ramsey very different to the one I first glimpsed, as a small boy, watching the 1966 World Cup Final. Back then our family had enjoyed the tournament's opening matches at home in Suffolk, then listened to the semi-final on a car radio driving north to Scotland. The Portuguese had been despatched, but the next few days were fretful. Where would we watch the final?

Somehow, my Anglo-Scottish father persuaded our holiday hosts, from whom we had rented a ramshackle caravan, to lend us their front room. So, on 30 July within whitewashed stone walls, on a tiny monochrome television, we witnessed what even the Scots agreed was one hell of a game. West Germany taking the lead, losing it, then equalising in the 89th minute. The agonies of extra time. Geoff Hurst blasting a hat-trick, Nobby Stiles jigging toothless, Bobby Moore brandishing the trophy. Yet amidst the victorious mayhem sat Alf Ramsey, silent and stern: what was going on in that head?

Six decades later, this book explores that mystery. Twist by surprising twist it reconstructs who Alf Ramsey really was, who he was not, and of how he turns out to be the most surprising of leaders. Alf was famous for football, but this version of his story explores what lay beneath. It is about what racism and poverty do to people, about patience and late development, about co-operation across classes and antagonism between them. It explores psychological difference, relentless learning, sex and discretion, and how disadvantage never leaves you. Alf's story is about open-mindedness, shame, fortitude and often suffocating, stereotypically English secrecy. All life is here, I promise, even the tricky bits he tried to hide.

This book tracks not only how Alf was made for that 1966 moment but why his story from the past helps us, in the present, to face perennially difficult issues: how football fails, why history matters, what it means to be English. Because sport and Englishness and history are just local solutions to wider human puzzles, and retelling Alf Ramsey's life helps answer questions which haven't changed much since Alfred was Great and England was born. What does it mean to be you, to be me, to be *us*, to be English? What do success and happiness look like, and more importantly *what do we look* like as we strain to attain them?

Even if you, personally, are not enamoured with football as a sport, or history as a subject, or Englishness as an idea, this book asks you to be open-minded about this man. For threaded through how Alf lived his 20th-century life are issues that still matter to us now. Arguments about identities and minorities, social justice, whether patriotism can be positive, sport should be fair, personal greed is wrong, hard work is good for you and, crucially, when the collective should come first and individual need second.

Alf's personal and professional life appeared old-fashioned even during his lifetime, but it was imbued with virtues considered modern today. That is why his story matters to our fractious present. Loving the nation in which we live need not mean disrespecting or disliking other countries, even whilst playing football fiercely against them. That is especially true, a modern Alf might argue, in the case of old rivals like Argentina, Germany and Scotland. Perhaps if we can learn to enjoy watching England play football, without hating the opposition, it might help us as English people to feel better about ourselves.

In this new biography, fresh evidence emerges about Alf Ramsey's remarkable achievements, secured whilst living a paradoxically unremarkable life, and telling stories which prompt us to re-imagine him totally. Understanding Alf's patriotism, his relentless hard work, his humility, how he led England to win the World Cup in 1966, lose it in 1970, then fail even to qualify in 1974; understanding all these might help 21st-century English football to reach the same simple goal that Alf loved and lived for: winning at football, whilst just happening to be English.

A Timeline Of Alf Ramsey's Life

1920	22 January: Alfred Ernest Ramsey born in Five Elms, Becontree Heath, near Dagenham.
1921	Building starts of the Beacontree Estate, adding 120,000 people to Dagenham by 1935.
1934	Alf leaves Becontree Heath School aged 14 after playing for school and district teams. Starts work as a Co-operative store errand boy, then apprentice. Stops playing football.
1936	Starts playing football again: Sundays for Five Elms FC, perhaps Thursdays for Co-op.
1939	Asked to sign amateur forms for Portsmouth; signed and sent off but never hears back.
1940	24 June: called up for the army, then travels for the first time across England to Cornwall. Plays regular football at various levels within the army until 1946.
1943	9 October: signs amateur forms for Southampton covering friendly and wartime league games.
1944	Southampton professional contract: £2 per match but still friendlies or wartime leagues.
1945	December: ordered to Palestine by the War Office as still serving in British Army.
1946	June: returns from Palestine and, after some negotiation, signs a full-time professional contract with Southampton. 26 October: full league debut aged 26 years and nine months.
1948	1 December: wins first full England cap at right-back in 6-0 victory over Switzerland.
1949	15 May: becomes Tottenham Hotspur's new manager's first signing, valuation £21,000.
1950	1 April: Spurs win Division Two with seven games to spare. 29 June and 2 July: Alf wins England caps seven and eight in 1-0 World Cup losses to USA and Spain.
1951	28 April: Spurs win Division One title. 10 December: marries Rita Norris (born Welch) in Southampton. Rita has a daughter from her previous marriage.
1952	April: Spurs finish Division One runners-up. Alf starts coaching top London amateur side Eton Manor on weekday evenings, and in November publishes autobiography.

1953	5 October: initiated as a Freemason with Waltham Abbey Lodge, Essex. 25 November: wins 32nd and last England cap in 6-3 Wembley defeat by Hungary.
1955	19 May: Ipswich Town approach Tottenham to sign Ramsey as player/coach, Alf spends the summer coaching in Southern Africa. 8 August: Ramsey appointed Ipswich manager.
1956	Ipswich Town finish third in Division Three South.
1957	Ipswich Town win Division Three South.
1961	Ipswich Town win Division Two.
1962	28 April: Ipswich Town win Division One to become Football League champions. 25 October: Alf appointed England manager, but continues managing Ipswich until March 1963.
1966	30 July: wins the World Cup as England manager.
1967	Alf Ramsey given a knighthood.
1968	8 June: England beat Soviet Union 2-0 to secure third place in European Championship.
1970	14 June: Mexico World Cup quarter-final, England lead 2-0 but lose 3-2 to West Germany.
1972	13 May: England lose European Championship quarter-final 3-1 on aggregate to West Germany.
1973	17 October: England draw 1-1 with Poland at Wembley and fail to qualify for World Cup.
1974	1 May: news breaks Ramsey is sacked as England manager by the Football Association.
1976	January: becomes a director of Birmingham City.
1977	September: temporarily manages Birmingham City. November: becomes full-time.
1978	March: leaves Birmingham City after disagreement about Trevor Francis, who in 1979 would become England's first £1m transfer.
1999	28 April: Alf dies in Ipswich, Suffolk, after a stroke the previous year and suffering from prostate cancer and Alzheimer's disease. 7 May: buried in a private ceremony in Ipswich cemetery. 15 May: memorial service at St Mary le Tower Church in Ipswich, attended mostly by ex-players and friends rather than FA officials or dignitaries.

Part One

LABELLED FOR LIFE: THE WORLD ALF WAS BORN INTO

CHAPTER 1

WHAT'S IN A NAME?

Alf Ramsey, Victim of Racism

Name-Dropping

ALFRED ERNEST RAMSEY was born on 22 January 1920, in a tiny wooden cottage, on the edge of the scattered rural hamlet of Becontree Heath. Becontree Heath lay in Essex, east of London and between the small market town of Romford, and the village of Dagenham. Between Becontree and the northern bank of the wide, tidal River Thames lay five flat miles of fertile, often soggy marshland. Alfred liked to be called 'Alf', even after becoming a 'Sir' in 1967. Yet, as a boy growing up in that edge-of-London countryside, Alf gained another name, a nickname he kept secret, never referred to and is known only because other people used it.

One of those was Jim Peters who, after moving to Becontree aged seven, became a 1950s Olympian athlete and marathon world record holder.[1] In a national newspaper interview Peters recalled playing 1930s school football 'against Alf Ramsey, then known to Essex schoolboys as D****e' (*Daily Mirror* 18 January 1952). A year later Peters again referred in print to 'Alfred *D****e* Ramsey' who 'until recently was still living' in the house where he was born.[2]

In his 1955 autobiography Peters repeated, for a third time, that 'There was a boy called *D****e* Ramsey who ... lived in a tiny cottage ... today *D****e* is much better known as ... a captain of England and a great footballer.'[3] From 1955, Alf's childhood nickname then disappeared, on the record, until a 1969 television documentary filmed another former teenaged team-mate serving in a Dagenham shop, and recalling 'D****e Ramsey'.[4] It then vanished again before resurfacing in a 1993 Jimmy Greaves book,[5] and a 2002 Channel 4 television documentary.[6] Modern dictionary definitions are clear what 'D****e' means: 'an extremely offensive word for a person who has black or brown skin.'[7] Bringing the unseen Sir Alf into view therefore starts with a simple question,

17

answered in this chapter. Did that odious term mean the same then, as it does now?

Previously with Alf Ramsey, the answers have depended more upon the politics of the commentator than the evidence. The *Morning Star* ('for peace and socialism') carried a brief biographical article on the 100th anniversary of Alf's birth: 'From childhood, the black-haired boy faced rumours that his dark looks were a sign of gypsy heritage', hence his 'sensitivity to criticism and reluctance to talk about his private life' (22 January 2020). That same day, in a politically contrasting newspaper, Alf's pre-eminent biographer and prominent right-wing journalist, Leo McKinstry, downplayed whisperings that Ramsey's 'family came from a gypsy background … Sir Alf was always angrily dismissive of this claim' (*Daily Express* 22 January 2020). Over a decade earlier, his excellent biography *Sir Alf* had poured similar scorn, claiming 'the eagerness to turn a childhood nickname [D****e] into a badge of racial identity seems to have been based on a fundamental error'. That was because, McKinstry argued, 'according to those who actually lived near him, Alf was called D****e because of the colour of his thick, glossy black hair.'[8]

Alf's childhood friend, Fred Tibble, later Dagenham's mayor and a councillor for 40 years (*Barking and Dagenham Post* 17 June 2021), squarely contradicted McKinstry's 'dark hair' explanation. Interviewed by a local newspaper in 1999, Tibble recalled working and playing sport with adolescent Alf, and that 'his nickname was D****e because of his tanned skin'.[9] Three years later he acknowledged 'everyone used to refer to him as D****e Ramsey.'[10] Two Tottenham team-mates endorse that interpretation, in McKinstry's own book. When one met the 34-year-old Alf in 1954 he recalled someone who 'looked a little Mediterranean in appearance'. The other, a close friend during Alf's six years at Spurs, said that Alf 'did look a bit Middle Eastern'.[11] This 1949 photo reflects that.

So why did McKinstry gloss over such interesting evidence, some from his own research? Perhaps because once Alf achieved national fame everyone assumed he was ethnically white. To conventional white gazes, including the current writer, at first sight a racist nickname for Alf Ramsey makes little sense. Alf presented himself, and was pictured by others, as the epitome of a conventional, white, middle-class, middle-aged Englishman.

Yet as most Alf Ramsey observers agree, things in his persona were not necessarily as they seemed. From the 1940s onwards, and after six wartime years spent with Army officers and BBC broadcasts, Alf gradually reinvented himself to disguise his origins. Using 'immaculate suits' and 'clipped, cultured' speaking styles,[12] especially after his 1955

move into management, he blanked out that childhood nickname; but because this book evokes 'the unseen Sir Alf' it needs to dig deeper, and construct his story afresh.[13] With someone like Alf, that is challenging. His fame retrospectively influences people's memories and any 'historical facts' that survive through individuals are 'always selectively' recorded.[14] In Alf's case, looking afresh at which biographical 'facts' matter most in his life story helps us learn not just *about him*, as an English football hero, but *from his story* about 20th-century English football and society.[15]

Which is why strong historical evidence is laid out below, showing how 'D****e' was used during Alf's lifetime racially to label people whose skin tone was not 'white'; evidence which also explains why he never publicly acknowledged, nor commented upon, his apparently unwanted boyhood nickname, even in his own 1952 autobiography. Alf 'hated to discuss the subject' of his rumoured Gypsy background, according to the young journalist who at various times ghost-wrote his newspaper column and became a close friend.[16] Only after Alf's death did that journalist feel able to confirm Alf's possible 'roots among the travelling community.'[17] During his lifetime, Alf's childhood nickname, although known by some, could also never be broached. For example, another journalist, when planning an interview in 1981, later recalled how a colleague had confided Alf's youthful nickname was 'D****e ... of which Ramsey thoroughly disapproved ... it was essential we did not use it ... in his company'.[18] By 1993 that protocol had been breached, in a book co-written by another eminent sports journalist with Dagenham local boy and 1960s England star Jimmy Greaves: 'When I was growing up ... locals used to refer to the Ramseys as gypsy stock ... one of his early nicknames in his playing days was D****e.'[19] It seems that throughout his lifetime Alf's nickname, often associated with whispers about his ethnicity, was common local gossip and national media currency.

This matters because, as multiple examples shortly demonstrate, 'D****e' as a word did the same racist work in Alf's early 20th-century England as it sometimes does today. Alf acquired it because of his dark skin, dark eyes and dark hair; but as chapters two and three explore, its racist impact was magnified by his family, their livelihoods and Alf's Becontree Heath birthplace being strongly identified with Gypsy, Roma and Traveller (hereafter GRT) people. The evidence below also strongly suggests that anyone living around east London in the first half of the 20th-century, and using the term 'D****e', could not plausibly deny its racist implications.

Rising Racial Tension

Alf was born in January 1920. During 1919, as his mother Florrie's pregnancy progressed, deadly race riots killed hundreds in the USA,[20] and at least five people in Britain.[21] The British riots erupted during January and February in South Shields and Glasgow,[22] followed by violent deaths, shootings, stabbings and house attacks on hundreds of people from ethnic minority backgrounds in East London, Liverpool, and other English and Welsh ports.[23] In London's East End, a few miles west of pregnant Florrie Ramsey, rioting gripped Stepney during April 1919, followed in May and June by racial violence in Limehouse, the West India Dock Road, Poplar and Stepney again.[24] Thousands of returning 'British soldiers and sailors', including ex-combatants traumatised by World War One,[25] perhaps unexpectedly found themselves competing for wages with ethnically diverse migrants from across the British Empire, who had been employed in wartime London's ships, docks and allied industries. Many 'White East Enders', this London newspaper editorial regretfully explained, were therefore returning home to:

> Enforced idleness, with memories which do not help them towards greater freedom from colour prejudice ... brought up against the coloured man in circumstances only too likely to provoke disorder. Hence the distressing problems with which we are now confronted. (*London Daily News* 18 June 1919)

Casually racist language such as 'D****e' had also been common in east London for 20 years before these riots. The *Tower Hamlets Advertiser* (8 October 1904) described a Jamaican-born, Black, British East End sailor as 'now unemployed', because Australia had barred 'coloured men' landing and 'they won't carry D*****s'. A 1907 assault case heard at West Ham described an attack on three 'Lascars' by two white men. Police evidence cited a white assailant swearing at 'you foreigners' and asking the policeman, 'Why don't you take these blacks?' A different police constable then described 'several d*****s taking refuge in a shop' (*Essex Times* 30 October). Journalists used 'D****e' indiscriminately to denote anyone with darker skin, including foreign visitors to the Royal Albert Dock or Whitechapel (*East End News* 11 December 1914, 16 February 1917), and local residents in Cable Street (*Daily News* 7 March 1913).

Then, as now, sport was a significant public arena for racial tensions and therefore labels like 'D****e'. Jack Johnson became the first Black American World Heavyweight boxing champion after defeating the white Canadian Tommy Burns, in Australia in 1908. Boxing's racialised nature coined the phrase 'The Great White Hope', reflecting media speculation about whether a white fighter could ever beat the black, graceful Johnson.[26] His second World Heavyweight Championship win, beating another white challenger on 4 July 1910, sparked race riots across the USA and racial tension in England. Their graphic reporting showed racist language as media mainstream in English newspapers,[27] including frequent deployment of Alf's nickname 'D****e'. This national newspaper's editorial, although mocking racism, used the N-word three times and imagined:

> A feeling of terror lest Johnson may become a multi-millionaire. A *d***y* millionaire with ... gold front teeth to match his waistcoat buttons and clouded cane ... he may come over to England ... and tell us how to run our empire. (*Daily Mirror* 6 July 1910)

Racist responses to Johnson's fame were common across England. A north London newspaper's 'joke' (*Islington Gazette* 14 July 1910) imagined a white street musician, usually blacked up as a minstrel, outside a pub in Holloway explaining his lack of make-up because 'with all this colour prejudice about' due to Jack Johnson's world-title win 'some boozy bloke might take me for a real *d****y* and go for me'. From Birmingham, a large, unusual crowd was reported outside newspaper offices awaiting the result of that distant boxing contest:

> Never before has the writer seen so many black men gathered together in this city, and the presence of the 'd*****s' testified to the absorbing interest ... the news of Johnson's victory was received with great jubilation by them ... and the white men ... were left to mourn. (*The Weekly Post* 9 July 1910)

Even a decade later, nine months before Alf's birth, Jack Johnson was still massive news. A famous British journalist 'doorstepped' the boxer, then used 'd****e' three times in his report alongside the N-word and numerous other racial slurs (*Sunday Express* 23 March 1919).

Labelled for Life

Everyday use of 'D****e' as a racist term had a long history, persisted throughout Alf's childhood, and continued into his professional playing career. It would have been impossible for Alf, and his family, to avoid reading and hearing regular public examples of Alf's nickname being used in racially prejudicial ways, because in football it was regularly deployed about any player from a Black or other minority ethnic background. As early as the 1880s, for example, the Black goalkeeper Arthur Wharton, who had excelled as a sprinter before joining Preston North End, had been called 'D****e Wharton'[28] and he still was 30 years later (*Lancashire Evening Post* 14 September 1918). Walter Tull (1888–1918), the best known of a handful of pre-war English Black professional footballers, suffered the same. In 1909 Tull made a whirlwind transition from playing for Clapton as an amateur, ten miles west of Alf's Becontree Heath birthplace, to signing professionally for Tottenham, then joining their Argentine tour hours before departure.[29] At which point, from the boat they were sailing on, Tottenham's tour manager publicly, racially labelled his own player, telling a journalist: 'If Tull shines at all he will be made much of, as d*****s get a good show at Buenos Aires.'[30] Weeks later, the *Bradford Daily Telegraph* commented, 'Tull, who is said to be a "D****e", played some fine games last year for Clapton' but 'is finding First League football a hue of another colour. D*****s are not often found in first-class English football' (8 September 1909). Tull experienced sporadic racial abuse from spectators and although some newspapers condemned it (*London Daily News* 2 October 1909), other journalists persisted in calling him 'd****e' (e.g. *Tottenham Weekly Herald* 24 September 1909, *Woolwich Gazette* 6 September 1910).

In 1921, the year after Alf Ramsey's birth, Arsenal signed Sadek Fahmy, 'an accomplished fellow speaking four languages' (*Dundee Evening Telegraph* 30 August), but who was casually and racially labelled: 'Trouble has arisen in footballing circles as to the correct spelling of his name ... we had the same difficulty until the popular nickname of "D****e" came to be generally understood. "D****e" is an Egyptian' (*Wallingford and Berkshire Advertiser* 2 September 1921). In 1928, Tottenham Hotspur's London-born Arthur Lowdell[31] was similarly 'nicknamed D****e because of his complexion' (*Reading Standard* 22 December). In the same period, just as Alf was first playing football for his school, two other Black, British footballers were internationally selected: Jack Leslie for England and Eddie Parris for Wales.[32] Both were sometimes called 'D****e' (e.g. Parris in *Daily News London* 1 April 1929) but also other terms like 'DUSKY FORWARDS ... Parris, Bradford's dark-skinned outside left, is one of the two coloured players in League football today. The other is of course, Jack Leslie, Plymouth's brilliant London-born Bermudan' (*Daily Mirror* 29 December 1929).

How Leslie could be 'London-born' but still be inaccurately termed 'Bermudan' the journalist did not explain, but historical evidence shows

Leslie spending his first 20 years in Canning Town, a few miles from the Ramsey family. Two weeks after Alf's Becontree Heath birth, Jack Leslie was then sold from Barking's amateur club, which neighboured Becontree, to the Football League's Plymouth Argyle (*Westminster Gazette* 2 February 1920). There he thrived and five years later was chosen for England, a selection reversed days before the game, in an act now recognised as racial discrimination.[33] Prejudice was commonplace then, and even a west of England newspaper had reported his England call-up using Alf Ramsey's racist childhood nickname: 'Leslie, the d****e forward of Plymouth Argyle, will fill the vacancy' (*Western Daily Press* 12 October 1925).

'Gypsies', Skin Colour and Racism

Alf 'D****e' Ramsey was not ethnically Black, nor apparently bi-racial, nor were his parents of clear Romany descent. Yet his nickname, family and birthplace were identified, as Alf grew up, with another social group often experiencing discrimination: 'Gypsy-Travellers, in the nineteenth and early twentieth centuries were a distinctive group, marked off from settled society by their types of employment and the nature of their way of life.'[34] Nowadays people from Gypsy, Roma or Traveller backgrounds are often referred to using an umbrella acronym, namely 'GRT'.[35] A century ago they were mostly called 'Gypsies', and often labelled by skin colour. This included using 'D****e' as a nickname, alongside other adjectives such as 'dusky' and 'swarthy'. In 1905 for example, local to where Alf grew up, the *Grays and Tilbury Gazette* reported an incident at Thurrock involving several Dagenham participants. The Dailey family (husband Patrick, wife Johanna and four young children) were living in a tent, whilst working on a local farm. Another male worker insulted, or possibly assaulted Johanna, and a fight ensued. At 1am the next morning the Daileys' tent was torched, the youngest child burned on both legs and the father's shirt set alight, scorching his back. A prosecution witness from Dagenham testified the accused man had threatened 'to burn Dailey out before morning' and then, referring to another Dagenham witness, threatened 'your bloody mate D****y ... I'll cut his throat ... and throw him in the Mardyke'. He had labelled a Dagenham resident, part of an itinerant group living in tents, as 'D****y'. In modern parlance this was a hate crime attack on people seen as 'Gypsies', just east of where Alf Ramsey's parents lived and for which a 53-year-old labourer was imprisoned for 12 months.[36]

Sport was another high-profile public arena for GRT racial nicknaming. In 1905 a Whitechapel boxing contest was reported under the headline 'GEORGE MOORE SCORES FROM D***Y HALEY', the latter's nickname being based upon his 'bronzed, Romany-like complexion' (*Sporting Life* 12 December). Edward 'D***y' Haley was born seven miles west of Becontree Heath, in Stratford in 1884, and lived there all his life. In census returns his father worked as a hawker, sharing a house with other hawkers, an 'Umbrella Maker' and a 'Doll Maker', all popular 19th-century Gypsy-Traveller occupations.[37] He was born in Bethnal Green, a traditional location for settled Cockney Gypsies.[38] In 1878, Haley was described as 'a general dealer of Bethnal Green' who had travelled to Maldon to sell 'bacon and cheese from a cart in the market square' (*Essex Newsman* 21 September). Alf Ramsey's grandfather, in the 1891 census, would similarly be categorised a 'general dealer', who by 1901 had become a 'hay and straw dealer'. Essentially, 'D****e' Haley, much like the Alf Ramsey sketched in the next chapter, had acquired his nickname due to a slightly darker skin tone and an ancestry with GRT connections, dealing in foodstuffs, often through 'family-based self-employment'.[39]

During Alf's 1920s and 1930s childhood, numerous other examples surface of 'D****e' being used to label GRT people. The *Sevenoaks Chronicle* of 29 April 1921 casually referred in a court report to 'Jobey Collins, alias D****e Smith, 25, a gipsy.' The *Police Gazette* of 25 January 1921 described someone wanted for horse stealing and called 'D***y Simpson ... complexion swarthy, hair dark brown ... dealer ... frequently attends horse sales ... resides in neighbourhood of Deptford'. In 1934, a fairground worker was referred to as 'D****e' four times in an article, describing him as 'illiterate' and 'having been with the fair nearly all his life' (*Birmingham Daily Gazette* 22 January). Such casually racist language and labelling continued across Alf's playing career. A front-page story in the *Daily Herald* of 28 September 1945 contained veiled, possibly fanciful, but clearly stereotypical 'Gypsy' allusions. It reported how in Essex:

> The charred remains of a man were found in a burnt-out caravan
> by the side of a lonely country road at Great Leighs ... occupied
> by a man known locally as 'D***y' ... He did casual farm work
> in the district ... It is said he had a premonition that he was
> going to die soon.

Hackneyed, demeaning references, associating darker skins with GRT people, had deep journalistic roots. They adorned stories in some left-of-centre newspapers,[40] and were deeply embedded within English class structures. Reporting on a New Year's Day fox hunt in Warwickshire *The Field* of 4 January 1908 lamented how an otherwise excellent chase by the Warwickshire hounds was disrupted by 'a camp of ... dusky Gypsies':

> For these dusky nomads had built their wigwams in the gorse and follow the pursuit of cutting umbrella handles. The tribe turned out in full force, most of the children being without shoes or stockings, and with true vagrant whine ... won a handful of coppers.

This journalist's chosen language reveals what Alf would face as he grew up: not just everyday English racial prejudice specifically against GRT people, but racism as a world mental map encapsulating the British Empire's social and ethnic hierarchies. Note how 'camp', 'dusky nomads', 'wigwams', 'tribe' and 'whine' were deployed as descriptors, words deliberately implying that these GRT people, despite living in the geographic heart of England, were alien, foreign or 'other'.

Such terms were paralleled, 62 years later, by Alf Ramsey's first (1970) biographer. Whilst deriding Alf's partly ghost-written 1952 autobiography,[41] he sneered that 'the word pow-wow appears so often it makes the reader wonder if maybe there is something behind the story of Ramsey looking so much like a Red Indian.' Some of Alf's England players, the biographer claimed, had joked that 'Ramsey would make a fortune playing a Red Indian chief'.[42]

During the 1920s, 1930s and 1940s, as Alf learned to live with his own nickname of 'D****e', stereotypical connections continued to abound between GRT people, skin colour, and terms like 'swarthy'.[43] A *West London Observer* headline shouted 'SEQUEL TO A GIPSY MARRIAGE', then pictured the defendant as 'a swarthy complexioned man described as a dealer'. His first wife said in court, 'We are both gipsies' (19 May 1925). In 1943 the *Sunday Dispatch* carried the death of the Reverend G. Bramwell Evens, a BBC radio celebrity who had broadcast as a 'true Gipsy' whose 'mother lived in a caravan. He was tall, swarthy with jet black hair' (21 November 1943).

Discrimination, Global and Local

Bramwell Evens's media career rested on him publicly 'being' a 'Gypsy'. Alf Ramsey did exactly the opposite by strenuously avoiding any public reference to his childhood nickname. Yet his secrecy did not stop the rumours referred to above nor, in 1981, prevent a national award-winning, 'fervently anti-apartheid' sports journalist (*The Guardian* 25 January 2013) slyly describing Alf as 'the swarthy knight'.[44] Widespread local and national examples show how Alf's 'D****e' nickname was associated, throughout his lifetime, with racial and racist world views; how GRT people were often stereotyped as 'dark', 'dusky', or 'swarthy'; and how such attitudes slotted into the everyday mindsets underpinning a global British Empire. These stereotyped images were also explicitly taught to children. In 1931, when Alf was 11, a newspaper column aimed at children of Alf's age explained that 'gipsy folk' are always 'dark haired, dark-eyed and dark skinned ... largely due to ancestry ... their tents and caravans are their homes'. Although Gypsies were, somewhat patronisingly, portrayed as 'an honest enough crowd', they were also categorised as 'a race apart' (*Sheffield Daily Independent* 18 July).

As Alf was growing up in the 1930s, that phrase 'race apart' acquired ominous weight, when perhaps half a million GRT (Roma and Sinti) people perished in the Nazi Holocaust.[45] Whilst some of the conditions enabling that holocaust were specific to inter-war Germany, the generic racism assisting it was present in England. Alf's Becontree, by now concreted over with thousands of new houses,[46] witnessed local fascism publicly paraded in street marches. Four years after Hitler's 1933 accession to power, in precisely the same streets where adolescent Alf now lived and worked, local fascists held regular demonstrations. From June 1937 Romford's British Union of Fascists were active in Dagenham, holding:

> Weekly meetings at Chequers Corner and Becontree Heath. This political activity was supported by street newspaper sales, house-to-house leaflet distribution and, on occasion, propaganda marches. By October 1937, Romford District felt able to claim that Dagenham-ites were 'willingly turning to National Socialism' and towards the end of the following year reported that the locality now possessed a 'strong organisation'.[47]

During 1939, Israel Rees, a Jewish fruiterer and grocer, was fitting out his new shop at number 786 Green Lane in Becontree. Two local fascist agitators, a father (Frederick Hunt) and his daughter (Irene), were bound over for a year, and paid costs, after being found guilty of threatening the shopkeeper. Rees testified in court how:

> On several occasions, Hunt had remarked that the Blackshirts would drive him out of Becontree. The court was also informed

that the grocer had received similar threats in anonymous postcards and telephone calls ... British Union of Fascist parades marched past his shop on Saturday nights.[48]

Alf Ramsey, nicknamed 'D****e' during the early 1930s, worked in a grocery store less than a mile from that 'Blackshirt' hate crime, and, through the windows of his own workplace, would have watched fascist parades marching past. Nor did local fascism simply disappear when war broke out in September 1939. In May 1940, a few weeks after German armies invaded Denmark and Norway, and a few weeks before Churchill became British prime minister,[49] the British Union of Fascists was strong enough to hold a 'Combined Rally' in Dagenham; one of only two they managed across Norfolk, Suffolk, and Essex.[50]

Conclusion

As a white liberal writer, with a lifelong love for football, researching this chapter has been unsettling and sometimes shaming. Cataloguing each grim example of 'D****e' being used in racist ways, before and during Alf's 20th-century lifetime, illuminated the resultant pain both from individual instances, and a prevailing climate of bullying based on skin colour and ancestry. Given this book reimagines Alf's biography, how might that have influenced him during his lifetime, and his historical reputation since?

Awareness has been widening on both fronts. A fascinating recent exploration of 150 years of 'England Football' highlighted racism as a thread, fleetingly pointed at Alf's racist nickname, but lacked space to further pursue it.[51] In 2023, another account of England's 1966 World Cup team and its manager finally acknowledged claims that 'Ramsey ... acquired the nickname D****e purely on the ... suspicion ... of at least a pint and a half of Romany blood'.[52] Yet in the rest of its brilliant 400 pages that suspicion lay unexamined, and its lifelong legacy for Alf ignored.

Assembling new evidence about Alf's life helps redress that, and prompts rethinking his story to reflect changing knowledge. Some scientists now argue 'whiteness' as a skin tone was a relatively recent, evolutionary variation from universally darker shades.[53] As recently as 8,000 to 12,000 years ago 'all humans were dark-skinned. Pale complexions ... only evolved as humans migrated beyond Africa.'[54] But whilst discrimination based upon skin tone may make little evolutionary or intellectual sense, that does not reduce the destructive impact of the belittling 'D****e' nickname with which Alf was lumbered. Those painful, prejudicial aspects of Alf's life story also play directly into current discussions around 'Englishness' and the problem of how to construct, as a recent expert commentator phrased it, a 'more generous and harmonious English identity which is not inward looking or defined by resentful nationalism' or 'pre-occupied by loss and nostalgia'.[55]

Given Alf's iconic status in the history of English sport, uncovering his hidden diversities may assist with that mission of reimagining modern Englishness. It is now clear that Alf's 1930s childhood nickname was known, by journalists and others, from the 1950s until his death. Strong historical evidence similarly shows it was often associated with racism, or actively racist in intent. Importantly, though, as the next two chapters reveal, a darker skin tone and racist nickname were not the only aspects of Alf's background to make him vulnerable to prejudice.

1 Peters, J. and Edmundson, J. (1955) p.1
2 **Valence House Archive and Local Studies Centre** *Dagenham Characters* (1953) p.14. I am indebted for this and many other references to Teresa Trowers, Local Studies Officer, and other archive staff
3 Peters, J. and Edmundson, J. (1955) p.3
4 **London Weekend Television** (1969) *Sir Alf Ramsey – England Soccer Team Manager* Producer Adrian Metcalfe
5 Greaves, J. with Giller, N. (1993) p.31
6 **Channel 4** (2002) *Sir Alf* Director Ken McGill
7 Cambridge Dictionary website (no date)
8 McKinstry, L. (2007) pp.15-16
9 *Barking And Dagenham Post* 5 May 1999 'World Cup King Sir Alf dies at 79'
10 **Channel 4** (2002) *Sir Alf* Director Ken McGill
11 McKinstry, L. (2007) Ed Speight p.138, Eddie Baily p.14
12 *Daily Express* 22 January 2020
13 Bage, G. (1999)
14 Beales, D. (1980) p.277
15 Ibid. pp.282-3
16 Nigel Clarke, quoted in McKinstry, L. (2007) p.15
17 **Channel 4** (2002) *Sir Alf* Director Ken McGill
18 Cooney, B. (2011) chapter 4. Cooney was also an associate producer for **Channel 4** (2002) *Sir Alf*
19 Greaves, J. with Giller, N. (1993) p.30
20 The National WW1 Museum and Memorial website (no date) 'Red Summer: The Race Riots of 1919'
21 Open University website (no date) 'Making Britain: discover how South Asians shaped the nation 1870-1950'
22 Griffin, P. and Martin, H. (2021)
23 Jenkinson, J. (2008)
24 Fryer, P. (2018)
25 Lawrence, J. (2003)
26 Kent, G. (2007)
27 E.g. *London Evening Standard* 5 July 1910 'The fury of the whites at the victory of the [N word] is said to be indescribable'; *Lloyd's Weekly News* 10 July 1910; *The Illustrated Police News* 16 July 1910 'Race riots all over America – N word and whites at war'
28 *The Athletic News* 6 July 1886, also in Goldblatt, D. (2014) p.149
29 *Tottenham Weekly Herald* 18 June 1909
30 Ibid. 4 June 1909
31 See 1901 and 1911 census
32 See BBC Sport website (18 October 2020) 'Eddie Parris: The forgotten story of the first black footballer to play for Wales'

33 See BBC Sport website (8 October 2022) 'Jack Leslie - the first black player to be picked for England' and Tiller, M. (2023) pp.21-25, 129-151

34 As defined in Mayall, D. (2009) p.181

35 The acronym 'GRT' reflects the 2021 UK Census see UK Government website (29 March 2022) 'Gypsy, Roma and Irish Traveller ethnicity summary'

36 *Grays and Tilbury Gazette* 26 August, 2 September, 18 November 1905

37 Mayall, D. (2009) pp.47-59

38 Taylor, B. (2014) p.119

39 Mayall, D. (2009) p.181

40 E.g. *Daily Mirror* 29 September 1915, 3 March 1947, *Daily Herald* 1 August 1938

41 Ramsey, A. (1952)

42 Marquis, M. (1970) pp.41, 17

43 E.g. *Westminster Gazette* 24 April 1923, *Daily Mirror* 12 January 1926, *Sleaford Gazette* 27 August 1927, *Illustrated Police News* 17 June 1937

44 Keating, F. *Illustrated London News* 18 November 1981

45 Kenrick, D. (2004) also Taylor, B. (2014) chapter 5

46 See chapters 3-5

47 Mitchell, A.M. (1999) p.242

48 Ibid. pp.273-4

49 Roberts, A, (2001)

50 Mitchell, A.M. (1999) pp.242, 338

51 Hayward, P. (2022) p.155

52 Hamilton, D. (2023) p.21

53 Jablonski, J. and Chaplin, G. (2010)

54 Badawi, Z. (2024) p.17

55 Cowley, J. (2022) p.265

CHAPTER 2

LIFE ON THE EDGE

Between Different Worlds

From Good Stock?

THIS BIOGRAPHY untangles Alf Ramsey's secrets. Regarding his rumoured GRT (Gypsy, Roma and Traveller) background, that entails less the establishment of absolute 'truth', more a balancing of probability around two questions. During his lifetime, might friends, neighbours, team-mates or journalists plausibly perceive the Ramsey family as having GRT heritage? And did Alf himself feel his background might lead others to think that? Alf's unwanted lifelong nickname nudges the answers towards 'yes', sealed by evidence in this chapter about some of his relatives.

Alf Ramsey was a puzzlingly closed book. His secretary at Ipswich Town 'worked for him for eight years' from 1955 but 'didn't really get to know him'.[1] In 1999 his second biographer noted 'he never wanted to talk about' his 'obscure early days … Alf always tried to forget his Dagenham roots'.[2] In 2002 Alf's trusted, 1980s newspaper column ghost-writer reiterated that: 'His family was always a closed book. I used to ask him what his father did for a living, and he changed the subject.'[3] Alf's third biographer, Leo McKinstry, similarly thought a desire to 'escape his background' pervaded his secretive behaviour,[4] acknowledged that rumours of Alf's GRT heritage were widespread, but insisted 'that did not make them true'.[5]

What historical evidence now proves *is* true, was that multiple Alf Ramsey relatives 'dealt' in food and agricultural produce, and 'travelled' to do so using ponies, horses and carts. Alf's grandfather John Ramsey, born in East Suffolk, by 1881 had moved 80 miles to Dagenham to lodge with his Suffolk-born sister and her Barking-born 'hay and straw dealer' husband. In 1883 John Ramsey married into a similar local family, and by 1891 was working as a 'General Dealer', an occupational description common to people of GRT heritage.[6] By 1901 he was 'hay and straw dealing', travelling miles to rural areas by horse and cart to buy raw materials, cart them back to Becontree Heath, then prepare the hay and straw for sale in London. John signed an 1890 will using 'X his mark', but by his actual death in 1913 his goods were valued at £1,072,[7] at least £150,000 today. Assets included five horses, 12 vans or carts, and sundry other animals and equipment (*Essex Times* 24 May 1913), earned through hard graft and enterprise. No wonder Alf asserted, during a 1969 television documentary, that he came from 'good stock ... I am not ashamed'.[8]

So why would he never discuss his ancestry? Perhaps to protect his parents. For about ten years from 1913 Alf's father continued the family business, earning him exemption in 1917 from wartime military service (*Essex County Chronicle* 6 July). It was still his trade at Alf's 1920 birth and in the 1921 census. But the business was failing and by 1928 Herbert had become a 'Labourer', then in 1939 a 'Dustman – Heavy Work'. His nickname was 'Cock', according to one local resident, who fondly recalled him collecting waste with a horse-drawn cart.[9] Other local people told McKinstry similar, in that because Herbert scraped a living some saw him as 'little more than a rag and bone man',[10] a trade long associated with GRT people.[11]

Chapter one showed Alf's racial labelling by skin tone, and chapter three touches on similar for his eldest brother Albert 'Bruno' Ramsey. So, were the Ramsey family Romany Gypsies? Probably not, as extensive ancestral research shows no clear-cut Romany influences. Equally, modern historical scholarship argues that the term 'Gypsy' referred not just to 'Romany' migrants, who first arrived in England during the early 16th century.[12] Seasonal and itinerant workers had travelled within the British Isles long before Romany people arrived, and their histories have interlinked ever since.[13] Historians use 'Romany Gypsy' to indicate individuals or groups where that ethnicity is distinct, and 'Gypsy-Traveller'[14] to describe other different, sometimes also ethnically distinct groups of English, Irish, Scottish or Welsh Gypsies.[15] What matters most to Alf's story, though, is not clear demarcations but how such identities have blurred:

> Romani Gypsies and Irish Travellers have always lived alongside and inter-married with each other ... five hundred years after arriving in Britain, the Romanies of Britain today are much as they always were – a hybrid nation made up of the descendants of original Indian nomads, sturdy beggars, landless poor and the economically displaced. In many ways, Gypsies and Travellers are Britain's internal refugees.[16]

As well as intermixing between groups, in each generation some GRT people have found partners in the settled population or simply decided to live in houses.[17] 'GRT' as a modern acronym actively nods towards such fluidity, and because Alf Ramsey's family background is both fluid and not clearly 'Romany', it is used throughout this book. The other generic term deployed is 'Gypsy-Traveller', derived from historical research cataloguing the eclectic spectrum of 19th and early 20th-century people often carelessly labelled as 'Gypsies'.[18] Alf Ramsey experienced exactly such labelling, despite having little or no obvious Romany heritage. How can we be sure? Because in 1973, Bobby Moore, Alf's and England's 1966 World Cup-winning captain, told exactly that to a busload of team-mates and journalists.

Bobby Moore and Team Buses

As glimpsed already, Alf was a secretive character. One of the few football journalists who graduated to genuine friendship was Nigel Clarke.[19] Clarke confirmed that, to English football insiders, rumours of the England manager having a Gypsy background were an open, if highly sensitive, secret. Clarke describes the only time he ever saw Alf 'really angry' was:

> Going through Czechoslovakia in 1973 with the England team … We were all sitting on the coach as it drove past some Romany caravans. And Bobby Moore piped up, 'Hey Alf, there's some of your relatives over there.' Alf went absolutely crimson with fury … It was always accepted in the football world that he was a gypsy.[20]

Moore's 'joke' could needle Alf only because 1970s English football reflected society's racism. Bobby Moore, the blond-haired and blue-eyed folk hero of English football, the man who in 1966 politely wiped Wembley mud from his fingers before shaking the white-gloved hand of the Queen, had not made an innocent wisecrack: he had used long-standing 'gypsy' rumours about Alf publicly to belittle his boss. Another prominent English football manager described Moore as 'calculating in everything he does on the field … and off it' (*Sunday Times* 31 May 1970). Moore's own boss at West Ham said the same.[21] Alf and Bobby, despite long-standing connections, also had an 'edgy relationship.'[22]

This incident belongs both to Alf Ramsey's history and modern England. In 2021, the English, Muslim, Pakistan-born Yorkshire cricketer, Azeem Rafiq, described almost identical racist labelling from his white, Zimbabwean-born captain Gary Ballance. During employment tribunal testimony, Rafiq described racial bullying by Ballance, inflicted through a 'joke' on a team bus that replicated Moore's 1973 mockery:

> We drove past Asian men with beards and Gary said in front of the whole squad ... 'is that your uncle there?' Everyone laughed, which only encouraged and egged Gary on. On those bus trips, he would look out for corner shops and make comments like 'does your dad own these?' Again, everyone would laugh. They treated it as if it was just banter, but I found it hurtful and humiliating – and racist.[23]

As Azeem's example illustrates, such incidents are rarely mere jests, but in Alf's case Bobby Moore's barb had added weight. Most people, perhaps everyone on that bus, would have known not just that Moore was repeating sly football gossip about Alf's GRT ancestry, but that the two men both grew up in what is now the London Borough of Barking and Dagenham. Moore's local knowledge lent his 'joke' some authority, but Alf's vulnerability to it was explained and magnified by stories unknown until now. During the 1920s, Alf had three Ramsey cousins, living in caravans, in the square mile of Bobby Moore's Barking home patch. Not only that but Bobby Moore's newlywed parents ended up living about 100 metres around the corner from his notorious great-uncle James, in 1939–40: Alf's family history was impossible to hide.

Alf's Great-Uncle James Ramsey

So, who was James Ramsey and why was he notorious? James had grown up, married and been widowed in Suffolk. Then by 1891, like three of his brothers and sisters, the 38-year-old had migrated 50 miles south to Essex, where he worked as an 'Engine Driver' for steam-driven farm machines. James had been threshing at a local farm in Hazeleigh, near Maldon, when it was robbed one Saturday evening. Police Sergeant Adam Eves, whilst trying to stop the burglars escaping, was beaten savagely around the head, had his throat cut 'from ear to ear', and his corpse rolled into a five-foot-deep ditch (e.g. *Barking Advertiser* 22 April 1893, *Essex Herald* 1 August).

Suspicion soon narrowed to James Ramsey and two associates, the Davis brothers. Ramsey was acquitted, the Davis brothers convicted, but in a pre-gallows confession one brother testified to having 'held the officer down while Ramsey cut his throat' (*Ilford Recorder* 18 August 1893). Other fresh evidence then emerged implicating Ramsey even further. He could not be retried for the murder but, after prosecution for theft, was sentenced to 14 years' imprisonment. The judge concluded 'nobody definitely knew' if Ramsey did the murder 'but he could not have described the affair as he had [in court] if he had not been there' (*Essex Standard* 11 November 1893).

Everyone in Becontree Heath, Barking and Dagenham, where Alf's family lived, would have heard about this gruesome case. Both of Ramsey's 1893 trials were vividly reported across national but also local newspapers (e.g. *Barking Advertiser* 22 April). Some reports mentioned Alf Ramsey's grandfather John, James's brother, as living on Becontree Heath and looking after James Ramsey's son (*Essex Newsman* 12 August, *Essex County Chronicle* 18 August). After his release 11 years later,[24] evidence shows James Ramsey had moved to Barking, three miles from Becontree Heath, presumably to be close to his family; for within months of arriving, 25 kilogrammes 'of iron the property of James Ramsey, contractor', had been stolen from 'a yard at Gascoigne Road, Barking' (*Essex Times* 18 June 1904). Was James dealing from there in scrap metal? Possibly, as the 1911 census shows him still in Gascoigne Road, self-employed, with a horse and cart. That yard is circled below, on this undated local planning department diagram from perhaps 20 years later.[25]

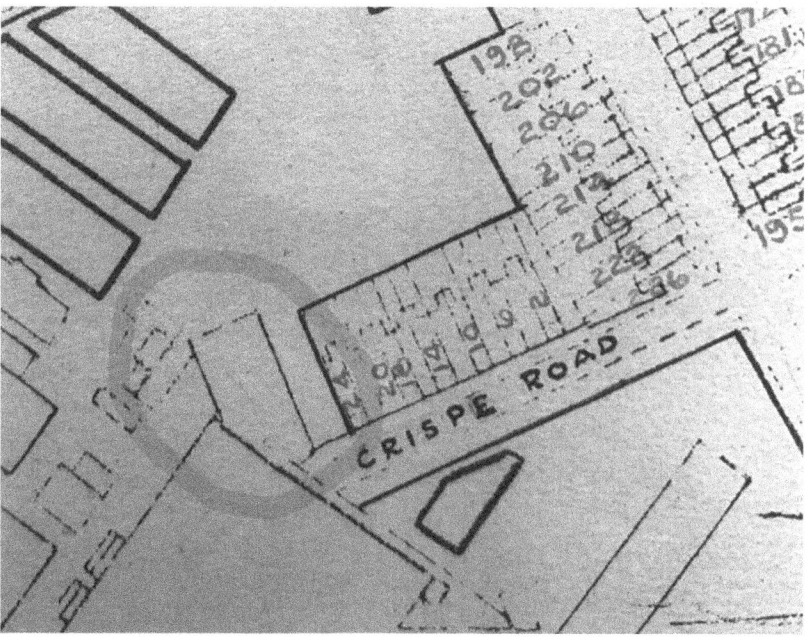

More significantly for the GRT rumours that suffused Alf Ramsey's life, in that same yard during the late 1920s, as Alf was growing up just three miles away, were at least two caravans inhabited over four years by three different cousins, all born as 'Ramseys' via Alf's great-uncle James. The first cousin was Lilian Ramsey, listed on the spring 1926 electoral register as inhabiting a 'Caravan, Crisp Road', although aged only 14.[26] The second was 27-year-old James Joseph Ramsey in autumn 1926, similarly living in a 'Caravan, Crisp Road', probably with his wife Elizabeth. Then in 1928 and 1929 a third Alf Ramsey cousin took over occupancy. Elsie Ramsey (1907–1995) married Elias Suckling in September 1927, the couple moved into that 'Caravan – Crispe Road', then relocated to a nearby house in 1930.

Such caravan-dwelling by Alf's cousins might have passed unnoticed by Bobby Moore's family and other locals, but for three factors. The first was that living alongside Alf's cousins in those years were Harriet and James Smith, a couple with long and clear GRT heritage. Census returns in 1901 and 1911 described James as a 'Dealer in Horses', and Harriet as a 'Hawker'. In 1925, a local newspaper reported James Smith having been found drunk and sound asleep in a 'horse and trap', describing him as 'a horse dealer of the Caravan, Crisp Road, Barking' (*Ilford Recorder* 23 October). This was the same yard where James Ramsey was working during the 1910s, and in which during the 1920s various Alf Ramsey cousins also lived in caravans. Most electoral registers until 1932 record the Smiths' caravan parked there; then from 1932–37 their van, and several others inhabited by different families, was often located on a plot about 100 metres away, by 221 Gascoigne Road.

The second attention-grabbing factor about Alf's convict great-uncle was his unusually tangled family life. The 14-year-old Lilian Ramsey, who in 1926 was living in a 'Caravan, Crisp Road', was his daughter. But her mother, Ada, had previously been married to James's son and had several children with him. He deserted her around 1910, but birth certificates suggest that Alf's great-uncle James then stepped into his own son's bed and fathered three more 'Ramsey' children with Ada.

A third and possibly decisive factor, in fuelling Bobby Moore's 1973 jibe that Alf Ramsey's family were 'Gypsies', was that great uncle James and Ada lived for a year about 100 metres around the corner from Bobby Moore's first home. Number 43 Waverley Gardens now boasts a Blue Plaque telling visitors that England's World Cup-winning captain grew up there. His parents had moved in after their 1939 wedding, four years after James and Ada Ramsey had moved to neighbouring 37 Westminster Gardens. The 1932 aerial photo below shows the close proximity of all these people and places.[27] The yard where Alf's cousins lived in caravans, during the late 1920s, lies in the smaller circle. Tantalisingly, but indistinctly, it contains at least two or three structures, possibly caravans. Meanwhile, above and to the right is a larger circle, the site of the new housing estate to which James and Ada Ramsey moved in 1935, and Bobby Moore's parents in 1939. James died in June 1940 but until 1950 Ada continued living there, or close by.

From 1904 until around 1930 Alf's great uncle James Ramsey was therefore connected to a small yard, possibly sometimes dealing in scrap metal, and definitely at other times hosting caravans. These were lived in by his own children and grandchildren, often alongside a long-established local GRT family. James Ramsey's reputation, and that physical location, would have been locally known in the years when Alf Ramsey was racially labelled during the late 1920s or early 1930s. Even more importantly, that site and its people lay in the square mile locality where Bobby Moore's mother had lived since 1912. Moore could easily have been drawing on family stories, street gossip and local knowledge to make his 1973 team bus jibe about 'Alf's Gypsy relatives'. Indeed, he may genuinely have believed it.

Alf's Bixby Ancestors on 'Me Nativ Heath'

The dealing and travelling backgrounds of Alf's paternal Ramsey ancestors, the era's prevailing racial attitudes, young Alf's dark complexion and his great uncle James Ramsey's local, caravan-dwelling offspring, helped rumour the Ramseys as Gypsies; a possibility then reinforced by his mother's 'Bixby' ancestry and her family's home turf.

Florence Bixby, Alf's mother, had long-standing family associations with both Becontree Heath and Chadwell Heath, two patches of open ground about a mile apart. In 1904, the local vicar published a voluminous 'History of Dagenham', which described these neighbouring heaths as having an 'unenviable reputation' due to 'the rough characters' living there. That same year, Becontree Heath was independently reported as renowned across East Anglia for being a 'well-known rendezvous of gipsies' (*Cambridge Independent Press* 23 December). The Reverend's local history book also described 'the plebeian natives' of Chadwell Heath, his own parishioners, as descended from the Romany 'gipsy colony' close by at Hainault. Chadwell Heath's locals, wrote their vicar, had the 'dark eyes, tawny complexion, and short, curly, black hair' which 'all point to foreign descent'.[28]

The young girl below, photographed on Becontree Heath, came from Alf's mother's 'Bixby' family. Her appearance matches the 'dark eyes, tawny complexion and … curly, black hair' claimed above for local GRT people. These fascinating but enigmatic images were purchased online in 2005 by a local historian.[29] Unfortunately, no background information was supplied by the vendor, but on each is handwritten 'Beacontree Heath'. They show an adolescent girl, in a stylish dress, dancing or standing alone in the open air. A note on one image explains 'Me fut is on me nativ heath and me name's Mrs Bixby'.

Bixby was Ramsey's mother's maiden name and, as a policeman wryly testified during a minor 1904 court case, there were 'a lot of

Bixbys around Becontree' (*Ilford Recorder* 24 June 1904). The quote is from a Walter Scott historical novel in which the Scottish rebel leader, Rob Roy MacGregor, urges the story's English hero to 'Speak out, sir, and do not Maister or Campbell me—my foot is on my native heath, and my name is MacGregor!'[30] Whether these annotations were made by somebody shown in the photo on the previous page, or someone else, is now impossible to say.

The second image shows an adult male talking to the same young girl. Was he related to her, a friend of the photographer, or a local historian like the Reverend above?

BEACONTREE HEATH

This mystery may never be unravelled, but the caption 'Me nativ Heath' suggests a strong Bixby bond to Becontree Heath. In 1952, Alf's autobiography was similarly, uncharacteristically emotional about his rural home soil.

> I lived for the open air from the moment I could toddle. The meadow at the back of our cottage was our playground. For hours every day, with my brothers, I learnt how to kick, head and control a ball, starting with a tennis ball ... We were happy in the country.[31]

Two More of Alf's Mother's Relatives, Labelled as Gypsies

Another relative locally labelled as a Gypsy was Emmanuel Bixby (1850–1929), cousin to Alf's unreliable grandfather Samuel Bixby, who had been absent since the early 1900s. In 1921, when Alf was aged one, Emmanuel was still working on Chadwell Heath, sharing a house with people related to Alf's mother.[32] Emmanuel had lived there or on Becontree Heath all his life, and did not die until Alf was nine years old. During his lifetime, Emmanuel was variously labelled as a Gypsy, hawker, costermonger, jobber, dealer, carter, and labourer. In 1894, for example, he had been 'a costermonger of Bennet Castle Lane', trading in Barking with a 'pony-barrow' (*Essex Herald* 24 April). In 1901 'Emmanuel Bixby, hawker' had refused to pay market tolls, swore at the collector, and was fined (*Barking Advertiser* 14 December). In 1896 a London newspaper, in a story reprinted across England, mockingly reported from Stratford Court how Emmanuel Bixby, described as 'a gipsy', was suing a friend also termed a 'gypsy':

NOT A FAIR 'DEAL'

William Cope, a gipsy of Dagenham, was summoned for illegally obtaining a pony and barrow, valued at £12, the property of Emmanuel Bixby, also a gipsy, of Chadwell Heath. Complainant ... was in the Cherry Tree Inn at Dagenham, drinking, his pony and cart being outside. Defendant joined the company, and after some talking, offered £2 for the pony, barrow and harness ... Bixby being worse for drink took £2 ... the Bench ... ordered defendant to return the pony and barrow on receipt of £2, or to pay Bixby £10. (*London Weekly Dispatch* 19 April)

A different relative, similarly although more subtly labelled, was David Bixby (1855–1922), a cousin of Alf's mother. Most Becontree people knew each other, many were related,[33] but David Bixby was the richest and best known. During a court case in 1915, adjudicating on damages after a traffic accident by Becontree Heath, a lawyer referred to David Bixby in his absence as 'a tall, dark, tragic-looking gentleman named Bixby of Becontree Heath'. On being challenged by the judge, the lawyer conceded, 'I withdraw that description' (*Ilford Recorder* 15 March): but why had he deployed it? His purpose was to undermine a key witness by insinuating the GRT heritage of Thomas Bixby, Alf Ramsey's uncle and his mother's brother. That deduction is possible because the phrase 'tall, dark, tragic-looking' echoed newspaper stereotypes of GRT people commonly using those words. For example, a report about a 1910 parliamentary debate, asking county councils to provide 'camping grounds' for Gypsies, mocked the 'ignorance of tradition' stereotyping male Gypsies as always 'lithe, tall, and dark' and a 'bit of a poacher ...

a burglar ... a liar' (*The Clarion* 19 August). Five years later the lawyer undermining Alf Ramsey's uncle used the phrase 'tall, dark, tragic-looking' to imply that Thomas Bixby was of GRT heritage and possibly therefore 'a bit of a liar'.

Nowadays this would be seen as 'camouflaged racism', disguised as 'something else entirely'.[34] Plainer to see was how the astounding, cash-rich success of the 'tall, dark, tragic-looking' David Bixby's business empire vividly associated Alf's maternal family with hawkers, costermongers and GRT people in general. David Bixby's 1922 local newspaper obituary shows this Becontree-born boy, who lived there lifelong, was in modern shorthand a ruthless but successful 'gangmaster':[35]

> One of the best-known market gardeners in Essex ... Previously a dealer ... the pioneer ... of the practice of buying crops as they stood in the fields, and for this purpose he travelled extensively throughout Essex, Bedfordshire and Cambridgeshire.[36]

After paying farmers cash for their crops, the Bixby Partnership hired numerous casual labourers to pick, process and cart their produce to London markets like Covent Garden.[37] This business model entailed Bixby getting 'the peas picked as quick as he can', meaning his workers were herded 'like pigs in barns and sheds' often sleeping in 'open fields, it is a dreadful life' (*Essex Chronicle* 12 September 1890). By necessity Bixby's workforce was occasionally, seasonally or permanently itinerant. It included many with GRT heritage but also the urban and East End poor, especially women working part-time. The crops they harvested were then hawked door-to-door, and on streets from baskets, barrows, carts, and market stalls: a list neatly summarising traditional GRT occupations,[38] Emmanuel Bixby's working life, and the occupations of numerous other Alf ancestors too many to mention. Then in the 1920s and 1930s, when thousands of incoming East End Londoners moved into newly built council houses, on an estate now covering Becontree and Chadwell Heaths, is it any wonder that some of them saw the Ramseys as rich in GRT heritage?

At the Margins

From the start of his England managership, Alf Ramsey felt chronically insecure, about which Terry Venables (England football manager 1994–96) told an illustrative tale. A sanitised first version describes 21-year-old Venables joining Alf's 1964 England squad. Hoping to forge links through mutual Dagenham childhoods, Venables mentioned his father working with an old neighbour of Alf's 'down at the docks'. Alf's reaction is predictable to us now, but shocked young Terry: 'Had I cracked Alf over the head with a baseball bat he couldn't have looked more gobsmacked. He stared at me for what seemed like a long, long time ... didn't utter a single word.'[39] A second, uncensored version, narrated to journalists and retold recently, has Venables passing best wishes to Alf from 'some colourful Dagenham *faces*' to which Alf responded, '*Fuck off son* ... and walked away.'[40]

Geoff Hurst, who also first met Alf Ramsey that year,[41] winning 49 senior caps by 1972, recently told the author, 'I had absolutely no, thinking about it, no idea where Alf's accent related to.'[42] Alf had vocally erased his past but, as Venables's recollection shows, was still paralysed by it. He could not escape his 'D****e' nickname, plausibly refute his family's rumoured 'Gypsy' heritage, nor deny some criminal ancestry. His crude response was to ignore everything, and Alf's stubbornness, alongside an intense loyalty evoked from friends, helped this non-communication strategy to 'work': inner-circle rumours about Alf's GRT ethnicity rarely surfaced in public. Yet his apparent dread of them doing so seemingly worsened Alf's tongue-ties, a limitation which helped scupper his England managerial career.

Alf was a 'country boy', reared on the edge of a global city. He appeared Romany neither by ancestry nor language, but his extended family had multiple Gypsy-Traveller members and connections. Neither parent lived in caravans, but cousins sometimes did. Close, straw-dealing relatives on both sides used vans and carts in their trade, and numerous other ancestors 'dealt' and 'travelled' for work. Alf was not Black, nor brown-skinned, nor apparently of mixed race, yet his dark eyes, hair, and darker skin tone attracted racist labelling. Crucially, although Alf himself admitted to none of these things, team-mates and journalists believed them. Southampton's Eric Day, who from 1946–49 often travelled with Alf back to Ilford, where Eric's parents lived close to Alf's, simply asserted Alf was 'a bit secretive ... because he was a gypsy'. The two are pictured on the next page during season 1947/48, with Alf on the right.

Similar was true at Tottenham where Eddie Baily, Alf's 1949–55 club and England team-mate, 'was always told that he was a gypsy ... he did look a bit Middle Eastern'. Alf's later friend and 1980s ghostwriter acknowledged 'it was always accepted in the football world that he was a gypsy'.[43]

Although Alf is long dead and never discussed these rumours when alive, the bruising impacts of adolescent labelling can be gauged via the experiences of another modern, white international footballer. Alf

Ramsey's story (born 1920, 32 England caps) parallels aspects of Gary Lineker's (born 1960, 80 England caps). Lineker achieved post-playing celebrity as the BBC's highest-paid presenter,[44] but his early football career path was not straightforward. A brief passage in a lengthy 2022 interview aired youthful vulnerabilities paralleling Alf's. In the mid-1970s, not long after Alf's England manager dismissal, Lineker was, in his own words:

> A tiny geeky kid with darkish skin, I pretty much got racist abuse although I'm as English as they come ... All the time. Even in professional football I had that a couple of times. I wouldn't name any names.

The interviewer responded twice, incredulously, 'Really ... really?!', to which Lineker replied, 'Yeah. I got that kind of nonsense, which was a bit weird.'[45] His throwaway revelation had not been designed to court controversy, but it followed. Black writers instantly recognised what Lineker was talking about, with Okundaye commenting how critics:

> Ridiculed him for supposedly 'identifying as black.' But the mockery is misguided. Lineker's comments were important and insightful ... a glimpse of how race and racism can work ... For whiteness to survive, its boundaries must constantly be policed ... racial categories are constantly invented and reinvented. (*The Guardian* 23 June 2022)

Not only does that sound similar to what Alf Ramsey experienced, but Okundaye also questioned the fallacy that 'Racial discrimination in England is only experienced by those with the darkest skin. Many groups have been let in and out of the club of whiteness: southern Europeans, eastern Europeans, Traveller groups.' Nels Abbey agreed: 'this surprising strand of racism – the failure to outwardly exhibit the necessary purity of whiteness' and the accompanying 'purity requirements of full racial acceptance' were, in his experience, 'more common than given credit for'.[46]

Lineker's 2022 revelation, that for some in the 1970s he lay outside of the 'club of whiteness', were echoed precisely in Bobby Moore's 1973 bus barb about Alf's 'Gypsy caravan relatives'. Nor, in essence, was such snide racism any different from the racist courtroom conjuring, in 1915, of a 'tall, dark, mysterious looking … Bixby of Becontree Heath'. The ongoing toxicity of 'purity requirements' about whiteness also underscores the toxicity of Alf's 1930s 'D****e' childhood nickname, just as 1970s racist labelling undermined the young Gary.

Socially conservative commentators heavily criticised Lineker. The Reclaim Party was founded in 2020 to challenge an imagined 'woke orthodoxy of *white privilege* and *systemic racism*.'[47] Its deputy leader painted Lineker as assuming 'every form of victimhood possible even when it is clearly ludicrous … I wish he would just put one of his football socks in his gob.'[48] Some respondents on the Fan Banter website posted comments like 'Absolute fruitloop' (@CS1312); 'I've read some nonsense in my time but this is wild' (@BrewersFayre1); and 'a total insult to players that did suffer racist abuse' (@leeashford8).[49] In parallel and from a more conventional direction *The Spectator* questioned Lineker's truthfulness, then grumbled about even having to *hear* his words:

> Lineker's talent on the pitch means we will never know whether what he is saying is true … whether he would have been targeted in the playground or not, hearing Lineker pose as a victim is a bit much … hard to take.[50]

Lineker's story parallels Alf Ramsey's in another way, with research suggesting GRT ancestry. James Lineker, a long-lived and distant great uncle of Gary's,[51] was baptised in Mansfield in 1821,[52] jailed in 1839 for sleeping 'in the open air for several nights' with 'no means of support' (*Nottingham Mercury* 8 February) and imprisoned again in 1842 as a 'rogue and a vagabond' (*Nottingham Review* 19 August). In 1871 and 1881 James was living in caravans as a 'Travelling Confectioner' and

'Traveller Tobacconist', with numerous other Fairground Travellers in Grantham. By 1911 the widowed James had moved into a Nottingham house, but his son Barton Lineker (1847–1924) was continuing to live as a Gypsy-Traveller. He house-dwelled in 1871, working as a 'Smallware Hawker', but from 1891 to 1921 he and his wife lived in caravans in Derbyshire, Lincolnshire and Nottinghamshire, trading as a 'General Dealer' or 'Licensed Hawker'. Gary Lineker's family background, like Alf's, therefore has visible Gypsy-Traveller heritage. His 'Lineker' father, grandfather and great-grandfather were also, throughout the 20th-century, market traders dealing in fruit and vegetables, as needlessly noted by *The Times* in its report on this controversy (22 June 2022).

Young Alf Ramsey in the 1920s and 1930s, and young Gary Lineker in the 1970s, were both victims of snide racist comments and nicknames relating to skin tone, but probably also to heritage. Their parallel experiences point to an important storyline in a narrative still gripping modern England: the longevity of everyday racism in football as a sport, and society in general. Historically that racism has been expressed not only towards people of visibly different ethnicities, with black or brown skin and perhaps speaking English as an additional language, but towards anyone with a slightly darker skin shade than a casual white observer, an occasional but unwitting racist, or a convinced white supremacist might consider 'normal'. As explored in the next chapter, that history of suspicion and sometimes prejudice against people perceived as having GRT heritage stretched throughout his lifetime, in the place Alf Ramsey called 'home'.

1 Pat Godbold in **Channel 4** (2002) *Sir Alf* Director Ken McGill

2 Edworthy, N. quoted in *Barking and Dagenham Recorder* 6 May 1999 (reporter Jonathan Weinberg)

3 Nigel Clarke in **Channel 4** (2002) *Sir Alf* Director Ken McGill

4 McKinstry, L. (2007) p.15

5 Ibid. p.15

6 Romany and Traveller Family History Society website (last updated April 2017) 'Was Your Ancestor A Gypsy?'

7 I am indebted to Royston Jones for this and other documents relating to Alf Ramsey's ancestors

8 **London Weekend Television** (1969) *Sir Alf Ramsey – England Soccer Team Manager* Producer Adrian Metcalfe

9 Thanks to Christine Bell (via Royston Jones) for her aunt's oral historical memories of Herbert Ramsey

10 McKinstry, L. (2007) p.5

11 E.g. *Sutton and Croydon Guardian* 22 Feb 2013 'Hundreds turn out for David Hilden's horse-drawn gypsy funeral procession'

12 Mayall, D. (2009) and Cressy, D. (2018)

13 Taylor, B. (2014) p.53

14 Mayall, D. (1981) and (2009)

15 The Traveller Movement website (2025) 'Romani (Gypsy), Roma and Irish Traveller History and Culture' also Bowers, J. (no date)

16 Bowers, J. (no date). Also Mayall, D. (2009) pp.71-78

17 Thanks to Jenny Neild for pointing me towards the Surrey County Council website (February 2025) 'Tracing Gypsy Romany and Traveller Ancestors at Surrey History Centre'

18 Mayall, D. (1981) and (2009)

19 McKinstry, L. (2007) pp.488-91

20 Ibid. p.15

21 Hurst, G. (2024) p.26

22 Hamilton, D. (2023) p.248

23 UK Parliament Committees Correspondence website (16 November 2021) 'Azeem Rafiq Witness Statement to the Leeds employment tribunal' 11 December 2020 p.17

24 I am indebted to Royston Jones for this reference and information

25 I am indebted to Teresa Trowers of the **Valence House Archive and Local Studies Centre** for saving and making available this uncatalogued document

26 Almost certainly a recording error as Lilian was too young to vote

27 **Valence House Archive and Local Studies Centre** MAP DS2010a, Aerial Photograph 1932 of William Warnes Factory Site

28 Shawcross, J.P. (1904) pp.275, 288

29 Tony Benton, to whom many thanks for permission to reproduce them here

30 Scott, W. (1817) Volume II, chapter 17

31 Ramsey, A. (1952) p.12

32 1921 census: James Ainsworth (Alf's grandmother's uncle) and wife Mary Ann (born Bixby)

33 West, J. (1993) p.49

34 Liew, J. (2021)

35 Since 2004 horticultural or agricultural 'Gangmasters' in England have been licensed: David Bixby's employment practices were unconstrained, e.g. *Essex Chronicle* 12 September 1890 'Death of a crop-picker's child'

36 *Barking and Dagenham Post* 5 August 1922

37 See *Barking Advertiser* 11 November 1899 for Bixbys protesting stallholder rent rises at Covent Garden market; 1901 census David Bixby junior 'Market Garden Salesman'; *Chelmsford Chronicle* 2 April 1886 for a Bixby-employed carter's accidental death

38 Mayall, D. (2009) pp.48-9; Mayall, D. (1981) pp.24-25

39 Venables, T., Nottage, J. and Montgomery, A. (2001) p.56

40 Hayward, P. (2022) pp.153-4

41 Hurst, G. (2024) p.81

42 Geoff Hurst oral history interview 7 February 2025

43 McKinstry, L. (2007) pp.47, 14, 15

44 BBC News website (12 July 2022) 'Gary Lineker stays top of BBC star pay list'

45 **High Performance** podcast (20 June 2022) *Gary Lineker*: interviewers Damian Hughes and Jake Humphrey

46 Metro website (23 June 2022) 'Gary Lineker proved that there is no such thing as whiteness' Opinion – Nels Abbey

47 The Reclaim Party website (2021) 'Principles'

48 Daily Express website (22 June 2022) 'Lineker's "racist abuse" claims blasted by Daubney'

49 Fan Banter website (no date) 'Gary Lineker receives backlash after speaking out on racist abuse aimed at him'

50 The Spectator website (21 June 2022) Tom Goodenough 'Why won't Gary Lineker name those who racially abused him?'

51 This James Lineker and the William Lineker cited as Gary's twice great-grandfather (BBC 2013 *Who Do You Think You Are?*) descend from their grandfather Samuel's first wife Ann Serflick. Samuel remarried after Ann's 1811 death. James Lineker in 1844 married Mary Folkes, a Nottingham neighbour of grandfather Samuel

52 All other records (census, newspaper, legal documents) give James's birthdate as 1824–26

CHAPTER 3

KEEPING ALF IN HIS PLACE

More Reasons for Silence

Becontree Heath and the 'Beacontree Estate'

ALF RAMSEY started life in 1920 on the fringe of rural Becontree Heath, an idiosyncratic scrap of English countryside about to be swallowed by one of Europe's largest housing projects. For Alf's family everything was changing. Just after his birth, planning permission was passed to build over 20,000 new homes for public rent, mostly across Dagenham but also in Ilford and Barking. Thousands of acres of agricultural and horticultural land were compulsorily purchased for the 'Beacontree Estate', and construction of a massive new town, aimed at London's East Enders, continued until the mid-1930s.[1] National and local politicians rushed it through, galvanised by Lloyd George's 1918 election slogan to make post-war Britain 'a land fit for heroes to live in' (*Westminster Gazette* 13 December). Yet by building on open 'heaths' like Becontree and Chadwell, governments were not just providing new homes for poverty-stricken urban East Enders, they were sanitising untidy semi-rustic enclaves of GRT-rich 'dealing' communities. By the early 1930s there was no 'organised resistance' to the Urban District Council taking over 'what was virtually common land' at Becontree Heath,[2] and by 1936 Dagenham's massive 'Civic Centre' towered over it. The legal key to its appropriation had been a 1931 bill passed by the House of Lords, during which the council's representative claimed Becontree was 'not in any sense a heath. There has been great trouble over this heath for years and various attempts have been made to deal with it.'[3]

A century later 'Becontree Heath' still figures as a place name on the red double-decker buses plying the busy streets of the London Borough of Barking and Dagenham. By 2021 nearly 220,000 people lived in that borough, of whom 9,800 were within 'Becontree Ward';[4] the same population as the whole of 1911 Dagenham.[5] Barking and Dagenham Borough's population, like Becontree Ward's, has also significantly ethnically diversified and it now has the tenth-highest 'Black, Asian and Multi-Ethnic' population in the UK.[6] Why is that relevant to Alf Ramsey? Because, as seen so far, and pursued below, stories of change, diversity and prejudice thread through his family and upbringing. Both Alf's parents lived in Becontree Heath throughout their long lives, dying there in 1966 (his father) and 1979 (his mother). No personal testimony from them has survived describing their own life experiences, their feelings about Alf being nicknamed 'D****e', nor their responses to the rumours of his GRT background that effectively targeted them. But what can be traced, during their lifetime and Alf's, is how GRT people were easy targets for virulent racial and social prejudice.

Since Roma people arrived in early 16th-century England, they had been 'a dispersed and vilified minority' viewed often by authorities as 'offensive to God'. Darker skin tones gave rise to the misconception they were Egyptians, spawning the abbreviation 'Gypsy'.[7] That term, as seen in chapter two, was then widely applied to other itinerant workers or travellers from very different backgrounds. For example, Alf's parents were born in the 1890s, when Essex County Council was Dagenham's governing local authority. In its 1894 council chamber a Liberal Party councillor labelled all GRT people, or 'Gypsies' as he called them, 'an intolerable nuisance … a disgrace to civilisation … simply abominable. They were of great expense … they had typhoid fever among them every few weeks. Altogether they were a great pest … everything that was bad' (*Essex Herald* 10 July). Gypsies camping in the Ramsey's Dagenham had been specifically and viciously berated two weeks earlier, in a 'Reader's Letter':

> Filthy nomads … always on the watch for an opportunity to turn their half-starved cattle into other people's fields … always got the cash to pay any fine … A stranger cannot pass without being surrounded by dozens of half-naked, dirty children who, if you refuse to 'give a copper' … call you some choice names, as they retreat to their tents where their lazy parents are lying about as happy as reptiles in a muddy pond. (*Essex Herald* 26 June)

As Alf's parents were born and raised, their home patch of Becontree Heath regularly witnessed petty prosecutions of itinerant GRT people living there in tents or vans.[8] Becontree was also a wild, rough place. In 1896, when Alf's mother was one year old, her father Samuel Bixby was heavily fined for sparking a drunken brawl involving 40 men outside a Becontree Heath pub. The Chair of Magistrates warned him, and wider

Becontree, that 'the Bench intends to put down these riots' (*Essex County Chronicle* 17 April).

They kept that promise using various tactics. One, directly affecting the dealing activities of Alf's grandfather John Ramsey and other close relatives, was that in 1897 Dagenham Parish Council started clearing Becontree Heath of agricultural clutter by turning it into a municipal 'Metropolitan Common'.[9] The council ordered 'all persons using the Heath' that 'carts, waggons, timber, straw, manure, soil, ashes or rubbish' or anything else 'deposited in or upon Becontree Heath ... to remove same'. GRT workers, with whom 'dealers' like the Ramseys and Bixbys worked closely, were specifically targeted:

> Councillor Smith moved that no gypsies or squatters be allowed to encamp upon Becontree Heath or trespass there ... this council to remove by reasonable force, if necessary, all caravans, carts, horses, tents and other belongings of any gypsies or squatters.[10]

Another, explicitly anti-GRT tactic was that in 1898 a new police constable was appointed to Becontree Heath, who immediately threatened local Gypsies he 'would burn them out'. William Rawson retired in 1913,[11] lived in Becontree until his 1937 death, and would have known and been known by Alf. This previously hidden posthumous account was published in the year he died:

> The superintendent asked him to take over the Beacontree Heath beat ... notorious for its lawless characters and the hordes of gypsies who camped there. Rawson accepted and ... During his first few weeks [1898–99] received hundreds of threatening letters ... Rawson tore them all up. He soon got rid of the gypsies who were constantly robbing the villagers. He told all the boys to collect faggots and put them in a pile on the village green. Then he informed the gypsies that if they did not go, he would burn them out. (*Northampton Mercury* 13 August 1937)

As a local historical memoir recalled, 'dealing' families like the Ramseys, and their 1920s next-door neighbours the Readers, made their living by purchasing 'surplus straw cheap in Essex' then using 'ample horses and carts' to freight it to 'spacious yards on The Heath'. Becontree Heath's open space, and day labour from GRT people and others, was crucial to then 'prepare it for sale' to London stables. These dealing families easily co-existed with, and sometimes were related to, itinerant GRT people who 'lived in caravans within the yards of dealers' or just camped on the common.[12]

Ominously for Alf's family and their way of life, during his childhood the building of the Beacontree Estate gobbled open spaces, and internal combustion engines took over roads. Census returns show his father Herbert (1921), grandfather John (1911) and great-uncle William (1901) as 'Hay and Straw Dealers'; but their trade was doomed and GRT people were being increasingly victimised. In the previous chapter Alf described 'living for the open air from the moment I could toddle', learning 'how to kick, head and control a ball, starting with a tennis ball' in the 'meadow at the back of our cottage.'[13] But when Alf was toddling there, in 1923, local headlines alleged a 'GIPSY NUISANCE ON BEACONTREE HEATH ... a growing scandal ... endangering health ... as many as eleven caravans'. Another reported 'some residents near the heath must supply them with water, but it was difficult to find out who' (*Ilford Recorder* 20 April 1923).

'Near the Heath' at Five Elms was precisely where the Ramseys lived, and like other 'dealers' they had multiple reasons for 'supplying Gypsies with water': they needed their labour, knew them as neighbours, and often themselves had GRT heritage. Yet nothing stopped the relentless building. By 1927 a local journalist gazed out 'from the top of a bus' and wondered 'if the next new street would cut right through the gipsy's camping ground on Becontree Heath' (*Ilford Recorder* 20 May). By 1929 the situation was desperate. The 'Kings', like Alf's family, were Becontree Heath straw dealers, and in 1929 opened their yard to itinerant GRT families. That prompted Dagenham council to order they 'remove refuse and provide efficient sanitary accommodation for caravan dwellers in the yard ... there were three vans occupied by 13 persons ... at one time there were as many as 98 people living in caravans in the yard' (*Ilford Recorder* 12, 19 July).

Such stories help us understand Alf Ramsey because, lifelong, he stayed publicly mute about what happened around his native Becontree Heath; a silence now possible to see as stemming from his racist childhood nickname and associated rumours. For, throughout Alf's adolescent and early adult life, prejudices against local GRT people persisted. As later recalled by a resident:

> Before the estate was built many gypsies lived on the land, but they had to move on when the houses were begun ... a few lingered on ... Becontree Heath ... they came round sometimes

selling wooden pegs … We were told we must never talk to them. They must have had a rough time because if anything went wrong it was always put down to … the gypsies.[14]

Children were told a scraped knee turning septic was because 'the gypsies had put a curse on the land … and people believed it!' Her memories also poked fun at widespread later rumours that structural problems at the new swimming pool, 'opened to the public at Becontree Heath' in 1972, were because 'the Old Heath Gypsies had put a curse on the pool'.[15]

John Blake moved to the Beacontree Estate as a child, in the same year Alf Ramsey stipulated moving back there as a condition of agreeing his 1949 transfer to Tottenham.[16] Blake described how Gypsies still lived on Becontree Heath and his parents' mistrust of them:

A number of my classmates at Junior School came from the permanent gypsy encampment on the heath, on the site of the present swimming pool. My mother declared the camp 'out of bounds', but my brother and myself ignored all warnings of children never being seen again after visiting the place, and often played there.[17]

A few surviving photographs show Becontree Heath GRT people in the late 1940s.[18] Below, a young woman and a child are seated by a conventional, wooden caravan.

A man can also be seen (below) seated by the same caravan's adjacent open fire. Although the image is indistinct, he may be Black or bi-racial.

There has always been diversity in Becontree, so how has Alf Ramsey's stayed hidden?

'Obsessive Self-Defence': Alf Hiding Himself

Four months after Alf died, and just as a new millennium approached, virulent biases and prejudices against GRT people persisted. In 1999 Norfolk farmer Tony Martin shot a 16-year-old Gypsy-Traveller child, Fred Barras. Fred was running away after an attempted burglary at Martin's isolated, derelict farmhouse. He died at the scene and Martin was convicted of murder. During his first winter in prison, Tony Martin received over 4,000 Christmas cards from the UK public,[19] despite having been jailed for killing a child by shooting him in the back. It is tempting to ask something Alf might have thought: what sort of an England was this?

Alf's family history, as sampled in previous chapters, helps explain why, when under the public gaze, he remained 'private to an almost hermit-like extent'.[20] A 1960s BBC interview exemplifies Alf's obfuscations. A reporter enquires, 'Are your parents still alive, Mr. Ramsey?', to which he tersely replies, 'Oh yes', so the reporter asks, 'Where do they live?', and Alf answers 'In Dagenham, I believe.'[21] Such hedging epitomised Alf's insecurities around ancestry, but also about accent.[22] Sometimes this has mistakenly been assumed as fear of 'sounding Cockney',[23] yet in a rare biographical interview Alf categorically denied being 'a cockney, who has polished up the rough edges of a London accent ... he came from a country background' (*Daily Mirror* 6 November 1972). Oral historical evidence similarly suggests that, until the mid-1950s, Alf had a country accent. A 1930s childhood friend remembered how 'I sometimes went to his house ... little more than a wooden hut ... Dagenham had its own special brogue and Alf spoke with that.'[24] Tottenham team-mate Dennis Uphill said Alf 'spoke very slowly with a rural twinge ... a sort of country brogue ... the same you would find in people from Norwich, a burr'.[25] Another colleague from late 1940s Southampton recalled Alf's 'voice had a slight accent ... not Cockney but Essex'.[26]

It was these rural accentual flavours that worried Alf most because, when allied with his dark complexion, racist nickname and family background dealing in produce, they marked him as 'other'. For example, when Ed Speight, a 1954–55 Tottenham team-mate, first met Alf, Speight referred amicably to their shared Dagenham birthplace. In response 'Alf did not say anything ... He looked a little Mediterranean in appearance, but he never talked about his background ... He was always on his guard, always. He had this mask and would never reveal much.'[27] Alf's later artificial 'style of speech' gradually evolved because he was always 'seeking to improve himself',[28] but he was not escaping the East End, he was backing away from his poor rural roots, darker skin tone and GRT-labelled nickname. Analysing his 1960s communication style as England's manager, a contemporary expert shrewdly interpreted Alf's apparently unemotional 'public composure' as actually 'obsessive self-defence'.[29]

Adding to Alf's insecurities was his older brother and lifelong Dagenham resident, Albert. Not only was Albert Ramsey nicknamed 'Bruno',[30] which as an English nickname similarly relates to 'dark complexion, brown-haired, nut brown',[31] but published testimony shows he bore an uncanny resemblance to Alf. It comes from songwriter Bill Martin, who in early 1970 co-devised 'Back Home', to mark England's Mexico World Cup campaign. For commercial reasons he wanted the England squad to sing it, but Alf's managerial permission would be needed. Visiting his celebrity friend, Dagenham resident and 1967 Eurovision song contest winner Sandie Shaw one evening, by accident or design Bill Martin spotted 'Bruno' Ramsey in a local pub.

> He was the absolute double of Alf. Once I saw it wasn't Alf, I thought it must be his twin. We got drinking and talking. He

did not say a word about Alf but then drunks don't talk family
… He did not want to talk about Alf, only himself.[32]

Martin described Alf, a few months later, initially scorning his proposal
for a World Cup song. Alf changed his mind only after the songwriter
raised meeting his look-alike brother in a Dagenham pub, including
how he 'fell over and was lying in the gutter when I left him'. Brother
Albert was, the songwriter claimed, Alf's 'Achilles' heel … a serious
drunk'.[33] Although that World Cup song then became a massive hit,
Alf afterwards, recounted Martin, 'made a point of completely blanking
me'.[34] Why? Because he had exposed Alf's personal vulnerabilities by
intruding into his background. Chapters one and two showed the malign
power of Alf's 'D****e' nickname and this 1970 incident confirms how
another Ramsey brother, also labelled to denote dark complexion, was
'the absolute double of Alf … I thought it was his twin'. Significantly,
by the time 1950s Alf became a football manager, local and national
journalists also knew of Albert's 'Bruno' nickname, lifestyle and closeness
to his now-famous brother Alf.[35] In 2002, Peter Batt, a legendary sports
reporter,[36] recounted a story that Fleet Street journalists 'all accepted
and laughed at over a drink'. It featured Albert, when Alf was managing
Ipswich (1955–63), regularly pulling 'up in a caravan outside the Ipswich
Ground', then waiting 'for Alf to crack, and go out and give him a
tenner'.[37] Another Suffolk journalist recalled 'Alf did not really want to
know his brother Albert, the dog man. He was embarrassed by him.'[38]
A Dagenham neighbour claimed Bruno 'never went out to work' and
'earned his keep from gambling and keeping greyhounds.'[39] In the
1950s all the Ramseys, including Alf, were registered owners of racing
greyhounds, which is how Alf ended up at Ipswich Town.[40] 'Bruno'
Ramsey may well have used a caravan or trailer for himself and his dogs,
so fuelling gossip about Gypsy-Traveller family links after stopping by
to see Alf at Ipswich.

Whilst this book's new evidence, viewed through contemporary
perspectives, helps us to see Alf's chronic insecurities as potentially
rooted in racism, previous biographies have largely ignored, denied or not
followed through on the implications. Neither Marquis's[41] nor Bowler's[42]
20th-century books mentioned Alf's racist nickname or rumoured GRT
heritage. Bowler hinted at both during a 2002 television programme,[43]
and repeated that briefly in print 20 years later when summarising Alf
as 'Dagenham D****e, a boy of Romany stock'.[44] Unfortunately, no
further evidence or discussion backed that up. Hamilton's majestic recent
444-page book, tracking Alf Ramsey and the 1966 team, similarly

abbreviated Alf's 'Gypsy' rumours to two sentences and 'a pint and a half of Romany blood'.[45]

The time-consuming, sometimes frustrating slog of researching Ramsey's family background may explain such brevity, but phrases like 'Romany stock' or 'Romany blood' inaccurately over-simplify Alf. His eclectic heritage, and career-long experiences of snide labelling, played deeper roles in shaping both Alf's fragile sense of self, and stunningly successful football career. His ancestry, like most of us, was also more tangled than crude terms such as 'stock' or 'blood' can convey. Despite his own darker skin shade, Alf's family appears not to have been 'Romany' in ethnic or cultural senses. Instead, and to their significant social disadvantage, they had a hybrid heritage in an age when any perceived 'Gypsies' or 'Travellers', especially if other than Romany, 'were dismissed as the off-scourings of society, needing to be swept away'.[46]

Alf's mother, described by him in 1972 as 'in many ways very like me',[47] epitomised the Ramseys' rustic otherness. Florence Ramsey clung to her tiny, primitive Becontree Heath 'wooden hut'[48] of a cottage, from her 1915 marriage almost to her 1979 death; and as early as 1952 the family's stubborn sense of difference was locally, publicly noted. Coinciding with Alf publishing his autobiography, a newspaper characterised his birth cottage as a place surrounded by modern council houses where:

> The Old World Holds Out Against The New ... Standing drowsily a little away from the road ... where even today cooking is done on a range and oil-lamps are still in use. There is no electricity or even gas. (*Dagenham Post* 22 October 1952)

Two decades later, the *Sunday Mirror* (6 June 1971) repeated that story nationally. Headlined 'NO TRANSFER FOR SIR ALF'S MOTHER'. It explained how 'Alf had hoped':

> To buy his mother a new house. But Florence Ramsey wants to stay in her 120-year-old cottage, despite the possibility of a threat to pull it down. She has lived in the two-bedroomed wooden-fronted cottage for fifty-six years. Two other cottages in the terrace are empty and the gardens overgrown.

Alf lived in that hut from his 1920 birth until 1940 army conscription, regularly returned afterwards, then moved in again from 1949–51. After marrying in December 1951, he relocated three miles west to Barking, before leaving Essex for good in 1955. His mother's refusal to move from there, or from 'Becontree Heath', was a perennial, public reminder that the Ramseys belonged to the old, rural Becontree of 'dealers' and 'Gypsies'. Not until Alf was aged nine or ten did new brick buildings surround their isolated home (*Ilford Recorder* 20 May 1927, 12 and 19 July 1929). That rural way of life had vanished by the time Alf's later pretentious, rather ridiculous 1960s speaking voice 'provided endless mirth' to London lads like Bobby Moore and Jimmy Greaves. Yet Alf's accent originally differed from theirs because his linguistic heritage was not 'working-class East Ender from Dagenham'[49] but rural East Anglian, from a family peppered with Suffolk and Essex 'dealing' and Gypsy-Traveller influences.

The public mask of Alf's eventually absurd vocalisation was, in McKinstry's striking phrase, a 'strangulated parody of a minor public-school housemaster'.[50] Equally, and like other biographies, McKinstry minimised the rural, GRT influences that helped conjure it. For him, 'much of the talk about Alf's gypsy connections has been wildly exaggerated, even invented.'[51] To support that, he quoted Pauline Gosling, a former neighbour, maintaining the Ramseys 'were definitely not of gypsy stock' even though she used to call him 'Uncle D****e'. Pauline's memory was that Alf got his nickname at school 'only because he had very dark hair ... nothing to do with being a gypsy. I know that for a fact.'[52] Yet a little digging reveals that Pauline was born 23 years after Alf. Anything she knew about him getting his 'nickname at school' only through 'very dark hair' was at best second-hand and contradicts other historical evidence. Pauline's account would have been given in good faith, so what might have been influencing her? And why have Alf Ramsey's biographers similarly underplayed, or even denied, his racial childhood labelling?

A contemporary explanation is that white people, including the author writing this, often find racism personally difficult to confront or acknowledge: a phenomenon one expert practitioner calls 'White Fragility'.[53] Such fragility emanates, she argues, from the social and personal risks entailed when white people try genuinely to 'hear' people of colour describing concrete, painful experiences of racism. Willed ignorance is far easier, she argues, because a 'racial status quo is comfortable ... whiteness ... as the norm or standard, and people of colour as a deviation from that norm'.[54] White writers like me, in the 'hyper-white space of sports media',[55] benefit particularly from wishing racism away. Yet the idea of 'White Fragility' lights up, and joins up, the myriad scraps of historical evidence telling Alf Ramsey's story. For example, in another invaluable McKinstry testimony, Jean, 18 years younger than Alf, worked in an office with his younger brother Cyril. Finding Cyril 'quiet and decent' she disbelieved rumours that 'Alf was a gypsy. To know Cyril, I could not believe it. Cyril did not seem to be from gypsy stock at all.'[56] Similarly, late 1940s contemporary Stan Clements told McKinstry he 'never thought Alf Ramsey was a gypsy. I cannot see that at all. When I first met him, his entire appearance was immaculate. And gypsies don't own land for generations.'[57]

Given revelations in previous chapters, Stan was perhaps muddling causes and consequences, because having been nicknamed 'D****e', Alf had an incentive to look immaculate. The 1980s childhood memories of Hope Powell, the first Black, English, female manager of an England football team, similarly describe how her mother 'drummed into' her children that 'we had to look like a million dollars and present yourself', so nobody could say 'you look like a scruff ... that was her way of protecting us from what was really going on'.[58] Powell's life can appear 'both exceptional and ... archetypal',[59] and so can Alf's. His archetypal defence strategy of dressing well, speaking precisely and adopting BBC pronunciation, insured not just against class vulnerabilities, but offered shields against being mocked as a 'Gypsy', or othered as not irrefutably white. Yes, Alf was 'quiet', 'decent', 'immaculate' and had relatives who 'owned land'. Yet from a 21st rather than a 20th-century perspective, why should such attributes mean Alf could not *also* have GRT heritage? Such logic only works by accepting the underlying racist assumption that its opposites are self-evidently true, that Gypsy, Roma, or Traveller people, or those with some of that heritage, are by some twisted racial definition[60] loud, badly behaved, or scruffy; and that their ethnicity dictates they could not possibly live settled lives, dwell in houses, or own land. That premise is not just morally hollow, it is historically inaccurate.

Given the deep, overlapping tides of prejudice, ignorance, and confusion about GRT people that persisted throughout Alf's lifetime, is it any wonder that, from the 1930s on, he never publicly acknowledged nor tried to explain who he *really* was? As an amateur in 1943, then a part-time professional attached to a professional football club (1944–46), as a full-time professional for two clubs whilst winning 32 England caps (1946–55), as a successful club manager winning the English Football League championship (1955–63), and then as England's World Cup-winning manager (1963–74), Alf Ramsey had an increasingly high profile on an expanding public stage. Everything Alf had personally learned, though, from how family, friends and neighbours were treated, showed that anyone assumed to be a 'Gypsy', or related to GRT people, was vulnerable to disadvantage, prejudice, and persecution.

'Racism' is the simple contemporary term to describe such processes. A powerful response to racism, particularly as experienced by GRT people, is 'secrecy', and that links Alf's life in the last century with modernity. For example, in 2022 a serving London police officer blogged openly for the first time about his GRT heritage and experiences:

> I didn't know we were a Romany family until I was 12 years old ... I was like *Why don't you talk about it ever?* My dad said: *Don't put it down in job applications, always put that you're White British* ... In 2015 I became a police officer and decided after hearing all the stuff in canteens and offices that enough is enough ... hurtful comments ... like *oh we got to deal with bl**dy p*keys again or gypp*s are causing problems.*[61]

Or as Romany Gypsy Grace O'Neill recalled recently, whilst writing about becoming secretive after school bullying: 'Somehow one of our classmates had found out and started calling us *Gyppo* in the playground. This only strengthened the idea that I should try to preserve and protect this element of my identity from the outside world' (*The Guardian* 15 June 2020).

Which all helps explain why, the better known he became, the more tenaciously Alf Ramsey refused to engage in any public discussion about his own or his family's past; and why his ancestral and early life story has had to be recreated here, nearly from scratch, using neglected or unknown historical sources. He was born into a remarkable, hardworking, entrepreneurial, sometimes eccentric, and occasionally lawbreaking East Anglian family, with Gypsy-Traveller links on both sides. They had rural upbringings and outlooks, and Alf was a rustic East Anglian from Becontree Heath, not an urban East Ender from the Beacontree Estate. These characteristics combined, by the early 1930s, to make Alf and his family feel like social and ethnic outsiders as, fieldby-field, the new estate swallowed their 'Native Becontree Heath'. Alf Ramsey's skin shade, rustic roots, scattered Gypsy-Traveller ancestry, and birthplace, combined to mark him down as 'other'.

Luckily for Alf, though, and amidst an otherwise unremarkable first 20 years, two things shone out. The first was that on the scattered occasions during his childhood that he was given a formal stage on which to show it, Alf was rather good at playing football. The second was that when lack of access to pitches, kit, coaching, balls, goalposts, and games in which to play seemed to conspire against him, resilience kicked in. The resilience he had learned in the face of family hardships, being nicknamed 'D****e' as a child, and of coming from a Becontree Heath community bulldozed by modernity. Alf's indomitable perseverance then secured, nearly 27 years after his birth, his first game of fully professional football in a national, competitive, peacetime league: exactly the sort of resilience that would be needed, 20 years later, were England to win its first football World Cup.

1 Thanks to staff at the **Valence House Archive & Local Studies Centre** and to Tony Benton for his highly informative 13 October 2021 talk on the 'Becontree 100' anniversary

2 West, J. (1993) p.51

3 *Ilford Recorder* 17 July 1931

4 Barking & Dagenham website (no date) 'Population and demographics' 2021 census

5 Kelly's Directory of Essex (1914) p.196

6 Barking & Dagenham website (no date): 'About the Borough – About Becontree ward'

7 Cressy, D. (2018) pp.1,42

8 For example: *Stratford Times* 2 February 1881, *Gravesend Reporter* 9 June 1883, *Essex Herald* 6 July 1885, *Barking Advertiser* 31 May 1890, *Essex Newsman* 9 June 1893, *Barking Advertiser* 23 March 1895, *Essex Newsman* 18 April 1903, *Essex Newsman* 27 August 1904

9 **Dagenham Parish Council Minute Book 1894-1908**

10 Ibid. 18 May 1899

11 *Walthamstow Guardian* 29 August 1913

12 West, J. (1993) p.49

13 Ramsey, A. (1952) p.12

14 **Valence House Archive & Local Studies Centre** E1 920 'My Dagenham Childhood' by Violet Kentsbeer p.55

15 Ibid. p.94

16 Ramsey, A. (1952) p.49

17 **Valence House Archive & Local Studies Centre** 1800/41 C2 02 'Childhood Memories of Becontree Heath in The 1950s' recorded by John Blake in 1993

18 Images courtesy of **Valence House Archive & Local Studies Centre**

19 BBC News website (17 August 2019) 'Tony Martin - man who shot burglars knows he still divides opinion'

20 Edworthy, N. (2000) p.68

21 Marquis, M. (1970) pp.14-15. See also Edworthy, N. (2000) p.69 and McKinstry, L. (2007) p.18

22 Marquis, M. (1970) p.15, Edworthy, N. (2000) p.70, McKinstry, L. (2007) pp.18-24

23 For example: McKinstry, L. (2007) p.23, Tommy Steele in *Daily Mirror* 19 December 1974

24 Ibid. p.5, p.20

25 McKinstry, L. (2007) p.22

26 Ibid. p.21

27 Ibid. pp.137-8

28 Ibid. p.21

29 Hopcraft, A. (1968) p.134

30 McKinstry, L (2007) Jean Bixby p.7
31 *Shorter Oxford English Dictionary* 3rd edition 1983
32 Ibid.p.402
33 Ibid. Bill Martin pp.401-3
34 Spurling, J. (2022) p.33
35 E.g. Scovell, B. (2005) p.204; McKinstry, L (2007) pp.401-3
36 Sports Journalists' Association website (4 May 2011) 'Fleet St's legendary sportswriter Peter Batt has died'
37 **Channel 4** (2002) *Sir Alf* director Ken McGill
38 McKinstry, L (2007) p.401
39 Ibid. p.7
40 See chapter 9
41 Marquis, M. (1970) op. cit.
42 Bowler, D. (1999)
43 In **Channel 4** (2002) Ken McGill *Sir Alf*
44 Bowler, D. (2021)
45 Hamilton, D. (2023) p.21
46 Mayall, D. (2009) p.186
47 *Daily Mirror* 9 November 1972 Interview with Frank McGhee
48 McKinstry, L. (2007) p.5
49 Dickinson, M. (2014) p.71
50 McKinstry, L. (2007) p.18
51 Ibid. p.15
52 Ibid. p.16, no source or date supplied
53 Diangelo, R. (2018)
54 Ibid. pp.14 and 25
55 Jacobs, C. (2022) pp.14-18
56 McKinstry, L. (2007) p.16
57 Ibid.
58 Powell, H. (2021) p.65
59 Wanga, J. (2022) p.119
60 Diangelo, R. (2018) p.15
61 MyLondon website (26 June 2022) Christopher Baughurst 'I'm a Met police officer from the Romani community, I used to hide it but now I want to inspire others'

CHAPTER 4

SAVED BY SUNDAY FOOTBALL

But Banned by the FA

Early Alf

THIS CHAPTER takes Alf Ramsey from Becontree birth in 1920 to armed adulthood in 1940 via school, shopwork, Sunday football and a world war, all backdropped by a daring social experiment. Building the new Beacontree Estate entailed more than just adding an 'a' to Becontree's spelling: effectively it bulldozed or land-grabbed the old Becontree Heath, and everything around it, ballooning Dagenham's population from 8,000 in 1921 to 80,000 by 1931 (*Ilford Recorder* 17 July).

Alf had been born at isolated Five Elms, a cluster of farm buildings and cottages fringing Becontree Heath, home in 1920 to just 17 families.[1] In 1924 London County Council compulsorily purchased all surrounding fields and auctioned their standing crops of rhubarb, broccoli and cabbages (*Ilford Recorder* 31 October). By 1934, when Alf left school, those fields had sprouted thousands of new homes and families. His first employer, 300 yards away, was a shiny Co-operative grocery store, in a busy terrace of modern shops, abutting the wide boulevard of Wood Lane. Alf's walk to work passed snug, brick-built council houses graced with gas, electricity and indoor toilets, utilities conspicuously absent in the Ramseys' flimsy timber cottage.[2]

Life was tough in this modernist Beacontree, because frenetic housebuilding far outstripped planning for schools, public transport, healthcare, recreation and employment. When Alf was seven, a local reporter lamented council failures to plan properly: 'Parents have had great difficulty in placing their children in schools ... young boys and girls are being thrown out into the world without the prospect of learning a trade or getting a job of any kind' (*Ilford Recorder* 20 May 1927). Jim Peters, cited in chapter one as persistently calling Alf 'D****e', moved there aged nine in 1927 when it was still 'almost completely country ... more farms than houses'. He waited 'nearly eight months before a [school] place could be found'.[3] Leaving school in 1933, Peters's dream was to play professional sport but three months later he and 'three hundred other' local youths were still unemployed. Most had to find work in London, entailing a 13-mile commute on packed trains.[4]

Alf's experiences mirrored those. Dagenham was 'sadly deficient in school building' and not until three years into his education was a new school opened in Becontree Heath (*Essex Chronicle* 4 November 1927). In 1923, the Beacontree Estate's 3,000 early tenants had staged a rent strike against 'paying more than half their income on rent, rates and travelling expenses' (*Daily Herald* 28 April). When Alf left school in 1934, public transport was still inadequate, despite most locals having to 'travel to and from London each day' for work.[5] Poverty was real, and ubiquitous. In 1925 'an Irishman, William Tobson, age 26' (*Westminster Gazette* 25 April) lay close to Alf's home for five days 'starving in a barn at Becontree Heath, before his pitiful cries for water attracted passers-by' (*John Bull* 9 May). Tobson, who had been working and sleeping rough on different local farms for two years, died of exhaustion, pleurisy and tuberculosis (*Essex Newsman* 2 May). Dagenham would eventually become famous for hosting the Ford Motor Company factory, but that did not open until 1931. Even then it was one of just six factories in Dagenham, compared to 83 in West Ham,[6] and its first skilled workers came from Manchester (*Barking and Dagenham Post* 9 November 2011). As late as 1938, only 30–40 per cent of Beacontree Estate inhabitants worked nearby, and Fords employed just 12,650 people.[7] Finding local jobs was particularly difficult for youngsters like Alf, and the year he left school '75% of Dagenham's 7,500 adolescents worked outside the area. Some Becontree boys spent 22 hours per week commuting, and the average time was 10 hours.'[8]

The effects of patchy schooling and limited job opportunities were exacerbated by scant youth support. A national newspaper editorial lambasted poor provision for the 'well-being of young people during the first years of their working life', highlighting how Beacontree's '65,000 children and young persons' were supported by just a few church groups and 'one boys' and girls' club with accommodation for 100' (*The Times* 4 May 1934). The *Daily Herald* similarly critiqued the estate's 'inadequate … weekday recreation' for youngsters, Beacontree lacking both 'premises and social workers and leaders'. It claimed many Dagenham school starters in 1925, Alf's first year, had 'no proper school accommodation' with many running 'wild until about eight or nine years of age because there were no schools' (1 April 1935). Ramsey's own educational memories were decidedly impoverished: 'Being not particularly clever at school, I seem to have spent more time pumping up footballs and carrying goal posts on to the Common' (*Daily Mirror* 9 November 1972).

Beacontree Insiders or Outsiders?

Rapid population growth and haphazard planning heightened tensions. Dagenham village in 1926 was socially and psychologically still 'very much separated' from the new estate, recalled one local.[9] Recent research painted new residents as 'faced with a degree of hostility from the people of the old Dagenham village', with some village children 'banned … from stepping foot' there or 'mixing with its residents'.[10] Remarkably, Alf said practically nothing about the Beacontree Estate in his 1952 autobiography, nor in later interviews, yet rapid change troubled many. In 1937 Alf's mother's second cousin 'Miss Annie Bixby' was:

> Found dead in her bedroom … filled with gas … she was worried about the proposed demolition of the house … to make room for a traffic roundabout … she was born at Becontree Heath and her family had lived there for several generations. (*Dagenham Post* 17 January 1937)

Annie Bixby was not alone in experiencing psychological distress. Speaking in 1934 of three incomers from London, who had taken their own lives within days of arrival, a Methodist minister observed some new parishioners' acute loneliness:

> After all the colour and warmth and light of the East End they go out into new areas where there are miles of badly lit streets … scarcely a church … a public house … and no institutions. The L.C.C. has segregated all these poor people, cutting them off from the middle-classes and upper-classes. They are suffering not only from loneliness but from isolation. (*Daily Herald* 2 March)

In such an odd social setting divisions could grow. Another cousin of Alf's mother, 29-year-old John Bixby, was prosecuted for threatening to strangle a 21-year-old woman (*Barking and Dagenham Advertiser* 7 January 1938). His defence claimed bullying: 'people had called him a cave man and a hunchback' and his victim 'was the cause of that derision' (*Essex Chronicle* 7 January 1938). Might Alice taking her own life, John's violent threats after name-calling and Alf being labelled 'D****e', sometimes have reflected tensions between rural and urban, or old and new?

Alf loved football but its public nature exposed him. Knowledge of his racist childhood nickname survived only because football is a team game, played in shared spaces, in groups representing place and community. Playing football entailed people watching and remembering Alf, whether he liked it or not, witness this anonymous 1920s schoolmate recalling: 'he was a year above me but I remember him' as 'a kid you wouldn't get to like in a hurry.'[11] When aged 13 and playing for his school, Alf was sent off 'for querying a referee's decision' (*Daily Express* 16 January 1964). Another contemporary remembered him as 'very withdrawn, almost surly, but he became animated on the football field'.[12] Football became the emotional outlet of choice, then a lifelong obsession, for this shy and racially labelled adolescent called Alf. How did that happen?

Alf Discovers Football

Alf's autobiography mentions school only when linked to football being played there, or whilst walking back and forth with his two elder brothers. Aged seven, he was selected 'to play for the Junior side ... at inside-left', with 'brother Len at inside-right'. In his first school season, Becontree Heath's 'Junior side won the local Schools' Championship' and aged 'nine I had progressed to ... captain and centre-half'. Then 'came my first *honour* ... to play for Dagenham Schools against West Ham in a Corinthian Shield match'.[13] Archives show Becontree Heath winning several trophies in Brentwood's Elementary Schools League, before in 1927 leaving to join the recently formed 'separate association' of Dagenham.[14] A national newspaper reported their 'RAPID GROWTH', with ten schools in the first season, plans for 15, and the current 'junior trophy' being 'held by Becontree Heath'. Crucially, given Dagenham schools' dire overcrowding, was the local council's 'great assistance in allowing the use of Parish and open spaces for League matches' (*Daily Herald* 9 November 1927). Thus, aged 13, Alf reached a footballing peak unmatched until ten years later in the army. A six-paragraph newspaper report featured Becontree Heath School's 3-3 league draw:

> The outstanding players for *The Heath* were Ramsay [sic] centre-half, and Parrish goalkeeper ... Ramsay scored with a long, dropping shot ... Parrish playing a marvellous game ... Parrish played in goal for the South of England last year, and was the first reserve for the English Schoolboys' team. (*Ilford Recorder* 28 September 1933)

A month later, Alf played for Dagenham Schoolboys against Romford, beating them 4-0 (*Ilford Recorder* 26 October 1933). Parrish, the goalkeeper mentioned above, was not in the team, nor two weeks later when Alf captained Dagenham to a 4-0 victory at the Dagenham Town ground. Alf played 'a very clever game' and later 'scored easily' (*Ilford Recorder* 9 November). But the teenaged football careers of Alf Ramsey and Parrish would, over the next few years, highlight Alf's disadvantage. Being aged nearly 14 and therefore imminent school leavers, neither played when Dagenham Schoolboys lost 5-3 to Tottenham (*Ilford Recorder* 6 December 1933). Yet three years later match reports applauded Parrish as Romford FC's 'best player ... played a brilliant game ... many of his saves were outstanding' (*Essex Chronicle* 19 February 1937). In 1938 Parrish again made 'many fine saves' before 9,100 'Essex Senior Cup Final' spectators at Ilford (*Essex Chronicle* 22 April), repeating that in Romford's successful replay at Walthamstow FC. Meanwhile, his school team-mate Alf Ramsey had been forced into playing Sunday football, in leagues banned by the FA. Even there, another team-mate later recalled, Alf's name came up almost as an after-thought: 'We were looking for some blokes to play football' but after 'a few games we weren't doing too well ... Someone suggested that D****e Ramsey ... he agreed to play and that was it.'[15]

Alf the Co-operator

Times were tough for the Ramsey family. Three more babies were born after Alf, one of whom died in 1924 aged ten months. By the 1928 birth of Alf's last sibling, his father's straw-dealing had failed and he had become a 'labourer'.[16] In 1934, school-leaver Alf's application for a Ford Factory apprenticeship was rejected.[17] What options remained? Alf later claimed a 'family conference' led him to becoming 'an apprentice at a local Co-operative store':

> The grocery trade for some unknown reason had always appealed to me, but before I started on my apprenticeship ... I would put in a spell as an errand boy. So everyday I'd cycle my way around the Dagenham district taking to customers their various needs. My wages were twelve shillings a week. I handed over ten shillings to my mother, put one shilling in a box as savings, and kept a shilling for pocket-money.[18]

It would be wrong to idealise this job. In 1934 a 12-year-old cyclist was killed by a lorry in Becontree Heath, with the local coroner sadly observing,

'You see it every day at all street corners. Tradesmen's lads coming out of side streets without looking where they are going, and it is sheer luck that they do not get run over' (*Essex Newsman* 10 November). Yet Alf's weekly wage of 'twelve shillings' equalled others working in London, who were commuting ten hours a week and paying to do so.[19] Pedalling miles along windy streets helped Alf keep fit, and his job opened the door to two things at which he learned to excel: football and leadership.

By sheer chance, the London Co-operative Society (LCS) had a dynamic new leader who, in late 1933, took the highly innovative step of convening 'one thousand young shop and errand boys' at a London SHOP BOYS CONFERENCE. Addressing them, he fervently recommended further study, celebrated the LCS's job security and 'automatic wage increases', and recounted his own Barking and Dagenham backstory:

> The lads were thrilled with Mr. Webster's reference to his own early experience as a co-operative errand-boy, which started 34 years ago in East London [pushing] a loaded grocery barrow along country lanes which now form part of the Beacontree Estate. He described his advance, stage by stage, to become General Manager of the largest co-operative society in the Empire. (*West Ham Mail* 17 November 1933)

We do not know whether Alf attended that conference, but Webster's speech was reported across multiple London newspapers. His recent appointment had also been photographed nationally, and his Barking backstory reported locally.[20] Was that why the Ramsey family were so excited for Alf about possible careers at the Co-op? Part local celebrity, part business guru, leading a company with an annual turnover equivalent to half a billion pounds today, Webster exhorted teenagers to 'be imaginative, do your job to the best of your ability, devote your spare time to pursuits which will develop your character. Be just' (*Weekly Dispatch* 17 September 1933).

Alf's subsequent life followed that precise pattern. Working for a commercially successful, socially innovative organisation just five minutes' walk away led to him recalling fondly, 'I was happy in this job', whilst also lamenting the lack of opportunity to play football:

> I worked, of course, every Saturday afternoon. On my half-day, Thursday, there was no organised [youth] football in the district and for two years I never knew the thrill of kicking a ball.[21]

That sustained absence from competitive football must have been agonising but was eased when the Co-operative Society started its own Thursday afternoon sports leagues *(Daily Herald* 26 February 1937). Little evidence survives but Alf's childhood friend and later Dagenham's mayor recalled, 'I used to work with him in Five Elms, and we played cricket and football for their team on Thursdays and Sundays' (*Barking and Dagenham Post* 5 May 1999). Alf's Thursday cricket talent was confirmed by him later gifting a treasured bat to a colleague's son,[22] probably the same bat as recalled here by Alf's childhood friend:

> Once we had a match against Upminster Thursday and Alf got 100 runs, so we presented him with a cricket bat. After the 1966 World Cup I saw him at a reception … at Barking Town Hall. The first thing he said when he saw me was that 'he still had that cricket bat'. (*Barking and Dagenham Post* 3 July 2002)

Of Thursday football, even less remains. Alf's 1952 autobiography claimed that he and other Five Elms youngsters met 'every Wednesday night … to pay our subscription of sixpence, discuss the following afternoon's match and … talk football.'[23] Here Alf was probably obfuscating, since no evidence survives of Five Elms playing Thursday football. If Alf did play in Thursday leagues, it was probably for Becontree LCS, one of multiple Co-op teams in their own, sponsored Thursday football league (*Daily Herald* 25 November 1938, 20 January 1939). Encouraging its workforce into Thursday sport was a political statement by Alf's employer to embody the Co-op's innovative, progressive, democratic socialist principles. From the mid-1930s the LCS invested heavily in offering employees otherwise inaccessible sporting (and cultural) opportunities.[24] Who led that initiative? The former Barking barrow boy cited earlier:

> LONDON CO-OP SPORT – BIG DEVELOPMENTS
> Considerable development in London Co-op sports should result from the highly successful delegate conference held recently under the chairmanship of Mr J. Webster, general manager. Numerous sound suggestions … augur well for the 19 sections of organised recreation. (*Reynolds Newspaper* 13 October 1935)

Such ambition put them in local competition with the established, FA-oriented amateur Thursday leagues then common across urban

England.[25] In 1936 the Co-op's new, socialist-inspired Thursday league team played their first representative match against the existing Essex Thursday League, at Leytonstone's ground (*Reynolds Newspaper* 13 December 1936). The latter had started in 1924, grew with FA endorsement to 40 clubs, and its 1936 and 1937 annual presentations at Ilford[26] were addressed by Jack Bowers, Essex FA committee member and future national FA vice-president.[27] For Alf, this would later have personal dimensions. The same Jack Bowers became an FA senior international committee member, a committee to which Alf Ramsey as England manager reported from 1962–66.[28] Bowers was ironically known amongst FA staff as 'Jumping Jack', because he was 'so old' he had once fallen 'asleep at a committee meeting'.[29] As a Co-operative employee and LCS Thursday sportsperson, 1930s Alf was therefore already on the side of disruptors, challenging the FA's football establishment. That divide was then irredeemably deepened by the FA stubbornly persecuting adolescents, like Alf, who dared to play football on Sundays.

Unrepentant: Alf the Sunday Footballer

Alf's 1952 autobiography included a photo of a Five Elms trophy-winning team, but without admitting the significant fact that it played on Sundays not Thursdays. This matters because, as Alf's 1974 sacking shows and later chapters explore, leading FA volunteer governors never felt comfortable with Alf, nor he with them; an unease tapping into English football's history. In 1908, Essex FA suspended and fined a well-known Barking FC footballer for playing and organising Sunday football, alongside his elite amateur Saturday career (*Barking Advertiser* 26 December). Then, despite vehement FA opposition, several new Sunday football leagues were founded in Alf's locality during the late 1920s and early 1930s, in open rebellion against the FA.

Typical of these was the Dagenham and District Sunday Football League in which Alf's Five Elms team started playing in season 1937/38 (*Barking and Dagenham Advertiser* 14 January 1938). The league's founding president was Salvatore Marino,[30] who also donated a cup to local women's footballers. Census returns show Marino was a 'greengrocer and fruiterer', born in Southern Italy. In 1921, he lived in West Ham and by the 1930s in Five Elms, where he and his wife ran a café (*Ilford Recorder* 26 June 1935). Breaking rules about the café's opening hours brought fines for the Marinos (*Ilford Recorder* 19 July 1934). By charitably sponsoring Sunday *and* women's football, Marino was poking fun at Dagenham council and an FA that, in their own recent words, had enacted a ban which 'side-lined … the women's game … for nearly 50 years'.[31]

The image below, of the April 1936 Marino Women's Cup Final, also helps illustrate Alf's youthful leisure time, local facilities and playing career. The venue was a new stadium, opened in 1932 (*Essex Chronicle* 9 December), fenced off to charge entry, and located at The Merry Fiddlers, Becontree Heath. Alf frequented it as a youth,[32] and the same month these photos were taken a men's Sunday team called The Merry Fiddlers lost a cup final there, before 2,000 spectators (*West Ham Echo* 24 April). Four weeks later that team won the elite East London and Becontree Sunday League (*West Ham Echo* 22 May 1936).

Some high-quality 1930s Sunday football made money, entrenching the FA's opposition. In 1935, the Dagenham Premier Sunday Football League could attract 'a good crowd' of paying customers at Old Dagenham Park (*West Ham Echo* 11 October), where 15 months later admission was still being charged for league cup games (*Dagenham Post* 26 February 1937). Alf's Sunday team played in an uncommercial league but did lose a 1938 charity cup final at The Merry Fiddlers ground, for which entrance would have been charged (*Dagenham Post* 20 May, 27 May 1938). Fortunately for teenaged Alf, amateur and semi-professional local Sunday football was booming. The amateur league his Five Elms side joined reported that 'six hundred players took part in' their 1935/36 season, with the imminent new season promising another 'big increase' to 26 teams (*Dagenham Post* 4 September 1936). Five Elms at first played only in their invitational Marino Cup, mentioned previously, but joined the league fully for season 1937/38.

Throughout the 1930s, and Alf's adolescent Sunday playing days, official opposition to Sunday football remained serious and sustained. A Brentwood Urban council committee 'asked the police to assist in preventing the use of the recreation fields for organised games on Sundays' (*Essex Newsman* 14 January 1932). Weeks later, open rebellion against the FA would erupt when a National Sunday Football Association was formed by 'numerous representatives' dissatisfied that 'clubs affiliated to the FA are debarred from Sunday play' (*London Daily News* 15 February 1932). Some councils, following the FA lead, 'would remove the goal posts to stop them playing' on council pitches.[33]

Months later a newspaper local to Alf ran a lengthy editorial headlined 'SUNDAY FOOTBALL'. It cited 28 existing local Sunday clubs and explained why this issue mattered so much to Dagenham youngsters like Alf. The new Sunday league used 'grounds in one of the public parks. There have been no complaints.' Football provided:

> The best form of recreation for a large number of lads, mostly between the ages of 16 and 22, who otherwise would find Sunday in a place like Dagenham intolerably dull. At the worst, it is said, they are kept out of mischief.

Unfortunately, the editorial continued, the FA's 'very strong views' banning 'Sunday play' meant 'several hundred lads' were now 'virtually *football outlaws* ... debarred from taking part in any game played under the auspices of the Football Association. Since 'the community of *outlaws* is fast increasing all over the country ... they cannot be ignored for long.' Some Sunday games now 'charged for admission' and the risk of Sunday football becoming 'professionalised and commercialised ... to the intense regret of all true lovers of the game ... is rather encouraged than diminished by a system of *outlawry*' (*Ilford Recorder* 11 August 1932).

Such reasoning made no headway with the FA throughout Alf's playing days. Just as he was leaving school, a 1933 Essex County FA meeting at Ilford decided to 'suspend a player until he severed his connection with Sunday football. Sunday football is prohibited' (*Chelmsford Chronicle* 29 December). A year later Essex FA made Harwich and Dagenham replay a game in the prestigious FA Amateur Cup after Harwich had fielded 'a Sunday active footballer' (*London Daily News* 19

November 1934, *Chelmsford Chronicle* 23 November). Similar national examples included a Worcestershire footballer suspended 'for taking part in a Sunday game' (*Birmingham Daily Gazette* 28 November 1934), and Yorkshire youngsters being warned to be wary 'about playing in Sunday football' as the FA's prohibition 'may get the Thursday or Saturday club for which they play into trouble' (*Sheffield Star* 5 October 1935). Kent FA tried to ban Sunday football from council pitches (*Herne Bay Press* 29 April 1939) and in 1939 Essex FA again forcefully threatened Sunday footballers like Alf with exclusion from FA competitions:

> A warning is issued … any player or official who participates in Sunday football automatically suspends himself … He can only play again by being reinstated by his County FA. If he plays without being re-instated, he is an ineligible player. (*Essex Chronicle* 17 February, *Herts and Essex Observer* 18 February)

That stark FA prohibition was reprinted in a newspaper local to Alf, on the same page as its match report of West Ham's fifth-round FA Cup tie before a 'record crowd of 47,614' against the eventual 1939 cup winners, Portsmouth (*West Ham Echo* 17 February). Poignantly, playing for West Ham was 20-year-old Benny Fenton, with whom schoolboy Alf had shaken hands a few years earlier as 'Hammers captain' during an FA-organised 'Dagenham Schools against West Ham Corinthian Shield match'.[34]

Even two months after war was declared Essex FA continued to persecute organised Sunday football. Whilst wanting to 'encourage football played solely for recreational purposes', it would not 'countenance any form of organised football on Sunday … except players engaged in work of National Importance on every other day of the week'. Any club seeking exemption 'must make application, which will be dealt with on its merits' (*Essex Chronicle* 20 October 1939). Even after the war ended, Essex FA continued their persecutions. In 1937 a businessperson local to Alf, George Simister, had founded another Sunday football league for Barking and Dagenham. Ten years later it was still going strong, as recently recounted:

> One young boy who played on Sundays was Alf Ramsey …
> I know this because the man who refereed the game was my father … who after the Second World War became secretary of the league. He had many battles with Dagenham Council, the Church, and the Essex FA.

Only in 1947, after a meeting 'at Dagenham Town Hall', did churches and local councils finally agree to support Sunday football. Significantly, though, the Essex FA,[35] with officers like the Jack Bowers mentioned above, still refused to go anywhere near it.

Sunday Football as Culture War

Conflicts over Sunday football, fought on battlegrounds like Dagenham's Beacontree Estate, were not just quirky local skirmishes, of minority interest, but symbolic national struggles between modernisers and conservatives. On one side were ordinary Saturday workers like Alf, and their political allies. The *Daily Mirror*'s sports editor (5 December 1930) pleaded, 'Is it a crime to play football on Sundays?', advising the FA 'not to outlaw its enthusiasts'. Clement Attlee, East London Labour MP and future prime minister, has been credited with co-founding the 'East London Sunday League' that year.[36]

Opposed were powerful FA and English establishment voices, also local to Alf, who resolutely persecuted Sunday footballers. Thomas Kirkup, London FA's first paid secretary, in 1934 helped impose an FA Amateur Cup replay because a 'Sunday Footballer' had played (*Daily Mirror* 7 November). Kirkup sat on the FA Council until 1947,[37] and despite promising Sunday reform (*Yorkshire Post* 22 August 1939) never delivered it. Similarly, we met Jack Bowers earlier: Essex FA officer since 1934, Wanstead resident, Ilford FC supporter (*Ilford Recorder* 4 July 1935) and as a 1960s FA International Committee member, someone to whom Alf later directly reported. In 1948, Bowers officiated at Essex FA's annual meeting when its president 'denounced organised Sunday soccer' as having 'potential dangers we may not be able to control' (*Essex Newsman* 6 June).

A year later in 1949, when Alf made his England home debut, a prominent journalist described him as a 'tall, dark, handsome … one time grocer's assistant' who had also risen 'from a street team named Five Elms' (*Daily Express* 28 November 1949). The phrase 'street team' was a coded reference to Sunday football, coded because it was still being stringently persecuted. In 1950 an amateur player from Ilford, three miles from where Alf then lived, was suspended for eight months from all FA football after 'playing in obscure Sunday football for his church lads' team in an out-of-the-way London park' (*The People* 8 October).

Some key FA voices dissented from this repressive policy. Alf ally Arthur Drewry chaired the FA selection committee that picked England's team and was FA chairperson from 1955–61.[38] In 1951, he told a local journalist, 'I am glad to see young people enjoying recreative sports on Sunday' (*Yorkshire Post* 26 January). In 1952, Drewry then provided a glowing foreword for Alf's autobiography, describing it as 'a book no football lover should ignore', written by a 'quiet and unassuming young man who carries on his head the broad brow of the thinker, the football strategist'.[39] But as mentioned earlier, whilst the book pictured Alf's younger self, its text did not openly admit to his Five Elms team playing Sunday football. Intriguingly, months before Alf Ramsey's book was published, yet another FA persecution in Dagenham came to national attention:

> The FA ... does not recognise Sunday football ... a Sunday club in Dagenham was asked to loan players to enable two Saturday sides to make up teams. Now the men have been told by the FA they risk suspension by playing on SUNDAYS! Ever heard the story of the Good Samaritan, Essex FA? (*The People* 20 January 1952)

At the height of Alf's professional playing fame, Sunday football therefore remained highly contentious in the press, and divisive within the FA. On the morning of Saturday, 29 November 1952, Alf autographed copies of his recently published autobiography at a Tottenham department store (*North London News* 28 November), hours before playing for Spurs and three days after helping England beat Belgium 5-0. Just four weeks earlier the FA's ruling council had again refused to recognise amateur Sunday football (*Daily Herald* 25 October) despite an FA national report cataloguing how '200 members' had been 'dealt with for playing on a Sunday and two London referees disqualified'. Bizarrely, that FA council even scorned a compromise option that 'a special committee be appointed to study the questions raised in the report' (*Hull Daily Mail* 24 October 1952). The controversy became publicly heated, with one London newspaper condemning FA officials and supporters as 'the Saturday snobs' who 'have no truck with anyone who plays football on a Sunday, referees football on Sunday or organises football on a Sunday' (*Kensington Post* 31 October 1952).

In 1954–55, FA divisions forced council decision-makers again to revisit this divisive culture war, in which Alf's example was now being nationally cited. Although claiming 'many distinguished footballers come from Sunday football', the only name offered in one major regional newspaper was 'Alf Ramsey, who learnt some of his skill in East London ... on Sunday mornings' (*Lancashire Evening Post* 8 December 1955).

Meanwhile, nationally, the left-of-centre media perspective was that 25 years ago:

> A bunch of lads in East London defied convention by playing on Sundays – their only free time. No regular pitches. Coats for goalposts, sticks to mark the corners. But within two years there were 22 teams. Today, the 'East London Sunday Football League' has 41 teams … Joint president is Mr. Attlee. (*Daily Herald* 11 December 1954)

Arraigned against them, conservative FA leaders, the English establishment and London's FA president Sir Leslie Bowker[40] still 'opposed recognising *the outlaws*' (*Daily Herald* 11 September 1954) because 'The Queen is our patron and recognition of Sunday football would invite bitter opposition from the churches' (*News Chronicle* 10 September 1954). Bowker, a successful lawyer, had recently sat in the front row at Queen Elizabeth II's 1953 coronation.[41] FA secretary Sir Stanley Rous, despite in 1955 consenting finally to stop suspending Sunday players, similarly insisted: 'Our attitude to Sunday football is the same. We will not recognise, promote, or organise football in this country on Sundays' (*Western Mail* 7 June 1955). Four years later, the FA again suspended a fully qualified first-class referee, just for officiating a Sunday match. Even the most senior FA Council member despaired: 'The approach to Sunday football reminds me of the attitude toward professionalism sixty years ago' (*Daily Mirror* 23 January 1959). Not until 1960 did the FA Council finally 'recognise Sunday football' and remove 'all restrictions on referees and linesmen' (*Daily Mirror* 7 May). Secretly, though, Sir Leslie Bowker and Professor Harold Thompson, Alf Ramsey's future nemesis and an arch FA amateur and networker,[42] still opposed even this change. On 30 April, Thompson complained in a letter that Bowker had not circulated Thompson's document about Sunday football (now lost or destroyed), warning Bowker: 'By the time the meeting is held … Sunday football will have become accepted.'[43] Both men seemingly still disliked the imminent, long-overdue Sunday football revolution. Two years, later, a daring appointment signalled their total defeat. A new FA secretary would offer Alf Ramsey a contract as England manager despite public recognition that he had 'risen from Sunday morning football to the most vital and challenging Soccer job in the land' (*Daily Herald* 26 October 1962).

These divisions ran bitterly deep. Twelve years after the FA finally 'allowed' amateur Sunday football, Alf shared with football fans some rare personal reminiscences. Headlined 'JUST ALF – THE "OUTLAW", STILL OWES AN FA FEE', he confessed to never having paid a 'seven shillings and sixpence re-instatement fee' owed to the FA since 'he had outlawed himself from the game as a teenager by playing on Sundays' (*Daily Mirror* 9 November 1972). Twelve months later, Professor Thompson would have his revenge by instigating, then leading, Alf's sacking and subsequent brutal professional mistreatment.[44] Sunday footballers had been FA 'football outlaws' since Alf's childhood,[45] hence despite his autobiography featuring that Five Elms team photograph, in 1952 its words merely hinted at Sunday football. Alf was a current England international player, so he had to appear to conform.[46] Movingly, though, he acknowledged how his adolescent football skills were kept alive by the 'manager of a shop at Five Elms', who called together 'young fellows who might be interested in forming a football club'.

Alf's glowing gratitude 'to Mr. Edward Grimme'[47] prompted the author to research this unsung community hero. Luckily, his son John was still alive, living locally, and generous in sharing memories and photos. He told me that, at some point, Alf delivered newspapers for his newsagent father, who everyone called 'Ted'. Ted's father, Ferdinand, had been born in 1840s Germany, arrived in 1860s London, led a tangled family life, and in 1908 christened Ted 'Ferdinand Alpha Grimme'. World War One probably prompted the change to Ted, but his connection to Alf tracks through the open attic window, as indicated by the arrow on the postcard below. It lay above Ted's 'Newsagent and Confectioner' shop, and next door but one to Alf Ramsey's Co-operative

shop workplace. As Alf recounted, in that attic headquarters 'the Five Elms club was formed … what a happy club it proved!'

The 'average age was around sixteen' and when Alf 'looked back upon those matches … most were against older and better teams, but we all learnt a good deal from opposing more experienced players. They were among the most valuable football lessons of my life.'[48] A unique, previously unpublished photograph, dated 1936 on the back, captures that spirit. Alf is seated at its centre, behind the ball, and Ted Grimme is standing far right.

Further historical evidence now corroborates Alf's account of Ted Grimme's crucial role with the Five Elms Sunday football team. Helped by newspaper research from community history volunteers,[49] the story emerges that in early 1937, as Alf turned 17, the team started life being called Five Elms Traders and competing in the Marino Cup (*Dagenham Post* 8 January, 5 February). In season 1937/38, they joined Division Two of the Dagenham and District Sunday League and shortened their name to Five Elms (*Dagenham Post* 30 July, 17 September 1937). Alf's adolescent skills were therefore sustained over a four-year span crucial to his footballing development, and future career, on the rough grass pictured above, managed by volunteers like Ted Grimme running outlawed Sunday league teams.[50]

Ironically, in 1948, when the FA would select Alf Ramsey to play for England, it was still vehemently suppressing that same Sunday football.

In 1962, when the FA chose him to try to win England the World Cup, only two years had passed since their formal recognition of Sunday football. The saviour aspects of 1930s Sunday football, for Alf's career, also echoed the 1980s story of Ian Wright, 'British football's first Black superstar'.[51] Like Alf, Wright was still playing London Sunday league football aged 20, but by 30 was a famous England international. Like Alf, Wright has always been 'proud to be English ... why wouldn't I be?'[52] The origins of Alf Ramsey's patriotism, its sometimes-clumsy expression, and its continuing contemporary relevance, now underpin the rest of this book.

1 1920 'Beacontree Heath Ward' electoral registers
2 See chapter 3
3 Peters, J. and Edmundson, J. (1955) pp.1-2
4 Ibid. pp.5-6
5 Young, T. (1934)
6 Olechnowicz, A. (1997) pp.iv-v
7 Ibid. p.97
8 Ibid. p.99
9 West, J. (1993) p.90
10 Benjamin, M. (2016) pp.53-4
11 McKinstry, L (2007) p.7 taken from a '**Sun** profile of Sir Alf in 1971'
12 Ibid. p.8 recollections of Phil Cairns
13 Ramsey, A. (1952) pp.12-14
14 **Minute Book Brentwood and District Elementary Schools Football League 1901-1935** pp.134-239
15 **Channel 4** (2002) *Sir Alf* director Ken McGill
16 I am indebted to Royston Jones for researching this information
17 *Daily Mirror* 9 November 1972
18 Ramsey, A. (1952) p.14
19 Peters, J. and Edmundson, J. (1955) p.6
20 E.g. *Sunday Mirror* 17 September 1933; *West Ham Echo* 22 September 1933; *Ilford Recorder* 21 September 1933
21 Ramsey, A. (1952) p.14
22 McKinstry, L. (2007) pp.27-28
23 Ramsey, A. (1952) p.14
24 See *Reynolds Newspaper* 20 October 1935 for varied LCS activities including cycling, football, darts, chess, drama; and 8 December 1935 for mentions of swimming, cricket, hockey, snooker and table tennis
25 Oxbury, P. (2014)
26 *West Ham Echo* 20 May; *West Ham Echo* 11 June
27 **FA Council minutes** 29 June 1963
28 Ibid. various minutes
29 Margaret Fulljames oral history interview 20 January 2023
30 *West Middlesex Gazette* 18 April 1936
31 FA website (no date) 'The Story of Women's Football in England'
32 Ramsey, A. (1952) p.15
33 Ibid.
34 Ramsey, A. (1952) pp.13, 14-15
35 Barking and District Historical Society website (9 October 2014) Robert Tanner 'Beacontree Simister Football League'
36 **London Weekend Television** (1991) *The Game* Episode 1
37 See London FA website (2025) 'History of London Football Association'

38 Butler, B. (1991) p.287

39 Ramsey, A. (1952) p.7

40 The Hamlet Historian website (22 December 2014) Jack McKinroy 'Arise Sir Les'

41 Ibid.

42 Richards, R. (1985)

43 **Professional Papers of Sir Harold Warris Thompson** HWT 48 2 E7

44 See also chapters 12-15

45 E.g. *Daily Mirror* 5 December 1930, *Ilford Recorder* 11 August 1932, *Daily Herald* 11 December 1954

46 National Football Museum website (no date) 'Hall of Fame - Alf Ramsey'

47 Ramsey, A. (1952) p.14

48 Ibid. p.14

49 Many thanks to them and Teresa Trowers at the **Valence House Archive & Local Studies Centre** in Dagenham

50 Kindly lent by John Grimme, identified as 'Selinas Lane' from background railway embankments

51 Theodore, T. (2022) p.58

52 Ibid. p.76

Part Two

FINDING HIS FEET:
LEARNING TO CHANGE

CHAPTER 5

FIGHTING WITH HIS FEET

Alf's Deep Love of Country

1939–40: Phoney War, Phoney Signing

AGONISINGLY, AROUND the time Britain declared war with Germany on 1 September 1939, a professional football club had finally noticed Alf Ramsey. His autobiography references no precise dates but describes the Five Elms club secretary arranging for Alf, and two team-mates, to meet a professional scout at the 'enclosed ground at Becontree Heath' pictured previously. Alf set the scene:

> Every Sunday morning large crowds gather to watch the match ... From out of the crowd surrounding the pitch there emerged a tall thin man with piercing eyes ... he had us eating out of his hand as he gave us the necessary forms.[1]

This striking figure was the vastly experienced Ned Liddell, who after several managerial roles had become Portsmouth's chief scout in early July 1939 (*Portsmouth Evening News* 6 July). By 8 September, though, war had prompted the FA to suspend professional football and request existing players' contracts be terminated. Although some informal friendly games continued, before small crowds,[2] these timelines suggest Liddell met Alf during August 1939 or just after.

Unfortunately, Alf never heard from Portsmouth again and later lamented 'the war put paid to my dreams':[3] but was that realistic? Portsmouth's squad needed strengthening in attack rather than defence (*Portsmouth Evening News* 6 July 1939), and it is statistically unlikely that Alf would have turned amateur registration into a professional contract. Football clubs then, like football clubs now, signed numerous eager youngsters before ruthlessly culling most. Wrexham, playing in 'Division 3 North', registered over 30 amateurs in summer 1939 (*Daily Mirror* 7 August). The inexperienced and amateur Alf, working full-time in a grocery shop, would not have got near Portsmouth's professional reserve side. He was destined at best for the London Mid-Week League, 'a competition for trying out young players and those recovering from injuries', without even any 'medals or cups'. Portsmouth was one of 11 clubs registered for its 1939/40 competition (*Chelmsford Chronicle* 23 June 1939), hence Liddell scouting east London amateurs when Portsmouth lay 100 miles distant.

Building on the bedrock of Alf's Co-operative Society apprenticeship, and volunteer-led Sunday football, it was the British Army that would now develop his sporting and leadership talents. From 1940–46, the army offered Alf a progressively structured environment in which to grow as a person and develop as an athlete; opportunities far more important to him than most contemporaries. For example, Alf played all three games in England's 1950, first World Cup tournament. Every other team member in the disastrous 1-0 defeat to the USA had either made a professional debut before war broke out,[4] or had been active in a professional club before conscription into the military.[5] Alf alone had no professional club experience before his six-year army career.

Alf Ramsey's football education, until aged 23, was stitched together from occasional Thursday football, regular outlawed Sunday football, and then playing in various military football teams. He was totally and uniquely reliant on the army for his sustained football development, from enlisting aged 20 and six months, until signing as a casual amateur for Southampton in October 1943. Even for three years after that, the army employed and directed Alf, until his June 1946 demobilisation aged 26. In September 1944, Alf had finally signed as a part-time professional with Southampton, but was paid just £2 per casual game, in wartime leagues and cups. Training and preparation before these was haphazard at best, impossible at worst, and as his six-month, December 1945 posting to Palestine showed, Alf's future remained in the army's gift. Consequently, the stories that follow explore how his personal identity, and ultimately Alf's playing and managerial success, rested to a striking extent on what army life taught him about football and about leadership.

1940–41: To Cornwall on the Riviera Express

Alf was fortunate to start his war in Cornwall, travelling there in June 1940 on the tourist Riviera Express overnight train; and lucky too that 66 of his 72 military months were spent within the UK. His army service entailed challenge, jeopardy but also opportunity. For Alf and countless other 1930s school leavers, it was the closest they would get to free tertiary education. As he admitted:

Until Cornwall, the longest journey I had undertaken was a trip to Brighton by train ... I was indeed very much the lad from the country! The Army was one of the greatest things which ever happened to me ... pitchforked into the company of many older and more experienced men ... I learnt, in a few weeks, more about life in general than I had picked up in years at home. The Army, in short, proved a wonderful education.[6]

That 'wonderful education' started with three months' conscript training in a holding battalion for the Duke of Cornwall Light Infantry (hereafter DCLI). It consisted of repeated kit drills, marching, basic weapon instruction and physical exercise. Following that, in autumn 1940, Alf recounted allocation to 'beach defence at Penzance',[7] with the newly formed (9 October 1940) 6th Battalion of the DCLI.[8]

Conscious perhaps that, unlike many of his autobiography's potential readers, Alf's own military career entailed scant direct combat, he included few details of his wartime service. In over 100 pages, the years 1940–46 take up just five, mostly describing not soldiering but army football. To understand him as an athlete, person, leader and patriot, more depth is needed: what did undertaking 'beach defence at Penzance' mean in gritty practice? Previously unused 'War Diaries' show that during October and November 1940 Alf's battalion was at a constant half-hour's notice of being called to fight. That entailed its 950 men 'watching and protecting the beaches from any attempt at invasion' despite some soldiers having previously 'only fired five to ten rounds'. In December 1940, a relaxation to 'four hours' notice enabled a 'short course with a rifle and light machine gun' for everyone.[9] But the inexperience of Alf and his fellow soldiers was tragically illustrated by one private killing a civilian whilst trying to shoot 'the rear tyre' of a car that failed to stop at their checkpoint.[10]

These recruits' nervousness was natural. The threat of a land invasion receded slightly after the autumn 1940 Battle of Britain but that aerial victory was entirely defensive,[11] and any assumptions that it instantaneously prevented invasion are retrospective.[12] As Alf and colleagues endured the winter of 1940–41, defending Cornish beaches with a rifle, barbed wire and the occasional light machine gun or mortar, the German air force was pounding British cities in 'The Blitz', targeting Alf's Dagenham home to lethal effect.[13] They were also bombing the Cornish airfields and other sites guarded by the 6th battalion of the DCLI. In April 1941, a soldier from 'A' Company was killed, and two others injured by enemy bombing. In May, enemy aircraft on seven occasions bombed or machine-gunned different locations 'over the area occupied by battalion'.[14]

These attacks were happening alongside ongoing, physically demanding beach defence work. In March 1941, 'the normal weekly programme was two days defence work, one day route march, combined with company scheme and platoon training', interspersed by 'recreational training limited to company football, boxing and cross-country running'. When Home Guard beach replacement guards could be deployed, the full-time soldiers received further training: 'Platoons were sent out for 60 hours under their own commanders ... all companies fired their light automatics on the range.'[15] In June, 'Work was continued on defences. Several hundred yards of tubular scaffolding were erected on the beaches.' Then, in June and July, the whole battalion was brought together for its first battle training. That entailed several weeks living in tents in Somerset, before returning to new barracks in Bodmin, Cornwall.[16] In other words Alf's first military year consisted of serious, sustained soldiering that involved intense preparation for mortal combat, alongside demanding defensive duties. These entailed extremely hard physical work, injuries, and deaths for fellow soldiers and civilians.

Tangentially, the army also offered sporadic opportunities for football. On 16 May 1941, the 6th Battalion 'Soccer XI lost match versus 7 East Yorkshire (2-1) in final of C.C.A. Competition'.[17] The battalion was then based at Helston from where, in 2004, a local inhabitant recalled watching 'Alf Ramsey ... play many a time on Helston Downs', and described meeting him on holiday two decades later in a Helston pub.[18] Alf himself dated forming 'our first football team' at Company level to Penzance, in November or December 1940; then 'to my surprise' being made 'centre half and captain' of the battalion side at St. Austell shortly after.[19] Even more significantly, from August 1941, Lieutenant Colonel Gerald Joseph Fletcher became Alf Ramsey's new commanding officer. Colonel Fletcher would provide one of many crucial, if quirky, assists in Alf's football career, and so in England's sporting history. Who was he?

1941–43: Colonel Fletcher, Army Football, Amateur Opportunities

Fletcher commanded Alf Ramsey for the tumultuous period from August 1941 to February 1945.[20] During December 1942, in a grim reminder of the war's brutality, the 6th Battalion DCLI was renamed the 1st Battalion: a necessity because, in summer 1942, hundreds of the original 1st Battalion's regular soldiers had been killed, injured or captured during a battle in northern Africa.[21] A handful escaped and at Helston on 9 December 1942, 'to mark the conversion', those ten survivors symbolically presented the 6th Battalion's 1,000 inexperienced soldiers with the battle-scarred 1st Battalion's flag of colours:

Dressed in full battle gear, Alf and his fellow conscripts were elevated into a regular army unit. In the new 1st Battalion DCLI's official war diary, Fletcher, as commanding officer, privately pledged: 'All ranks will do their utmost to ensure ... the Battalion is avenged.'[22] In his public address before thousands, he also explicitly portrayed sport, alongside military training, as a dutiful way of paying respect to the DCLI comrades now buried in the desert, or languishing in prisoner of war camps:

> Go forward in your great comradeship, never faltering nor complaining ... facing it all with a laugh and a light heart, fighting on even when your strength to fight has gone, firm in your resolution that nothing but the best shall be good enough for you to give. When, whether in battle or in peace, in your discipline or your turn-out, in training or in sport, then and only then will you prove worthy of this great inheritance.[23]

Alf's belief, quoted earlier, that the army gave him a 'wonderful education', presumably included what he learned from stirring words such as these, about his battalion's sacrificial 'great inheritance'. Indeed,

Alf later paid explicit tribute to the leader who had delivered them, describing Fletcher as 'a former Army player' and 'great guide to us all', who 'encouraged football as much as possible' without hampering 'our military duties'.[24]

Was Alf's praise over-sentimental? In the 1970s, Alf Ramsey was alleged as xenophobic, not patriotic, a perspective from which Fletcher's rhetoric could also be viewed as nationalist, militaristic mind games. Equally in sport, as in war, patriotism is complex. Football represents something more than individualism, and its symbolism reaches beyond particular games. For example, in May 1938, and supposedly to promulgate peace, the England team was infamously pressurised by diplomats, and Stanley Rous as England's FA secretary, to perform a Nazi salute in Berlin.[25]

George Orwell, a powerful 1940s wartime propagandist and political writer still influential today,[26] argued that links between international football, nationalism and power were malign. In December 1945, just as World War Two closed and the Cold War kicked off, Orwell scathingly criticised an ill-tempered British football tour by Soviet Russia's Moscow Dynamo:

> If you wanted to add to the vast fund of ill-will existing in the world at this moment, you could hardly do it better than by a series of football matches between Jews and Arabs, Germans

and Czechs, Indians and British, Russians and Poles, Italians and Jugoslavs … watched by … 100,000 spectators. I do not … suggest that sport is one of the main causes of international rivalry … merely another effect of the causes that have produced nationalism.[27]

Yet that same year, and far less quoted, Orwell also argued passionately that:

Nationalism is not to be confused with patriotism … two different and even opposing ideas. By 'patriotism' I mean devotion to a particular place and a particular way of life, which one … has no wish to force upon other people. Patriotism is by nature defensive, both militarily and culturally. Nationalism, on the other hand, is inseparable from the desire for power.[28]

The rest of this book makes the case that, using Orwell's definition, Alf Ramsey was a patriot not a nationalist. Equally, Orwell confessed to knowing nothing about football, his childhood school experiences meaning he 'loathed the game' and:

I could see no pleasure or usefulness in it, it was very difficult for me to show courage at it. Football, it seemed to me, is not really played for the pleasure of kicking a ball about but is a species of fighting.[29]

Orwell may personally have disliked playing football, and felt uncomfortable about associations with nationalism, but international football was now ubiquitous at all levels. During Alf's Sunday football playing days, several east London Sunday teams toured Belgium (*Daily News* 20 April 1935, *West Ham Echo* 10 April 1936). In 1937, a French team visited Dagenham to play a Sunday side (*Sunday Dispatch* 26 December). In February 1938, prior to England's infamous 'Nazi salute fixture' shown on the previous page, players representing the Cornish regiment Alf would shortly join lost 3-1 to a visiting team from the German training ship *Schleswig-Holstein*.[30] A book recording the German sailors' signatures survives at Bodmin Barracks, but what emerged only recently was their probable spying to prepare for a Nazi invasion.[31]

Alf, during six years of army service, seemingly took to heart Colonel Fletcher's rhetoric to go 'forward in great comradeship … in training or in sport', for patriotism became integral to Alf's lifelong sense of footballing identity. Equally, so did sheer hard work. During an incessantly wet September in 1942, Fletcher led his battalion through battle simulations across Bodmin Moor, sleeping mostly under canvas, and marching 225 miles. Then in December, following Fletcher's ceremonial speech cited above, the now renamed 1st Battalion DCLI moved 200 miles east to the massive camp at Barton Stacey in Hampshire.[32] There, alongside ceaseless training, they were soon competing in and winning competitive inter-brigade sports matches (February 1943), and, after moving to guard the Isle of Wight, enjoying regular swimming.[33] Their strong football team, as in this 1942–43 image, centred literally around Lance Corporal Alf Ramsey.[34]

Ever mindful of morale, in August 1943 Colonel Fletcher organised a fund-raising friendly for his team. As his war diary recorded, 'Battalion Soccer Team ... played SOUTHAMPTON AFC at SOUTHAMPTON, losing an enjoyable game by 10 goals to 3.'[35] Alf was captain for a game that sparked his subsequent career.[36]

Alf later recalled this as his first encounter against a 'professional team', and often being 'bewildered by the speed of thought and movement shown by the professionals ... but we must have shown promise for ... we were invited to play once more at The Dell against Southampton Reserves'.[37] That fixture happened four weeks later and, after catching the Isle of Wight ferry to reach Southampton, this time the 'Army' (DCLI) team won 4-1.[38] Six days later, Alf then described:

> The biggest bombshell of my life. I was hard at work when a message was telephoned from the Commanding Officer's office … two miles away … ordering me to report at once. I racked my brain trying to think of any military offence I may have committed.

To Alf's surprise, Fletcher told him on arrival that Southampton FC had telephoned. Could Alf play 'at centre half for their first team tomorrow' as they were unexpectedly a player short? Alf equivocated, acutely aware of his footballing inexperience, but 'Colonel Fletcher looked hard at me … *This is a big opportunity, Ramsey. I suppose you have at some time or another considered becoming a professional footballer?*' Assertively, Fletcher picked up the phone and confirmed that Alf would meet the team at Southampton Central Station.[39] By now aged nearly 24,

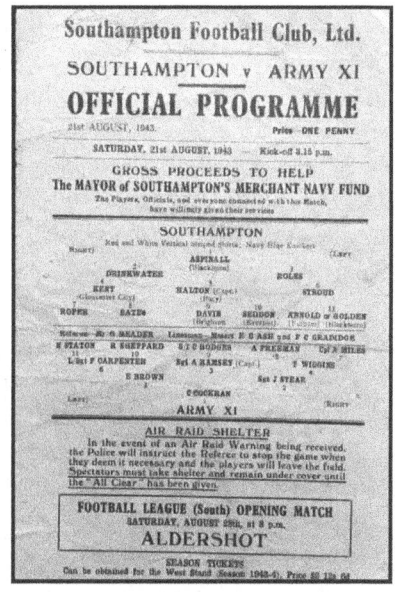

Alf described exiting Fletcher's office before doing 'a little tap-dance with delight … That Friday ranks among the longest days in my memory … there might after all be a place in the game for me if I came through my war service without injury?' Then on Saturday, 'as the London-bound train swished through Eastleigh Station', he signed forms registering as an amateur player for Southampton. 'A new and exciting world was opening up before me and, although I may have looked quite cool, my heart was thumping away.'[40]

Alf had found his perfect commanding officer because Fletcher, unusually in the army's officer class, loved football. Historical records show he was born in 1899 into a High Wycombe hotelier family, attended a Luton Grammar school, and by 1911 boarded at a Woodford Green school, a few miles from Becontree Heath. He joined the DCLI in April 1918, served briefly in France and never left, becoming a captain in 1928 and a major in 1938. Those milestones were interspersed with service in Ireland, western Africa and India,[41] and punctuated by playing football. In January 1920, Fletcher and a team-mate carved out 'numerous openings' in a game for the DCLI in Calcutta (*The Englishman's*

Overland Mail 3 January). Fletcher was one of only two officers in the team. Six months later, he played as a forward before a 'massive crowd' at Calcutta (*The Englishman's Overland Mail* 17 June). In 1921, again accompanied by just one other officer, he was picked for 'The Army versus The Navy' at Plymouth's Home Park (*Western Morning News* 27 April). In 1922, the only officer in the team, he featured in round four of 'The Army Cup' in Dublin (*Wiltshire Times* 28 January). At the end of the decade the evidently skilful Fletcher was still playing, and scoring, in Calcutta (*Civil Gazette* 6 May 1929).

Alf's timing was fortunate. The 1st DCLI were temporarily stationed at Southampton whilst rehearsing secret preparations for D-Day, meaning he could sign those amateur forms with Southampton in autumn 1943.[42] Although Alf conceded a penalty near the end of his debut at Luton, Southampton also fortuitously scored an even later goal to win 3-2. Alf was still in Southampton three weeks later, the next time he was asked to fill in, against Queens Park Rangers (QPR) in the wartime Football League South. There his successful streak ended, though. A national newspaper reported that QPR 'who have not fielded a guest player this season, overwhelmed Southampton 7-0 and went to the top with a slightly better goal average than West Ham' (*Sunday Mirror* 31 October). As Alf later admitted, given that 7-0 trouncing, it was probably 'just as well for me that shortly after ... I was moved North ... and for a time Southampton conveniently forgot about me.'[43]

1944–46: Serious Soldier then Serious Footballer

Alf's battalion's war diary described 1944 starting with two months in County Durham. During a freezing February war games entailed digging into defensive positions, counter-attacking and then '10 days sleeping merely under bivouac cover with one blanket' during which 'the weather was generally bad with snow and rain'. Colonel Fletcher believed it of:

> Great value ... in teaching all ranks how to look after oneself in difficult conditions for a prolonged period [for] many of the younger soldiers it was the first time they had spent more than a couple of nights out of doors.[44]

Aged 24, Alf now had over three years' military experience. Since arriving at Barton Stacey in December 1942 he had been promoted to sergeant and trained to lead a specialist anti-aircraft unit.[45] As the second-in-command of a platoon, Alf would have helped lead younger soldiers through that ten days of camping 'in difficult conditions' during those freezing February war games. He was learning invaluable lessons about leadership, and in March 1944 the battalion returned to face a different challenge on the south coast.

This involved building and running camps to prepare thousands of soldiers to land and fight on D-Day beaches. From June 1944, the DCLI retrained nearly 500 former 'Light Anti-Aircraft' personnel to go to France as 'Light Infantry', then rehabilitated 300 soldiers injured in Normandy's intense fighting to return them to combat. Colonel Fletcher called this process 'hardening' and his war diary lamented the work as 'a somewhat uncongenial but most necessary task on the invasion of the Continent'. His commanding officer praised the DCLI for doing their 'heart breaking job' with such 'cheerful, helpful willingness', and similar thanks followed a month later from General Eisenhower, 'the Supreme Allied Commander'.[46] No evidence from Alf, a mere foot soldier, describes the personal impact of preparing other young men, just like him, to be blown apart on French beaches. Nor do we know how he felt about working with wounded soldiers only to return them to the battlegrounds. Yet it is tempting to think that 'survivor guilt' may have played a part in the making of what one newspaper called, the day England won the World Cup, 'this fanatically single-minded Englishman' (*Hull Daily Mail* 30 July 1966). Modern research into such guilt has indeed described survivors as having 'a strong desire to make amends for surviving'.[47]

The battalion's 1944 war diary shows no football references, although by autumn Alf's autobiography does. Just before the 1944/45 season started, Southampton requested he 'play in a trial match at The Dell', then offered to sign him as a 'wartime professional', paid £2 per match.[48] This represented progress, but Alf's employment was still soldiering, and he was a 'professional' footballer only in the sense of being paid for appearances, not training. Given in the latter half of 1944 he was based in Hove, 60 miles away, training at Southampton was not an option anyway.

Yet for these few months, Alf was starting to play elite sides at professional stadia, before increasingly large crowds. A six-week injury followed his signing,[49] but he then made his Wartime League South debut in Southampton's victory over Arsenal (*Sunday Mirror* 31 December 1944). Seven days later, Alf played at Tottenham, losing 4-0 but later diplomatically claiming 'from that moment onwards I had a terrific regard for Spurs!'[50] The reality had been less amicable. Even in a wartime fixture, played primarily to maintain national morale, 'some fools in the crowd booed Southampton as they came out after the interval' (*Sunday Mirror* 7 January 1945).

Such boos possibly expressed fans' dissatisfaction with the opposition Southampton offered. Coincidentally, the quality of wartime games was locally debated later that week, when over 300 football officials and fans discussed, 'Was wartime football slower?' The event was led by two current professionals, from Arsenal and Brentford, who both answered 'yes'. England international Bernard Joy was an Arsenal regular in season 1944/45 and had probably played against Alf a few days earlier. He thought:

> The present game had slowed down ... any good First Division team of 1938-39 would beat the best of today's sides 99 times out of 100 ... however 1945 footballers were not entirely untrained. Many, in the services, had their Physical Training exercises, and most of the others did voluntary training two or three times a week. (*Middlesex Chronicle* 6 January 1945)

A front-page story from another newspaper, headlined 'SURPLUS OF SOCCER STARS', celebrated Alf's Southampton as one of several clubs using wartime football to give 'a steady flow of youngsters League football ... scores of youths have had the opportunity of sampling the coaching in actual matches of experienced and seasoned internationals'. Southampton were 'typical of this new spirit. Eight of their side are youngsters, picked up from junior teams. They have graduated through the Saints reserve side and gained promotion to the League team' (*Good Morning* 29 January 1945).

Meanwhile, Alf was once again playing for his battalion, and in 1945 football returned to the DCLI war diary. During January, Alf captained a team that reached the divisional football semi-finals, and they won the March 1945 final just as Colonel Fletcher was posted elsewhere.[51] Concurrently, Alf's wartime league football experience continued. Playing up front as an experiment, he scored four goals in a 12-3 rout of Luton Town, watched by 11,000 people at The Dell (*Sunday Dispatch* 4 March 1945). Attempting the same next week, Alf was, in his own words, 'a complete and utter failure' against Watford,[52] but Southampton's young team was receiving warm praise in match reports. The *Daily Mirror* (22 April 1945) called them an 'amazing side ... playing some of the best football I have seen this season', including winning away at three of the wartime league's top four clubs. One was Brentford, beaten 4-2 at The Dell before a crowd of 7,459. That included a London journalist, whose report colourfully evoked wartime football's quirky character and context:

> Southampton fielded a young side ... only [three] were pre-war professionals ... 10 are actually on Saints' books ... Apart from the blitzed stand, the Southampton pitch will need a lot of attention to put it in order for post-war football ... the players declared it to be the hardest and roughest in professional use. The centre line was the wriggliest thing I've seen across a presumably first-class pitch. (*Middlesex Chronicle* 21 April 1945)

Pertinent to Alf's story, this journalist also wrote how Brentford's players were noticeably ageing: 'Footballers are notoriously and understandably shy about their ages. They take an extraordinary long time to reach 30, and even longer to pass that ominous landmark.' Alf's 1952 autobiography lied about his age, in similar manner, by claiming he was aged 30 despite being nearly 33; but whatever his age in 1945, Alf's football world at last seemed to be opening before him. Soon after Southampton's victory over Brentford, Germany surrendered, the European war stopped, and he was featuring in Southampton's plans for peacetime football.

Starting the 1945/46 season at centre-half, though still in Wartime League South, Alf gained further valuable experience. On 8 September 1945, before 24,000 at Fratton Park, Southampton went 3-0 down to local rivals Portsmouth. The first goal came from 'a long clearance to Evans, who cleverly tricked Ramsey to beat Cruickshank at short range' (*Sunday Dispatch* 9 September 1945). Days later another reporter, watching Southampton lose 1-0, was 'disappointed after all that has been said about the bright, effective football they play ... Dodgin and Ramsey worked hard in defence, but I am afraid that is the best one can say' (*Daily Herald* 13 September). Southampton's 1945/46 league season indeed ended eight months later in a disappointing 16th place. What part had Alf played? Perhaps luckily, very little.

Alf Heads East

Alf had fortuitously managed to complete the 1944/45 season with Southampton, having been sent to Wales in April 1945, but in June the battalion returned to Sussex and its new commanding officer confided to his war diary that it would soon be 'taking its place overseas again'.[53] That summer of 1945 they began 'jungle training in deepest Sussex ... part of a light division to take part in the final stages of the war against Japan'.[54] This involved 'intensive training with the emphasis on tropical conditions' in wild boggy areas 'a few yards from the camp.' Here the 'summer undergrowth was shoulder-high ... jungle tracks were made intensely realistic ... The Sussex Downs ... now represented the sweltering beaches of enemy-occupied islands.'[55]

On 15 August 1945, Japan surrendered, after two USA atomic bombs had instantaneously killed about 100,000 Japanese civilians.[56] The War Office, though, merely changed the destination of Alf's battalion from fighting the Japanese in south east Asia, to Palestine. They departed Southampton on 4 December 1945, sailed for ten days via Malta and disembarked at Port Said. By 23 December, road convoys had taken them to a camp ten miles north of Haifa, to act as a 'Demonstration Battalion to the Middle East School of Infantry.' As in Britain during 1944, the 1sr DCLI was to lead the training of other soldiers.[57]

Despite acute tensions and violence in Palestine Alf had again been personally lucky. His six months there filled just three autobiographical paragraphs,[58] but perhaps deserved more. He was now one of eight colour quartermaster sergeants, positions senior to 30 other sergeants, 60 corporals and 873 other ranks, and subordinate only to the battalion's 32 officers.[59] Alf had been recognised as a leader, capable of controlling and distributing the materials needed for 1,000 men to subsist and fight. Echoing his days at the London Co-operative Society, Alf now managed 'the battalion stores'. James Last, a young conscript in 1944, 50 years later recollected how:

> Alf dished out the kit ... a new pair of socks, you had to go and see Alf. Quartermasters could be zealous ... but Alf was a very nice man ... a very fair man. We had Cockney blokes who used to call him Alf, but he said *You shouldn't be calling me that. I'm a quartermaster sergeant.* It wasn't pulling rank for the sake of it, but if the sergeant major heard that, he would have reprimanded him ... he didn't have a posh clipped voice then ... His dad was a dustman. (*East Anglian Daily Times* 30 July 2016)

Palestine in 1946 had acute inter-communal tension, with Jewish terrorists targeting and killing British soldiers. Nevertheless, Alf's commanding officer reported in January 'The morale of the Battalion is very high and there are many facilities for sports and entertainment.'[60] Football was a particularly powerful tool for boosting morale, and 'few things are more conducive to the building up of a common spirit than a successful football side.'[61] Colour Quartermaster Sergeant Alf

Ramsey became central to that by captaining battalion,[62] army[63] and combined area teams like the one shown alongside:[64]

Alf had previously captained school and Sunday teams, but the army taught him formally how to manage people under intense pressure. A recently discovered eye-witness from that period vividly described Alf's footballing leadership style:

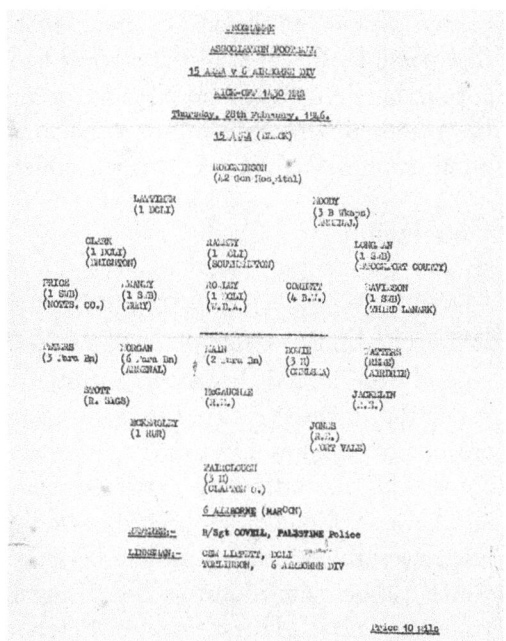

> It was our boast that we had the best battalion side in the United Kingdom, and now … the Middle East … C.Q.M.S. Ramsey has been an excellent team captain. His half-time team talk to his men is always a remarkably effective institution. To those of us on the touchline this ceremony looks like a very serious religious ritual.[65]

Twenty years later, during an English summer afternoon at Wembley, Alf Ramsey's team talk was once again 'remarkably effective'. The 1966 World Cup Final was broadcast globally to millions and is still easily viewed online. When the West Germans scored a late equaliser, with just seconds remaining, extra time beckoned. Alf's assistant recalled how 'some of the players sagged, but as I hurried around them on the pitch … I heard Alf Ramsey … in his quiet controlled voice: *You've beaten them once, now go out and beat them again.*'[66]

Recently, that phrase has been claimed as one of 'many myths and misconceptions' surrounding the 1966 World Cup,[67] an argument refuted in chapter 12. Unarguably, though, Alf's leadership pivoted the England team to rally, recover, then win the World Cup Final. As his fellow soldier remarked of Alf's 1946 team talks in Palestine, 20 years earlier, they were 'a remarkably effective institution … like a very serious religious ritual'. To Alf, football indeed felt sacred, magnified by reasons explored in the next chapter, but it was the army that had made that possible. In 1948, just six weeks before his first senior England appearance, Alf would be playing for an 'FA XI' at Arsenal, where the match programme summarised him perfectly: 'Alf Ramsey of Southampton. Right Back, Army Product.'[68]

Conclusion

Analysing Alf Ramsey's career, McKinstry identified an 'affinity of outlook' between Alf and World Cup winners 'George Cohen, Ray Wilson, and Bobby Charlton' because 'they had all done military service ... and experienced the maximum wage'.[69] Actually, Cohen was too young for national service. Ironically, given George Orwell's stringent critique of Moscow Dynamo's 1945 tour quoted earlier, Cohen later recalled his 'most dramatic' boyhood memory was watching them play at Chelsea.[70] Equally, Cohen respected Alf not just because he had 'done everything in the game' but because he had 'been through a war, which can be quite educative'.[71] Of England's 1966 finalists, the other youngsters, Ball, Hurst, Moore, Peters and Stiles, also missed the 'national service' which, until 1957, had continued wartime conscription.

The players in England's 1966 winning team who had experienced military service were Banks, the Charlton brothers, Hunt and Wilson. McKinstry's study of the Charlton brothers noted how Jack's 'two years of National Service were amongst the happiest of his life', quoting his recollection that 'with the Guards at Windsor, I really began to enjoy myself'.[72] Yet Jack, like England's four other previously conscripted 1966 finalists, and all Alf's 1950 England World Cup team-mates, had been attached to a professional football club before military service. Alf Ramsey alone was primarily formed as a footballer *by* military service, over the unusually long time span of six years, and during which strong ideas and attachments were developed.

Recollections are rare of Alf describing leadership, but Alan Ball cited him using a remarkable, comradely military metaphor: 'He wanted us to love each other. I remember him saying *a general can't win wars and neither can foot soldiers but together they might*.'[73] Norman Hunter won 28 England caps, and similarly described Alf's player management in military terms: 'He studied his men as an army commander does.'[74] Reflecting on Alf during a recent chat with the author, Geoff Hurst was still struck, over 60 years after first meeting him, about how, when recruiting Hurst to England, Alf probed 'not so much about my football skills', as 'trying to find out what sort of person or character I was.' Hurst also heard Alf on several occasions describe player selection as seeking people who 'will not let me down on the day'.[75] That notion resembled the very essence of Colonel Fletcher's 1942 exhortation to 'Go forward in your great comradeship, never faltering nor complaining … firm in your resolution that nothing but the best shall be good enough in battle or in peace … in training or in sport.'[76]

In a bundle of surviving congratulatory 1966 letters to Alf, at least three were from old army colleagues. One addressed 'My dear Sarge' wryly commenting on how the World Cup Final was 'a far cry from Penrose station anti-aircraft platoon and … inside right for the battalion side'. Another simply asked, 'Remember Aircraft Recognition?' The lengthiest was from a major with 34 years of service who, as a regular in the old 'first Battalion', had survived 1942's merciless desert battles. He mentioned having last seen Alf 'in Cyprus' and being 'proud to have served with you'. He was also sure 'Colonel Fletcher' will have been 'much impressed' with 'the wonderful example' Alf had shown 'in management and above all sportsmanship'.[77]

Following his 1949 transfer from Southampton to Tottenham, Alf's army background apparently encouraged a new nickname of 'The General' (e.g. *Huddersfield Examiner* 24 October 1950). Whilst preferable to 'D****e', team-mates were possibly teasing Quartermaster, Colour Sergeant Ramsey. For Alf so incessantly thought and strategised about football, in such unusually intense ways, that he could seem insensitively bossy and obsessively single-minded. Those character traits built on the methodical control, discipline and training Alf imbued in his army years, when he learned how to act like a leader. Equally, fascinating new possibilities about Alf Ramsey's personality, explored next, may also help to explain them.

1 Ramsey, A. (1952) pp.15-16
2 Imperial War Museum website (2025) '10 Facts About Football in the Second World War'
3 Ramsey, A. (1952) p.16
4 Williams with Walsall, Aston with Manchester United, Mannion with Middlesborough, Mortensen with Blackpool, Mullen with Wolverhampton Wanderers
5 Wright at Wolverhampton Wanderers, Hughes at Tranmere, Dickinson at Portsmouth, Finney at Preston North End, Bentley at Bristol Rovers and Bristol City
6 Ramsey, A. (1952) p.17
7 Ibid.
8 Godfrey, G. and Goldsmith, R. (1966) pp.30-34
9 **6th Battalion DCLI War Diary** National Archives WO1 166/4217
10 Ibid.
11 Imperial War Museum website (2025) '8 Things You Need To Know About The Battle of Britain'
12 Overy, R. (2010)
13 Valence House Collections website (no date) 'Dagenham Bomb Map'
14 **6th Battalion DCLI War Diary** National Archives WO1 166/4217
15 Ibid.
16 Ibid. also Godfrey, G. and Goldsmith, R. (1966) p.31
17 **6th Battalion DCLI War Diary** National Archives WO 166/8642
18 BBC Home website (15 October 2014) 'WW2 People's War – A Quarryman's Tale'
19 Ramsey, A. (1952) p.17 also Godfrey, G. and Goldsmith, R. (1966) pp.31-34
20 Ramsey, A. (1952) pp.17-18
21 Godfrey, G. and Goldsmith, R. (1966) pp.120-23
22 **6th Battalion DCLI War Diary** National Archives WO 166/8642
23 **Journal of the DCLI** (1945) p.57 for which thanks to **Bodmin Keep – Cornwall's Army Museum**
24 Ramsey, A. (1952) pp.17 and 17-18
25 Fisher, T. (2010)
26 E.g. The Orwell Foundation website (20225)
27 Orwell, G. (1945) pp.51-2
28 Ibid. pp.1-2
29 Orwell, G. (1952) p.36
30 **Journal of the DCLI** May 1939
31 Thanks to James Inglis: **Bodmin Keep - Cornwall's Army Museum**
32 **6th Battalion DCLI War Diary** WO 166/8642
33 **1st Battalion DCLI War Diary** WO 166/12518
34 Grateful thanks for this photograph to **Bodmin Keep - Cornwall's Army Museum**
35 **1st Battalion DCLI War Diary** WO 166/12518 (August 1943)

36 Grateful thanks to Duncan Holley for this image and other information from the excellent Southampton FC Player Archive website (2025)

37 Ramsey, A. (1952) p.18

38 **1st Battalion DCLI War Diary** WO 166/12518

39 Ibid.

40 Ramsey, A. (1952) pp.19-20

41 *Gradation List of the Officers of the British Army* (1939) p.572

42 **1st Battalion DCLI War Diary** WO 166/12518

43 Ramsey, A. (1952) p.20

44 **1st Battalion DCLI War Diary** WO 166/12518

45 Ramsey, A. (1952) p.17

46 **1st Battalion DCLI War Diary** WO 166/12518

47 Pethania, Y. et al. (2018)

48 Ramsey, A. (1952) pp.20-21

49 Ibid. p.21

50 Ibid.

51 **1st Battalion DCLI War Diary** WO 166/17153

52 Ramsey, A. (1952) p.22

53 **1st Battalion DCLI War Diary** WO 166/17153

54 Godfrey, G. and Goldsmith, R. (1966) p.124

55 **Journal of the DCLI** May 1946 (Volume XI) p.5

56 Imperial War Museum website (2025) 'The Atomic Bombs That Ended the Second World War'

57 **1st Battalion DCLI War Diary** WO 169/20042

58 Ramsey, A. (1952) p.22

59 **1st Battalion DCLI War Diary** WO 169/23199

60 Ibid.

61 **Journal of the DCLI** May 1946 (Volume XI) p.8

62 Ibid.

63 Ramsey, A. (1952) p.22

64 Grateful thanks for this photograph to **Bodmin Keep - Cornwall's Army Museum**

65 **Journal of the DCLI** May 1946 (Volume XI) pp.9-10

66 Shepherdson, H. (1968) pp.165-6

67 Hamilton, D. (2023) pp.242-43

68 Thanks to Alex Alexandrou and the *Army FA History Project*

69 McKinstry, L. (2007) p.441

70 Cohen, G. (2005 edition) p.73

71 Ibid. p.186

72 McKinstry, L. (2003 edition) p.44

73 Hurst, G. (2024) p.203

74 Wolstenholme, K. (1996) p.153

75 Geoff Hurst oral history interview 6 February 2025

76 **Journal of the DCLI** (1945) p.57

77 **FA Archive of 1966 Congratulatory Letters** E. Bunn 2 August; R. Osmond 31 July; W. Edwards 3 August

CHAPTER 6

IN A LEAGUE OF HIS OWN

How Difference Led to Learning

Kicking Off

BY AUTUMN 1946, Alf, aged nearly 27, was finally training and playing football full-time, but his professional journey had only just started. Everyone else in the 1950 England team had either played for, or been attached to, a professional club before joining the armed forces. How did he catch them up? Although tempting to cite the force *of* Alf's character, the forces *in* his character mattered as much: currents he learned to channel, utilise and sometimes disguise, but from which he could not escape. His personality was unusual, and Alf somehow seemed 'different'.

After his death in 1999, Alf's football contemporaries perhaps felt freer to talk about his awkwardness. McKinstry's biography capitalised brilliantly upon that, interviewing numerous contemporaries, then using their evidence accurately to depict Alf as mixing:

> Tremendous self-confidence within the narrow world of football, and tortured, tongue-tied diffidence outside … Alf never felt comfortable outside of the reassuring environment of running his teams. All his ease and self-assurance evaporated when he was not dealing with professional players.[1]

Numerous accounts concur, although Alf himself argued that six years in the army had reduced his social anxieties. A close friend testified he 'absolutely loved the army', and recalled him saying, 'I have never been very good at mixing with people, but you have to be in the army, or you are in trouble.'[2] Yet little intimate evidence of Alf's private character survives, either from those days, or family memories. His wife, Victoria, gave occasional interviews, often voicing resentment about Alf's treatment by the FA (e.g. *Daily Mail* 30 July 2016), but 'felt she could not co-operate' with McKinstry's biography.[3] Alf's USA-based stepdaughter conceded to one researcher that 'I think he was overwhelmed with the fame awarded to him',[4] but has also remained mostly silent. When approached during this book's research she twice, very politely, continued that family policy.

> My father was a very quiet and private man and as much as I would like to support your request, feeling in my heart that I would from some points of view keep his memory alive, I must decline ... my father would not be happy with me if I allowed all these requests.

Alf Ramsey's family's reticence means evidence of his early character rests on scattered fragments collected mostly by journalists, particularly McKinstry. They tell of early shyness, for example a primary school friend and neighbour recounted 'We grew up together ... Alf was very introverted, not very forthcoming ... very withdrawn, almost surly, but he became animated on the football field.' Another neighbour, a year younger than Alf, described an unusual youthful quietness that 'was not like the locals ... a bit intellectual, a bit distant. He spoke a little better than the rest of us. He was pleasant, but he was different.' A female acquaintance also recalled teenaged Alf being:

> Well spoken, just as in later life ... polite, dignified, a very reserved person. We once went on a coach trip to Clacton with the Five Elms team, and he sat quietly on the bus at the front. He did not play around much like some of the others. His life seemed to be just football.

Having watched young Alf playing in that team, on the nearby Merry Fiddlers football field, a local football enthusiast agreed with these other football observers, that he was 'subdued, never threw his weight about'.[5] The only two equivalent descriptions from army days echo those accounts, telling in 1946 of Alf's unusual seriousness and fairness.[6] Fortunately for this inquiry, perspectives on his personality then multiply after autumn 1946 when he became a full-time professional footballer.

Teaming Up

From post-war team-mates a picture emerges of Alf as painfully shy, obsessive about football, undoubtedly talented, but tangibly different. At Southampton, Alf Freeman, who shared digs with Ramsey, described a 'very, very quiet man',[7] a perception shared by others. Alf Ramsey, Ted Bates recalled to Leo McKinstry, 'would not go out of his way to talk to anybody'. Bill Ellerington, Alf's club and England rival at right full-back, described 'a hard lad to get to know ... not standoffish but you could never get at him ... not one of the boys ... he did not join in'. For goalkeeper Ian Black, 'Once he had finished training, you seldom saw him ... He did not like much involvement with others ... Though he would talk plenty about the game, he was not much of a conversationalist otherwise.'

Winger Eric Day saw Alf regularly on trains home, because their families lived a few miles apart. Describing him as 'a very honest bloke ... very modest', Day also casually attributed Alf's closed character to his GRT background:

> There was never much conversation ... it was only ever about football ... He was a bit secretive he just didn't chat. Maybe that was because he was a gypsy. Gypsies are extremely close-knit; they keep it in the family.

As explored previously, Alf's fear of labelling, and rumours, accentuated his shyness, but an ultra-controlled nature also contributed. Black noted, 'A very good gambler. Whatever the result, win or lose, he finished.' Stan Clements, Southampton's centre-half, agreed Alf was 'good with figures', perhaps because:

> His family were involved in racing greyhounds ... some of them used to live on that, so he knew about gambling ... very quick at working out the odds ... a cool gambler you never saw him get excited ... never over the top. He always had control.[8]

Such impressions from Alf's 1946–49 Southampton team-mates were reinforced by his 1949–55 Tottenham colleagues, some of whom were candid about his oddities. Youngster Mel Hopkins joined Spurs in 1952: 'Alf was the loner. He would not mix much ... He seemed a bit more sophisticated ... He went his own way.' For goalkeeper Ron Reynolds: 'Of all the players I had dealings with he's the one I could never figure out.' Even Alf's close friend, jocular Cockney Eddie Baily, admitted, 'Most people got annoyed with Alf ... he gave the impression that he read the game, and everyone else had to follow ... A lot of the others thought he was stand-offish.'[9] A Spurs-supporting local journalist who knew 1950s Alf well, on and off the field, described Alf's team niche as 'with them but never really of them. Aloof is the word ... He was, and still is, aloof ... apart from the herd.'[10] In 1952, he noted 'two things you just cannot get Alf Ramsey to do. The first is to get hot under the collar, and the second is to talk about himself.'[11]

Such idiosyncrasy would be interesting in anyone, let alone the only English manager (so far) to have won the men's football World Cup. Alf's character quirks, testified by team-mates above, raise an intriguing possibility, discussed below.

Special Qualities, Special Skills

A recent official definition claimed that, 'around 1 in 10 people across the UK are neurodivergent, meaning that the brain functions, learns and processes information differently.'[12] Multiple colleagues described Alf as 'different', some finding him 'difficult'. Might that have been because his brain boasted aspects of neurodivergence and possibly lay within, or was related to, the wide range of phenomena known as Autism Spectrum Condition (hereafter ASC)?[13] New scientific research and evolving knowledge means the 'definition of autism has changed over the decades and could change in future',[14] and the UK's current NHS-approved national autism strategy similarly emphasises ASC's fluidity:

> Autistic people see, hear and feel the world differently to other people. Autism varies widely and is often referred to as a spectrum condition, because of the range of ways it can impact on people ... While autism is not a learning disability, around 4 in 10 autistic people have a learning disability.[15]

Nothing suggests Alf had learning disabilities. On the contrary, if he was neurodivergent, aspects possibly helped his career, as with other successful and openly neurodivergent people like television presenter and naturalist Chris Packham, West Midlands Police murder detective Warren Hines, or the billionaire founder of Microsoft, Bill Gates.[16]

Historical distance, fragmented evidence, and Alf's 1999 death mean this chapter makes no attempts scientifically to 'diagnose' him. Rather, it uses the evidence available in a thought experiment to test for possible signs of neurodivergence in how Alf spoke, thought, behaved, and learned. To root that in current professional understanding the discussion below is structured using the UK National Health Service's seven 'Main Signs of Autism in Adults'.[17]

**NHS Guidance
Main Signs of Autism in Adults include:**

A. 'Finding it hard to understand what others are thinking or feeling'
Alf's attitudes, glimpsed in previous pages, often irritated others
without him seeming to notice. Early 1950s Tottenham team-mates
found him 'prickly and irritable ... his know-all sarcasm led to suspicion
and misunderstandings'.[18] After his 1962 appointment as England
manager, Alf's scorn scorched journalists, too. Peter Batt, a reporter
on *The Sun*, suffered 'general utter contempt, I've never known anyone
to make you feel more like a turd under his boot than Ramsey'. From
the 1950s onwards veteran journalist Brian Glanville often 'mixed in
the same cabin' as Alf the England player, then the England manager.
Glanville observed, 'He could be very spiky ... I have all sorts of amusing
memories of him, but he was a very strange man.'[19] For example, Alf
seemed incapable of seeing things from a jobbing journalist's perspective,
and in 1969 was filmed bluntly stating, 'I can live without them ... they
cannot live without me.'

Another vastly experienced journalist recently vouched that 'to meet
Ramsey solo could be daunting'.[20] Towards FA committee members a
senior figure also recalled Alf being 'brusque unnecessarily – not an
easy person to speak to, very aloof'.[21] Indeed, Alf's 'level of reserve was
almost unnatural'.[22]

Alf Ramsey's emotional ham-fistedness was, at some point,
experienced by everyone around him. He loved most of his players,
and they mostly loved him, but he was insensitive even to the greatest.
Nobby Stiles summarised him as 'so straightforward – he says things to
people – upsetting them', adding loyally and hastily, 'it's a good thing.'[23]
Jack Charlton recalled how, after their first meeting, Alf 'never spoke
to me again for six years. He didn't like me.' Brother Bobby thought
Alf could be 'blunt to the point of being rude'.[24] Alf's loved ones
experienced similar treatment. In 1951, he took his then-fiancée, Vicky,
to a Tottenham championship celebration event. Within seconds of
the dancing starting, 31-year-old Alf handed her to Ron Reynolds, the
22-year-old reserve goalkeeper, because 'Alf didn't want to dance, he
wanted to talk about football ... so he lumbered me ... I was practically
speechless.'[25] A year later, on the first Saturday after their marriage,
Vicky waited for Alf after the game, with the wives of the other players.
He had to be reminded as he was leaving, 'Hey, Alf, you've forgotten
your wife,'[26] so deep was 'his cocoon of concentration for every game'.[27]

Chapter 14 will demonstrate how Alf adored and was influenced by that wife, but his mind was always filled with football.

B. 'Getting very anxious about social situations'

Alf Ramsey lacked social confidence and was genuinely at ease only in football settings. He would talk brusquely to journalists, then immediately afterwards 'romp like a schoolboy with his players ... the only people in whose company he can really relax – the only people he really likes' (*Sunday Mirror* 18 January 1970). Pictured here with Gordon Banks in February 1966, Alf looks almost playful.

But when the setting was not a pitch or training ground, Alf became anxious. At this celebratory award ceremony in December 1966, even in his year of triumph Alf actually appears to be distinctly uneasy:

Close friend Eddie Baily believed Alf 'was better when you was with him on his own',[28] and Alf may sometimes have masked his social anxiety using alcohol. Baily recalled Alf, aged 30 at least, being drunkenly sick at a family party, about which another team-mate laughed, 'I can see Alf now, bent over the toilet.'[29] On 1 May 1957, at another impromptu party after Ipswich had won the Third Division South, the Ipswich chairperson lost 'Old Stoneface', as he nicknamed Alf, but 'eventually found him under a table singing'.[30] Might he have been hiding, not just under that table but behind real or assumed inebriation? In another extreme example, Alf similarly used work to mask anxiety about social pressures. Winning the League Division Two title in 1961 was:

> The greatest day in the 25 years of Ipswich Town Football Club. The board room was noisy, raucous … a heck of a party. The Chairman paused as he opened another bottle of champagne … 'Where's Alf?' Cobbold went out to find his manager sitting in an almost deserted stand. Alf Ramsey, in his greatest hour, was watching Ipswich boys play Norwich boys. 'Alf, come and have a drink,' said the chairman. 'Not just now, thank you, I am working,' he replied. (*Daily Herald* 24 April 1961)

In 1966, Alf repeated that personal abstraction technique on the world stage, at Wembley, during England's moment of victory. A highbrow interviewer a year later remarked how he:

> [He] sat stock still, unsmiling … 'It was all rather nice,' he says 'very nice for all the people watching the game on television … I don't normally jump in the air myself, but I enjoy watching other people being happy'. That remark is typical of this detached football master. (*Illustrated London News* 26 August 1967)

C. 'Finding it hard to make friends or preferring to be on your own'

As Alf admitted, and the observations of others reinforced, he felt little social or emotional need for people beyond his family. In the mid-1950s, even before achieving managerial success, his secretary at Ipswich Town reacalled that he 'didn't need friends'.[31] And whilst professionally he relaxed more when with other football players, or managers, that rarely extended to emotional intimacy. As recalled recently by World Cup Final hat-trick hero Geoff Hurst, Alf did not 'allow you to get to know him … you were never really sure what he was thinking, or even who he was.'[32] The only journalist to whom Alf granted biographical interviews observed that he could 'without effort, slam the door of his personality on his players', and his attitude could change:

> From moment to moment – click-click, click. He has never felt a compulsion to communicate – a need to be liked. And it must be emphasised that this is not something that happened when he was appointed England manager. Or when the World Cup was won. Or when he was knighted. As a player … and as a club manager … he was always reserved, reticent, thoughtful … To him his other life is simply no one else's business. (*Sunday Mirror* 18 January 1970)

A genteel publication concurred that 'socialising is not one of Sir Alf's favourite occupations nor one of his strong points' (*Illustrated London News* 26 August 1967). Ipswich chairperson John Cobbold lamented that Alf 'always seemed to find difficulty in making friends'.[33] For Hopcraft, Alf's 'public impassivity becomes a terse, contemplative wariness in private. Ramsey is not a popular man … people who know him well … have lots of stories to illustrate his incommunicability … his cold dignity is certainly not an act.'[34]

Alf's distance and emotional frigidity became famed throughout football, and remain mainstays of his image. A leading contemporary football writer recently summarised that 'Ramsey's aloofness and mistrust of emotion and ego were deep character traits',[35] whilst another wryly noted how, on World Cup victory day, Alf smiled just twice.[36] What has never previously been considered is that such traits may have stemmed from inherent neurodivergence, rather than behaviours later adopted as a football player and manager.

D. 'Seeming blunt, rude or not interested in others without meaning to'
Alf evidenced this in his own words. Only two years into a professional career, during his first full England appearance, he had just passed the ball to the world's most famous footballer, England veteran Stanley Matthews. 'Hold it, Stanley,' shouted the newcomer, an instruction perceived as rude by team-mates, but Alf's retrospective justification was even clumsier:

> Apparently, the thought that an unknown such as I should make a suggestion to Stanley Matthews shocked quite a number of folk. Matthews, a great fellow as well as a wonderful footballer, was wise enough to realise that my advice was sound and for the good of the team.[37]

Alf's rudeness could be indiscriminate. Clive Strutt was an adolescent junior press photographer when Alf was Ipswich manager (1955–63), and travelled regularly with the Ipswich team. He encountered 'a quiet and aloof man, who nobody really got close to', who made his dislike 'clear to me on more than one occasion'.[38] At the other end of the career spectrum, by the 1970s, leading journalist Frank McGhee had spent several years globe-trotting with Alf, in the days when journalists shared the England squad's planes, buses and hotels:

> Sir Alf is a complicated mass of contradictions ... Cold, hard, humourless, aggressive, downright rude in a Press conference or TV interview ... Few people ... see the warmth behind the stone mask, the man inside the machine. ... The eyes under the unruly bush of his brows can suddenly look as hostile as brown broken glass on a fourteen-foot wall. The wide mobile mouth straightens to a gash. (*Sunday Mirror* 18 January 1970)

Alf's coldness could mix personal and professional. Southampton player Joe Mallett exchanged Christmas cards with him all his life but knew that 'if you went against Alf that was the finish'. His team-mate Ted Ballard similarly vouched that any disagreement could mean 'he would never speak to you' again. Those perceptions stemmed partly from Alf Ramsey falling out with Alf Freeman, another team-mate. The pair had served in the same battalion, played in army football teams and turned professional together at Southampton. They shared digs that Freeman found for them, perhaps because it appeared Alf 'did not have any friends', as 'he kept himself to himself'. Then one Sunday, Freeman ate the meal left by their shared landlady and, deliberately or inadvertently, consumed Ramsey's portion, too. When Ramsey arrived home late, Freeman described 'a terrible row' breaking out. News soon reached the other Southampton players, who 'all knew about it' because Freeman 'was the chatty type'. Ramsey on the other hand, testified Joe Mallett, was a silent opposite and 'never spoke to Freeman again until he left the club, that's how he was'.[39] Yet poignantly, a few years later, Ramsey would autobiographically describe how 'for hours' he and his friend Freeman 'would tramp through the Hampshire countryside, all the time talking football'. To some 'this may sound boring', Alf admitted, but to them he insisted 'it was a great pleasure'.[40]

The first page of Alf Ramsey's autobiography referenced another 'unfortunate disagreement', this time with Southampton manager Bill Dodgin, sparked from Alf's perspective by being treated insensitively after an injury, but perhaps related also to broader career reasons.[41] Matters escalated to a transfer request (*Coventry Evening Telegraph* 8 March 1948), banishment to Southampton's reserves (*Portsmouth Evening News* 11 April 1948) and Alf's eventual sale to Tottenham. He confessed 'to some this may appear just a trivial incident, but with time on my hands it became an obsession'.[42]

E. 'Finding it hard to say how you feel'

Speaking of his own, famed 1966 World Cup Final coolness, Alf explained:

> My reaction at the final whistle may have appeared cold-blooded, but this is me. I am a normal person. I feel all the sorts of feelings others do, but I just don't show them ... I have always been like this. (*Sunday Mirror* 3 May 1970)

Alf's first biographer, Marquis, that same year labelled him 'as expressionless as a Trafalgar Square lion. His face gives few clues as to what is going on inside his head.'[43] What came out of his mouth could also be inscrutable. Drawing comparison with the speech-impaired King George VI, Marquis described Alf's words emerging 'reluctantly through a tightly controlled mouth ... his eyes move uneasily ... he ploughs on through the debris of inappropriate words and shattered syntax, utterly oblivious'.[44] By the 1970s, public puzzlement was growing about Alf's emotionally frigid leadership style, but he could not alter it:

> That unemotional mouth and those black-etched eyebrows will never give away a feeling, either in victory or defeat ... He casts himself in a lonely role ... His reaction is predictable. He will withdraw into his shell and shut those marionette lips to the public. (*Sunday Mirror* 16 May 1972, Colin Byrne)

Even Alf's ally and favoured interviewer, Frank McGhee, admitted 'the man is painfully conscious that he is not specially articulate' (*Daily Mirror* 6 November 1972). By the late 1990s, Bowler's biography positioned Alf's 'inscrutable expression, the clipped answers to questions, the wary responses' as Alf trying to distance himself from any 'open displays of emotion', potentially identifiable as 'lower order'.[45] But was it only social class cramping Alf? His language and behaviour at moments of peak football drama were extraordinarily emotionally flat. Asked by a TV interviewer 'how he felt' just after having won the championship in Ipswich's 1961–62 Division One debut season, Alf baldly responded, 'I feel fine', then refused to elaborate.[46] Four years later, when implored minutes after clinching the World Cup, to 'describe your feelings at this moment', he delivered monotone incoherence. That response is transcribed precisely below only to illustrate just how painfully Alf experienced '*finding it hard to say how you feel*':

> Well, I don't know. It is very, very, difficult, in as much as this has became, become, or it had become a desire, this tremendous desire to win the World Cup competition, which had rubbed off on to the players to some great extent. I think it leaves you a little flat, at the same time, you have this tremendous feeling of satisfaction.[47]

After viewing nearly all the available filmed interviews of Alf, a recent analyst described how, under questioning, he was 'often abrupt, stilted or silent', his 'facial expressions would stiffen, and his gaze beneath those caterpillar eyebrows become glassy'. He attributed Alf's odd vocal tones, and regular 'spoonerisms, malapropisms or mispronunciations', to personal and social insecurity.[48] Might a brain working differently, through neurodivergence, be another possible cause?

F. 'Taking things very literally – for example, you may not understand sarcasm or [colloquial] phrases'

Alf was aware that others perceived him as oddly lacking in humour. Autobiographically, he therefore insisted the opposite, claiming that visiting 'a variety show' was his:

> Biggest treat … Maybe I should whisper this, but I get my biggest kick out of the comedians when I can literally roll in the aisles with laughter. That confession, I know, will shock those who for some reason look upon me as one of soccer's intellectuals who thinks only of football. How this legend developed I do not know but take it from Ramsey it's all hooey. I'm an ordinary chap.[49]

Objectively, though, it is not clear that Alf understood humour as a neurotypical person might. His first biographer described how 'he is kind, but his sense of humour is rudimentary'.[50] In a much crueller critique, historian Frank McLynn declared utter dislike:

> He was a humourless boor … Ramsey raised humourlessness to a fine art. He liked to talk in a clipped, pedantic manner that he presumably mistook for style, but the only amusing thing about him was the way he mangled the English language … A humourless, cynical, negative opportunist. (*The Guardian* 2 October 2005)

Ipswich chairperson John Cobbold affectionately described 'some annoying ways' Alf had, particularly how 'in reply to every comment he'd say, "Why did you say that" … it drove us mad'. Cobbold also recalled how 'unintentionally, he'd put people's backs up' by answering innocent comments quite literally. Members of the public might 'pass him in the street and say, "good game last night", and he'd reply, "it was a bloody awful game"' (*Hull Daily Mail* 2 September 1972).

G. 'Having the same routine every day and getting very anxious if it changes'

Alf Ramsey practised football routinely, repetitively and relentlessly. After admiring how Manchester City full-back Sam Barkas played against Southampton (*Daily News* 7 April 1947), Alf fixed on him as his role model. Returning that summer to Dagenham 'in the small field near my home', he took 'a football every morning … and spent an hour or two trying to place it at a chosen spot'. Once back at Southampton, Alf realised practising alone was insufficient. He could not 'adopt the constructive type of game for which Sam Barkas was famous' if Southampton 'colleagues would not respond'. Alf therefore persuaded Eric Day, Southampton's right-winger, to use a miniature pitch marked out on the dressing-room floor to perfect new approaches and 'expound for hours our various theories'.[51]

Southampton's coach endorsed that account, recalling Alf 'spending hours discussing techniques and tactics. I have never known anyone with the same sort of application … He would never accept anything on its face value. He had to argue about it and make up his own mind.'[52] Perhaps to moderate or puncture such pretensions, Alf's manager and team-mates brought up his slowness in turning. His response was simple: 'For hours, and wearing spiked shoes, I would practise turning and getting off the mark from either a walking or running position.'[53]

Such structured, relentless self-evaluation and improvement were maintained at Spurs, where Alf revealed to a journalist: 'I don't care too much to be told that I have had a wonderful game. I prefer it when someone points out a fault. Then I can do something about it' (*Daily Mirror* 1 February 1951). Spurs manager Arthur Rowe witnessed how 'Alf would come back after practice to perfect his kicking. He would spend hours seeking accuracy and perfection.' He did the same for England, with captain Billy Wright saying of Alf's free-kick practices, 'He would never be content until he could do it ten times out of ten.'[54] Alf relied on routines to perfect his playing techniques and achieve football greatness. Did they also help him make sense of the world?

Alf seemed totally disinterested in anything conceptual, cultural or abstract; indeed, anything other than football. His double title-winning captain at Ipswich, Andy Nelson, described him as private, quiet and 'very unhappy to have any conversation that was unrelated to football'. When someone changed the subject from football, 'you would literally be rid of Alf in two minutes. He'd be off, gone.' Such testimony led Alf's most recent biographer, and staunch supporter, to paint him as 'one-dimensional … uneasy with any discussion about politics, current affairs or art … an unabashed philistine.' Similarly, for a later newspaper columnist collaborator, Alf was not 'a worldly man':

We never really talked about current affairs or wider political issues. He was just happy talking about football ... He never wanted to discuss governments or religion or anything like that. His life revolved around football. He had little conversation about anything else.[55]

Alf's unvarying routines also underpinned England's 1966 triumph:

To apply himself to win the competition ... he relied on routine. From Monday to Thursday (he always took Friday off), Ramsey would catch the 8.35am train from Ipswich ... he always left [FA headquarters] at 4.30pm ... he was able to look straight through his fellow passengers in silence, never acknowledging their presence.[56]

Alf's poor background, school-leaving age of 14, and insecurities after being racially nicknamed and rumoured a 'Gypsy' certainly heightened his lack of confidence about the wider world: but his obsessional interest in football, and disinterest in anything else, may also have originated in elements of neurodivergence. That included attributes which significantly strengthened his professional learning, made him a potent football player and manager, and mirrored many of the UK NHS's seven 'Main Signs of Autism'[57] discussed above.

Two other ASC characteristics can now also be added, clearly displayed by Alf and central to his success. The first is having a 'highly focused interest' to the point of compulsion or obsession, in Alf's case being 'how best should people play football?' The second he shared with a tiny minority (five–ten per cent) of neurodivergent people, sometimes termed 'savants',[58] who have an unusual and hyper-detailed photographic memory.

Highly Focused Interests

All authoritative explanations of ASC feature 'having a very keen interest in certain subjects',[59] phrased alternatively as 'highly focused interests or hobbies.' A national UK autism charity states simply: 'Many autistic people have intense and highly focused interests, often from a fairly young age. These can change over time or be lifelong.'[60] Alf displayed just such an early, highly focused interest in football. A childhood friend recalled, 'He did not have much knowledge of the world. The only thing that ever seemed to interest him was football.'[61] Alf told a journalist in 1967 that he 'had been playing football since he was able to run' (*Illustrated London News*

26 August), earlier writing of himself that 'from the moment I could toddle … for hours every day … I learnt how to kick, head, and control a ball'.[62]

That pattern pervaded the rest of a life in which Alf obsessively learned about football, with an intensity that appeared unusual even to elite team-mates. Jackie Milburn, a 1950s fellow England international and room-mate, described how 'Alf was never a great one for small talk … Football was his one subject of conversation.'[63] Eddie Baily, his friend, Spurs and England team-mate, described how after England's 1950 shock World Cup defeat to the USA, Alf demanded an inquest: 'Should have done this, should have done that, he got on your nerves at times.'[64]

Alf's relentless concentration intensified as England manager. Called into his squad, this 1960s player found him 'a strange bloke … he's so relentless about the game. None of this is a giggle for him in any way.'[65] Similarly, Geoff Hurst's first meeting with Alf was on a train, travelling from London in November 1964 for an under-23 fixture. The conversation 'was more like an interrogation than a friendly chat', focused entirely on Alf questioning Hurst about other players, and Hurst 'found out next to nothing about Alf'. Yet, despite earning 49 senior caps over the next eight years, this episode was 'probably the longest exchange' the two ever had.[66] As Hurst personally underscored to the author, for Alf Ramsey 'to achieve what he achieved in his career' he had to be 'totally focused and obsessed with the game … just completely and utterly focused'.[67]

The only journalist to whom Alf ever granted serial biographical interviews cited 'the tightly closed circle of his world – his horizons are the England fixture list' (*Sunday Mirror* 18 January 1970). Two years later, as poor results increased public pressure, he quoted Alf describing himself as engaged in ceaseless, compulsive reflections on the game:

> Alf always has a reason for whatever he does – and is inclined to emphasise this point when he is criticised or pressurised. 'These people have a go at me after spending ten minutes thinking about it. I seldom stop thinking about football'. (*Daily Mirror* 8 November 1972)

Alf's lifelong, obsessive interest in learning about football brought success, but also consumed him. In 1952, he confessed that 'being a footballer, and connected with football, is the thing which matters above all else to me'.[68] That fiery focus left Alf emotionally, psychologically and financially vulnerable after his 1974 sacking as

England manager. As explored in chapters 14 and 15, and recalled by his 95-year-old widow:

> It broke him. He was never the same man afterwards. Alf tried to get on with his life. He would go out with friends and watch matches, and he pottered around the house. But he lived for football, and he just felt lost. There was nothing left for him, really. (*Daily Mail* 30 July 2016)

Savant? Alf's Extraordinary Footballing Memory

'Savant syndrome' is highly unrepresentative of ASC as a phenomenon and has been dramatically over-used in popular culture.[69] As a term it embraces the '5–10% of people with autism' who possess 'special talents or skills … common areas of giftedness include … photographic memory'.[70] This small proportion of autistic people, in their field of obsessive interest, can 'create visualisations as intense as those brought about by the original stimuli';[71] a faculty Alf seems to have come close to. Frank McGhee, his trusted interviewer during 1970–72, was told by Alf's wife that he needed a list when shopping alone, 'otherwise he comes back with only half an order', but his football memory was stratospherically detailed:

> Perhaps the most astonishing feature of this man's intelligence is a built-in ability for total recall of teams, matches, incidents throughout his career. He can press a button in his brain and recall every game, any move, each goal … he couldn't recall the date of his first game as England manager – but he remembered the outcome … And he rattled off the names of the team and the changes he made for the second match … and the changes he made for the third match … If I hadn't interrupted, he might have turned this series [of interviews] into a list of players and results. (*Daily Mirror* 6 November 1972)

Others agreed, that 'his memory of games and incidents in them is incredible, even to knowing with which foot a vital tackle was made eight years ago' (*Sunday Mirror* 16 May 1972, Colin Byrne). Jimmy Greaves testified to Alf's 'total recall of just about every match and every key player he ever saw'.[72] Why was this helpful? Because such dynamically memorised detail enabled Alf's coaching to improve already brilliant players, and devise game plans, long before technical advances in film technology made those processes significantly easier. Geoff Hurst recalled how, before 1966, Alf 'spent three years sifting through players working out who he could rely on ... almost all of it without access' to the multiple film and media channels 'now at everyone's fingertips'.[73]

In another example, four years after the actual match concerned, Alf recalled not just Bobby Charlton taking a defensive covering position against Yugoslavia, one that Alf had coached him towards, but that position's tactical significance within the team's formation at that precise point. Alf identified that as 'the moment when I thought he became a great player' (*Sunday Mirror* 26 April 1970). Charlton independently reciprocated, citing numerous examples of microscopically detailed preparation: 'Tiny little things, but he was meticulous ... Ramsey's professional attitude was responsible for winning the World Cup, no question of that.'[74] Hopcraft beautifully summed up Alf's unique football knowledge, built from this personalised library of extraordinarily detailed memories: 'He had in his mind a picture of a team in movement, not of names on a sheet of paper ... a special vision of a moving team.'[75]

Alf's remarkable football memory persisted late into life. He was approaching 70 when he met an ex-footballer on a Suffolk golf course in the late 1980s. Although now emotionally estranged from football, following his dismissal and cruel treatment, Alf's astonishingly specific memory persisted. He recalled picking this player once for England under-21s in 1974, over a decade earlier. Even more extraordinarily, he then reeled off the team's other ten members. 'He was spot on,' remarked the amazed player.[76] The billionaire tech entrepreneur Bill Gates, to mark similarly approaching 70, recently wrote a revealing autobiography about his early life, which was discussed in a candid interview. There Gates revealed how 'he thinks his superpower is his neurodiversity and ability to hyperfocus', in support of which he cited the apparently mundane example that 'he can remember all the numberplates of his first employees' (*The Times* 25 January 2025).

Remind you of anyone?

1 McKinstry, L. (2007) p.xxv
2 Ibid. p.30
3 Ibid. p.xiv
4 Hamilton, D. (2023) p.391
5 McKinstry, L. (2007) pp.5, 8, 12-13
6 See chapter 6
7 Thanks to David Bull: unpublished Alf Freeman interview transcript, recorded whilst researching Bull (2004)
8 McKinstry, L. (2007) pp.46, 47, 50, 21-2, 50
9 Ibid. pp.92, 93, 88-89
10 McKinstry, L. (2007) p.135
11 Finn. R. (1951) p.125
12 UK Government website (22 July 2021) 'The national strategy for autistic children, young people and adults: 2021 to 2026'
13 Autism Spectrum Condition (ASC) is used here as less value-laden alternative to Autistic Spectrum Disorder (ASD)
14 National Autistic Society website (2025) 'What Is Autism?'
15 UK Government website (22 July 2021) 'The national strategy for autistic children, young people and adults: 2021 to 2026'
16 BBC2 (2022) 'Inside Our Autistic Minds' website; Tammet, D. (2024) pp.53-78 'Warren'; *The Times* 25 January 2025 'Bill Gates: Trump, Musk and how my neurodiversity helped me'
17 NHS website (11 November 2022) 'Signs of autism in adults'
18 Hamilton, D. (2023) p.43
19 The Set Pieces website (2015) I. Macintosh 'Vox In The Box: Brian Glanville'
20 Hamilton, D. (2023) p.167
21 **Channel 4** (2002) *Sir Alf* Director Ken McGill
22 Spurling, J. (2022) p.35
23 Glanville, B. (2008) p.71
24 Hayward, P. (2022) p.158
25 Bowler, D. (1999) pp.88, 108
26 Marquis, M. (1970) p.54
27 Greaves, J. with Giller, N. (1993) p.33
28 **Channel 4** (2002) *Sir Alf* Director Ken McGill
29 McKinstry, L. (2007) pp.94-5
30 Scovell, B. (2005) p.134
31 Pat Godbold interviewed 19 May 2023 Ipswich Town Foundation event, The Hold, Ipswich
32 Hurst, G. (2024) pp.81-82
33 Hopcraft, A. (1968) p.132
34 Ibid. pp.133-4
35 Hayward, P. (2022) p.156
36 Hamilton, D. (2023) p.260
37 Ramsey, A. (1952) p.46

38 Internet Archive Pride of Anglia website (2005) 'Alf Ramsey - Your comments'

39 Thanks to David Bull and drawn from transcripts of unpublished interviews with Ted Ballard, Alf Freeman and Joe Mallett recorded whilst researching: Bull (2004)

40 Ramsey, A. (1952) pp.25-6

41 Bull, D. (2004) pp.114-18

42 Ramsey, A. (1952) pp.11, 47-8

43 Marquis, M. (1970) p.17

44 Ibid. pp.16,17

45 Bowler, D. (1999) p.116

46 **Channel 4** (2002) *'Sir Alf'* Director Ken McGill

47 **BBC Radio 5** Live 'Replay' (released 31 December 2018) '1966 – England win the World Cup Final'

48 Hamilton, D. (2023) pp.72-3

49 Ramsey, A. (1952) p.61

50 Marquis, M. (1970) p.9

51 Ramsey, A. (1952) pp.27-8

52 McKinstry, L. (2007) p.39

53 Ibid. pp.29-30

54 Bowler, D. (1998) pp.40, 98

55 McKinstry, L. (2007) pp. xxix-xxx

56 Hamilton, D. (2023) p.148

57 NHS website (11 November 2022) 'Signs of autism in adults'

58 Ghaziuddin, M. (2018) p.17

59 Ibid.

60 National Autistic Society website (14 August 2020) 'Obsessions and repetitive behaviour'

61 McKinstry, L. (2007) p.8

62 Ramsey, A. (1952) p.12

63 Scovell, B. (2007) p.72

64 **Channel 4** (2002) *'Sir Alf'* Director Ken McGill

65 Hutchinson, R. (1995) p.71

66 Hurst, G. (2024) p.81

67 Geoff Hurst oral history interview 6 February 2025

68 Ramsey, A. (1952) p.62

69 Bradshaw, S. (2012) p.81

70 Ghaziuddin, M. (2018) p.17

71 Bogdashina, O. (2016 2nd edition) p.134

72 Greaves, J., with Giller, N. (1993) p.34

73 Hurst, G. (2024) p.67

74 **History of Football** (2001) 'Sir Bobby Charlton on Alf Ramsey'

75 Hopcraft, A. (1968) pp.135, 138

76 Scovell, B. (2007) p.14

CHAPTER 7

INTERNATIONAL ALF

Bigot, Innovator, or Just Misunderstood?

Alf's Xenophobic Image

ALF'S POSSIBLE neurodivergence is returned to shortly, after a discussion of some difficult topics. Brian Scovell, a prominent football journalist,[1] in 2005 claimed that 'Ramsey was a bit of a racist', citing his attitudes towards opponents Argentina and Scotland.[2] Incidents after England's 1966 World Cup quarter-final against Argentina, when Alf stopped England players from swapping shirts and made angry broadcast comments, have so dominated his international image that they are dissected in chapter 12. The starting point here is the arguably lazy tacit assumption that Alf was xenophobic. For example, one 1993 publication asserted Alf's 'in-built dislike and distrust of foreigners', exacerbated sometimes by him being 'continually on a collision course with the media'.[3] A decade later, Alf's last biographer, a respected right-wing journalist,[4] repeated that allegation by claiming he had 'an ingrained xenophobic streak and little time for any foreigners'.[5] More recently a left-of-centre observer, similarly unfavourably, compared Alf's supposed attitudes with the (then) England manager Gareth Southgate's letter[6] extolling a:

> New progressive, tolerant form of 'Englishness' ... how different it is from anything Alf Ramsey said in 1966. The World Cup-winning manager then called the Argentinians animals and refused to shake hands.[7]

Such allegations impacted Alf's personal reputation. They also matter collectively because football is England's national sport,[8] and an easy arena for airing insecurities about identity.[9] Poisonous varieties of those had prompted Southgate to write his 2021 letter:

> Dear England ... Everyone has a different idea of what it
> actually means to be English. What pride means ... Why would
> you choose to insult somebody for something as ridiculous as
> the colour of their skin? ... We have a desire to protect our
> values and traditions ... but that shouldn't come at the expense
> of introspection and progress.[10]

Alf Ramsey's reputation, in contrast and imperceptibly, has so long been
associated with the 'little Englander' values against which Southgate
railed that Alf's supposed jingoism has become accepted as historical
fact. From 1955 at Ipswich, through to his 1974 England sacking, Alf's
managerial image encouraged that. His highly conventional dress style,
for example, contrasted with psychedelic 1960s emblems of youthful
rebellion, and 'England were guided through this societal change by a
manager ... immaculately dressed, like a Tory MP in a 1950s film.'[11]

Alf's poor media skills magnified impressions of cultural
conservatism, especially during the Mexico 1970 World Cup. For
example, ITV's leading football commentator argued fairly that 'England
did not do themselves any favours', but then erroneously claimed that
advice to the England squad not to 'drink the water' was 'typical Anglo-
Saxon nonsense'.[12] Yet international medical and professional guidance
preached exactly that,[13] and not unusually. In England in 1966, the
visiting Spanish squad had been banned from drinking Birmingham tap
water,[14] and the West Germans brought their own bread and sausages
(*The Guardian* 29 July 2016). In Mexico in 1970 the difference was that
similar cautionary actions became disproportionately and personally
identified with Alf, as chapter 13 explores.

Equally and undeniably, Alf's bristly public image, and clunky
media style, caused career-long public confusion. This 1999, fan-focused
obituary almost shrugs in puzzlement about England's enigmatic World
Cup winner:

> If we wanted to think of him as a cold fish and an oddball, it
> was water off his back ... Virtually every one of his England
> players seems to have had nothing but respect for the way he
> treated them ... He comes across as a man of his time and it
> wasn't the Sixties ... There was a kind of wartime feel about him
> ... a riddle wrapped in a mystery ... I spent the early Seventies
> defending him, but my heart wasn't always in it. (*When Saturday
> Comes* 148, 28 April 1999)

Fans felt ambivalent about Alf, suspicious perhaps that he was jingoistic or worse, but might inaccuracies and misunderstandings have been hardwired into history? For example, in 1970 his first biographer claimed that Alf Ramsey's opinions about English football would often fly 'firmly in the face of the facts'. As a 'most striking example' he cited something jingoistic Ramsey was meant to have said in 1953, after playing in England's first-ever Wembley defeat to a foreign team. His account positions Alf as complaining afterwards that England 'should never have lost' 6-3 to Hungary because 'four of those goals came from outside our penalty area'.[15] Four decades later, Ramsey's most recent biographer repeated the quotation to show Alf's supposed 'blinkered partisanship'.[16] In 2023, it was recycled again, in a beautiful book, to paint similar pictures: *Four of their goals were struck from outside the box*, he [Ramsey] moaned.'[17]

Scrutiny now suggests the original quote was inaccurate. What Alf actually said was that Hungary were 'quite the best side in the world. They would certainly beat Uruguay or Argentina.' Hungary had, though, enjoyed some luck because 'two goals, the fourth and fifth, came from outside the penalty area' (*Daily News* 26 November). That is two goals, not the four claimed by Alf's first biographer, then repeated by others; and his detached tone sounds nothing like the 'blinkered partisanship' often claimed as his defining feature.[18] Simple internet searches soon locate 1953 match footage, which confirms Alf was right; only goals four and five originated from shots 'outside the penalty area'.

That example shows how short the steps can be from Alf's undisputed English patriotism, through claims of partiality and partisanship, to serious allegations of xenophobia. Mis-steps are also likely when observing someone whom, it was claimed in the year 2000 'even the most patient and enthusiastic of psychiatrists might think twice' about analysing. Alf was 'an enigma ... taciturn, gruff, aloof, stubborn, self-righteous, patriotic to the point of xenophobia ... his public character neatly fitted the foreigner's caricature of an Englishman at his coldest, most reserved and uptight'.[19] A few years later, the pre-eminent football journalist Brian Glanville similarly labelled him as 'ineluctably xenophobic', with a supposed 'deep, utterly English caution'.[20] Significantly, though, Glanville also described Alf as 'socially inept', somebody 'dedicated to the point of obsession', whose 'quasi-religious dedication to the game – which for him was hardly a game – excluded all non-initiates'.[21]

Glanville's identification of those latter three characteristics aligns with evidence of Alf's possible neurodivergence but may also have contributed to his shakier accusation of 'xenophobia'. For example, a support practitioner expert in neurodivergence recently summarised her clients' key strengths in ways evident in Alf: 'rational thinking', an 'eidetic [or photographic] memory' and a 'strong 'analytical ability'. But she also cited another typical strength of neurodivergent people as 'strict adherence to rules and order'.[22] Alf Ramsey displayed exactly that, as explored shortly. Might misunderstandings prompted by that trait have helped mistakenly fuel later impressions of xenophobia?

Alf's International Initiation: In at the Deep End

The year 1948 offers a helpful starting point, as Alf's international professional playing career began then. Visiting continental Europe with England, on a ten-day FA tour to Italy and Switzerland, he later termed it as 'among the most exciting adventures of my life'. He was shocked by seeing 'apparently well-fed and beautifully clothed people after the austerity of Britain',[23] but admitted to undisguised glee when Italy's World Cup-winning manager gave every England player and official 'a small sack of rice. In those days rice was almost as valuable as gold.'[24]

Alf had been a surprise, late inclusion in the 16-strong England touring party, having played just two seasons of full-time professional football (*Yorkshire Evening Post* 13 May 1948). Little wonder this novice was awestruck in Turin by the:

> Electric-like atmosphere … for the first time it dawned upon me just how seriously they take their football on the Continent. At home we look upon soccer as something to be enjoyed. On the Continent, and in South America, a game of football is something to be won at all costs for … national prestige.[25]

Because that account was published in 1952, after England's 1950 World Cup humiliation, Alf may have been using it to argue that English football's amateurish arrogance needed updating; but in May 1948 England had beaten Italy. Alf described the fixture as the 'hardest … faced since the war: a match against an ex-enemy country'.[26] British forces had been fighting in Italy just three years earlier, and Alf was only 23 months out of army uniform. The Turin ground had previously been called the 'Mussolini Stadium' but was still 'one of the best in Europe'. For Alf, this 'experience at Turin was to be the basis of my future international career',[27] albeit he watched England's 4-0 victory from the sidelines. Days later, though, he debuted for 'England B' against

Switzerland and relished 'playing against the Continentals ... first and foremost, the speed of movement and thought'.[28]

Europe was merely the first stop in Alf's year of international learning. After flying back to London from Zurich on 27 May 1948, and staying overnight with his parents at Dagenham, on 29 May he took off again 'from Heath Row for ... *Rio de Janeiro!*'[29] His club, Southampton, were unsuccessfully touring Brazil, having lost all five games so far. Alf, carrying precious letters from home for team-mates,[30] would join for the next one. But on arriving in Rio de Janeiro, he was pestered by an English-speaking Brazilian reporter who:

> Nearly spoilt my dinner by trying continuously to draw me into conversation about England's victory over Italy ... the Italians were rated by Brazil as the best soccer team in the world, and our defeat of them had shaken the whole of South America.

Alf would 'not commit [himself] as a newcomer to the FA scene', but the 'young man proved most insistent'. On the next day's flight to São Paulo, Alf saw the results. After being handed a newspaper he nearly:

> Jumped out of my seat with surprise. Looking out of the front page was my photograph ... 'Alf Ramsey' was in the headline ... my reporter friend had written considerably more than I had said to him ... Maybe, I thought, Brazilian words took up more space than they do at home.[31]

This episode may have encouraged Alf's wary, eventually icy attitudes towards journalists, but what happened during his first game in Brazil, against the São Paulo side Corinthians, has become significant for his reputation. McKinstry argued that crowd disturbances after a 'black Corinthian player [Aldo] had been sent off ... fed Alf's nascent xenophobia'.[32] Since this implies not just xenophobia, but racism, those events are now analysed.

For Alf, this 1948 game was a debut, not just in South America, but under floodlights. At first the artificial light made him 'all at sea', wrote the game's English referee afterwards, though soon he 'was magnificent and showed real class'.[33] In the first half, Alf also missed a penalty, shot the rebound straight into the goalkeeper's hands, and gave another penalty away. In the second half, the opposition left-back, Aldo, fouled Southampton's winger Eric Day. Alf's account pictured Aldo astride of Day and 'with his fists' demonstrating 'how Joe Louis had put so many opponents to sleep'.[34] Aldo's sending-off then prompted, again in the words of the match referee, 'a free fight on the popular terraces when bottles were thrown and the military police had to quell the riot'.[35]

Other rich evidence about that night comes from Southampton player Ted Bates who 'never said a bad word against anybody', a rigorously researched biography concluded.[36] Yet in a letter home Ted confessed he 'did not want to play in many more matches' like that one:

> They did everything to us except knife us ... pushing, shoving, kicking in fact doing every dirty thing you could think of and when we retaliated in the good old English way, did the crowd get mad ... there was almost a riot. Quite a few ... swarmed onto the trainer's box ... the nearest thing to a battle I ever want to see.[37]

One São Paulo newspaper observed that the referee had 'exasperated many fans' after 'he missed several fouls, which prompted boos'. Equally, it said Aldo was guilty, and the pitch-invading fans were 'deplorable' (*Diario da Noite* 3 and 4 June 1948). Another agreed that referee Reader had 'acted correctly' (*Correio Paulistano* 4 June 1948). Two years later Reader would skilfully referee the explosive Brazil-Uruguay World Cup Final.[38]

Alf's own account of the match against Corinthians, written four years afterwards, broadly matched everything cited above, but also contained racially questionable phraseology. The first instance was him recalling 'just when I thought things had quietened down, some wild-eyed negroes climbed over the wire fencing'.[39] Although some modern polling positions any contemporary broadcast use of 'Negro' as potentially highly offensive,[40] other anti-racist activists and researchers argue that 'historically, the word Negro was never a racist slur, just a word meaning black'. They describe how, in the UK from the 1960s, 'Negro' as a term gradually gave way to 'Coloured and later to Black and later to BAME'. In the USA of 1963, it was even 'a term still used ... by Martin Luther King in his *I Have A Dream* speech'.[41] Alf Ramsey's 1952 deployment was not therefore in itself racist, although placing 'wild-eyed' next to it possibly was, potentially reflecting a prejudicial trope circulating in early 1950s London, identifying Black people with a 'lack of control'.[42]

Equally, and unknown to Alf, ticketing arrangements had sparked genuine local dismay. Another Brazilian newspaper, translated from the Portuguese, claimed a prominent Rio de Janeiro sports official had corruptly 'deceived São Paulo leaders by offering them a derisory amount for the Southampton game' (*Mundo Esportivo* 24 June 1948). Local fans, therefore, had to 'to pay for admission ... a real swindle to the public' (*Mundo Esportivo* 3 June 1948). Had perceived corruption sparked real anger, and generalised crowd disorder, from those fans on the 'popular terraces',[43] some probably Black, who did then climb over fences?

None of that excuses, or definitively explains, Alf using the racist trope 'wild-eyed negroes'. His account may also have racially stereotyped a late Corinthians substitute,[44] whom Alf described as a 'young negro'. He 'ran about the field in an amazing manner. His lack of footballing knowledge would have filled a hundred books; his broad shoulders, had we stood and waited for him to hit us, could have filled the local hospital!'. Finally, Alf also recounted how that young player, at an otherwise friendly post-match meal, had:

> Sat beside me, to make this banquet one of the most embarrassing I've ever attended. I tried to speak to him and in return received only a fixed glare. Even when my colleagues tried to be pleasant all they received was the same glare. There was something hypnotic in the way this negro stared at us ... the most unpleasant man I've ever met on or off the football field.[45]

Hypnotic' and 'glare', in this context, could be seen as imbued with racial assumptions, especially as apparently Alf had not inquired whether this man spoke or understood English. As seen previously though, 'Negro' was not in itself a racist term during the early 1950s, and was often used by academics and journalists;[46] nor did Alf's account attribute this young player's behaviour to his skin tone or ethnicity. Indeed, prior to that passage he had described how 'the Corinthians included four negroes, all of whom proved to be first-class ball players'.[47]

Contrary to McKinstry's account,[48] Alf's autobiography also did not specify the ethnicity of Aldo, the dismissed player. Alf seems genuinely not to have known the combative substitute's name, or been able to communicate with him, hence referring to 'the young negro'.[49] Negative observations about his behaviour may have expressed unconscious racial bias, but McKinstry's argument that the riot had 'fed Alf's nascent xenophobia', after a 'black Corinthian player [Aldo] had been sent off',[50] now feels unsafe.

A ground-breaking 1947 oral history of Brazilian football, only recently translated into English,[51] further contextualises this 1948 match. Published just as Brazil prepared to host the 1950 World Cup, its strong anti-racism message celebrated the rise of Black and biracial Brazilian footballers, whilst recording the persistent prejudice they faced.[52] It also catalogued how 1940s Brazilian football was politically charged, racially diverse and divided, and socially explosive. Interstate rivalry was warlike, as mentioned in the 1948 São Paulo newspaper stories above about ticketing disputes:

> The newspapers of Rio and São Paulo treated each other as if ... belligerent powers ... It was not a question of Brazil it was one of Rio and São Paulo. Of the war of the Brazilian Championship ... This gives an idea of the pressure exerted ... on soccer players, white, mulatto, or black ... like a soldier in a war.[53]

In other words, the intense atmosphere experienced by all the Southampton players, in São Paulo that June 1948 evening, was relatively normal in Brazil. Five years earlier, 4,000 fireworks had been detonated inside one stadium, even before kick-off,[54] but to a wide-eyed Alf this was all new:

> Forty-thousand spectators ... roared every time a Brazilian touched the ball. We got the bird if a tackle resulted in an opponent going down. Fireworks were tossed on to the field with gay abandon ... The pitch seemed to jump beneath my studs as the crowd's roar grew with intensity.

Alf's *inexperience* as a professional footballer probably heightened his sensibilities and may have contributed to him repeating some of the casually prejudicial racial assumptions present in English, early 1950s society.[55]

Another hypothesis is possible, though. Could Alf's racially loaded language, published in late 1952, consciously or sub-consciously have emphasised his own whiteness, through fear of his 'D****e' nickname catching hold? Chapter one showed that nickname being printed on 18 January 1952, in the mass-circulation *Daily Mirror*, and how rumours about Alf's nickname and ethnicity had circulated during his playing career. It also pictured him standing rather uneasily with Southampton winger Eric Day, the player punched in the fracas that sparked the 1948 crowd disorder. Day's family lived locally to Alf Ramsey's, and the two men often travelled home together. Day casually described Alf as 'maybe ... secretive ... because he was a gypsy ... gypsies are extremely close-knit'.[56]

If Day made such assumptions, so might other Southampton team-mates. The same holds true for Tottenham, where Alf was playing in 1952 when his autobiography was published. Several team-mates grew up or lived in Dagenham,[57] so knowledge of his childhood nickname, and rumoured GRT background, could easily have spread to them. Plausibly, as the writing of Alf's autobiography progressed during spring and summer 1952, he felt under pressure to distance himself from his childhood nickname of 'D****e', and its associated ethnicity rumours. Could Alf's racially loaded language, in the three passages cited above, therefore have reflected an instinct to protect himself, rather than xenophobically attack others? 'Xenophobia', as a charge, is also contradicted by other rarely quoted passages from his autobiography. Alf clearly, unself-consciously loved Brazil, and deeply admired its Black footballers. Describing the England players' stay by Copacabana Beach, during the 1950 World Cup, he was effusive:

> Dozens of football pitches laid out on the sands ... beneath floodlights league matches are played ... The negroes who have such wonderful ball control, are the star turns on Copacabana Beach, and whenever they knew we were watching they went out of their way to give a wonderful exhibition of ball play.[58]

Of that 1948 match against Corinthians he similarly stressed:

> The sportsmanship of football folk in South America ... thousands of games take place at which nothing at all happens ... I must emphasise that although the match had its unfortunate moments, there was nothing on the field, apart from the one incident, to really upset us ... The Brazilians as footballers? Great ball players who had above all else learnt to master it. Their method of always trying to use the ball coincided with my own idea of how the game should be played.[59]

Alf describes himself, in footballing terms, as at least partly Brazilian because like them he believed in 'always trying to use the ball'.[60] Given his hyper-focused, fanatical interest in football, Alf could have paid no higher compliment.

King Arthur, King Alfred

Alf's football thinking, and his incessant international learning, were channelled and expanded during his 1949–55 Tottenham playing career by cosmopolitan manager Arthur Rowe: 'Rowe was the preacher, Ramsey the practitioner. Rowe preached the "simple, quick, accurate" formula to his players without let-up. Ramsey showed them how on the field' (*Daily Mirror* 31 July 1951). Alf had been Rowe's first signing and he described them soon becoming 'the closest of friends ... Mr. Rowe had definite and original ideas as to how the game should be played ... ideas which I liked.'[61] His warmth was reciprocated and Rowe described how 'I always used to speak to Alf and Ron [the Tottenham captain], telling them what I was thinking of doing. I would ask them their thoughts.'[62]

Alf and Arthur shared army backgrounds and Essex connections. Rowe had captained Spurs during the 1930s, started coaching, then served as an army physical training instructor from 1940–45. He managed Essex's Chelmsford City from 1945–49, including 1966 hat-trick hero Geoff Hurst's father, before returning to manage Tottenham in 1949. War had also thwarted both Alf Ramsey and Arthur Rowe. In 1939, 19-year-old Alf's amateur playing affiliation with Portsmouth went nowhere, and war scotched 33-year-old Arthur's golden job offer to coach for the Hungarian FA, following a successful summer secondment (*Weekly Dispatch* 9 July 1939).

More significantly, both men thought deeply about football, although Rowe better disguised his seriousness with comic one-liners. Of 'peripheral vision', a favourite phrase of England manager Walter Winterbottom, he commented, 'You know what that means ... seeing out of your arse!'[63] A 2003 obituary, written by a journalist soaked in Tottenham reporting, recalled Rowe telling him 'football's a simple game, it's the players who make it difficult' (*The Independent* 11 November 1993). Yet just like Alf, what seemed obvious to Rowe was invisible to others. Rowe thought about simplicity, having coached in Hungary when 'the crucial point was that it was *thinking*. In Budapest, as in Vienna, football was a matter for intellectual debate.'[64] Rowe's fresh thinking in turn inspired Alf, who eulogised how Rowe 'before he ever brings to our notice any plan [he] ... studies his subject from every possible aspect'.[65] These cosmopolitan influences had already surfaced when Rowe's managerial career started at Chelmsford City. In 1946, he unfavourably compared British sporting 'happy-go-lucky attitudes' with the professionalism of the USA and Russia. For good results:

> We must revise our outlook and approach towards top-class sporting competitions ... coaching by people who are experts in

their job … more and better facilities for training and practice … Natural talent abounds in Britain but … it needs coaching, training, and intelligent handling. (*Essex Newsman* 12 July)

Having honed his management skills, on returning to Tottenham in 1949, Rowe innovated immediately and 'almost uniquely in Britain, Spurs began building from the back, with Ramsey given licence to push on'.[66] At his 'first serious tactical talk' Rowe told the Spurs players to, 'Play football all the time. Make it quick. Make it easy.'[67] The resultant 'push and run style' ended up seeming spontaneous but was, like most excellent recipes, built upon structured thinking, deep planning and incessant practice.

Alf also garnished Arthur's dish, using his 1948 South American experiences. Shortly after joining Tottenham, Alf noticed goalkeeper Ditchburn's tremendously long and accurate throw, reminiscent of:

How the crack teams in Brazil worked … having got possession of the ball it was their job to retain it … I reasoned that as Ditchburn was such a good thrower, if I put myself in an unmarked position where he could throw the ball to me it would be more beneficial than if he punted it to the half-way line.[68]

Rowe influenced Alf Ramsey at multiple other junctures, including mentoring during early days at Ipswich,[69] and Alf copying Rowe's 1949 positive opening at Tottenham, when he started in 1963 with England. Alf was ostentatiously ultra-focused 'from the moment he took over England's team', immediately adopting 'a more professional approach' than his predecessor Walter Winterbottom.[70]

Alf Ramsey, mimicking Arthur Rowe, was a single-minded, dedicated professional, whose obsessive love of football was almost unnaturally intense. A reporter recalled travelling with them both during Alf's Ipswich days, and returning from an away game:

Four or five hours lay ahead before we arrived in London. Throughout, Ramsey and Rowe talked and talked and talked about football. Nobody else entered the conversation: there was no opportunity. And rarely, if at all, did they smile. They were lost in a world of their own.[71]

Alf consulted Arthur in 1962 about whether to accept the FA's offer to manage England,[72] a significant conversation given the pair's shared history. Rowe was then achieving success with Crystal Palace, but in January 1954 'had suffered a nervous breakdown, brought on by the worry and ceaseless work' of leading Spurs back to the high spots of 1949–52. He returned to work in July 1954 but after defeat by Third Division North's York City, in the FA Cup fifth round of February 1955, 'He suffered his second breakdown and was admitted to hospital in April. In July 1955 he resigned.' Rowe, it would later emerge, had undergone 'the horrors of electric shock treatment at a sanatorium in Kent'.[73] Given everything Arthur endured for his love of football, Alf could have consulted nobody better about the prospect of managing England. Equally, might witnessing Rowe's mental health disintegrate during 1954–55 have reinforced Alf Ramsey's later instincts towards defensive, bunker mentalities, and contributed towards unfair allegations that such protectionism amounted to something worse: an active dislike of those foreign to or different from oneself, known otherwise as 'xenophobia'?

Xenophobic, or Just Misunderstood?

Arthur and Alf disguised and protected themselves: Arthur behind quips, Alf behind privacy, but both were vulnerable characters driven by ambition. The last chapter witnessed Alf's relentless self-improvement using routine-based practice. He admired others who did likewise and was favourably struck by Tottenham goalkeeper Ditchburn's:

> Severe criticism of himself. Ted is never satisfied … He practised for hours to achieve his accuracy at various distances. In practice matches his 'heaves' to our wingers every week grew in perfection until we thought they must be guided by radar.[74]

Ditchburn, though, simply found Alf annoying:

> He had a lot to say in the dressing room … He got on well with Arthur Rowe … But Alf was no friend of mine … I never got on with him … It was as simple as that. I was not the only one who felt like that. He was that type of bloke. He had his own little world.[75]

To Tottenham team-mates, Alf had a personality which, in 21st-century terms, seemed irredeemably nerdish: 'Ever so inward … Not nasty … but if the conversation wasn't about football he would just switch off.'[76] Could such a focused mind look open-mindedly outward?

This chapter opened with claims Alf had an 'ingrained xenophobic streak'.[77] Yet he praised Brazilian teams in 1948, and during the 1950 World Cup marvelled at the ball control skills of everyday Black Brazilians. Commenting about playing Argentina in 1951, Alf proclaimed 'how much I admire the brand of football served up by South American teams. I think it is cracking stuff.'[78] He said similar after playing Italy in November 1949:

> In every match in which I play it is to learn something new ... the Italians on several occasions produced touches which I have since stored away for personal interest ... in trying to cope with these high-speed artistes one quality in their play forcibly struck me ... their brilliant positional sense ... really slick footballers ... not for the first time – they provided a lesson.[79]

Three years later, this time as a tourist, Alf was similarly enthralled by Florence's annual medieval ball game, boasting 'satin and silk costumes in all the colours of the rainbow'.[80] At the same time, he was stringently critical of how some modern Italian footballers behaved. 'To put it bluntly', he wrote, they:

> Seemed to forget all about the rules of the game ... nudging, shirt-pulling and other distracting features ... the Italian players should have studied the laws of the game much more carefully. Incorrect interpretation of the rules more than anything else was responsible for the rather nasty taste the game left in my mouth.[81]

Alf definitely sounds pompous, and insufferably pious, but was this xenophobia? His ire was aimed also at the 'rather elderly gentleman' referee, who finding 'himself unable to keep up with the play consequently missed many vital points'.[82] Alf, with utter and innocent conviction, then argued that:

> I do not stoop to dirty tricks or foul play. Association Football, I shall always contend, is something to be played as an art and should be enjoyed by everyone. As I play fair, I expect my opponents to do the same; an argument with which no one can justly take offence.[83]

Given Alf's multiple positive comments about foreign teams and players, his almost comic parallel piety about rule-breaking may have reflected not xenophobia, but more complex cognitive phenomena. Naively, but not xenophobically, he is making the logical argument that, as a global game, football's rules should be universally understood and applied; and Alf's previously unrecognised tendencies towards neurodivergence may have magnified the strength of his feelings. Like many people with ASC,[84] rules mattered inordinately to Alf.

For example, other than 'a year's bad luck' in a single game, he had no footballing 'alibis to offer for England's defeat' to the USA in their 1950, second World Cup game. The American winning goal is shown below, as Alf watches on with horror.

Off the field, though, Alf argued that England 'could have lodged a protest against the USA' for selecting players not born there, a practice against World Cup rules.[85] When Spain knocked England out in the next game, although he blamed his own defensive error, more 'weak shooting', and the referee disallowing an England goal, Alf's heaviest criticisms were about Spain's team failing to:

> [Play] Football in keeping with the rules of the game ... Time and again they put an end to moves ... by intercepting our passes with their hands ... our rivals seemed to use their hands far more often than they did their feet ... Apart from their handling, their habit of bodychecking, pulling our shirts, and using their elbows did not please the Brazilian spectators.

The insufferably priggish Alf then tartly remarked that if 'the Spaniards wanted to do this, all very well, but we did not intend to follow their example'.[86]

Rather than being feigned, though, his shock seems genuine. Was it rooted in a neurodivergent world view that simply saw things differently? Playing against Austria in 1952, Alf was similarly appalled, claiming their centre-forward 'threw himself full length' to earn a penalty, despite not being touched by a defender.

> If the laws of the game had been correctly interpreted, he would have been warned by the referee for ungentlemanly behaviour. But then, maybe I'm getting worked up, for to me more important than winning a game is to play it in the best possible spirit and obey the rules. Perhaps I am a trifle old-fashioned in holding such views.[87]

Reinforced perhaps by neurodivergence, Alf was again emphasising an imperative to 'obey the rules'; but his self-described 'old-fashioned' queasiness about rule-breaking may also have had cultural, not just psychological, overlays. A massive academic study has recently positioned advocacy of 'fair play' less as chauvinistic bigotry, more as a long-lived English social ideal and cultural phenomenon, stretching back beyond Shakespeare. It cites multiple historical examples, of diverse English people, claiming 'fair play' as part of their cultural identity,[88] including all shades of political opinion from the 20th-century that Alf lived in.[89]

Examples are not hard to find. In the same week that Alf played against Austria, as cited above, the *Daily Mirror* (21 May 1952) featured a Sussex train driver, who was also a keen angler, physically fighting another man on a riverbank. Why? Because that man had been fishing for pike during the close season. Headlined 'Believes In Fair Play', he justified his physical confrontation with the rule-breaker by arguing, 'Angling is my whole life ... but I believe in fair play and the observance of the close season.' Alf's paragraph of football piety above, berating an opponent for alleged cheating, was of similar ilk; not intentionally xenophobic, but an expression of sentiments common to many 20th-century English working-class men, especially about sport.[90]

Finally, arguments for Alf being 'a xenophobe' are further and fatally weakened because his black-and-white, rules-based view of international football, used above to criticise various foreign opponents, was replicated in how he treated his own English players, English FA high-ranking voluntary officials, and English-speaking journalists. Alf's awkward, rules-based persona was directed universally towards everyone, whether English people or foreigners. For example, in 1972, despite years working with him, interviewer Frank McGhee still confessed to finding Alf Ramsey 'not an easy man to like'. By now Alf had vast managerial experience but still fumed when journalists wasted his time with 'questions that he considers foolish, flippant, unfair or insulting' (*Daily Mirror* 6 November 1972). Alf's sense of social and psychological isolation seeped out everywhere, McGhee observed:

> He classes any group he doesn't especially like as 'these people' – and the range is wide, including opponents, journalists, certain managers, members of the League Management Committee, and some Football Association officials. Alf doesn't fancy many of 'these people'. (*Daily Mirror* 7 November 1972)

Alf's disdain for the English FA's committee members[91] was also matched by the strict rules he laid down for England players. Soon after his 1962 managerial appointment, Alf stopped London-based squad members, before home internationals, 'sleeping at their homes. It really astounded me … I had to alter it straight away … It was unfair' (*Sunday Mirror* 19 April 1970). Enforcing hotel stays also, it should be noted, bolstered Alf's control of his squad. Managing his first European tour in 1963, he refused a request for the players to be let out to celebrate a victory: 'If you want a fucking beer you can come back to the hotel',[92] Alf barked. He ordered in 40 bottles, then enforced a 10pm bedtime. Similar happened in 1964, after beating the USA 10-0 in New York, when an impromptu hotel suite party was halted at his direct instruction (*Daily Mirror* 7 November 1972). Two weeks earlier, at the start of that tour, he had already threatened seven rule-breaking players, four of whom would eventually win World Cup medals: Banks, Wilson, Moore and Bobby Charlton. They had sneaked out for drinks in London the night before departure, but on their return just before midnight each player found 'passports lying on our beds'. Alf let them stew, days later telling all seven he would have liked to have 'left you behind in London … I will not tolerate a repeat performance.'[93] One recalled it as 'the most severe and punishing reprimand he had ever had', that Alf's 'face turned white. He lost it.'[94]

Perhaps as Alf intended, this story soon 'became known to anyone selected to play for England',[95] but the same iron discipline persisted throughout his reign. Shortly before the 1966 World Cup tournament started, Alf castigated two other eventual medal winners (Ball and

Stiles) for leaving the Lilleshall training complex, to drink a single pint: 'Ramsey's eyes flashed as he said *Get out of here, all of you. Get out of my sight*' (*The Independent* 7 June 2006). Alf also imposed isolation upon England's players, banning wives and running England's World Cup camps 'like a monastery'. In February 1971, Martin Peters and Geoff Hurst inadvertently breached that rule, in Malta, prompting Alf to threaten they 'could kiss goodbye to our international careers' if repeated.[96]

Alf was not intolerant of foreigners who broke rules because he was xenophobic, he was intolerant of *anybody* who transgressed *his* rules and codes, whatever their nationality. That was proven by him threatening to drop, for minor disciplinary reasons and at various times, at least eight of the 11 Englishmen who won the 1966 World Cup. Citing one of them, an expert recently noted how Alf possessed:

> Brutal honesty and an authoritarian streak. Euphemisms and 'emotional literacy' weren't part of his lexicon. The players' feelings weren't the first concern. Ramsey's lacerating candour cut through with the toughest men ... *You were frightened to death really*, said [Bobby] Charlton.[97]

Alf viewed football players with cool objectivity. Although that could lead to unintentionally cutting, even cruel feedback, it also meant he disregarded surface features that might influence others: not just

sexuality (see chapter nine) but also skin colour and ethnicity. On 11 December 1968,[98] ten years before Viv Anderson became the first male, Black, full England international, Alf picked Paul Reaney for England. Reaney resembled Alf in three ways. Firstly, his skin tone was darker than white team-mates. A newspaper recently claimed, 'Paul Reaney is now regarded as the first non-white player to play for England' (*Daily Mirror* 31 October 2021).[99] Secondly, Reaney, like Alf Ramsey, was 'always reluctant to talk about his family background during an era when views about racism were less enlightened'. Finally, mirroring Alf, Reaney was an 'outstanding right-back'. In November 1970, the pair were pictured, both wearing white tops, during England training (see previous page).

Alf first picked Reaney for England under-23s in March 1964 (*Daily Mirror* 11 March) and in the preliminary 1966 World Cup squad (*Coventry Evening Telegraph* 7 April). Alf nurtured him further before declaring, months before the 1970 Mexico World Cup and in typically flat fashion, that 'as a defender … Paul Reaney … satisfied me' (*Coventry Evening Telegraph* 11 December 1969). Reaney seemed certain to travel to Mexico but sadly, in April 1970, broke his leg *(Daily Mirror* 3 April)*. Football being a capricious sport, even a fit Reaney may not have made the squad, or the team. Equally, had he done so, the injuries of others might have meant his selection for the quarter-final against West Germany. It is tempting to imagine Reaney, during the match's closing stages, heroically appearing from nowhere to stop Seeler heading back across the six-yard box and equalising for West Germany.

How 'satisfied', on so many levels, might the potentially neurodivergent, often misunderstood, but probably not xenophobic Alf 'D****e' Ramsey have been about that?

1 Football Writers' Association website (10 August 2018) 'Brian Scovell becomes 1st Life Vice-President'

2 Scovell, B. (2005) p.156, then 156-8

3 Greaves, J. with Giller, N. (1993) p.36

4 E.g. McKinstry's range of articles on *The Spectator* website (2025) 'Leo McKinstry'

5 McKinstry, L. (2007) p.xxx

6 The Players' Tribune website (8 June 2021) 'Dear England' Gareth Southgate

7 Anti-Capitalist Resistance website (10 July 2021) Kellaway, D. 'More Than Just A Game – What We Can Learn From The Euros'

8 Goldblatt, D. (2014)

9 Calvin, M. (2018) chapter 18

10 The Players' Tribune website (8 June 2021) 'Dear England' Gareth Southgate

11 Hayward, P. (2022) pp.218, 233.

12 Dawson, J. (2000) p.61

13 See chapter 13

14 Passingham, I. (2016) p.55

15 Marquis, M. (1970) pp.39-40

16 McKinstry, L. (2007) pp.126-7

17 Hamilton, D. (2023) p.38

18 McKinstry, L. (2007) pp.126-7

19 Edworthy, N. (2000) p.66

20 Glanville, B. (2008) pp.35, 55

21 Ibid. pp. 35-6, 39

22 Breslow, M. (2020)

23 Ramsey, A. (1952) p.34

24 Ibid. p.35

25 Ibid. p.36

26 Ibid. p.35

27 Ibid. p.37

28 Ibid. p.38

29 Ibid. p.39

30 Holley, D. (2022) p.33 Many thanks to Duncan Holley for access to this excellent history and other assistance.

31 Ibid. pp39-.40

32 McKinstry, L. (2007) p.59

33 Holley, D. (2022) p.34

34 Ibid. p.41

35 Ibid. p.35

36 Bull, D. (2004) p.xii

37 Holley, D. (2022) p.34

38 Glanville, B. (1973) p.68
39 Ramsey, A. (1952) pp.41-2
40. Ipsos MORI (2021) pp.16,19
41. Institute of Race Relations website (9 March 2021) Liz Fekete 'Who gets to define racism?'
42 Olusoga, D. (2021) p.501
43 Holley, D. (2022) p.35
44 Helio for Hilton, at centre-half, and Bode for Rui in the forwards (*Diario da Noite* 3 June 1948, *Correio Paulistano* 4 June 1948)
45 Ramsey, A. (1952) pp.41-2
46 Kynaston, D. (2009) pp.100, 448, 450
47 Ramsey, A. (1952) p.40
48 McKinstry, L. (2007) p.59
49 Ramsey, A. (1952) p.42
50 McKinstry, L. (2007) p.59
51 Filho, M. (2021)
52 Filho, M. (2021) e.g. Leonidas da Silva pp.187-95
53 Ibid. pp.236, 238
54 Ibid. pp.235-9; Ramsey, A. (1952) p.40
55 Kynaston, D. (2009) pp.25-6, 99-101
56 McKinstry, L. (2007) p.47
57 Ibid. pp.137-8
58 Ramsey, A. (1952) p.67, also 68-9 for the beauty of Brazil
59 Ramsey, A. (1952) pp.42, 43
60 Thanks to Gavin Barber for illuminating this point
61 Ibid. p.50
62 McKinstry, L. (2007) p.82
63 Ibid. p.81
64 Wilson, J. (2009) p.87
65 Ramsey, A. (1952) p.53
66 Wilson, J. (2009) p.132
67 Ramsey, A. (1952) p.51
68 Ibid. pp.51-2, 53
69 See also Hamilton, D. (2023) pp.56-57
70 Shepherdson, A. (1968) p.42
71 McKinstry, L. (2007) p.202
72 Hutchinson, R. (1995) p.58
73 The Fighting Cock website (1 March 2012) 'A Very English Visionary' Cloake, M.
74 Ramsey, A. (1952) p.53
75 McKinstry, L. (2007) p.90
76 Ibid. p.139
77 Ibid. p.xxx

78 Ramsey, A. (1952) p.80
79 Ibid. pp.55-6
80 Ibid. p.99
81 Ibid. pp.101-2
82 Ibid. p.102
83 Ibid.p.103
84 Breslow, M. (2020); Petrolini, V., Jorba, M., Vicente, A. (2023)
85 Ramsey, A. (1952) pp.71-72
86 Ibid. p.74
87 Ibid. p.107
88 Duke-Evans, J. (2023)
89 Ibid. especially chapter 13
90 Ibid. pp.278-81
91 E.g. McKinstry, L. (2007) pp.373-4
92 Greaves, J. with Giller, N. (1993) p.37
93 Ibid. p.38
94 McKinstry, L. (2007). p.227
95 Hurst, G. (2024) pp.88-89
96 Ibid. pp. 146, 150-151
97 Hayward, P. (2022) pp.158-9
98 Ibid. p.296
99 Ibid. chapter 23, also Tiller, M. (2023) chapters 10-11

CHAPTER 8

PRACTISING KINDNESS

Secret Societies, Charitable Etonians

Introduction

THIS CHAPTER breaks fresh ground in Alf Ramsey's story by moving beyond 1952, the year his only autobiography was written, and recognising two previously ignored episodes as Alf moved from playing into management. The most visible and significant, running from 1952 until 1955, was part-time football coaching work at a charity in Hackney Wick called the 'Eton Manor Boys Club', started in 1909 by four Old Etonians. Eton College, founded in 1440 and less than 40 miles due west of Hackney Wick, is still an elite, boys-only, fee-paying boarding school. It has educated 20 British prime ministers including David Cameron (2010–16) and Boris Johnson (2019–2022).[1] In contrast, Hackney Wick's Eton Manor Boys Club targeted 'the very roughest class of working boy'.[2]

Another, more shadowy development in Alf Ramsey's life was that in 1953 he became a freemason. Freemasonry to modern eyes looks almost as 'establishment' as Eton College. Was Alf consciously aiming to join that establishment, or were these two storylines simply chance at play?

Alf the Freemason

Unsurprisingly, given Freemasonry's long history of secrecy, and the sparsity of evidence about Alf's personal life, previous biographers seemed unaware he was one. A scant documentary trail tracks Alf entering Waltham Abbey Lodge (2750) at the 'first level' on 5 October 1953, being 'raised' to the third, master mason level in October 1954, and finally leaving in 1981.[3] His 1953 initiation fee was '20 guineas',[4] or £21, well over a week of Alf's wages.

What did membership buy? Freemasonry then, as now, centred around three ideals: 'Look after those less fortunate, improve yourself, and live life well so as to be remembered for the right reasons.'[5] Although

Alf's life outcomes eventually matched that template, no evidence has yet come to light of his tangible Freemasonry actions. Frustratingly, few documents record what his Waltham Abbey Lodge and its members actually did. The lodge was founded in 1899, its 'first meeting' was at the 'Royal Forest Hotel, Chingford, on 18th May 1905', and by 1909 it had 20 members. In the 1950s, it was very active, with five new members joining in 1952 and seven more with Alf in 1953.[6] When he died in 1999, 'his widow donated his master mason's apron, Grand Lodge certificate and the summonses showing his initiation and passing to the Lodge.'[7] Given Alf kept this paraphernalia, being a freemason seemingly meant something to him: but what?

Although their meetings formally eschew discussion of religion or politics,[8] in the period Alf joined, and mostly since, modern European Freemasonry had generally been associated with liberal sentiments, 1980s Italy excepted.[9] For example, from the 1920s freemasons were 'ruthlessly persecuted by the Nazis and in several Fascist states, such as Vichy France ... Mussolini's Italy ... and interwar Romania'.[10] The same happened in Franco's fascist Spain, where in the 1930s and 1940s fantastical but influential propaganda claimed Masonic, Jewish and Bolshevik conspiracies against the Catholic Church.[11] Religious suspicion, prohibition and even persecution of Freemasonry still occurs today, and membership is not risk-free.[12] Equally, no evidence survives about Alf's motives for joining. One highly active Essex freemason was Sir Herbert Dunnico: football enthusiast, former Labour MP, Baptist minister, political pacifist and chair of Essex FA 1947–53. Yet nothing specific links the two men and he died three days before Alf joined.[13]

Others are more likely to have encouraged Alf into Freemasonry. England superstar Stanley Matthews was a member. He enticed Alf to play in southern Africa during the summer of 1955, as explored in the next chapter, and the two often featured in charitable UK benefit matches.[14] Jackie Milburn, team-mate in England's fateful last 1950 World Cup game and Alf's 1963 successor as Ipswich manager, was a freemason; so were Joe Mercer, Don Revie and Ron Greenwood, Alf's England managerial successors. Sir Stanley Rous, FA secretary from 1934–62, then FIFA president until 1974, was likewise.[15] Arthur Drewry, Football League chairperson and the FA England selector who penned the introduction to Alf's 1952 autobiography, had no fewer than 14 freemasons attend his funeral, presumably from his local lodge (*Grimsby Telegraph* 30 March 1961).

Were these all odd, unconnected coincidences? Probably, and a recent comprehensive history debunks the last 50 years of conspiracy theories surrounding British Freemasonry.[16] The most likely explanation for the membership of 1950s professional footballers is that playing careers were short, wages were capped, and Freemasonry offered local networking opportunities, alongside charitable outcomes. Yet Alf maintained his membership long after that phase of his life had ended, and his FA secretary from 1967–74 recounted the arrival of a strikingly odd letter:

> I could not understand it … weird … a bit illustrated, it just didn't make any sense, the wording or anything … I just gave it to Alf, and he never responded to it through me … It was quite big paper, and I am sure there were colours on it … obviously words … handwritten.[17]

An FA colleague in whom she confided 'told her it was Masonic', but until now she had not known he was a Freemason. Although that letter is long lost, and history is unlikely ever to document or explain Alf's Freemasonry, might his reserved, obsessively private character have found a comforting retreat in the ritually reinforced secrecy, and single-sex camaraderie, of Freemasonry membership?[18]

The Eton Manor Boys Club

Meanwhile, Alf Ramsey's career and character was simultaneously being shaped by another charitable foundation that has also lain hidden in his life story. When he first visited Eton Manor Boys Club, in 1952, Alf would have been struck by its spacious, two-storey, oak and stone headquarters building, and acres of sporting facilities. The charity was founded in Hackney Wick in 1909, having spun off from the 1880 Eton Mission: a faith-driven partnership offering Eton College's privileged schoolboys voluntary work in one of London's more deprived localities.

Eton Mission had focused on young children and families, but the four Old Etonians who set up Eton Manor worked with the adolescents that male children would grow into, then the men those adolescents became. It did so through a belief in the potential of sport, culture, and open-air activities to enrich some of England's poorest people. Eton Manor's facilities became the envy of similar 'Boys Clubs' across London, facilities which sometimes included hiring elite sportspeople like Alf Ramsey as coaches.[19]

Eton Manor was the brainchild of Gerald Wellesley (born 1885), actively supported and funded by three others: Alfred Wagg (born 1875), Edward Cadogan (born 1880) and Arthur Villiers (born 1883).[20]

All four attended Eton, then Oxford or Cambridge universities, and came from landed aristocratic or financial-sector families. In 1943, Wellesley would become the seventh Duke of Wellington. Although he was the only Eton Manor founder who married, from the 1910s onwards Wellesley could be 'flamboyantly homosexual'.[21] His eventual wife, and his previous fiancée, had both been female lovers of Vita Sackville-West, and although he and his wife separated in 1922 they stayed friends.[22] Meanwhile, the other three Eton Manor founders remained lifelong bachelors and generously funded the charity.

The privileged, well-connected, sometimes eccentric lives of these four Old Etonians matter to Alf's story because at Ipswich Town, from 1955–63, the chairs of the board were also Old Etonians: Alistair Cobbold until 1957, then succeeded by his bachelor nephew John Cobbold. John, as we will see in the next two chapters, was probably gay. Alf's 1952–55 Eton Manor apprenticeship was not just in coaching young and adult footballers, but in managing and being managed by aristocratic, powerful, privileged, mostly single and sometimes homosexual Old Etonians.

More prosaically, because Hackney Wick lay roughly six miles between Barking to the south, where Alf had just moved house with his new wife and stepdaughter, and Tottenham Hotspur's White Hart Lane ground to the north, the club was a geographically convenient mid-point in his commute. Aged nearly 33, Alf's playing career was coming to an end, and getting married in December 1951 meant he needed to plan for his family's future. Meanwhile, season 1951/52 had ended in a disappointing sixth-place league finish for the Eton Manor Old Boys adult football team. Also, as the in-house newsletter reported, financially it was 'in some respects, a disastrous year' (*Chin-Wag* July 1952), hence their joy in reporting 'the most wonderful news the footballers have had for years', namely that Alf had 'accepted the invitation to become Adviser/Coach to the Club' and would be 'coming along every Thursday evening to supervise the Coaching and Training of our footballers' (*Chin-Wag* September 1952).

Alf's work was paid, as revealed by an intriguing source. An Eton Manor regular told an oral history project about driving out of the club's isolated training ground one night and noticing:

[There was] a person walking out. Well, the buses weren't very frequent so … I stopped the car and opened the door, 'Would you like a lift somewhere?' and this very quietly spoken person got in … I got talking to him and I said, 'Oh you're – you're the football coach, aren't you?' And he said, 'Yes,' he said, 'I play for Spurs but ... you don't earn that much money as a footballer, and it's nice to earn a little more, by coaching.' You can guess who it was – Alf Ramsey.[23]

Alf's weekly coaching role at Eton Manor lasted three seasons, until summer 1955, and links persisted for years afterwards. Whilst managing Ipswich, Alf signed, then selected, an ex-Eton Manor player (*Daily Herald* 4 April 1959). Twelve months previously an Eton Manor member had met Alf at nearby Leyton Orient, when they were playing Ipswich. Alf, he observed, had a reputation as one of football's best-dressed managers:

> And on this occasion it was right, because he was wearing a very famous tie, none other than Eton Manor ... I said, 'the old tie looks familiar Alf.' He replied, 'it should do in this part of the world.' I found it was one of his most prized possessions, and also his association with the Club ... he used to enjoy Mr. Viliers' parties ... He particularly asked to be remembered to all the people he knew at the Club. (*Chin-Wag* October 1958)

Despite such warm associations, Eton Manor has slipped out of Alf's publicly told story. Marquis's biography ignored it, and Bowler's offered just one sentence, inaccurately fixing Alf's start date as 'February 1954'.[24] McKinstry repeated that, even more briefly.[25] By 1970 and 1972, when Frank McGhee interviewed Alf at length for the *Daily Mirror* and *Sunday Mirror*, the Eton Manor Boys Club had been disbanded and its magnificent Hackney headquarters demolished or abandoned.[26] Three of its Old Etonian founders and lifelong funders had died, as would Wellesley in January 1972. The moment had passed perhaps for even Alf himself to acknowledge Eton Manor, yet its impact on him, as on thousands of East Enders, was deeply significant.

Alf's Work at Eton Manor 1952–55

For Alf, the Eton Manor opportunity arose almost accidentally. Major Arthur Villiers was Eton Manor's joint founder, major benefactor, leader, and had been resident on site since 1939. In 1952, he argued with previous coaching contacts at Arsenal and turned to Tottenham: might any Spurs player be interested?[27] So it was that Alf gained his first experiences of coaching, every Thursday evening, under the rudimentary lighting at Eton Manor's Hackney Marsh 'Wilderness' sports ground.

Midweek, floodlit Football League football did not start until 1956, the year after Alf stopped playing. He was, therefore, free to coach on Thursday evenings, although as he played himself on most Saturday afternoons he rarely managed to watch the competitive fixtures of those he coached.

For everyday matters, Eton Manor's five 'Old Boys' adult teams, and seven 'Senior' (16–18) and 'Junior' (14–16) teams were managed, and selected, by Eton Manor staff or volunteers. Alf's task was to lead weekly coaching sessions and raise the club's wider morale and profile. His impact was instantaneous:

> Alf Ramsey ... must take much of the credit for Eton Manor's 1-0 victory at Cheshunt. Ramsey coaches the Manor team, an East London boys' club, and in readiness for this game gave them an additional tactical talk after 'club night' on Thursday. (*Daily Herald* 13 October 1952)

Alf's brief was wide. On Thursday evenings, Eton Manor's adult footballers were urged to 'take advantage of the expert coaching and knowledge ... when Alf Ramsey is available to help you to improve your game'. Seniors, aged 16–18, could also join in:

> Boys who have already taken advantage ... have learnt many useful hints ... Without correct balance it is impossible to get any power behind a shot or clearance, and certainly not direction. With Alf Ramsey coaching, probably the best exponent of kicking a dead or moving ball playing football to-day, everybody in the Club now has the chance to eradicate this weakness. (*Chin-Wag* October 1952)

As well as helping individuals, it was hoped Alf's knowledge and prestige would raise Eton Manor's status in the football world. 'Something like this has been wanted at the Club for years', wrote a regular newsletter columnist (*Chin-Wag* October 1952). Ordinary club members agreed. 'Readers Letters', two from outside London and one from Iraq, praised Alf's appointment (*Chin-Wag* October 1952, January 1953), and Eton Manor's raised media profile was maintained for months:

> Congratulations to the first team not only on putting up an excellent game against last year's winner of the London Senior Cup, but on being the subject of Gittins' cartoon in the *Evening*

News. It is certain the Club will make headway under the schooling of Alf Ramsey. (*Chin-Wag* November 1952)

That cartoon's final caption affectionately lampooned Eton Manor for being 'too polite to take advantage' of their opponents having only ten men on the pitch and predicted future contests with that match's opponents 'at anything from boxing, to athletics, squash and tiddly winks' (*London Evening News* 27 October 1952). As such teasing implied, Eton Manor encouraged attempting multiple sports and friendliness, not just excellence. Even unconfident, unsociable and newly married Alf was persuaded to attend the 'Football Club's first Annual Dinner and Dance', where 'Mr. and Mrs. Alf Ramsey' were toasted (*Chin-Wag* March 1953).

Alf took his coaching seriously. Eton Manor youth teams regularly received 'pep talks from Alf Ramsey' to add 'that little extra for the forthcoming battles' (*Chin-Wag* April 1953). George Gatward, just 17 when Alf arrived, recalled he 'loved the Club ... loved the boys ... thought it was a marvellous Club ... he was a fantastic coach ... made everything so simple'. Similarly, Kenny Elgar, born in 1929, remembered how:

> I just wanted to be near him because he never talked anything but sense ... if he stayed behind and did a little bit more, we all stayed behind with him ... he used to come straight from Tottenham ... he just used to love to watch Boys and Old Boys playing.[28]

As with Tottenham before and Ipswich after, Alf's arrival signalled almost instant success:

> Heartiest congratulations to the first team on winning the London League, Premier Division Championship. Also, to the second team as runners-up in the Second Division ... the happiest and most successful season since the Club started again from scratch after the war ... no fewer than 36 players turned out for the first team this season ... Charlie Phillips and Alf Ramsey both ... have the knack of inspiring and enthusing the players. Charlie, with his forthright and outspoken advice and criticism, and Alf in his quiet, knowledgeable, and patient handling of even the most difficult problem. They make an ideal combination. (*Chin-Wag* May 1953)

Alf genuinely cared about Eton Manor. During May 1953, despite being on tour with England in South America and playing against Argentina, Chile and Uruguay, Alf wrote to the Eton Manor 'Annual General Meeting':

> Taff Wilson ... had received a letter only the day before from Alf Ramsey in the Argentine, saying how very happy he had been to help with the coaching and training, and how much real pleasure he personally got out of it. Alf Ramsey was tremendously impressed by the keenness and enthusiasm of all who had come along on Thursday evenings. Taff ... was very happy to say that Alf Ramsey would continue next season ... There was no better man in the country at this particular job ... Eton Manor were extremely lucky to have such a treasure. (*Chin-Wag* June 1953)

That 'treasure' was soon getting national media attention. As the *Daily Herald* noted under the headline 'RISE OF ETON MANOR DUE TO ALF RAMSEY'S COACHING':

> Eton Manor ... command almost as big local support as some senior league sides, and this despite being hemmed ... by professional, Isthmian and Athenian League teams. Their remarkable rise over the last two years has been largely due to the regular coaching of Alf Ramsey ... he has never seen his pupils play, but their present commanding style shows how beneficial is this type of continuous training for our younger players. (5 September 1953)

The 1953/54 season opened erratically but the senior team showed 'greater confidence':

> Alf Ramsey's wise coaching becomes more noticeable each game they play, and his tactical talks on Thursday evenings are looked forward to as much by the players as the games on Saturdays. For the first few weeks ... the talks ... are about the first team, but any other player is quite welcome to come along and listen ... Very soon we shall have similar meetings for the remaining teams ... In having Alf Ramsey as our Coach and Adviser we have something which most other Amateur Clubs would give much to possess ... one of the greatest tacticians

and football brains in the game to-day. (*Chin-Wag* September 1953)

Success was a two-way street, resting not just on Alf's coaching insights, but on Eton Manor's long-standing culture of community and solidarity. These were qualities, perhaps even blueprints, which Alf replicated during later successes with Ipswich Town and England. For example, a headline in the 1954 article cited below celebrated players who 'WON'T LEAVE ETON MANOR'. One was my stepchildren's grandfather, Bill Turner, standing in this family photo eighth from the left on the back row. Alf Ramsey stands bashfully, also at the back, third from the left.

The charity's overall rules stipulated that joining Eton Manor Boys Club was only allowed between the ages of 14 and 16. Consequently, every player pictured above, in the other four senior sides and the seven boys' football teams, had first joined before reaching 16. They had also been playing for Eton Manor ever since, as England's leading 1950s football magazine noted:

> The reason for the continued success of Eton Manor, the London League champions, is the amazing loyalty of their players. No inducements can tempt the Eton Manor lads away from their own club ... And of course, the coaching of Alf

Ramsey is an invaluable asset. (*Charles Buchan's Football Monthly* February 1954)

What did teenagers gain from Eton Manor? Probationers were expected to sample numerous activities, including football but also cricket, rugby, swimming, athletics, squash, tennis, table tennis, rifle shooting, reading, drama, debating and many more. All were virtually free so long as members attended, participated, and paid a nominal few pence per month. As boys gained experience, they were then encouraged on to the largely self-governing management committees that ran everyday activities.[29] Many lived in cramped, damp homes, due either to inter-war poverty or World War Two bomb damage, so Eton Manor was an island of excellence and opportunity. Members were also supported as they matured, often in generous and unusual ways. Arthur Villiers, who lived on site from 1939 onwards,[30] personally and frequently intervened to find homes, jobs, or simply hand out cash to needy members and their families. The broader social benefits of membership were massive,[31] as were the footballing ones. Many players who Alf coached in the 1952/53 and 1953/54 London Premier League Championship-winning teams could have played professionally, or at higher amateur levels, but they stayed at Eton Manor. No wonder Eton Manor revelled in its own ethos of 'friendliness and comradeship … the one thing our better-known rivals in senior amateur football cannot buy or hope to have' (*Chin-Wag* May 1955). Whilst Eton Manor's idealistic values and culture can help explain Alf's later squad-building successes with Ipswich, then England, another and more pragmatic advantage accrued from this early coaching experience: Alf was forced to learn how to capitalise upon the restricted talent available. Eton Manor's policy of selecting for senior teams only members who had joined as boys aged 14–16 simplified things drastically. For Alf, it meant develop or die, because outsiders were ineligible.

The playing quality of the lesser players in Ipswich Town's Third Division South squad, when Alf started there in August 1955, probably resembled the best at Eton Manor. Lacking any significant transfer budget, Alf somehow managed to mould those players into a winning unit. Then, when managing England from 1963, having the 100 or so best English players to choose from created a different sort of problem: how to shape a squad, blending the team spirit and egalitarian solidarity of Hackney's Eton Manor, or Ipswich Town, with the sometimes-egotistical excellence of brilliant young professionals, from across the country, at the top of a ruthlessly competitive sport. What Alf learnt at

Eton Manor from 1952–55 might, therefore, be seen as the first steps in a management career that won England's 1966 World Cup. It is no coincidence that the 1966 squad's £22,000 winning bonus was not disproportionately allocated just to World Cup medal winners, as it might be today, but evenly shared at £1,000 each.[32] The players decided it, but Alf had created that culture. The day after their 1966 victory, England's trainer put everything down to Alf Ramsey's leadership and cultivation of 'team spirit ... togetherness' (*Nottingham Evening Post* 1 August 1966). Was that approach, mirrored also at Ipswich, first learned at Eton Manor?

> FOOTBALL OLD BOYS ... No one would be happier than our coach Alf Ramsey to see at least 50 of the 80 or more players signed on turn up for training on Tuesday and Thursday evenings ... A good class team relies upon a flow of first-class reserves to fill gaps ... even though a player may be in one of the lower teams, next season or the one after could give him the chance to play in the first team, if fit enough. Two good examples ... who just a few seasons ago were in the fifth team are now knocking on the door of the first. (*Chin-Wag* April 1954)

Given two successive league titles in 1952/53 and 1953/54, no wonder Eton Manor's football Annual General Meeting welcomed Alf's keenness to continue into 1954/55:

> The Chairman ... paid tribute to the splendid job of work done by Alf Ramsey and others ... He was glad to report Ramsey had agreed to continue with his coaching on Thursday evenings ... and emphasised that Alf Ramsey's talks were not confined to the first and second teams alone, all could learn a great deal at these meetings and training sessions. (*Chin-Wag* August 1954)

When that new season went awry, though, neither Alf nor anyone else at Eton Manor panicked:

> Alf Ramsey has never tried harder than he is doing now with the boys, and so are the players, but that is the way things go at times – the harder you try the worse the results. Perhaps it is possible to try too hard; it happens even in first class professional football. (*Chin-Wag* November 1954)

Writing in the same magazine, another stalwart, after watching Eton Manor lose 2-1 to Leyton in the Amateur Cup, highlighted that:

> The exasperating part was that our boys all-round were superior, in football science, displaying excellent ball control, but ... they played too slowly against the fast-moving Leyton side ... I am wondering if the boys get enough experience of top-class football. I was talking to Alf Ramsey ... he thinks it is all there but needs stronger opposition.

Amateur football was thriving, though, and the match was featured on 15 November 1954 by cartoonist Harold Gittins, in the now-disappeared London paper *The Evening News*:

In testimony to Eton Manor's culture, whilst being given a lift back to the station, the cartoonist explained that he had chosen to feature their game:

> Because the last cartoon of the Manor had given him a great deal of pleasure ... for months afterwards he was receiving letters of thanks from Club members all over the world. He was so impressed with the spirit, the thanks ... the pride in their Club. (*Chin-Wag* December 1954)

Eton Manor finished fourth in the London Amateur Premier League that season, and in 1955/56 won it for the third time in four years. Alf's coaching was central to such success, but he sometimes contributed more widely. January 1955's football club dinner and dance hosted nearly 200 guests, with Arthur Villiers and other Old Etonians on the top table. Who replied to the formal toast proposed? 'Alf Ramsey who provided a very pleasant little speech, which left no doubt that the guests were thoroughly at home and part and parcel of the Manor' (*Chin-Wag* February 1955). Meanwhile, on the pitch, Alf's career at Eton Manor closed with him helping to win one more trophy:

> ESSEX MINOR F.A. CUP FINAL PLAYED AT LEYTON ORIENT STADIUM – ETON MANOR 5, UPMINSTER 1
> Monday, May 2nd, 1955, 6.30 p.m. A few words by Alf Ramsey during the interval had a desired effect, and the football showed some improvement over the last 20 minutes of the first half. (*Chin-Wag* May 1955)

Despite having left Spurs for Ipswich Town in August 1955, at Eton Manor's January 1956 football club annual dinner and dance:

> It was hoped that Alf and Mrs. Ramsey would be able to come along, Alf had kept the date free, but with the Ipswich match with the Orient postponed, Alf would have to use the free day to move his home to Ipswich and hope to come along later. (*Chin-Wag* February 1956)

Alf may have moved on from living in Barking, playing at Spurs, and coaching Eton Manor part-time, retracing his family's Suffolk roots to manage Ipswich Town. But what Eton Manor lessons and legacy did he take with him?

How Eton Manor Enriched Alf

Alf Ramsey's rapid football transformation from playing until April 1955, to becoming Ipswich Town manager in August 1955, to achieving third place in May 1956, then to winning their league in May 1957, has always appeared miraculous. Alf's previously hidden Eton Manor coaching experience helps explain not just that immediate success but probably contributed to greater ones that followed. Three seasons of coaching Eton Manor's strong adult amateur teams, and helping with younger teams and players, were especially useful and informative to Alf because his own route to professionalism had been so different from his peers.

Eton Manor also mattered because few other managerial progression paths lay open to Alf. His Spurs rival for a coaching job, Bill Nicholson, had telling advantages. He had been a professional at Spurs before war broke out, was an army physical training instructor until 1945, passed an FA coaching course post-war, and then became Cambridge University's part-time football instructor. No wonder that, in 1955, Spurs chose Nicholson as coach rather than the slightly odd, isolated and relatively inexperienced Alf Ramsey (*The Guardian* 25 October 2004, 'Bill Nicholson Obituary'). What is less clear is why Alf, unlike Nicholson, Greenwood, or others, did not take an FA coaching course, particularly as his close friend, Arthur Rowe, chaired the London Football Coaches Association.[33]

Might leaving school at 14, never having formally studied since, and being aged nearly 27 before making a full professional league debut, have dented Alf's confidence about studying and being assessed? In 1953, the FA coaching examination pass rate in England averaged a mere 42 per cent.[34] Or perhaps Alf perceived that earning extra money at Eton Manor, close to home, gaining experience and doing social good, outweighed the advantages of an FA badge. Additionally, during 1953/54, Alf could plausibly have thought that any available spare time to enhance his career might be more usefully put into mastering Freemasonry 'workings',[35] than studying for an FA certificate?

Looking more widely, Eton Manor had also pulled off a beguilingly powerful social trick. In deprived, working-class Hackney Wick, it seemed successfully to have synthesised aristocratic, establishment English sporting attitudes, such as aspiring to excellence through amateurism, 'fair play', and patriotism, with parallel but independent working-class traditions. Those included cultivating sporting excellence to escape from poverty, gaining social respect and status through 'playing hard but fair', and loving England not necessarily for what it was, but for what it could be: something closer to the satanic, gritty mills of Blake's Jerusalem, than to Eton's privileged green playing fields.[36]

Marxist cynics might claim this synthesis was more imagined than real, relying on Eton Manor selecting suggestible working-class boys aged 14 to 16, then brainwashing and bribing them through lavish charity that nevertheless maintained the status quo. Romantic liberals might counter with the testimony of multiple individual Eton Manor members then, and since, including one of the author's own family, that Eton Manor was the best thing that ever happened to them. But since historical understanding is not a zero-sum game, both may be true. Indisputably, many working-class Eton Manor members adored the heady, idiosyncratic mix of egalitarian people power, with privileged excellence, that their membership seemed to convey. Not unlike, perhaps, the international English footballers with whom Alf Ramsey managed to win a World Cup?

Alf eulogised his World Cup-winning *team* for their achievements, rather than highlighting *individual* contributions.[37] From the high-profile 1966 example of Jimmy Greaves onwards,[38] he was also increasingly criticised for omitting or undervaluing so-called 'flair' players, and stubbornly prioritising communal team and squad values.[39] That blend of egalitarianism and excellence had been a feature of Eton Manor. The club's honorary secretary throughout Alf's time, Ernie Osgood, claimed in a 1954 newspaper interview that 'all our five teams play as a unit. There are no individualists ... I couldn't even tell you who scores the goals! We play to win ... that's all!' (*Daily Herald* 12 November).

Alf's famed, stubborn single-mindedness, and disregard for popularity, may also have been influenced by Eton Manor. Encountering powerful individualists like Arthur Villiers, a constant presence on site throughout the 1950s, possibly gave Alf confidence about doing things differently. Villiers, although a director at the internationally prestigious Barings Bank and friend of innumerable aristocrats, politicians and millionaires, was highly eccentric. He drove around the large Eton Manor site, and sometimes Hackney and inner London, in a battery-powered 'car' that resembled a milk float. His teeth were all covered in gold, and he could often be glimpsed in a tatty, long fur coat, entertaining society leaders to dinners in his garage. Typical ingredients were tinned tomato soup and ham, prepared by a butler from Barings. Well-connected guests would sit alongside Eton Manor youngsters and chat about their lives: Lord Longford, nephew of Villiers, was a frequent volunteer and visitor during Alf's time there.[40]

Previous pages have demonstrated how Alf Ramsey met Arthur Villiers, and other Old Etonian patrons, at Eton Manor dances, dinners, meetings and sporting events. After such experiences, the aristocratic eccentricity Alf would encounter at Ipswich from 1955, especially from bachelor Old Etonian brothers and directors John and Patrick Cobbold, would come as no surprise. Conceivably, Alf's cussed later refusal as England manager to conform to what FA committee members or journalists expected, also partly reflected his 1952–63 experience of mixing with and being managed by eccentric Old Etonians. These were individuals so advantaged, wealthy, aristocratic and educated, and sometimes so arrogant, that they felt no need to cede to the expectations of others: rather like, in that latter respect, Alf himself.

The intriguing twists and turns of the next chapter will explore whether Alf's apparent ease with personal social eccentricity might also have extended to the homosexuality, as cited earlier, of Eton Manor founder Gerald Wellesley. Alf would have known that name because Wellesley visited Eton Manor summer camps and reunions in 1952, 1953 and 1955, twice with his wife (*Chin-Wag* July 1952, July 1953, July 1955). Wellesley featured regularly in club newsletters and in 1955 received from ordinary members:

> Bags and bags of birthday cards on his 70th, and jolly good luck to him and all those who sent them. It shows that, although he is … miles out in the country, the East End of London still, and always will, remember him. (*Chin-Wag* September 1955)

Did any ordinary Eton Manor members know how, in 1940s army staff circles, Wellesley's homosexuality had earned him the nickname the 'Iron Duchess'?[41] In 1927, Old Etonian Geoffrey Gilbey, Wellesley's close friend and with whom he co-led numerous 1920s/30s Eton Manor summer camps and concerts, started a homosexual affair with the 16-year-old Harrow schoolboy and later openly gay playwright, Terence Rattigan.[42] Just like Wellesley, Gilbey was married and featured regularly in 1950s Eton Manor reunions and newsletters (e.g. *Chin-Wag* September, November 1953, November 1954).

No evidence of homosexual wrongdoing has yet come to light at Eton Manor, and Wellesley's and Gilbey's bisexuality is mentioned here only because it relates to Alf's story in two respects, pursued in the next chapter. Firstly, at Ipswich from 1955, Alf would be led and line-managed by another bachelor, and reputedly gay Old Etonian, called John Cobbold. Secondly, and seemingly with Cobbold's help, Alf would, in his opening managerial months, rehabilitate an Ipswich Town professional footballer back into the squad, and on to stardom, after he had pleaded guilty to then-illegal homosexual 'indecent behaviour' with another man.

Did the leadership and values Alf witnessed at Eton Manor shape his own? Almost certainly, and the Etonian accents heard there may subliminally also have influenced how Alf spoke; yet his management was already evolving its own quiet style. My stepchildren's grandfather, Bill Turner, was not just a lifelong Eton Manor boy but Alf's 26-year-old right-back in their 1953/54 league-winning team pictured earlier. Bill was regularly coached by Alf, and it was he who first alerted me to Eton Manor as a neglected historical episode. Shortly before he died, Bill described Alf's distinctive approach:

> He was so ... [*searches for the right words*] if you never met him and didn't know him, you wouldn't have realised he had this spark of genius ... an older man who had made a tremendous success of his life, of his football, and was passing what good advice he could on to his pupils ... such a self-effacing man you wouldn't have known he had the fame that he did have.[43]

1 BBC Culture website (14 April 2021) 'The School That Rules Britain' John Self

2 Crossley, A. (2007) p.14

3 *Freemasonry Today* 11, Summer 2010 p.28

4 **Museum of Freemasonry** *1899-1999 Centenary Souvenir Province of Essex Waltham Abbey Lodge* Cross, J., Fowler, S. and Britton, V. (1999) 2750 p.24

5 United Grand Lodge of England website (2025) 'What Is Freemasonry?'

6 **Museum of Freemasonry** *1899-1999 Centenary Souvenir Province of Essex Waltham Abbey Lodge* Cross, J., Fowler, S. and Britton, V. (1999) 2750 pp.24-5

7 *Freemasonry Today* 11, Summer 2010 p.28

8 Hamill, J. and Prescott, A. (2006) pp.9-41

9 Dickie, J. (2020)

10 Kenney, J. (2016) p.6

11 Preston, P. (2011) pp.461-472

12 Dickie, J. (2020) pp.377-78

13 Hamill and Prescott (2006) p.30

14 See *West London Observer* 1 April 1955, *Uxbridge Gazette* 20 January 1956, *Middlesex County Times* 5 January 1957

15 *Freemasonry Today* 11, Summer 2010 pp.28-29

16 Dickie, J. (2020) pp.379-82

17 Margaret Fulljames oral history interview 20 January 2023

18 Dickie, J. (2020) pp.27-31

19 Bedell, G. (2007) 'To The Manor Born' *The Observer* 29 July; Johansen, M. (2007) Lecture 'Up The Manor' project launch September 2007 Villiers Park Cambridge

20 Eton College website (2025) 'Collections - Ventures in giving: the Eton Mission and Manor Boys' Club'

21 Alldritt, K. (1997) p.337 and Bloch, M. (2015) pp.131, 166

22 Foster, R.F. (2003) p.528

23 **Up The Manor Oral History Project** transcript Ken Beamish

24 Bowler, D. (1999) p.107

25 McKinstry, L. (2007) p.133

26 **Up The Manor Oral History Project** Johansen, M. (2007) Lecture 'Up The Manor' project launch September 2007 Villiers Park Cambridge

27 **Up The Manor Oral History Project** transcript Charlie Phillips

28 **Up The Manor Oral History Project** Transcripts George Gatward, Kenny Elgar

29 **Up The Manor Oral History Project** Transcript Alan Sims

30 Shaw-Kennedy, R. (1969)

31 Bedell, G. (2007) 'To The Manor Born' *The Observer* 29 July; **Up The Manor Oral History Project** transcripts, e.g. Colin Draper, Derek

Edwards, Doug Bristow, George Gatward, Henry Lee, Jeff Lee, Kenny Elgar, Terry Bell

32 McKinstry, L. (2007) pp.372-3

33 Morse, G. (2016) pp.138-9

34 Ibid. p.133

35 Dickie, J. (2020) p.23

36 Duke-Evans, J. (2023)

37 **BBC Radio 5 Live 'Replay'** (released 31 December 2018) '1966 – England win the World Cup Final'

38 Glanville, B. (2008) pp.45-46

39 McKinstry, L. (2007) pp.438-50

40 Shaw-Kennedy, R. (1969); Johansen, M. (2013) Blog 'Adventures in the Wild East: the Story of the Eton Manor Boys' Club'

41 Heffer, S. (2022) p.1398

42 Darlow, M. (2000) chapter 2; Wansell, G. (2009) pp.36-38

43 Oral history interview with Bill Turner 18 June 2018

Part Three

LEADING THE WAY: LIBERAL, MODERNISER, UNDERDOG

CHAPTER 9

A PATH PAVED WITH DIFFERENCE

Ramsey's Rainbow Career Ride

Pushed Out of Spurs

ALTHOUGH 1955 would catapult Alf from playing to job-seeking, to leaving London, season 1954/55 started well. Spurs opened with two victories and Alf was made captain.[1] In January 1955 he and manager Arthur Rowe enjoyed a glamorous 'Variety Club' lunch with film legend Ava Gardner, 'the only star in the world' (*Kinematograph Weekly* 13 January). Alf personally had just featured in a 1954 children's Christmas football annual, advising on the pressures of penalty-taking. 'Turn a deaf ear on colleagues and opponents' and 'ignore all the chatter', Alf advised. Soon 'you will be able to detach yourself sufficiently to be unaffected'.[2]

That proved untrue for Alf and tragically so for his manager. Results worsened, boardroom troubles broke out and their careers imploded. Spurs finished 16th in Division One, after a season in which Alf was repeatedly 'left badly beaten for speed' (*Sunday People* 26 December 1954). On 19 February 1955, in a humiliating FA Cup shock, Spurs were beaten 3-1 by Third Division York City. Alf was 'sometimes not in the same county' as York's victory-clinching left-winger (*The Times* 21 February 1955) but he visited the City dressing room anyway, graciously admitting 'you really showed us how to play' (*Daily Herald* 21 February). The result shattered Rowe, who was hospitalised for months with a severe nervous breakdown.[3] His replacement was assistant manager Jimmy Anderson, but Anderson and Alf 'barely tolerated one another'.[4] Alf was dropped (*Lancashire Post* 30 April 1955) and then shabbily omitted from Tottenham's tour of Hungary.[5] If Rowe had stayed healthy, Ramsey might have coached at Spurs,[6] yet regime change, and witnessing his friend's mental health disintegrate 'from the strain of running' a big club like Tottenham (*The People* 24 April 1955) pushed Alf to think differently.

That started with a two-month summer coaching trip to southern Africa, facilitated by Stanley Matthews. Matthews, although markedly less beautiful than Ava Gardner, was similarly a global celebrity.[7] A lucrative South African football tour, centred on him, had been discussed for months (*Bradford Observer* 4 February, *Coventry Evening Telegraph* 19 March), assisted by Matthews's Blackpool team-mate and 1953 FA Cup Final-winning goal-scorer, Bill Perry. Perry had emigrated from Johannesburg in 1949, and some modern fans perceive him as bi-racial.[8]

Whatever the truth of that is, once in southern Africa the presence of Perry, Matthews and Ramsey encouraged 15,000 paying spectators to watch Southern Rhodesia beat Portuguese East Africa 4-2 (*Daily Mirror* 26 May 1955, *Nottingham Journal* 6 June 1955). This 1955 tour also changed Matthews's life, both through earning significant cash and becoming a 'football missionary'.[9] Every summer thereafter for 25 years was spent 'coaching in Africa ... I did all my 1955 pre-season training in the township of Soweto where I was coaching black youngsters'.[10] It is unclear whether Alf helped Matthews with that summer Soweto coaching, but returning to England on 29 July Alf was 'tanned and looking as fit as ever'. Under the prophetic newspaper headline 'ALF RAMSEY WILL BE IPSWICH BOSS', he admitted that 'being left out of the Spurs' tour of Hungary ... was the greatest disappointment of my career' (*Daily Herald* 4 August 1955). Alf's comment was a bitter, coded criticism of how Spurs had treated him and Rowe. That bruising episode, and Stanley Matthews's southern Africa invitation, had pivoted Alf at a career-critical moment.

Pulled towards Ipswich

Strong forces then pulled Alf towards Ipswich. His solitary, obsessive, controlling character traits pre-disposed him to football management. Bob Ferrier, possibly Alf's 1952 autobiographical ghostwriter, interviewed him in 1951, hearing 'he wants to stay in the game when he is too old to play ... for my money here is the perfect managerial material' (*Daily Mirror* 1 February).

Alf's management destination would be Ipswich, Suffolk's county town, an hour's train ride from London and close to grandfather Ramsey's rural roots. Ipswich Town had clinched their first league promotion to League Division Two in 1954, followed instantly by relegation back to Division Three South. Having been managed by Scott Duncan since 1937, fresh thinking was needed. Board meeting minutes now reveal how, on 19 May 1955, Ipswich's directors heard 'there was a possibility of securing the services of Mr. A. Ramsey'. They formally requested the permission of Spurs and authorised their chairperson 'to make a first approach to Ramsey, with a view to having an interview when he returned from South Africa'.[11]

Ipswich's boardroom boasted characters similar to Eton Manor, where Alf had thrived: Old Etonians whose wealth and privilege brought ambition but enabled longer-term perspectives on achieving it. Ipswich's culture was consequently less ruthless than other 1950s football boardrooms. The same newspaper report describing Rowe's nervous breakdown had lamented the 18-strong and rising 'casualty list of managers' sacked that season (*The People* 24 April 1955). Ipswich Town may also have contacted Eton Manor about Alf, using Old Etonian networks. Its chairperson from 1947–57 was Alistair Cobbold. His cousin, and chairperson from 1957–76, was 'Mr John' Cobbold. Both were Eton educated, as was senior director Sir Charles Bunbury (born 1886), a schoolmate of Eton Manor founders Wellesley (born 1885) and Villiers (born 1883). Remarkably, from Ipswich Town's 1878 founding until 1991, 'the top man was either a Cobbold or someone married to a Cobbold',[12] most of whom were schooled at Eton and sometimes Harrow.

'Captain Ivan' Cobbold was chair of the Ipswich Town board from 1935–44. In 1936, after nearly six decades slumbering in amateur, gentrified leagues, he suddenly turned Ipswich Town professional. Two years later, Ipswich secured Football League entry and 'Captain Ivan' was lauded by this celebrity cartoon (right) in a now-disappeared newspaper (*Weekly Dispatch* 15 May 1938).

Understanding this Cobbold family contextualises the club Alf joined in 1955 and helps explain his subsequent success. The Cobbolds had been politically and commercially influential in Suffolk throughout the 19th century, but in 1919 'Captain Ivan' joined England's aristocratic Premier League, by marrying a daughter of the Duke of Devonshire. 'Captain Ivan' then competently managed the family's vast brewing and landed wealth alongside hunting, shooting, fishing and social climbing, preferably whilst being photographed. He featured below, in another now-defunct magazine, salmon fishing with the future Conservative prime minister Neville Chamberlain (*Illustrated Sporting and Dramatic News* 16 February 1929):

THE MINISTER OF HEALTH ON THE BANKS OF THE BLACKWATER: (ABOVE) MR. NEVILLE CHAMBERLAIN TAKING A SALMON, AND (RIGHT) CAPTAIN COBBOLD IN THE WATER WITH THE GAFF.

WITH A 20-LB. CATCH: MR. NEVILLE CHAMBERLAIN, HIS GILLIE AND HIS SALMON.

LANDING A SALMON ON THE BLACKWATER: MR. NEVILLE CHAMBERLAIN, WITH ROD, AND CAPTAIN COBBOLD, WITH GAFF, FISHING NEAR CARBYSVILLE, FERMOY, IN COUNTY CORK.

'Captain Ivan' was also a patriot. Wounded in World War One, he rejoined his regiment in World War Two before being killed, alongside one hundred others, when a German rocket demolished the packed Guards Chapel in London on Sunday, 18 June 1944. He had been helping plan the D-Day landings.[13]

His fellow Ipswich Town directors were mostly similar upper-class, elitist Conservatives, whose hierarchical politics were sometimes softened by personal generosity and sincere beliefs in community. Like Eton Manor's Arthur Villiers, with whom Alf had worked from 1952–55, their significant personal wealth also fostered individualism and eccentricity. As an example, Ipswich Town's decision to cease playing football, barely two weeks into World War Two, 'set Ipswich apart from every other Football League club in the country'.[14] When consequently the club later slipped into financial deficit, 'Captain Ivan' simply wrote well-publicised cheques[15] (*Edinburgh Evening News* 23 January 1943, *The People* 25 June 1944). The rainbow career ride that Alf Ramsey had just begun rested, partially, on crocks of Cobbold gold.

'Mr John' Cobbold: Alf's Unusual Key Ally

Everything about 'Mr John' Cobbold, Alf's keen ally from the start, and soon the board's overall boss, needs viewing in the shadow of

'Captain Ivan', the intimidating but 'adored' father to whom 'Mr John' was 'absolutely devoted'. Constrained by social and class expectations, the 16-year-old 'Mr John' did not 'burst into tears nor break down', at news of his father's death because 'one suddenly has an awful lot of responsibility'.[16] Four years later 'Mr John' hosted 1,400 guests at his own 21st birthday party (*Diss Express* 13 August 1948) and became the Football League's youngest director (*Aberdeen Press* 2 November). This privileged but vulnerable young man was simultaneously learning to manage multiple businesses, extensive landed estates, a fledgling political career, personal grief and his uncertain sexuality: a crushing mix that perhaps nudged him into the spectacular alcohol abuse that came to characterise his life.[17]

Just like Alf, by the spring of 1955 'Mr John' Cobbold's career had also struck a wall. Adopted aged 24 as Ipswich's Conservative parliamentary candidate (*Scunthorpe Evening Telegraph* 19 June 1952), in the 26 May 1955 general election, he lost to Labour by 3,582 votes (*The Times* 27 May). Given hundreds of local Cobbold-branded pubs and ales, his family's status as leading employers, landowners, and charitable benefactors, and his uncle being, from 1957, Conservative Prime Minister Harold Macmillan, 'Mr John's' electoral failures were embarrassing. He lost Ipswich's 1957 by-election, and the 1959 general election, before giving up then candidly admitting 'I would certainly have done my best for my constituents but … in no way was I anywhere close to being properly qualified for the job.'[18]

Those things matter because 'Mr John's' career struggles almost certainly influenced Alf's 1955 Ipswich appointment. In national newspapers at the time,[19] and throughout his 1952 autobiography, Alf had projected progressive football attitudes. Recruiting such a high-profile moderniser might help 'Mr John' Cobbold win a seat as Ipswich's MP, especially if Ipswich Town thrived. That theory helps explain why, within 24 hours of his 1955 election failure, Ipswich Town had not only courted Alf Ramsey but promised him, via a national newspaper, sole control of coaching and team selection, light administrative duties, and no expectation of being a player-manager (*Daily Mirror* 27, 28 May 1955).

Privately, Ipswich had probably contacted Alf in early May, against FA regulations.[20] By early August they were promising his salary would double to £1,500 plus a £150 car allowance and an attractive rented house.[21] Yet it was not only the 'Cobbold family' who clinched Alf as manager. Playing a pivotal part in the backstory[22] was another, mostly unacknowledged, Ipswich Town director from an entirely different background.

Nat Shaw: Jewish Migrant, Imaginative Entrepreneur

Like Alf, Nat Shaw had refashioned his identity. The 1911 Mile End census listed Nathan Schnur as an apprentice tailor, and his nationality simply as 'Jew'. He was born Naftaili Sznur in 1895, in what is now Poland, then his parents emigrated to London's East End. By 1926, Naftaili had legally changed nationality to British, and by 1929 had formally changed his name to Nathaniel Shaw.[23] In the ethnically loaded and stratified atmosphere of 1920s England, Naftaili just wanted to blend in, motives parallel to Alf's lifetime spent ignoring that nickname of 'D****e'. Family stories of Nat arriving at Ipswich station, in the early 1920s, similarly paralleled Alf's journey there:

> My father was a very unusual Jewish man, and I am not sure where he got all his ambitions from. Brought up in the East End to a very poor family, he and my mother decided to open a dress shop in East Anglia ... the train stopped at Ipswich and he saw they did not have a dress shop so they opened one there.

Nat's siblings then set up similar enterprises in Peterborough, Wisbech, Boston and Suffolk's Bury St Edmunds, of which a niece recalled, 'I hated it there at first and experienced my first taste of antisemitism.'[24] But Nat was drawn also to sport, especially greyhounds. In 1929, he owned two, in 1930 twenty-five,[25] and by 1932 he was competing in national hare-coursing tournaments against rich industrialists and aristocrats (*Yorkshire Post* 20 October). Then, in the autumn of 1935, Nat opened the 'Suffolk Stadium' (*Bury Free Press* 7 September), a 15-minute walk from where Ipswich Town's then-amateurs played football at Portman Road. Shaw's stadium had been built for greyhound racing, yet its mere existence changed the town's football forever. Since 1919, local newspapers had carried repeated but unsuccessful petitions and letters lobbying Ipswich Town to turn professional.[26] Nat's town-centre stadium now transformed the power balance. On 9 April 1936, 1,500 people crammed into Ipswich Town Hall to declare support for a newly proposed professional club called 'Ipswich United', to play at Nat's Suffolk Stadium,[27] where Southern League membership, they believed, would draw 'large crowds' (*Bury Free Press* 4 April 1936).

Until now, Ipswich Town had tenaciously maintained 'one of the last strongholds of ... gentlemanly amateurism ... beyond the London area'.[28] Yet even the slightly fantastical notion of a rival professional Southern League team, playing in a greyhound stadium, heralded the surrender of the amateurs. On returning from a family visit to Canada, 'Captain

Ivan' Cobbold, recently appointed Ipswich Town president, switched sides and publicly pledged 'utmost support' for Ipswich Town to turn professional, but stay playing at Portman Road. Ipswich's 19th-century amateur football tradition, ludicrously over-extended for six decades thanks mostly to the Cobbolds, had crumbled before a modernity[29] leveraged by a Polish-born, Jewish, working-class entrepreneur and migrant. Shaw was immediately appointed to a new board of Ipswich Town directors.[30]

'Captain Ivan' Cobbold later, misleadingly, attributed professionalism mainly to his aristocratic friend and Arsenal chairperson, Sir Samuel Hill-Wood,[31] but Nat Shaw had links even to him. Nat's 1933 national champion hare-coursing greyhound, mentioned below, shared the same Suffolk trainer as Hill-Woods's 1910 and 1913 winners (*Bury Free Press* 18 February 1933). Nineteen years after helping push Ipswich Town into professionalism, Nat then performed a second act central to Alf Ramsey's career, and so to England's 1966 World Cup win. 'Mr John' Cobbold recalled that it was Nat Shaw's suggestion, when Ipswich were searching for a new manager in the spring of 1955, to approach Tottenham:

> He had heard one of their players was going to hang up his boots. Nat owned the Ipswich greyhound stadium … the Ramsey family had connections with the sport … that made him aware of the player's situation.[32]

Nat's suggestion was easily acted on because Alf Ramsey's connections with greyhound racing ran deep. A 1952 newspaper reported Alf ran 'several dogs at Romford' and that his 'Burning Desert, won five out of seven races during July' (*Scunthorpe Evening Telegraph* 27 September). A neighbour recalled the 'family were … always about walking the dogs' (*Barking and Dagenham Post* 29 July 2016). Indeed, Alf, his brother Albert, Alf's mother, father and sister Jean, between 1947 and 1956, had registered more than 30 different greyhounds at the Ramsey's tiny Becontree Heath cottage. Those dogs competed over 30 times at Romford, Dagenham, Southend, Clapton and New Cross.[33] As a Tottenham team-mate testified, Alf 'was worth listening to about greyhounds' and 'knew the form of all the dogs'.[34]

Like any other greyhound owner or fan,[35] Alf would have recognised Nat Shaw's greyhound racing fame long before considering Ipswich Town as a career move. Shaw was a 'sportsman of national repute' in his own right (*Boston Guardian* 18 February 1948), owning dogs that in 1933 and 1948 won the UK's elite hare-coursing trophy the Waterloo Cup. Since

1836, all racing greyhounds have been descended from Waterloo Cup winners.[36] Both Shaw's Waterloo Cup wins were nationally reported,[37] sometimes mentioning his Ipswich Town directorship.[38] 'Mr John' Cobbold claimed Shaw had heard accidentally, via greyhound racing, that Alf might become available in May 1955. Perhaps more likely is that Shaw, an innovative sporting entrepreneur, was asked to target him using professional networks, then initiate the discreet discussions that culminated, three months later, in Alf's Ipswich contract (*Ipswich Evening Star* 10 August).

Ted Phillips: The Making of an Extraordinary Difference

Alf Ramsey's managerial debut season took Ipswich Town to third in Division Three South, followed by becoming champions in 1956/57. Although several factors nudged his good first season into an excellent second, the person around whom the rest of this chapter revolves is not Alf himself, but someone for whom Alf changed everything, and vice versa: a Suffolk-born, hulking centre-forward called Edward ('Ted') Phillips. In 1956/57, aged just 23 and with barely any senior football experience, Phillips scored 41 of Town's 101 league goals. During a championship decided by goal average, that contribution was clinching. Later, in Ipswich's 1960/61 Division Two triumph, he scored 30 league goals. Then, in 1961/62, he helped win the Division One championship, with 28 more. Phillips's brace against Manchester United helped seal his reputation as the 'hardest shot in soccer' (*Daily Mirror* 24 November 1961), similar to the goal he scored in this win against Tottenham a few weeks before:

Over six seasons Ted Phillips became pivotal to Alf winning three successively higher titles, culminating in the ultimate league prize. Yet on 8 August 1955, the same day Alf was formally being job-interviewed, a previously unseen minute from Ipswich Town's board meeting reveals an extraordinary secret story. Phillips's career, two weeks before his 22nd birthday, looked to be over. If he pleaded guilty or was 'convicted in a charge of Gross Indecency at the magistrates court', he would 'be given … 14 days' notice terminating his agreements without prejudice to the Club's rights for a transfer fee'.[39]

Whilst Alf Ramsey was sat before Ipswich Town's board, nervously making his case to be their new manager, Ted Phillips stood before a magistrate in Saxmundham, a small rural town 20 miles north-east of Ipswich. That magistrate decided Phillips and Donald Bloss, a 30-year-old sheet metal worker probably had, between 1 December 1954 and 30 March 1955, 'committed an act of gross indecency with each other'.[40] He therefore sent them, and two others, for trial at Ipswich Crown Court. Twelve years before private, consenting, adult homosexual activity was legalised; 35 years before Justin Fashanu came out as England's first gay, male, professional footballer, with ultimately tragic consequences;[41] and a shocking six decades before a second dared follow (*The Guardian* 17 May 2022), the young Ted Phillips's homosexual contacts with another man were set to be tried in open court. Phillips had played just 16 league games for Ipswich Town and, so far, Alf had managed none.

At that point neither Alf Ramsey, Ted Phillips, nor anybody else could have predicted how their stories would become inextricably linked, to English football's glorious benefit. A convincing case can be made that without Alf as manager, England would not have won the World Cup. Equally, without Phillips's goals, Alf would never have become England manager. Did Ted Phillips, prosecuted for homosexual behaviour in 1955, provide a crucial assist to England winning the World Cup in 1966? That plotline played out like this. On 5 September 1955, Ipswich Town's directors 'welcomed Mr. Alf Ramsey to his first meeting as Manager', hoping he would stay 'for many years'. Meanwhile, the same handwriting recorded young Phillips's prospects were nosediving. He had 'asked to be released from his agreement with the Club', which Ipswich agreed 'without prejudice to the Club's rights for a transfer fee'.[42] The imminent court appearance, at which he would admit illegal homosexual activity, had crashed his career; yet professionally and contractually, Phillips remained Ipswich Town's property until sold or allowed to return and play.

Fortunately, the inexperienced Alf had an administrative veteran to lean on during this challenging episode. In 1937, Southern League Ipswich Town had poached secretary-manager Scott Duncan from Manchester United. The next year, Duncan successfully guided Ipswich to Football League election and had managed them ever since. During Ipswich Town's 1955 new manager recruitment process, 66-year-old Duncan agreed to continue 'company secretary' duties,[43] whilst ceding to 35-year-old Alf all team management and coaching.

Alf must have been delighted. Ted Phillips's case had, in the openly homophobic 1950s, the potential to make lurid headlines. Major newspapers regularly featured stories of men involved in 'gross indecency', apparently just because they had newsworthy occupations: vicars (*Daily Herald* 26 January 1955), a retired army colonel (*Daily Mirror* 25 September 1954), RAF orderlies, an aristocrat and a journalist (*Daily Express* 25 March 1954), and police and army officers (*Manchester Evening News* 16 November 1953, *Daily News* 21 March 1953). As a professional footballer, in 1955 Ted Phillips could have expected similar. Even in 2022, six decades after homosexuality first started to become decriminalised, a similarly young, male, third-tier English professional footballer, became famed for declaring himself gay.[44]

For straight readers living in modern Britain, it is easy to underestimate the challenge that Alf Ramsey, Ted Phillips and Ipswich Town faced in 1955. Homosexual acts only began to be legalised in England in 1967, and even then partially and timidly.[45] In the early 1950s, they were relentlessly prosecuted: 'Court cases involving sodomy, gross indecency and indecent assault had risen from 719 in 1938 in England and Wales to 2,504 in 1955.[46] Early 1950s England was peppered with thousands of prosecutions, demonstrating an 'extraordinary degree of hostility ... against homosexual activity' by local police, magistrates and judges.[47] The sensational 1951 defection to the USSR of the gay spies Guy Burgess and Donald Maclean, had reinforced, for those susceptible, 'enduring notions of queer treachery',[48] and, at headline levels, the 'paranoid and edgy ... atmosphere of the era' illogically associated communism with homosexuality.[49] Interestingly, if coincidentally, the Ipswich newspaper's report of Phillips's court case (*Ipswich Evening Star* 24 September 1955) appeared on the facing page of an advertisement for new television programmes about 'Burgess and Maclean', despite the story having broken four years before.

Prosecutions of homosexuality in East Suffolk, to where Alf Ramsey had just moved and where Ted Phillips was prosecuted, mirrored other localities in provincial England. In 1954–55, nine different Crown

Court trials were held in Ipswich, prosecuting 18 different men aged over 16, including four in the case during which Ted Phillips pleaded guilty. Ages varied widely, from teenagers of 17 to older men in their late 50s, but all were convicted and persecuted for sexual behaviours that today are legal and socially unremarkable. Equally, in four of these nine trials, four of the 18 people convicted had also committed sexual offences against boys under 16, for which three adults were sentenced to between nine and 12 months' imprisonment.[50] The 30-year-old Donald Bloss, with whom the 21-year-old Ted Phillips had admitted committing 'an act of gross indecency', had also indecently assaulted a 15-year-old boy on Christmas Day 1953, and privately admitted other attempted offences against victims aged 16 and 19. Although the offence Ted Phillips admitted to committing was as a consenting, adult 21-year-old, might he have been groomed from an earlier age? Since detailed evidence was not discussed in court, the answer may never be known.

Detailed discussion of evidence in homosexuality cases was rare because, to minimise publicity, most of those prosecuted pleaded guilty. In Ted Phillips's case, the single local newspaper story was relatively short, at 300 words, although still eye-catchingly headlined 'INDECENCY CASES: TOLD YOU ARE A MENACE'. Four adult men had pleaded guilty. Donald Bloss, the married and perceived ringleader, had a previous conviction for indecent assault and was jailed for nine months. 'You are a menace to young men,' the judge told him, based on what was heard in open court but presumably also on other assaults he had admitted to police, as mentioned earlier. Ted and the two other adults convicted alongside Bloss all pleaded guilty to 'gross indecency' and so received discharges, conditional on not reoffending. Writing of Ted Phillips, the newspaper reported he had previously 'been fined for assault occasioning bodily harm. At his own request his contract with a local football club had been terminated. He had been in the Army, which he left with a very good character.' The presiding judge also summarised leniently for Phillips, opining 'this is an isolated case … you have suffered a great deal because of this isolated act' (*Ipswich Evening Star* 24 September 1955).

That judge was Gerald Howard, who may have experienced discreet lobbying from two personal contacts who happened to be Ipswich Town directors. One was Sir Charles Bunbury, a regular judicial deputy for Judge Howard himself,[51] and who had attended the August and September Ipswich Town board meetings at which Phillips's impending case was discussed. The other was 'Mr John' Cobbold, Ipswich's aspirant Conservative MP, who Judge Howard would have known because

Howard was already the Conservative MP for Cambridgeshire (*The Times* 27 June 1973, Obituary).

Some influence on Judge Howard seems likely because Phillips's record was not spotless. Weeks after first signing for Ipswich Town, he had pleaded guilty to an 'assault occasioning actual bodily harm', on 19 February 1954 in Leiston town centre.[52] Phillips had inflicted what the magistrate labelled an 'unprovoked assault' on a 21-year-old man, late on a Saturday night (*Ipswich Evening Star* 17 March 1954). The four-month window within which Phillips admitted 'gross indecency' also undermined Judge Howard's own depiction of an 'isolated act'.[53] If 'isolated', why could a specific date not be cited?

Ted Phillips probably also knew some of his fellow accused before their August 1955 arrests. He told the court in September he was living with his parents in Nayland,[54] over 40 miles away from the other three Leiston-based offenders. Yet from 1951 until just before the court case, Phillips had been living and working in Leiston, and playing football for Leiston FC, from whom Ipswich Town signed him in late 1953.[55] His 1954 conviction for 'assault' had recorded him living at 23 Long Row, Leiston: less than 200 metres from the imprisoned ringleader in the 1955 homosexuality court case, under 800 metres from the second adult convicted for 'gross indecency', and within five miles of the third.[56]

Phillips's decision to move to his parents probably helped Alf Ramsey, Scott Duncan and 'Mr John' Cobbold to save his career. At Ipswich Town's board meeting of 31 October 1955, 'the manager and secretary reported that on being approached by the Chairman and manager of the Stowmarket FC', an 'agreement had been signed' to loan them Ted Phillips.[57] This arrangement with a club 15 miles from Ipswich, and near a main railway line, had probably been lined up when Stowmarket visited Bury Town for a game, before Phillips's Crown Court trial. Hidden alongside that game's match report lay a brief, mid-page paragraph:

> Mr. A. Ramsey, newly appointed Ipswich Town manager, accompanied by the Ipswich secretary, Mr. Scott Duncan, and Mr. John Cobbold, a director, visited Kings Road to see Tuesday evening's match. Mr. Ramsey told a *Free Press* reporter that it was just a routine visit. (*Bury Free Press* 9 September 1955).

Given Phillips's impending prosecution, and his first loan game at Stowmarket happening just six weeks later (*Bury Free Press* 14 October 1955), Alf's classic stonewalling line of 'just a routine visit' sounds less likely than this being a carefully devised strategy to handle a sensitive situation and keep Phillips fit. Ipswich's 3 October 1955 board meeting had agreed to circulate to 'various league clubs that we were prepared to consider offers ... and if necessary a month's trial'.

Exiled by Ipswich, Reprieved by Ramsey

By 1962, Ted Phillips's 99 goals, during Ipswich Town's three table-topping seasons of 1956/57, 1960/61 and 1961/62, would have helped Alf Ramsey to become England manager; but in season 1955/56, the now-isolated Ted was playing for his future in non-league football. Against Gorleston he 'worked hard' (*Bury Free Press* 21 October 1955), next week suffered an apparently 'serious injury' (*Bury Free Press* 28 October) but bounced back against Tottenham 'A' to 'flash the ball in from about 30 yards ... a great shot' (*Bury Free Press* 11 November). A fortnight later, playing a strong Norwich 'A' side with considerable league experience, Ted hit the post and 'was a thrustful leader' (*Bury Free Press* 25 November 1955). That long season continued in similar vein, scoring with a 'hard free kick' against 'West Ham A' on Easter Monday (*Bury Free Press* 6 April 1956), then injuring his ankle three weeks later (*Bury Free Press* 27 April).

Phillips kept in regular and anxious touch with Ipswich Town. On 5 December 1955, Scott Duncan reported a telephone conversation, during which Phillips confirmed staying at Stowmarket for the rest of the season. Answering one of several letters from Phillips asking about his future, a board discussion on 9 January 1956 concluded he should stay on the transfer list and 'any reasonable offer would be accepted'. Then, on 5 March 1956, Alf led the first sign of change. Alf Ramsey as manager, rather than previously Duncan as secretary, had recently met Stowmarket's chairperson, and 'a letter having been read from [Phillips] enquiring his position with the Club, consideration of inviting him to re-sign for next season was continued to next meeting'. Alf clearly wanted to re-instate Ted Phillips, proved by decisions at that next meeting on 9 April:

> Regarding Player Edward J. Phillips ... it was agreed after the manager had seen him play that he be offered an engagement for next season and in the meantime included in the transfer list to be logged with the Football League by 5th May at a fee of £3,000.

This paragraph is deeply significant, not just for Ted Phillips as a player, but for the unfolding story of Alf as a manager. Alf wanted Phillips 'engaged for next season' because he valued his ability. Probably, he also suggested a £3,000 transfer fee to deter potential buyers. Phillips had made just 16 league appearances and been prosecuted twice in two years, latterly for a socially isolating and, some believed, abhorrent offence. At that inflated price, with a problematic past and scant track record, no purchaser was likely.

Then, on 7 May 1956, Alf clearly and forcefully led his directors: 'Regarding player Edward Phillips on the Manager's suggestion it was agreed to offer him a Four Weeks' engagement ... and if he proved satisfactory to extend the period of his contract.' Despite the social stigma associated with Phillips's conviction for homosexual behaviour, Alf wanted to re-integrate him. Three months later, just as the new season started and only a year into his managerial career, on 14 August 1956 Alf's determination to secure Phillips's return was again underscored:

> The manager reported that he had signed Player Edward J. Phillips to the end of the season at £10 per week in the playing season and £9 in the close season plus £2 10s in the First Team and the usual Bonuses.

Yet this new season kicked off disastrously with Ipswich bottom after three games, all missed by Ted Phillips through injury.[58] After six games Ipswich were still 'disjointed and ineffective' (*Birmingham Daily Post* 7 September 1956), and at the 8 October 1956 board meeting, Alf bemoaned player injuries.[59] By the board's next meeting, though, on 5 November, Phillips had scored an incredible 15 goals in just 13 appearances. Consequently, Alf asked for his weekly wage (and one other player's) to be increased to match other squad members; but some directors could not agree so the issue was 'held over until the next meeting' on 3 December. By then Phillips had added two more goals, so Alf tried again to equalise his pay. Eight of the nine board members were present but, 'after much discussion and consideration on the question' of wages, the directors once more 'decided by a majority to leave them as they are for the present'.

Such disagreements were rare. This 'Minute Book' covered 11 years of board meetings, recorded on over 350 pages, during which most issues never needed a vote: the board was deeply divided. Alf tried again four weeks later, after Phillips had added another eight goals, this time swinging the doubters round. On 7 January 1957, 'after some discussion it was unanimously agreed' to pay every professional playing 'in the League team ... the same weekly wage of £14'. Alf's managerial judgement was then proved spectacularly correct. A few months later, 'goal average' won Ipswich promotion and the Third Division South championship. Phillips's 41 league goals had been decisive, and his transfer value rocketed. Wolverhampton Wanderers and Birmingham City enquired about buying him, but on 1 April 1957, a date tinged with irony given how foolish the Ted Phillips sceptics now looked, the board 'unanimously decided that he was not for transfer'.

Winning Through Diversity: Ramsey's Remarkable Stance

Prior to this book's publication, until Justin Fashanu in 1990, English football offered no examples of a high-profile male professional continuing to play after publicly admitting to homosexual behaviour or being convicted of it. For that reason alone, Ted Phillips's 1955 conviction, 1955/56 exile, then 1956/57 rehabilitation and league-winning goal tally are important. Their historical significance then increases exponentially because Alf was still being appointed when Phillips's case first surfaced, he had been in post just six weeks when it went to court, but within 12 months he had secured Phillips's return. In a virtuous circle, Phillips's brilliant footballing contributions then paved Alf's career path to winning *that* 1966 World Cup tournament, hosted in a country still 12 months away from legalising even private homosexual acts by consenting adults.

Given the intensity of social shame generally associated with 1950s homosexual criminal convictions, Alf's approach seems unusually brave, particularly in a male single-sex sporting context. Examples abound of numerous other mid-1950s men convicted of homosexual behaviour losing everything: careers, relationships, social standing and, tragically, sometimes taking their own lives.[60] The year 1955 was also a very difficult one in which to exercise open-mindedness, given that the annual incidence of newspaper reported homosexuality convictions had peaked in 1954.[61] Unsurprisingly, 94 per cent of those charged just admitted their guilt, like Phillips, because pleading 'not guilty' risked detailed evidence being discussed in open court, generating lurid headlines. Admitting guilt, on the other hand, meant a judge simply passed sentence then explained their decision, in comments often brief and sometimes unreported.[62]

Alf's leadership seems to have been key to Ted Phillips's career resurrection. Board meeting minutes conclusively show that, by April 1956 and possibly earlier, Alf wanted Phillips to return. Despite some board scepticism, by August 1956 he had secured that, followed shortly by an equalising of his wages. Alf then exercised such strong authority over Ipswich players, and directors, that Phillips became central to three title-winning teams. Whilst we cannot know whether liberalism, tolerance, ethics, or politics guided Alf's decision-making, a simple, undeniable fact, persists. He delivered, decades ahead of countless other managers, what human rights campaigners have always requested: equal opportunity, unclouded by prejudice, around characteristics irrelevant to a profession's performance. As 1966 hat-trick hero Geoff Hurst said, when I sketched him this story's outline, given attitudes at the time, Ted Phillips's resurrection was 'amazing … amazing'.[63]

Leadership support for Alf Ramsey, and personal empathy for Ted Phillips, was very probably provided by 'Mr John' Cobbold. In 1955, Cobbold was not publicly rumoured as gay, presenting then as an eccentric 28-year-old bachelor, but strong rumours of his homosexuality later emerged. McKinstry judged 'he was almost certainly a homosexual', citing the vastly experienced local reporter Tony Garnett's statement that 'there was no question he was a homosexual, but he used to go to America for his recreation'. Ted Phillips himself told McKinstry that 'all the players were aware that he was a bit the other way.'[64] Others who knew Cobbold well, like former Ipswich Town manager Bobby Robson, and press secretary Mel Henderson, confirmed he lacked interest in women but tactfully presented him as asexual.[65] A multiple award-winning sportswriter recently said simply, 'Cobbold was believed to be homosexual.'[66] The weight of such evidence makes it difficult to believe that 'Mr John' would not have viewed Ted Phillips's 1955 conviction, and rehabilitation, with anything other than kindness and empathy.

Another possible reason for Phillips's re-acceptance into the squad was that team-mates simply viewed him as a good person, a fine player, and cared little about a strange court case. That seems possible because, parallel with depressingly common 1950s persecution, other evidence survives suggesting tolerant English attitudes towards homosexuality and bisexuality. When actor John Gielgud returned to the London stage in 1953, after his conviction for homosexual importuning, he received a standing ovation and his career blossomed.[67] More pertinently for the case of Ted Phillips, historical evidence is growing of 1950s homosexuality having been known and accepted in working-class communities. Unremarkable, everyday gay activity in southern English places like London and Portsmouth regularly involved men from all three 'armed forces', and others with working-class backgrounds.[68] In northern industrial towns and cities, male, working-class gay or bisexual behaviour was also more common than previously thought.[69]

The other three men convicted with Phillips had manual occupations: a 'sheet metal worker', a 'farm labourer' and an 'apprentice fitter' (*Ipswich Evening Star* 24 September 1955).

Records show that the much-maligned 'ringleader' was married. The three other convicted men all married after the case, and Ted Phillips married twice. Some socially 'ordinary' 1950s people evidently knew more about homosexual behaviour, and were accepting of it, than modernity might assume. Contemporary ideas about homosexuality also tend towards deeper, sometimes radically divergent 'queer' social and psychological identities.[70] A young person in the 1950s, experimenting with their sexuality, might have thought differently. Phillips may also privately have offered team-mates a wide range of explanations. Although in 2008 he publicly attributed his season-long loan at Stowmarket to picking up 'a knee injury in pre-season training',[71] when fellow players asked about his conviction at the time he could have blamed: a dreadful error, a drunken one-off, mistaken identity, police conspiracy, or a total miscarriage of justice. It also seems plausible that at a younger age Phillips was illegally groomed by Bloss, or others, and if questioned or challenged, he told people that difficult truth. Possibly significant to his rehabilitation was that Phillips had also recently spent nine months frontline soldiering in Malaya, as part of two years of national service (e.g. *Bury Free Press* 2 May 1952, 6 February 1953). In an often-brutal campaign, nationally reported in jingoistic language, the Suffolk Regiment killed nearly 200 communist insurgents whilst losing 12 of its own soldiers (e.g. *Coventry Evening Telegraph* 25 August 1952, *Birmingham Daily Post* 29 December 1952).

In addition, on 30 December 1957, Ted Phillips married 19-year-old Joyce Rayner. Reported locally as the 'Wedding of Nayland Soccer Star', the journalist noted how 'Ipswich Town footballers were among the congregation ... when famous Ipswich inside-left Ted Phillips was married' (*Suffolk Free Press* 8 January 1958). Unfortunately, that marriage failed. When he married again in 1966, Phillips's certificate recorded 'previous marriage annulled'. No available evidence explains the grounds for that annulment, although non-consummation heads a short list of what is legally acceptable.[72] More happily, Phillips's second marriage was long and very successful. A 2018 local newspaper obituary quoted his widow praising, in very loving ways, her memories of:

A great man ... We had a wonderful life together, we were married for 51 years and in that time, we went everywhere and did everything ... He had a wicked sense of humour and loved playing tricks, so there was never a dull moment. (*Maldon and Burnham Standard* 13 January)

It seems highly unlikely Phillips's 1956/57 Ipswich team-mates did not know of his conviction. The case had been reported in a local newspaper, and ten players from season 1954/55 were still there when he returned. One, signed by Alf from Bury Town in 1956, had played against Phillips in that Stowmarket team during 1955/56, then played alongside him in all three of Ipswich's title-winning seasons.[73] Ipswich players seemingly ignored, were unaffected by, or later ignorant of the episode. The absence of any remotely similar historical example from English professional football's entire 20th-century history suggests that Alf Ramsey's 1950s leadership, probably aided by 'Mr John' Cobbold and Ipswich Town's culture, was crucial to ensuring Ted Phillips's professional survival. But Ted Phillips also helped himself by his footballing excellence, muscular presence and humorous personality. Frequently playing the practical joker, Phillips once completely soaked Alf with a hose, whilst repeating a trick often played on team-mates. Alf's response? He removed his tie and jacket, brushed off the worst, silently walked to his car and drove away.[74] McKinstry, whose *Sir Alf* biography was unaware of Ted Phillips's 1955 conviction, devoted three pages to similar practical jokes perpetrated by Phillips either on Alf, or involving him. Yet, 'Such was Alf's fondness for Phillips that he gave him a great deal of leeway.'[75] Alf rarely told him off and Ted Phillips reciprocated the affection: 'At Alf's memorial service I could not speak ... Alf meant so much to me ... He was unique.'[76]

As perceived by Phillips, Alf's 'unique' nature encouraged, perhaps necessitated, a career forged from diversity. Spurs pushed Alf out in late April 1955, after pressure crushed his friend and mentor's mental health. Alf then toured southern Africa, possibly coached Black youngsters, and was covertly recruited to Ipswich Town via greyhounds and a migrant, Jewish, working-class sporting entrepreneur, who in 1935/36 helped push Ipswich Town into professionalism. Once at Ipswich, Alf's strongest ally was a discreetly gay, alcohol-addicted, failed politician, and his most immediately successful player a local youngster convicted of homosexuality, who became integral to winning three divisional titles. Given Alf's own experiences of racist labelling, his likely neurodivergence, playing outlawed Sunday football, not turning full-time professional until aged nearly 27, and only learning to coach part-time with amateurs on weekday evenings, his was a remarkable path to managerial success. From such unseen or underplayed English diversity, sprang England's 1966 success.

1 Hamilton, D. (2023) p.42

2 *Billy Wright's Football Album* (1954) pp.78-82

3 Turpin, N. (2023) p.245

4 Hamilton, D. (2023) p.41

5 Bowler, D. (1999*)* p.110

6 Hamilton, D. (2023) p.42

7 Henderson, J. (2013) pp.262-66

8 Another View From The Tower website (1 July 2020) 'Blackpool's first ever black player'

9 Henderson (2013) pp.263, 271-72

10 Matthews, S. (2000) pp.392, 328

11 **Ipswich Town Minute Book 1947-58** 19 May 1955

12 Hodges, C. (2014) p.198

13 **Ipswich Town Minute Book 1947-58** pp.200-201

14 Mills, R. (2016) p.214

15 Hodges, C. (2014) p.200

16 Henderson, M. (2009) p.43

17 Ibid. also Scovell, B. (2005)

18 Ibid. p.65

19 e.g. *Daily Mirror* 1 February 1951, 27 September 1952

20 See Ramsey's own accounts in McKinstry, L. (2007) p.143 and Henderson, M. (2009) p.79

21 **Ipswich Town Minute Book 1947-58** 8 August 1955

22 Henderson, M. (2009) p.80, also McKinstry, L. (2007) p.138

23 *London Gazette* 'Notice of Naturalisation' 6 July 1926 and 'Announcement of name change' 8 February 1929

24 National Anglo-Jewish Heritage Trail website (no date) 'Nat Shaw - the Waterloo Cup and Ipswich Town Football Club' memories from Mavis Sotnick (daughter) and Monica Bogen (niece)

25 *Greyhound Stud Book* published annually since 1882 by the National Coursing Club

26 Eastwood, J. and Moyse, T. (1986) pp.60-74

27 Ibid. pp.74-75

28 Mills, R. (2016) p.215

29 Eastwood, J. and Moyse, T. (1986) pp.74-75

30 Ibid. also *Daily Mirror* 26 November 1993

31 Mills, R. (2016) p.227

32 Henderson, M. (2009) p.79

33 *Greyhound Yearbook* annual entries, and for example *Daily Herald* and *The People* for results

34 Greaves, J. with Giller, N. (1993) p.32

35 Belton, B. (2002) Appendix

36 Laybourn, K. (2019) p.108

37 *Daily Herald* 8 February 1933, 14 February 1948

38 *Evening Dispatch* 13 February 1948

39 **Ipswich Town Minute Book 1947-58** 8 August 1955

40 **East Suffolk Petty Sessional Division of Blything** 'Register of the Court sitting at Saxmundham, 8 August 1955'

41 Okwonga, M. (2022) pp.46-7

42 **Ipswich Town Minute Book 1947-58** 5 September 1955

43 Ibid.

44 *Daily Telegraph* 22 November 2022 'Why there are still no openly gay footballers in the Premier League?'

45 UK Parliament website (2025) 'Regulating sex and sexuality: the 20th-century'

46 Cook, M., et al. (2007) p.158

47 Ibid. p.168

48 Ibid. pp.168-69

49 Jivani, A. (1997) p.97

50 **East Suffolk Quarter Sessions 1950-62**

51 Ibid. 23 September 1955

52 **Blything Petty Sessions Court Register 1954** 'Court held at Saxmundham 15 March 1954'

53 Ibid.

54 See also Ted Phillips's first marriage reports *Suffolk and Essex Free Press* 8 January 1958, and his brother's marriage *Suffolk and Essex Free Press* 8 April 1959

55 *Ipswich Evening Star* 21 August 2013 'Ted Phillips at 80' interviewed by Chris Brammer; Leiston match reports mentioning Phillips *Bury Free Press* 27 March, 27 September 1953

56 *Eye Constituency Electoral Registers* 1950-55

57 **Ipswich Town Minute Book 1947-58** 5 October 1955, 31 October 1955

58 Eastwood, J. and Moyse, T. (1986) p.110

59 **Ipswich Town Minute Book 1947-58** p.296

60 Cook, M. et al. (2007) pp.170-71. Also, Higgins, P. (1996) pp.95, 179-230

61 Higgins, P. (1996) p.214

62 Ibid. p.160

63 Geoff Hurst oral history interview 7 February 2025

64 McKinstry, L. (2007) pp.148-9

65 Robson, R. (2005) p.75; Henderson, M. (2009) pp.17-18

66 Hamilton, D. (2023) p.67

67 Cook, M. et al. (2007) p.171

68 Higgins, P. (1996) pp.76-80, 170-230

69 Smith, H. (2012) especially chapter 6

70 Buckle, S. (2015) pp.2-3, 213-23

71 Henderson, M. (2008) p.32

72 UK Government website (2025) 'When you can annul a marriage'

73 Henderson, M. (2008) p.23

74 Scovell, B. (2005) p.152

75 McKinstry, L. (2007) pp.179-82, and 180

76 Ibid. p.xxvii

CHAPTER 10

OBSESSIVELY PROFESSIONAL

Ramsey as Moderniser

Starting at the Bottom

ALF RAMSEY'S life had somersaulted in the summer of 1955. Just 15 chronological weeks separated his final appearance for glamorous, top division Tottenham, when a speedy winger inflicted one of Alf's 'hardest games ever' (*Sunday Mirror* 24 April 1955), and Alf's 8 August appointment as Ipswich Town manager. Culturally, though, he crossed chasms. The season Alf joined Spurs they won the Second Division, then in 1951 the Football League championship before home crowds averaging over 55,000. Spurs finished runners-up in 1952, lost an FA Cup semi-final in 1953, and Alf won over 30 England caps there, three times as captain. Tiny Ipswich Town, meanwhile, had played only 12 league seasons before 1955, progressed beyond FA Cup round three just once, and never had a professional play for England. Instant relegation had followed their single 1954 promotion, and the changing rooms for players were huts, as flimsy as Alf's wooden cottage birthplace in Becontree.

Within 21 months, Alf had galvanised Ipswich to win the Third Division South, on 1 May 1957, and seen his annual salary hiked to £2,000. Three months later, Ipswich Town directors celebrated their stadium's new West Stand nearing completion, financed by the Supporters' Association. In another mark of progress, they politely declined the Suffolk Sheep Society's request to hold their annual 'Sheep Show and Sale' on the adjacent practice pitch.[1] The club was edging forward, although money remained tight. After winning Division Two (today's Championship) in season 1960/61, for their top-flight debut season each player's boot budget was set at £18. Ray Crawford, a brilliant 1958 signing, coveted an Italian-made pair costing £30. Alf asked Crawford to pay the £12 difference himself, Crawford agreed,[2] and when his 33 league goals were added to Ted Phillips's 28, Ipswich secured the League championship. Speaking 50 years later, Crawford captured Ipswich Town's provincial otherness, and rustic facilities:

> When clubs came to Portman Road they could not believe … our club dressing room was an old cricket pavilion with a wooden floor and no heating. There was one communal bath and shower, and the toilets were at the back without any lights! At half time some of the lads would have a crafty fag there. I'm sure Alf knew but didn't say anything.

This image, from a previous generation of Ipswich players, captures that spirit and the same bath.

What Ipswich Town *could* boast was a manager with obsessional precision, steely self-discipline, and the guile to help his team capitalise upon 'one of the best pitches in the league'. Another key player recalled Alf telling them:

> 'The ball will get there faster than the man, so pass the ball quickly, short or long, it's up to you.' He worked on players' weaknesses and left the good things alone … Alf would give a team talk on a Friday after training, going into great detail about the opposition, then on match days he would just tell us to enjoy ourselves.[3]

Alf's ascent to England, then that 1966 victory, was forged in these provincial, unfashionable surroundings. Awkwardly, even comically for English nationalists, given Alf Ramsey's supposed attitudes, another element originated in … Scotland?

Scott Duncan

As seen in chapter nine, Alf's flying start as Ipswich manager had a significant assist from Scott Duncan, his patriotic Scottish predecessor and company secretary until 1958. Duncan had played at Newcastle, managed at Manchester United, and was lured to Suffolk in November 1937 to become one of football's 'highest paid officials' (*Daily News* 10 November 1937), and help Ipswich secure entry into the Football League. Stanley Rous, Suffolk-born FA secretary and a 'great friend' of Ipswich Town chairperson 'Captain Ivan' Cobbold, advised Duncan's experience and contact book could 'secure precious votes' from northern league clubs.[4] That was crucial because any new league entrant just needed more votes than the existing member that had finished bottom.

On the pitch, in May 1938 and six months into his management, Duncan's Ipswich finished third in the Southern League, five points behind champions Guildford City. Off the pitch, weeks later, the crafty Duncan helped secure enough votes for Ipswich to join League Division Three South, and he pocketed a large bonus. Significant transfer cash then helped Ipswich finish seventh in their 1938/39 Football League debut season but, days after war broke out, 'Captain Ivan' Cobbold decided to close Ipswich Town until peace returned. To the horror of the protesting 'Supporters Association',[5] the (mostly) public school-educated Ipswich Town board sacked their professional players, put Duncan on a retainer, and by 1942 were having to donate their own money to keep the club solvent.[6]

This matters to Alf Ramsey's story because, effectively, Ipswich started afresh in 1946/47. That season, just as Alf became a full-time player at Southampton, Scott Duncan led Ipswich to sixth in Division Three South. Fourth and seventh places followed but from 1950–53, just as Alf's playing career was peaking, Ipswich finished in the bottom half. In 1954, they won promotion, a joy tempered by instant relegation. The club had, therefore, played a mere ten full Football League seasons before Alf took over. Miraculously, in just seven more, he would make them the best team in England, but Duncan had first recruited three players pivotal to Alf's 1961/62 League championship: Scotsman Jimmy Leadbetter from Brighton in 1955;[7] Welshman John Elsworthy from Newport in 1949; and in 1953 one of Ipswich's tiny number of Suffolk-born players, Ted Phillips. Board minutes from 1955–58 also evidence how Duncan's time-consuming company secretarial work left Alf free to concentrate on football. Duncan performed multiple administrative, legal and organisational functions, including: frequent liaisons with the financially crucial 'Supporters Association', overseeing regular ground improvements, organising insurances, and managing the large portfolio of domestic property rented to players.[8] As Alf publicly later acknowledged, from his lofty position as England manager, he was 'lucky' that 'during my first two years at Ipswich' Duncan handled business-critical tasks of which Alf had little knowledge or experience (*FA News* March 1971). Duncan is pictured below on the right, standing with the young 'Mr. John' Cobbold, already the public face of the Ipswich board. Whether accidentally or deliberately, what appears to be a wallet protrudes from Duncan's left pocket: he was a money man, through and through.

Equally, it was Alf who led the club's football. John Elsworthy played under Duncan from 1949–55, under Alf Ramsey from 1955–63, and compared the two as managers:

Scott Duncan was never on the training pitch … When Alf came in he'd put his tracksuit on and train us. We never used to train on the pitch until Alf, we always used to train on the practice pitch. Alf came along, went straight on the main pitch and said, 'This is where you play Saturday, this is where you train.'

Sir Alf was a tracksuit manager, the first one. Scott Duncan before him was a financial man... He knew everyone in football and kept the club's head above water ... He was good, but he wasn't a coach like Alf was ... Alf practised throw-ins and corners. We'd never done that before. That season we scored ten goals off corners! We'd never score from corners with Scott Duncan.[9]

Alf Ramsey's and Scott Duncan's strong characters, and contrasting coaching styles, led to a cool relationship, and evidence of their footballing collaboration is rare. Early on, when Ipswich played non-league Peterborough United in the FA Cup, Duncan checked out the opposition (*Peterborough Advertiser* 18 November 1955). Whether it was his pre-match briefing or Alf's team's shortcomings that led to the 3-1 defeat is unclear, but after that Duncan performed few team, coaching, or management functions. 'Mr John' Cobbold recalled:

In the first year Alf was with us there was obviously a certain amount of tension between him and Scott. I cannot remember how many times Alf offered his resignation, which was never accepted ... we were right not to do so ... things improved virtually straight away under Alf.[10]

But exactly what and how did Alf change things at Ipswich, to enable them to 'improve virtually straight away'?

Cultures to Create Professionalism

In the next chapter Alf becomes England manager, during the autumn of 1962, but only on condition of him gaining sole control over team selection; a position rehearsed during the summer 1955 negotiation process with Ipswich Town. Alf refused to become their player-manager and secured a three-year transition before taking on Scott Duncan's 'Secretarial' duties. Alf concentrated solely on the club's players, teams and tactics, and his new employers left football decisions entirely to him. Alf's line manager from 1957, young 'Mr. John' Cobbold, became famous for regularly admitting, 'I don't know anything about football ... We don't interfere with the manager.' A 1974 interview celebrated how, during Cobbold's three decades on the Ipswich board, neither Alf nor his four successors had been sacked, nor their football choices questioned (*Sunday Mirror* 13 October).

Although devolving power to Alf worked spectacularly well, by any norms of management logic its success was surprising. For what experience did this 35-year-old have to draw on? Alf's formal education ended aged 14, he had not systematically studied since, started playing professionally very late, and had never been taught coaching or management. Alf's leadership resources consisted of his character and 21 years spent working in the retail, military and professional football sectors, which was hardly a conventional CV. But with Ipswich, as later with England, Alf put into his own everyday workplace practice what he asked of others, and what his upbringing had asked of him: ceaseless toil, resilience in the face of obstacles or injustice, and fairness. Adolescent Alf's first paid work was six years at the London Co-operative Society, absorbing communal values later central to the success of his teams. Six more years learning the discipline and organisational principles of army life extended and reinforced that learning. After becoming a full-time playing professional with Southampton and Tottenham (1946–55), Alf then started to accrue deep craft knowledge from his rich, daily experience of training, playing and observing elite football. His perpetual analysis of such knowledge, fuelled by his obsessive footballing interest and uniquely photographic memory, was of inestimable value in the technology-free world of 1950s football management. Alf could recall in minute detail aspects of matches, teams, players and tactics, which to other witnesses of the same game were either 99 per cent forgotten or never seen in the first place. His unusual mindset then helped him analyse those memories to develop insights into patterns and structures of play, and individual strengths and weaknesses of players, invisible to most other human eyes until technological advance enabled the easy filming of football. In coaching terms, this knowledge and those skills found a safe space to seed, at Eton Manor from 1952–55, before being transplanted into compatible soil at Ipswich Town. There, despite not forging a deep football trust with Scott Duncan, during his novice years Alf had an alternative confidante: his friend, mentor and unfailing ally, Arthur Rowe.

Like much else in Alf's story, the tide and currents of this crucial relationship are traceable only in fragmented sources. Their mutual shyness and discretion in the face of fame meant both men left few written records, at least after Alf's 1952 autobiography. But it has recently become clear, via family testimony, how extensively Arthur Rowe supported Alf as England manager. 'If the FA's phone bill had been itemised in the 1960s, Rowe's number would have appeared there regularly. Rowe didn't seek publicity. He advised Alf without recognition, accepting only the occasional lunch or dinner at the FA's expense.'[11]

That managerial mentoring had started when Alf was at Ipswich, something saved for history by an accidental witness. Ted Phillips, in later life, described how Alf would be 'on the phone most Monday mornings to Arthur Rowe, talking football and picking his brains'.[12] Phillips's recollection can be pinpointed to 1956 or 1957, given his 1955/56 loan to Stowmarket, and has been triangulated by Ipswich Town secretary Pat Godbold. She recalled how Phillips's daily rail journey from Colchester meant:

> He arrived earlier than his team-mates. To kill time, he would sit in the corner of the club offices and quietly read his paper. Every morning Ramsey would arrive and stride past and say 'Morning Ted.' From behind the *Daily Mirror* came the reply 'Morning Alf.' Always the same, every day for years.[13]

Rowe had some influence on Alf's tactics, aspects of which during Ipswich's extraordinary 1961/62 League championship were borrowed from Tottenham a decade earlier. John Elsworthy, a key defender for Ipswich from 1949–65, in 2009 recalled Alf encouraging Ipswich 'to pass the ball right the way through from the goalkeeper to the front men',[14] paralleling an approach Alf had first learned under Rowe at Spurs during the early 1950s.[15] Alf's astute use of 'spindly, wizened' Jimmy Leadbetter, 'ostensibly playing at outside-left, but told to drop back and spray passes forward',[16] also had a Tottenham precedent. As recently noted, 'Leadbetter was the reason why Ipswich won the title. He was to Ramsey what Sonny Walters had been to Arthur Rowe at Tottenham.'[17] Yet useful as Alf found it to recycle some of Rowe's tactics, there was more to his success than mimicking his mentor. Alf transformed Ipswich Town's squad culture, as well as their playing methods, and his conscious nurturing of co-operative, egalitarian approaches suffuses multiple accounts.

This was not an instant or easy option, given Alf's emotionally inexpressive character, but a culture that grew gradually through Alf's reliability and kindness, rather than showy gestures or rhetoric. Leadbetter vouched Alf 'was very considerate. He knew I was a married man ... He'd tell me to get off home if anything happened there, to look after my family, where other managers think they own you. They couldn't care less about anything else.' Ipswich's goalkeeper agreed about Alf's family-friendliness: 'If he'd have asked them, even our wives would have played for him.'[18] The manager's own wife sometimes nearly did. For example, at the end of his first season Alf, 'accompanied by his wife and daughter, performed the opening ceremony at a fete', organised by supporters in a rural Suffolk outpost. Alf gratefully acknowledged how 'the Ipswich Town Supporters Club did a great deal for the parent Club during the year' (*Diss Express* 29 June 1956). Five years later, he still diligently fulfilled such local duties, attending a Colchester celebratory dinner for the 'Essex and Suffolk Border League' and its secretary (*Haverhill Echo* 27 May 1961), despite Ipswich's third team having only just rejoined it (*Weekly Dispatch* 31 January 1960).

Alf later applied similarly thorough, culture-building management approaches to England, with 'his belief in team play and eschewing too much individuality' showing 'itself in his selections for the 1966 World Cup'.[19] Leadbetter, Alf's tactical Ipswich linchpin, in 1962 summarised that egalitarianism, describing how Alf 'insists there are no stars at Ipswich. A team is eleven players. No one is any better than anyone else.'[20] Alf's policy of prioritising collectivism over individualism was, albeit unintentionally, corroborated by a 1962 nationwide poll of 180 football reporters choosing 'Player of the Year'. Each had two votes and 'Burnley men between them got 221 votes, Spurs 131 and champions Ipswich ... just 14! Manager Alf Ramsey said *We're ordinary players who play ordinary football. We concentrate on the simple things*' (*The People* 29 April 1962). As Geoff Hurst shrewdly observed to this book's author, 63 years after Ipswich won the League championship, 'I always say it's not so much what Ramsey did with England' that was his 'remarkable job', but 'what he achieves at Ipswich'. Going from 'the third to the first' then winning it, Hurst described as 'absolutely astonishing'.[21]

Alf's instinct for egalitarianism was also, until January 1961, reinforced by player contracts that would mystify modern football fans. For decades English Football League clubs had imposed national, maximum wage caps, and stringently restricted not just salaries, but the rights of players to secure or benefit from transfers. That changed only in 1960/61 when the Professional Footballers' Association (PFA) successfully threatened strike action.[22] At Ipswich Town, the wage cap had meant, in 1956 for example, that 'after some discussion all full-time professional players be paid the same weekly wage of £14 when playing in the league team', with an 'increase in the win bonus to players from £2 to £3.'[23] Given £14 then was worth less than £500 today, Ipswich footballers were poorly paid for such a precarious occupation. Equally, during the PFA's 1960/61 campaign, they still seemed 'reluctant' to strike (*Daily Herald* 17 November 1960).

Was that partly Alf's influence? Although recently cited as having 'always supported the PFA',[24] as manager Alf showed firm leadership about wage levels. With several games left in Ipswich's eventually victorious 1960/61 Division Two campaign, he publicly insisted, despite the PFA's victory, 'We shall pay our players just what we can afford. And if they don't like it, they can go' (*The People* 16 April 1961). A few weeks into the next season, during which the wages of English players were uncapped for the first time, Ipswich were placed fifth in Division One. Alf attributed that good start not to rising wages but because:

> Co-operation and trust … runs throughout the club. At Portman Road we are all here to help one another. We are a small club, but our staff is as good as any in the country. They act like men and give all the help a manager could require. (*Torbay Express* 16 September 1961)

Alf maintained that mantra all season, four months later telling the *Birmingham Sports Argus*, 'We have no stars at Ipswich, and for me this means no troubles. I have a team of real triers and a team of real men. The average age is just over 27, and with this maturity and experience they know how to conserve their energy' (13 January 1962). Less than four months after that, the day before winning the League championship at their first attempt, Ipswich's success was brilliantly analysed in a national newspaper's 'special report'. It centred on Alf Ramsey, 'the quiet one':

> Who brought to Ipswich the simple philosophy that every football team consists of 11 players. His success is the success of the old-fashioned virtues. Like not knowing when you are beaten. And making do. And not showing off. And doing your best. (*Daily Herald* 28 April 1962)

Nevertheless, the mere existence of such qualities did not guarantee success, and retrospect can oversimplify leadership stories. Since sporting victories are never inevitable, how can Alf's Ipswich victory narrative be unsmoothed? A helpful example is Ipswich Town's winter of season 1958/59. On 14 February 1959, a dressing-room revolt erupted, just an hour before kick-off, as a bumper home crowd gathered outside for an attractive fifth-round FA Cup tie. Some players threatened not to play without a significant bonus, but Alf called their bluff: 'In that

case I shall go and tell them [the fans] there won't be a game today.'
Intriguingly, the same source two sentences later eulogised that squad's
strong 'camaraderie, the team spirit. We had no prima donnas ... a very
close-knit bunch – Alf went out of his way to ensure that ... on and off
the field of play.'[25]

These two memories were offered in good faith, but other sources
suggest that achieving Alf's 'camaraderie' was a steeper and rockier
path than rosy retrospection paints. The ticketing for that fifth-round
FA Cup match, against eventual losing finalists Luton Town, triggered
significant fan unrest about increased prices and ticket distribution.
Anger was so extreme that Alf called a team meeting to tell players,
'Don't for goodness sake worry about this ticket business,' admitting
that 'players have been subject to a great deal of abuse from people in
the town' (*Daily Herald* 9 Feb 1959). The team's league form since 26
December had been no cheerier, drawing one and losing five. As a
football journalist put it:

> MISERABLE. That's the word Alfred Ramsey, once the
> sure-footed polished idol of Spurs and England, used to
> describe the performance of his team against Lincoln last
> week. MISERABLE. That's the word I use to describe the
> performance of his team against Sunderland last Saturday.
> MISERABLE. That is how the Soccer citizenry of Suffolk
> are this morning as the TOWN slam up their cup prices. (*Daily
> Herald* 11 February 1959)

The hidden player rebellion, and public fan revolt, probably contributed
to Ipswich losing 5-2, but a week before, transfer stories had also surfaced
about Ted Phillips. Whether he had been covertly approached, was
himself trying to engineer a transfer, or the whole episode was conjured
by journalists is now difficult to tell. But Alf was asked by Phillips,
on the first Monday in February, if it was true that Fulham wanted to
buy him (*Daily Mirror* 3 Feb 1959). In season 1958/59, Phillips scored
only eight goals and made just 22 league appearances, his confidence
still fragile after a cartilage operation 12 months before. To cap things
off, although nationally crowds rose that season, helped by television
coverage of Brazil winning the 1958 World Cup in Sweden, Ipswich
bucked that positive trend with their average gate dropping by 4,000
to just over 14,000.[26]

In other words, football is never fixed nor certain. How a manager
pulls their staff through flat patches better illustrates their leadership

than periods when everything seems serene. Amazingly, after the squalls alluded to above, between August 1959 and April 1962, Alf steered Ipswich Town to 11th, then winning League Division Two, before securing the League championship. How had he managed it? A recent analyst attributed their unexpected, March 1962, 3-1 victory at reigning champions Tottenham to the fact that 'Ipswich had become a family, which made the club different ... its players played for him [Alf Ramsey] first and themselves second'.[27]

Tactics and Team Selection

Alf Ramsey created cultures where people felt valued, but he had also become proficient in the technical qualities fundamental to football management. Alf professed to tactical pragmatism, developing tactics to suit available players rather than theoretical models; but he also planned longer term for campaigns, not just immediately for matches. Alf knew his Ipswich squad members were not individually brilliant, but to capitalise upon their collective strengths he devised a counterattacking, fast-passing system to move the ball forward quickly. A leading national TV commentator described 'pure football, played in a simple direct way, that leads to goals and movements of beauty'.[28] Another leading journalist, termed 'mean-spirited'[29] for criticising Ipswich's 'crushing solidity', in 1968 also praised them, whilst reflecting on Alf and England:

> Footballers can be berated for not being highly talented, but it is no use blaming them for winning. This experience with Ipswich confirmed Ramsey in the lesson to apply to his job as England manager. Individual ability was relevant only when it connected collectively ... what Ramsey looks for is maximum effectiveness from eleven players.[30]

Whilst Alf's club and national tactics prioritised turning his available players into winners, they also reflected his own unusual cognition, unwittingly illustrated by two further observations from that same journalist. He described Alf, unlike most others, having 'in his mind a picture of a team in movement, not of names on a sheet of paper'; an internalised, imagined film fuelled by Alf's extraordinary photographic memory. The advanced footballing craft knowledge that created then nudged Alf to discard long-standing conventions about formations: 'He did not give players positional titles; he gave them jobs.'[31] This deep understanding of what individual members could, or could not, contribute to the wider team was enhanced by Alf's observational practices. Four weeks after starting as Ipswich manager he was watching games and practice matches 'from an observation post 30 feet off the ground. *You get a better picture of play up here*, explains Alf, *and you spot things you may miss from ground level*' (*Daily Herald* 5 September 1955). During season 1957/58, Alf again perched in lofty spots, alongside hospital radio commentators, better to read games.[32]

Alf's coaching was consequently detailed and structured, as discussed below, but he disliked over-complex, match-specific tactical plans. Instead, Alf trusted his own judgement of the skills of individual players, of how they combined, and his thorough training and coaching, to prepare teams for their next game. Such groundwork enabled minimal matchday instructions, leaving players freer to focus on personal duties and partnerships rather than complex match plans. Two key figures in Ipswich's League championship side, the first at the time and the second 40 years later, captured how Alf devolved professional trust to players. This attacking midfielder described how:

> No hard and fast tactics are laid down. Mr. Ramsey insists that if you 'play football' then the moves are bound to come. This ensures that variety is introduced into every game. In all the games I've played for Ipswich Town I've never really been told what to do. 'Just go and play your natural game' has been the call.[33]

Meanwhile, this defender recalled:

> I used to sit there in the dressing room … and he never said a word to me before I ran out on a pitch ever. Never said a word, he just left me to get on … the same went for most of the rest of the players, except Phillips and Crawford who were the two that he spoke to most often before the game.[34]

Hinting at another key Alf attribute, taking the pressure off players, he described their manager's deliberately low-key preparation in the minutes before the championship-clinching final league game in 1962: 'He didn't say anything really, just that we knew what we had to do.'[35] Strikingly, Geoff Hurst observed after recently rewatching the 1966 World Cup Final, that 'within our allotted roles Alf encouraged free thinking', demonstrated by having just hours previously told Bobby Charlton to man-mark Franz Beckenbauer despite Charlton having 'never once man-marked in his entire career'.[36] In Alf Ramsey's leadership style, trust meant everything.

Training and Coaching

As a full-time professional footballer from 1946–55, Alf prized varied exercise, structured rest, a balanced diet, rarely smoking or drinking, and relaxing with hobbies.[37] Managerially, he preached the same and constantly refreshed training to maintain the motivation of players. On arrival in 1955, 'He immediately introduced new ideas into the training at Portman Road' (*Leicester Mercury* 17 September 1960) and also borrowed from others. One Ipswich player, present throughout Alf's time, studied for coaching qualifications and recalled how after attending 'specialised courses Alf ... would call [him] into his office and pick his brains'.[38] Pre-season training involved stamina building through road running, but 'once the season got under way he introduced more ball work and five-a-side sessions'.[39] A 1958 newspaper described how 'a recent addition to the club's training methods is the use of medicine balls', with Alf 'setting an example by training with [his players] whenever possible' (*Huddersfield Examiner* 27 December). He once 'staged a special sprint' to settle arguments about Ipswich's fastest player (*The People* 3 January 1960), and to enliven training had 'an outline of a goal painted on a wall ... parts of the goal have been divided off into different areas'. During shooting practice, players were 'awarded points for various areas, more points being given for those spots well out of the goalkeeper's reach' (*Birmingham Sports Argus* 22 September 1962).

Alf's coaching resolutely concentrated upon improving skills. 'I have never had much time for the kick and run stuff,' he said in 1958 (*Manchester Evening News* 23 January), and this key player confirmed:

> Two touches were all he wanted. If the ball came at your chest he wouldn't let you bring it down then trap it and pass it. Oh no, after you chested it down you had to control and pass all in the one movement[40] ... If we were having a practice match and anyone did anything silly he'd blow his whistle and correct it ... He was a perfectionist really.[41]

Although Alf never cluttered the minds of players with complex game plans, his match preparation was pedantically thorough. Roy Stephenson played in 41 of Ipswich's 42 1961/62 League championship games, recalling 'Alf's attention to detail was amazing. In his Friday team talks he concentrated on trying to find weaknesses in the opposition. There were no long dossiers, he had all the information in his head. He had an incredible memory.[42] Ted Phillips similarly testified how Alf was:

> So organised that I swear he could think up free-kick routines in his sleep. We would spend three hours training on a Friday and most of the time was spent working on a new routine he had dreamed up ... it invariably worked. Alf could make a team talk last a couple of hours he was so thorough. I'd have been nothing without Alf ... He was like a god to me.[43]

Alf Ramsey's leadership practices at 1950s Ipswich, and 1960s England, contradicted the conservative public image that dominated his 1970s decline. He was 'a resolutely modern coach, open to new ideas. His work togs were a tracksuit and boots ... even after his 40th birthday, Ramsey would take part in the practice matches.'[44] As the leading historian of football tactics recently summarised, 'When England appointed Ramsey, they were getting a thoroughly modern, radical tactician.'[45]

Management of Players

To prevent this narrative sliding into hagiography, it is important to note how, outside of training, Alf could bore his players rigid. One confessed how on train journeys, 'You used to avoid him. You'd run along the corridor,' because Alf just 'lived for football' and could talk of nothing else. Another described Alf working his way through eight or nine compartments of players and staff: 'He'd bore us all ... we'd change the conversation ... and he'd get up and walk next door.'[46] Yet the same player recounted how Alf's obsessive nature and photographic memory, which to modern eyes suggests neurodivergence, was professionally life-changing:

> Every mistake we made in a match or every good thing we did he could point it out to us, he had it all up here, and he'd say why did you do this? He could tell you a week later, tell you every mistake you'd made in a match. It was uncanny.[47]

Alf never received formal training but was brilliant at coaching because it satisfied his acutely observant, consuming football interests, then channelled them into individual performance management. A team-mate remarked that goalkeeper Roy Bailey was:

> Another one who Alf made. When he came from Palace he was good, but he was a much better keeper once he'd joined us

... Alf was ... so clever. If you improve each player five percent overall, it's a tremendous improvement. He never tried to make miracles ... just to make an improvement ... some improved ten percent, others five percent, but every one of us improved.[48]

Alf's running film of internal memory also helped him imagine new positions for players. Jimmy Leadbetter signed in the summer of 1955, just before Alf's accession as manager:

[I spent] most of my first season in the reserves. Twice I played inside-forward. In January, Mr. Ramsey called me into the office and said, 'How do you fancy playing on the left wing?' It was a bit of a shock ... I was not very fast.[49]

Changing Leadbetter's position underlay Ipswich's subsequent titles, but it was not only him who Alf re-imagined:

A remarkable thing about Ipswich is the number of switches that come off. I'm an inside forward who became a left winger. Roy Stephenson, on the opposite wing, was also an inside forward. John Compton, full back, was a wing half. Bill Baxter, wing half, was a centre half.[50]

Compton's positional change was especially significant. Veteran left-back Ken Malcolm, his back damaged during the summer of 1961 by paid casual labouring whilst building the club's new North Stand terracing,[51] broke down three games into the season. Inspirationally, Alf switched Compton, signed in the summer of 1960 but with just three first-team appearances, from midfield (wing-half) to left-back. He then personally prepared Compton for his debut, against an England international winger, by having a speedy Ipswich reserve constantly run at him, whilst former full-back Alf personally coached Compton in real time.[52] The result was that Ipswich beat recent league champions Burnley 6-2. Compton then played 36 more games for his League championship medal, and during the next match 'Compton, sure-tackling, fast-recovering and ever-alert, emerged as another of Alf Ramsey's discoveries' (*Daily Herald* 4 September 1961).

Alf's personal qualities inspired but could also intimidate players. Interviewed shortly after England's 1966 World Cup win, Arthur Rowe explained how 'Alf has always had relentless application, the desire to be better tomorrow than he was yesterday and, above all, complete honesty. Those are the things which enable him to get the best out of others' (*News of the World* 7 August). But whilst Alf's honesty could feel bruising, as noted in chapters six and seven, it always rested on facts. Ray Crawford, to this day Ipswich Town's leading goal-scorer, recalled missing his second-ever penalty: 'It was pathetic, the poorest penalty you have ever seen ... *You'll never take another one for this club,*' Alf told him, and he did not.[53] But players tolerated Alf's brutally honest analyses because they trusted his judgement and had witnessed his 'resolute faith' in them. That is why, as another of his signings explained, 'you always wanted to play for him.'[54]

Proof of Alf's outstanding player management is clinched by testimony from an unlikely source. In the summer of 1955, Ron Blackman was signed, aged 30, by Scott Duncan. Injuries meant he played fewer than 30 games in three seasons under Alf who, he recalled, then:

> Took me to one side and sacked me when my league career ended at 33 with a dislocated shoulder. But he did it gently and explained things properly. One thing that underlined his kindness came after we won Division 3 South. I didn't play enough games to qualify for a medal. A local jeweller made silver-plated tankards for all the players ... I didn't get one. Alf wasn't very happy about it and presented me with his – a superior one being the manager – which I thought was very generous. (*Reading Evening Post* 7 May 1999)

Management of Pressure

However effective the tactics, thorough the coaching, well picked the side and strong the player-manager bonds, winning competitions entails handling huge pressure. Between 1955 and 1966, Alf Ramsey won four trophies: the League championship and World Cup being the ultimate his teams could achieve. These were extraordinary feats, given the parlous starting positions of Ipswich and England, and key to such success was how Alf helped players, under pressure, still to perform. As with other attributes, Alf's character provided the base metal, turned to gold by his calmly methodical management. Sarina Wiegman, interviewed just before managing England women's Euro 2022 Final win against Germany, similarly explained, 'I have to prepare really well,' because when 'we've done everything necessary, everything in our control to be as good as possible ... That gives me calmness.'[55] Such calmness soothed her players, one commenting, for example, 'I don't know how she does it ... it feels less tense.' Wiegman's assistant confirmed 'the key to [Wiegman's] calmness' is how 'she really trusts and believes in the process'.[56]

Alf similarly believed in calmness, and process, which is why as a player he took penalties for Southampton, Spurs and England. For England he was flawless, scoring all three, but that was not true in club football. We saw in chapter seven how he missed in 1948, under pressure for Southampton touring Brazil. Six years later, he confessed, 'Of the three penalties Tottenham were awarded last season [1953/54] I missed all of them … I not only used the wrong tactics but also changed my mind halfway.'[57]

Such honest analysis of his own elite experience gave Alf great cachet with Ipswich Town's journeymen, and even more with an England squad managed previously by Walter Winterbottom. Winterbottom had many qualities, reviewed in the next chapter, but internationally was a 'poor judge of players', who failed to 'communicate at their level', and by whom several star England players were 'appalled and also a little confused'.[58] Alf was the opposite. He lent players confidence by dissecting individual performances in intimidating detail, whilst constructively suggesting improvements. Crucially, players also knew Alf had worked incessantly for his own medals and caps. His leadership and management inspired players because he was, patently, an authentic football learner, powered, in Arthur Rowe's 1966 words, by 'relentless application'. Yet after 1955, Alf also used that learning to improve not just his responses to pressure, but how as a manager he could protect his players from pressures that might freeze them, in make-or-break matches: a thread traceable throughout his managerial career at Ipswich, then with England.

At the start of season 1956/57, Ipswich had lost five of six league games but 'there was no panic from Alf, who stayed perfectly calm and assured the players things would improve … He very rarely raised his voice … if things hadn't gone well he would say *what went wrong, boys?*'[59] Journalists from across England started to notice this cool leadership style, one commenting, 'The success of Ipswich is the culmination of a remarkable recovery reflecting particular credit on Alf Ramsey' (*Western Mail* 2 May 1957). Next season, previewing a fourth-round FA Cup match at Manchester United, the biggest fixture in Ipswich's history, another praised this 'urbane, philosophical … well-groomed' manager 'who chooses his words carefully'. Ipswich, Alf reassured, were 'not in the least worried … NO special training. NO seaside excursions. NO brine baths. NO golf. NO steaks' (*Daily Herald* 25 January 1958). Alf managed everything so smoothly on the day that John Elsworthy stayed in the dressing room whilst team-mates surveyed the pitch, and:

You'll never guess what happened next – I fell asleep. It sounds crazy but I really did doze off ... the next thing I knew I could feel a presence near me. I woke up and who should it be but Alf ... He just grinned.[60]

Alf's equanimity had been evident to 1950s England team-mates. Nat Lofthouse, when Ipswich sat on the brink of promotion to Division One in 1961, could not 'remember Ramsey ever becoming ruffled or despondent during a match ... cool, classy Ramsey ... an ideal manager ... has imbued the Ipswich team with his qualities' (*Staffordshire Sentinel* 9 April). Two weeks later, after promotion was sealed, experienced football journalist Peter Lorenzo similarly labelled Alf a 'cool genius' who:

> However awkward the situation, remains as unruffled as a clergyman ... Ramsey's secret? An indisputable ability to take 11 ordinary players and make them into a team. He is also fanatically enthusiastic, though he doesn't show it, scrupulously fair and a players' man to the core.

Then, in an insight that connects us to the next chapter's story of how Alf became England manager, Lorenzo asked an interesting question:

> How have Ipswich managed to keep a man of this calibre? Simple, Ramsey keeps his word. *A year after I came here I was approached by a First Division club. I ignored it. I had an agreement with Ipswich – and I kept it. I still have an agreement – and I intend to keep to that.* (*Daily Herald* 24 April 1961).

Alf wasn't lying about 'being approached'. Until recently it was claimed 'just one club attempted seriously to take Ramsey away from Ipswich', named as Charlton in September 1956.[61] But new documentary evidence suggests Preston North End's directors beat them to it in August 1956, following rejection by Alf's closest footballing friend. Arthur Rowe had 'regretfully declined' Preston's invitation re the managership 'on health grounds'.

> Mr. A. Ramsay [sic] had been approached, but he was not inclined to accept on account of lack of experience. It was agreed ... a direct approach to be made again to Mr. Ramsay.[62]

A week later, the Preston board discussed 'a visit to Mr. A. Ramsay and the managership of this club ... agreed that Mr. Ramsay be interviewed and offered the position with a salary in the region of £2000'.[63] Given that, in the 1950s, Preston reached one FA Cup Final, and were twice League championship runners-up, this was an amazing offer. Alf was not, therefore, lying in 1961 about 'keeping to an agreement' despite a firm offer.

That plotline ties into his later England appointment. Days after Walter Winterbottom had resigned as England manager, the FA's own recently appointed leader, Denis Follows, had cautioned patience about recruiting his replacement: 'We may have to wait. We want the best man we can get, and he may have a club contract. If a man would break his contract to come to us, he might just as likely break his contract with us' (*Daily Mirror* 3 August 1962). Might Follows, even then, have inclined towards Alf Ramsey as a potential England manager? And would Alf's promise to Ipswich always to 'keep to an agreement' stand in the way of his ascension?

1 **Ipswich Town Minute Book** 1 April p.314, 12 August, 2 September 1957 pp.329-333.

2 Hamilton, D. (2023) p.82

3 Brooks, M. (2011) pp.7-8

4 Henderson, M. (2009) p.75; see also Iain Campbell Whittle's excellent website Scots Football Worldwide (2025) 'Scott Duncan – and a certain other'

5 Hadgraft, R. (2002) p.25

6 Mills, R. (2016)

7 Hamilton (2023) p.75 mistakenly implies Leadbetter as a Ramsey signing

8 **Ipswich Town Minute Book,** for example: pp.261, 267, 269, 271, 279, 285, 291 and 320

9 Those Were The Days website (28 April 2022) 'TWTD Replayed - John Elsworthy Interview'

10 Henderson, M. (2009) p.80

11 Hamilton (2023) p.151

12 Ted Phillips interview in Henderson, M. (2008) p.30

13 Hadgraft (2002) p.43

14 John Elsworthy interview in Henderson, M. (2008) p.9

15 Ramsey, A. (1952) pp.51-3

16 Barber, G. *When Saturday Comes* 421, 15 July 2022

17 Hamilton, A. (2023) p.84

18 Bowler, D. (1998) p.129

19 Brooks, M. (2011) pp.21-22

20 *Topical Times Football Book* (1962) p.9

21 Geoff Hurst oral history interview 6 February 2025

22 Goldblatt, D. (2015) p.10

23 **Ipswich Town Minute Book** pp.304, 305 3 December 1956

24 Hamilton, D. (2023) p.124

25 Larry Carberry interview in Henderson, M. (2008) p.23

26 Eastwood, J. and Moyse, T. (1986) p.115

27 Hamilton, D. (2023) pp.87-88

28 Brooks, M. (2012) pp.15-17, p.18

29 Hamilton, D. (2023) p.84

30 Hopcraft, D. (1968) p.136

31 Ibid. p.135

32 Hadgraft, R. (2002) p.45

33 *Topical Times Football Book* (1962) p.9

34 Those Were The Days website (28 April 2022) 'TWTD Replayed - John Elsworthy Interview'

35 Ibid.

36 Hurst, G. (2024) pp.272, 264

37 Ramsey, A. (1952) pp.29-30, 61-64

38 Garnett, T. (2002) p.85

39 Hadgraft, R. (2002) p.88

40 Henderson, M. (2008) p.12

41 Those Were The Days website (28 April 2022) 'TWTD Replayed - John Elsworthy Interview'

42 Hadgraft, R. (2002) p.50

43 Henderson, M. (2008) p.32

44 Hamilton, D. (2023) p.76

45 Wilson, J. (2022) p.131

46 Brooks, M. (2011) p.19

47 Ibid.

48 Those Were The Days website (28 April 2022) 'TWTD Replayed - John Elsworthy Interview'

49 *Topical Times Football Book* (1962) p.9

50 Ibid.

51 Hadgraft (2002) pp.91, 87

52 Ibid. pp.91-92

53 Henderson, M. (2008) p.46

54 Brooks, M. (2011) p.22

55 *The Athletic* (29 July 2022) Sarina Wiegman interviewed by Charlotte Harpur

56 Wrack, S. (2023) p.238, Keira Walsh then Arjan Veurink

57 *Billy Wright's Football Album* (1954) p.79, 80

58 Hamilton, D. (2023) pp.133, 26, 27

59 Henderson, M. (2008) p.25

60 Ibid. p.8

61 Hamilton, D. (2023) p.69

62 My gratitude to Ian Rigby, club historian, who at the National Football Museum Archive alerted me to the **Preston North End Minute Book** 14 August 1956

63 Ibid. 21 August 1956

CHAPTER 11

OUTSIDERS, INSIDERS, UNDERDOGS

Alf's England Ascension

Introduction

FOR 21st-CENTURY progressives, Alf Ramsey appears an unlikely hero, but in nearly every action that mattered he was a liberally inclined moderniser, not an unreasonable reactionary. Equally, he was a poor politician whose social awkwardness, and reluctance to engage beyond the world of football, narrowed his leadership style to personal influence rather than coalition building. Such characteristics could have cramped his life, but Alf had liberal assists. Two loving parents helped his childhood, and colourful others his adolescence: the former Barking barrow boy who inspired Co-operative Society sport for example, or Alf's teenaged football being saved on Sundays by a community-minded newsagent of German heritage. In 1955, Alf reached Ipswich via an East End, Jewish migrant from Poland, with a fortune made from frocks and greyhounds. For ten years, from 1952, he also fell under the influence of various Old Etonians, of varied sexuality but constant wealth, who purchased and progressed his management talents. One was 'Mr John' Cobbold, Ipswich Town chairperson, pictured here toasting Alf's England appointment on 26 October 1962.

Alf's managerial club success had rested on saving the career, probably with John Cobbold's help, of a hulking Suffolk centre-forward, in classic English mould, publicly prosecuted for homosexual behaviour. Behind these powerful characters in Alf's professional life lay a rich ancestral supporting cast of industrious and dealing relatives, many with Gypsy-Traveller and GRT connections.

Given such an unconventional background, to become England manager and then to succeed, Alf needed another assist: Denis Follows obliged. Controversially elected as the FA's salaried, full-time professional 'Secretary' in February 1962, which involved beating the media favourite, and moving from being an FA volunteer to an FA employee, by October Follows had appointed Alf as England manager. Yet despite organising the 1966 World Cup, then helping England win it, Follows has been largely overlooked or undermined in previous histories. Partly, perhaps, because he secured the FA job whilst working as a trade union leader, who had threatened national strikes, and personally defended the pilot involved in the 1958 Munich air disaster? Alf's was not the only extraordinary personal story behind England's 1966 World Cup win.

A Preacher, a Saint, a Sage: Three Knights of the FA

In 1962, the FA employed Alf Ramsey as England manager in a job he never even applied for, shortly after England had failed at yet another World Cup. In 1966, England then hosted the World Cup, and slightly unexpectedly won it. In 1967, Alf was knighted, and in 1970 lost an epic World Cup quarter-final. Then, in 1974, he was brutally sacked after Poland, the World Cup's eventual third-placed team, edged England out during qualifying. In different roles the three knighted FA characters below acted in these dramas, especially its opening scenes. To understand Alf's rise to England manager, each is now introduced.

Sir Stanley Rous: From 1930s Preacher to 1960s FIFA President

Rous, as FIFA president, features in multiple classic 1966 photographs. The tall, white haired football politician is pictured overleaf standing between Prince Philip and Queen Elizabeth II moments after she handed Bobby Moore the Jules Rimet Trophy.

Like Alf Ramsey, football helped Rous to become socially mobile, just massively more so. Born into a shopkeeping family on the Suffolk-Norfolk border, Rous fought in World War One, qualified as a schoolteacher and trained as an elite football referee. During a hectic

1934 he was hired as FA secretary, refereed the English and Welsh FA Cup finals, and officiated several international fixtures.[1] Then, from 1934 until 1961, Rous profoundly influenced and modernised English football, ushering England back into FIFA and in 1949 being knighted.[2] Finally, from 1961 to 1974, he was a reforming if Eurocentric FIFA president who, some claimed, helped bias 1966 referees against South American sides.[3] African nations, which had boycotted 1966 in protest at under-representation, despised Rous for wishing to maintain sporting contacts with South Africa, and in 1974 FIFA members voted him out.[4]

Personally, Rous and Alf Ramsey differed widely. For Alf, as a shy, disadvantaged 1930s teenager, Sunday football was a blessing, but Rous voted against accepting it (*Yorkshire Post* 22 August 1939). Rous regularly preached to Sunday gatherings of professional footballers and league representatives,[5] including in 1936 at East Ham, three miles from adolescent Alf (*West Ham Echo* 20 March). Eighteen months later, a national newspaper directly criticised Rous and urged the FA to support Sunday football to 'encourage fitness among our youth. When, I repeat, will the FA tackle it?' (*John Bull* 11 December 1937). For years Rous did the opposite, although by 1954 he was admitting, 'If we cannot break the Sunday football racket, then let us join it, control it and keep it in its proper place' (*Portsmouth Evening News* 9 April). It was not until 1960, just before Rous left for FIFA, that the FA finally gave way.

More gloriously, four months later, FIFA announced England would host the 1966 World Cup, helped significantly by Rous (*Daily Herald* 23

August 1960). Equally, he would probably not have chosen as England manager the ex-Sunday footballer, Alf Ramsey, and nor would Rous's preferred successor as FA secretary, the incumbent England manager Walter Winterbottom. The twists and turns of Winterbottom's story paradoxically reveal just how much of England's 1966 victory was owed to him, but how little he wanted Alf as England manager.

Walter Winterbottom: Alf's Saintly Predecessor

Walter Winterbottom, England's first football manager (1946–62) and knighted in 1978, was a slightly otherworldly figure whose inspirational development of English coaching contributed significantly to victory in 1966. Equally, under his team management at four World Cups (1950–62) England won just three matches out of 14.[6] In fairness, a major reason for Winterbottom's managerial underperformance was a wheeze, hatched by his future employer during that 1946 job interview, to give him two massive roles.[7] The first was as FA director of coaching, translating a national football coaching vision into local and regional reality.[8] Winterbottom himself, even after England's calamitous group stage exit at their first World Cup in 1950, still maintained that being director of coaching 'was his more important role'.[9] Managing the senior English male football team was merely Winterbottom's second job.

Winterbottom's employer was the FA, and his mentor was FA secretary Sir Stanley Rous. For them both, England competing 'correctly' mattered as much as World Cup success. Results mattered, but so did the FA maintaining British football's imagined moral and organisational pre-eminency, both as the game's founder and as a buttress in building Britain's post-imperial legacy. For example, within a single 1938 sermon, Rous blithely preached, 'England's greatness depended on two things – religion and sport.' The English were 'still the best games players in the world' although that would only continue 'if we took coaching and training seriously', hence his appointment of Winterbottom eight years later. Yet in the same sermon, Rous simultaneously lauded amateurism, warning against 'over-specialisation and professionalism' which led people to 'play games in the wrong spirit … defeat is insignificant compared with the joy of battle' (*Lincolnshire Echo* 7 February).

Winterbottom was appointed in Rous's own image as another talented, personable and highly intelligent former schoolteacher.[10] Walter correctly instructed England's first 1950 World Cup squad, including Alf Ramsey, to 'behave like ambassadors',[11] but team selection for the tournament was ceded to a senior FA councillor. For Bobby Charlton, by the 1960s Winterbottom had become:

> A symbol … of the old amateur world in many eyes … A new and stronger form of leadership was required. Part of Walter would always be locked in the theoretical … the days of the teacher would have to give way to the days of the pro.[12]

Winterbottom, sighed Charlton, 'did not know how to handle players, how to talk to them'.[13] A more pragmatic football professional who clearly did was Alf Ramsey. McKinstry's interviews with Alf's players underpin Charlton's point: he coached professional footballers in terms they understood, whilst Winterbottom could not.[14] Equally, this had always been the case. In 1948, star striker and England international, Tommy Lawton, criticised Winterbottom's coaching so openly that his international playing career ended aged 28.[15] Fifteen years later, Jimmy Greaves joked of Winterbottom, 'Just because I play for England, he thinks I understand peripheral vision and positive running.'[16] Nor were such instances isolated gripes from jaundiced ex-players. Reporting from a three-day 1962 World Cup preparation camp at Lilleshall, a journalist quoted Winterbottom: 'We have been working at this idea of getting the players to know each other's play, and in particular trying to produce the retreating defence situation and to penetrate it' (*Birmingham Daily Post* 13 December 1961).

Whilst Winterbottom's pedagogic enthusiasm was indisputable, and admirable in his director of coaching role, for his other job it became a handicap. Hard-bitten professional footballers, most of whom left school aged 14 and by 1961 were in sustained dispute with football authorities about repressive contracts, and standardised capped wages,[17] could be excused for finding Winterbottom's school teacherly, safe-salaried ways incredibly irritating.[18] All of which adds gorgeous irony to this comment, a decade earlier, from a teacher's pet named Alf Ramsey:

> Like everybody in football I had heard of Mr Winterbottom's famous pre-match talks but did not know quite what to expect. After a pow-wow of about ninety minutes, I had a great respect not only for Mr. Winterbottom's knowledge of the game, but his ability to put over points in a concise and easy to understand manner.[19]

Alf's approval then, and historical analysis now, reinforces that Winterbottom's national leadership of coaching was pivotal to England's World Cup win. All of England's 1966 World Cup Final goals came from West Ham players (Hurst three, Peters one), in a team captained by a third (Moore). West Ham's manager since 1961 had been Ron Greenwood. During the 1950s, Greenwood was revolutionised by Winterbottom's coaching course:

> [It] taught us how to teach ... they seemed to take us right inside the game ... everything was geared to getting the best out of individuals and teams ... at the end of the week I remember wishing the course could go on forever. My wife spotted something different in me the moment I got home. 'You've changed,' she said. 'You've come alight!'[20]

Winterbottom similarly enthused West Ham's then-captain, Malcolm Allison, who:

> [After] one of Walter's courses at Lilleshall ... came back to West Ham inspired by what he had learned and immediately began coaching sessions for the young players every Tuesday and Thursday evening. They took place on the carpark.

Those carpark-coached 'young players' included Alf's World Cup Final trio of Hurst, Moore, and Peters, who had all been 'captured by Mal's infectious enthusiasm. Mal saw coaching ... as an added extra that would improve the player's football intellect as well as their playing abilities.'[21] England's 1966 World Cup-winning right-back, George Cohen of Fulham, was similarly managed by another Winterbottom-inspired coach, Vic Buckingham. Future England bosses Joe Mercer and Bobby Robson, like Greenwood already mentioned, also attended Walter's Lilleshall courses.[22] English football in general, not just the 1966 winners, was immeasurably enriched by Winterbottom's visionary coaching of coaches.

Equally, after a decade of serial World Cup failures, ushered in by the 1950 and 1953 international humiliations in which Alf had played, a replacement England team manager was desperately needed. When, in 1961, Stanley Rous resigned as FA secretary to become FIFA president, he,[23] and most English newspapers, advocated Winterbottom to replace him.[24] The 19 February 1962 election, by the 80-strong FA Council, seemed a done deal. Had Winterbottom won, his preferred successor definitely would not have been Alf, but English football shook when 50 FA Council representatives voted for the comparatively unknown FA insider, honorary treasurer Denis Follows, and just 20 for Winterbottom (*Daily Mirror* 20 February 1962).

Denis Follows: Ultimate Underdog

Denis Follows, despite hiring Alf in 1962, organising the 1966 World Cup, helping Alf win it, and being knighted in 1978, was, in Alf Ramsey's most recent biography, belittled as an 'officious mediocrity'.[25] In doing so, McKinstry followed Alf's first biographer, who in 1970 mocked Follows as merely heading an 'anti-Rous' faction, whose 'qualifications were quite irrelevant' to him getting the job.[26] Even a modern, brilliantly researched biography of Walter Winterbottom misleadingly portrayed Follows as 'installed' by Professor Harold Thompson, Alf's key FA persecutor.[27]

New analysis suggests all these generalisations are inaccurate. At election time, Stanley Rous had privately identified 'Thompson and Follows' as Winterbottom's key rivals,[28] but he meant separately not collectively; no documents show Thompson and Follows collaborating. On the contrary, plentiful evidence suggests Follows, like Alf, detested Thompson and found him extraordinarily difficult. For example, in 1965–66 Follows was regularly heard muttering by his driver, 'Oh not again Thompson!', or 'Heavens Thompson, have I got to sort this again?'[29] What the 1962 election victory of Follows had signified was an FA Council grassroots rebellion against the autocratic Rous, as much as a Thompson conspiracy. Follows himself told an eminent journalist shortly afterwards, 'The Secretary is meant to be the servant of the Football Association, but we all know what happened. The servant became the master.'[30]

Hindsight suggests the FA Council made a wise choice. Follows had broad FA voluntary experience,[31] and the key skills necessary for secretary: ceaselessly building football coalitions, steadily modernising an antiquated FA, and organising a successful and victorious first home World Cup tournament. Pat Day started work at the FA in 1965, as a junior secretary, and like all job applicants was interviewed by Follows. She became his secretary in 1970, and by her 1998 departure had risen to deputy chief executive, the FA's first senior female leader.[32] Her previously unseen testimony paints Follows as a 'very strong administrator', who with staff assistance each day would go through every single letter sent to the FA:

> He liked to have his finger absolutely on the pulse … Not looking for any limelight, just doing the job as best he could … a really nice man but … on the surface all you would see is a hardworking businessman … strict but you knew where you stood … his general knowledge was very wide.

So why have the qualities of Follows, and his pivotal partnership with Alf, been ignored in previous histories? Probably because they inconveniently contradicted press narratives, prevalent since the 1950s, painting the English FA as unfit for purpose. But for close observer Pat Day, the two had clear similarities. Alf, like Denis Follows, came across as:

> Very quiet, very modest, just got on and did his job and ignored the media as best he could. I've always said that the reason he was so successful in 1966 was that he had players that played as a team. They didn't do it for themselves, or for their agents to get them more money, they did it because they absolutely respected Alf Ramsey.[33]

Follows, like Alf, rose through hard work, although from a more conventional background. Born in 1908, census records show Follows's father as a stationmaster and several relatives as railway workers. He went to school in Lincoln, university in Nottingham, and in the 1930s led various British and international National Union of Students (NUS) conferences and initiatives.[34] Follows taught in grammar schools before 1939, then held leadership and training roles in the wartime RAF (*Lincolnshire Echo* 2 January 1967), as had Winterbottom. Yet, unlike Winterbottom, from 1946 until 1962, Follows gained rich experience beyond football by leading the new professional trade union BALPA (the British Airline Pilots' Association). That entailed promoting international aviation co-operation,[35] and in 1950 earned Follows an MBE.[36] His daughter also described the family never having 'missed the TUC annual conference ... BALPA had to be represented ... that was our summer holiday'. Unsurprisingly, their family newspaper was the *Daily Herald*, a left-leaning daily which, after Alf Ramsey's appointment, noted he had 'risen from Sunday morning football to the most vital and challenging Soccer job in the land' (*Daily Herald* 26 October 1962). Alf may subsequently have won England the World Cup, by managing what happened on the pitch, but as shown below it was largely through Denis Follows's leadership that he was appointed in the first place. It was also only through Follows's political and administrative skills that the FA successfully hosted the tournament, and enabled England's winning preparations.

For example, Follows's trade unionism and quiet Christianity, as 'a very regular churchgoer', helped build a productive working relationship with Minister of Sport Denis Howell, the UK's first in that role and its Labour postholder from 1964–70. Both were from 'Chapel backgrounds' and 'used to sing hymns together in the back of the car going around the country to various events'.[37] Even more significantly, and in parallel with how Alf eschewed popularity in pursuit of what seemed right, Follows's BALPA trade union leadership had been successful in very challenging areas. He agitated for better safety measures and improved working conditions, represented individual pilots at crash investigations, and organised industrial action (e.g. *Birmingham Post* 25 October 1958, *Daily Herald* 24 November 1961). Particularly pertinent to the world of football, even after becoming FA secretary, Follows represented and supported Captain Thain, the pilot scapegoated for the 1958 Munich air disaster, 'because he was sure there'd been a miscarriage of justice'.[38] Three England international footballers died, and 20 more Manchester United players, officials and others were killed or injured in the accident but Follows consistently, sometimes unpopularly, supported Thain (e.g. *Daily News* 13 April 1959, *Western Morning News* 6 February 1961). In 1969, Thain was eventually cleared of all blame (*Daily Express* 11 June).

Like the Alf Ramsey seen in previous chapters, Follows was also on the professionally progressive wing of English football. He wanted the FA to recognise Sunday football[39] and in 1971 persuaded it to allow women's football,[40] becoming 'a great friend to the Women's Football Association … a Life Vice-President'.[41] In short, far from being the 'officious mediocrity' painted by McKinstry, Follows was a skilled, forceful leader of change, akin to another quiet radical he appointed: Alf Ramsey. As a close-up observer from 1965–66 recently testified:

> They were both very mild mannered … men of few words …
> not clipped or standoffish but … whatever scenario they listened
> intently, took everything in, and their comments coming back
> … were just a rifle shot to the heart of the matter.[42]

The England Manager Who Never Was: Jimmy Adamson

All previous books about Alf, and many about football's wider history, uncritically repeat a story spawned by FA official records but screaming for scrutiny. Why? Because it fits neither football logic nor Denis Follows's character. This previously unchallenged narrative has Jimmy Adamson, Burnley captain and Winterbottom's hastily appointed assistant coach at the 1962 World Cup in Chile, formally being offered the England manager's job before Alf.[43] But despite stemming from published 'FA Council Minutes' of 1 October 1962,[44] the story shows intriguing inconsistencies, its riddles unsolved for decades, perhaps because of the secrecy that surrounds elite role recruitment. Finding the best candidate to manage the England team during its first home World Cup, following four tournament failures, was always going to be a challenging process.

Yet some things are clear. In the autumn of 1961, Winterbottom did not refute press stories that if he became FA secretary, as everyone thought he would, his chosen successor as England manager would be Billy Wright, England veteran of 105 caps and already England's under-23 and youth-team manager (*Aberdeen Express* 2 September, *Daily Mirror* 29 November). Shortly after Winterbottom's FA secretary campaign unexpectedly failed, in February 1962, Wright decided to become Arsenal manager (*Daily Mirror* 17 March). On 18 March the *Sunday Telegraph* then carried a telephone interview with Alf, citing his England manager potential 'if Mr. Winterbottom resigns'. Meanwhile, perhaps specifically to counter that option, Walter began frantically to promote Jimmy Adamson.[45] At some point after that, perhaps during England's 1962 World Cup preparations and campaign, did Winterbottom prime Adamson to become the next England manager, without the FA's knowledge or permission?

That seems likely and is explained below, but Follows had prepared contingency plans. On 30 July 1962, Winterbottom communicated his resignation, just before it went public (*Liverpool Echo* 1 August). Yet within 48 hours, Follows had decisively split Winterbottom's previous jobs into two, advertised them, requested more time from league clubs for the new manager to train England players, and secured an attractive salary for that person 'to keep moving forward toward a strong England' (*Daily Mirror* 3 August). By 8 August, two six-person FA selection panels had been appointed, FA chairperson Graham Doggart leading both. Applications would close on 31 August, and on 20 September the recruitment panels would agree shortlists.[46]

Retrospect strongly suggests media leaks from the recruitment panel. Why else, after applications had closed but before applicant selection had happened, would a major newspaper have published in-depth interviews about the role with two leading candidates who had *not* applied: Joe Mercer and Alf Ramsey (*Daily Mail* September 10–11 and 13–14 1962)? In his interview, Alf effectively exploded the official recruitment process halfway through by making a remarkable 1966 prediction examined in the next chapter: 'I think we can win' (14 September). As those fateful 1 October FA Council minutes recorded, things then went awry. Despite reviewing 59 applications on 20 September, the minutes claimed, 'the Committee' had rejected them and 'decided therefore to approach Mr. J. Adamson'. Two days before the FA Council's 1 October meeting, someone had already leaked that 'Adamson ... approach' to the *Daily Mail* (29 September). Perhaps Winterbottom or an ally, to create momentum? Confusion reigned, with the same council minutes recording Adamson 'was not willing to be considered'. FA chairperson Doggart had anyway instantly claimed the FA 'had not definitely decided to give Adamson the job' (*Daily Mirror* 2 October). What was going on?

A recent study asserted that 'only the FA's track record' of consistently 'bad decisions can explain why Doggart and his committee chased Adamson'.[47] This assumes they genuinely 'chased' him, despite no documentary evidence of that process surviving. Jimmy Greaves, an England star player at the time, thought Adamson was 'simply too nice' for such a challenging job.[48] Adamson himself, although picked by Winterbottom for the 1962 World Cup as a player and assistant coach (*Daily Herald* 30 March 1962), after the tournament publicly wanted to continue playing, not work for the FA (*Newcastle Journal* 21 July 1962). He remained 'mystified' by Winterbottom's England plans for him, even 50 years later:

> Winterbottom always wanted me to take the England training sessions ... odd as I was only in my late 20s ... at the pre-match meetings when he announced the team, I sat there waiting for my name to appear, but it never did ... I've often wondered why ... When he left the position he recommended me as England manager, but I turned it down.[49]

Adamson's revelations perhaps solve this football 'whodunnit'. Might Winterbottom, smarting after his February 1962 FA election failure and eager to maintain influence, simply have 'gone rogue' in the summer of 1962, and informally offered Adamson the job? Adamson, unlike Alf, had frequented FA coaching courses at Lilleshall,[50] and been a 'personal friend' of Winterbottom's since 1948 (*Daily Mail* 29 September 1962).

Despite this appalling public mess, the pragmatic Follows did not panic. He may even have used Adamson's 'refusal' further to pressurise FA councillors to cede England team selection to a new manager. Both Alf Ramsey and Joe Mercer, the leading candidates who had not officially applied, had demanded that change during recent media interviews (*Daily Mail* September 10–14). Significantly, after the abortive FA recruitment committee meeting of 20 September, it was leaked to the same newspaper that the FA would probably agree to managerial control of selection (24 September).

The English FA's own official history lends support for a possible Winterbottom 'rogue offer' to Adamson because he had strayed similarly before, approaching Ron Greenwood in 1961 to become his successor.[51] A well-known journalist, talking with Winterbottom after the 1962 World Cup, has also been cited 'speculating on who would take over ... I don't think Alf Ramsey's name was mentioned', Winterbottom instead confirming 'we went for Jimmy Adamson'.[52]

An official, anonymised FA source also revealed 'the Burnley captain was not a unanimous choice at the FA', some members wanting 'a man with more experience. *The England manager*, said one, *should know his job NOW*.'[53]

Which all helps explain why a discreet FA backchannel to Alf seems to have been active from about mid-September, evidenced by his later confession to 'having thought about' the England job offer 'for a whole month' (*Sunday Mirror* 19 April 1970). As Doggart's first interview with Alf was on 17 October, two days after Follows had attended an FA committee meeting ceding team selection to the new manager, perhaps Follows started talks with Alf on 20 September? Certainly, Follows's 26 October personalised letter, offering Alf the England job, contained the crucial binding clause, 'You will have full responsibility for the selection of the England team.'[54]

All this fractures former assumptions that Adamson was genuinely offered the England job. Despite having to juggle complex FA Council politics, would Follows, given his 15 years of experience leading complex trade union negotiations, have risked him or Doggart offering a pivotal leadership role, during England's first World Cup hosting, through an off-the-cuff job offer to someone who had no senior England caps, nor football management experience at any level? Not only would such a gamble have been completely out of Follows's character, but Adamson himself was 'mystified' by Winterbottom's flattery. Additionally, Follows had publicly predicted when recruitment began: 'We may have to wait. We want the best man ... and he may have a club contract. If a man would break his contract to come to us, he might just as likely break his contract with us' (*Daily Mirror* 3 August 1962). Whilst letting the recruitment process follow its official but unproductive course, at just the right moments Follows seems to have initiated discreet discussions with Alf, whilst simultaneously persuading the FA Council to abdicate team selection powers. These were impressive influencing and negotiation skills, perhaps of a kind learned through successful trade unionism?

Alf Ramsey, Denis Follows, and Much Ado about Table Mats

Despite plentiful evidence indicating Alf's strong relationship with Follows, a strange story about 1966 World Cup table mats has disproportionately coloured how history views Denis Follows. It originated with Neil Phillips, medical doctor to England's senior team from 1968–74. Phillips's self-published autobiography cited the story three times,[55] and in McKinstry's *Sir Alf* biography it dominated perspectives on Follows. Another major work recently repeated it, arguing that as an example of FA incompetency 'nothing was more egregious than the saga of the commemorative mats'.[56] But might Phillips's original account have been imbalanced, and its importance exaggerated, so skewing our perceptions of Denis Follows, Alf Ramsey and the 1960s FA?

McKinstry's retelling inaccurately placed the event 'several months after' the 1966 World Cup Final and, more importantly, depictedFollows unfairly. It featured Alf, his two assistants and Dr Phillips, packing kit into the basement at the FA's Lancaster Gate headquarters. Alf, McKinstry said, spotted some 'crested boxes on the shelves' and 'moments later Denis Fellows [sic] came in'. When Alf asked what they were, Follows replied, 'Aerial photographs of all the World Cup grounds in England … made into table mats.' Alf asked, 'Could you give each member of my staff a set?', and supposedly Follows retorted, wrote McKinstry, 'Oh no, Alf, you and your staff don't qualify. These mats are only for the directors of the FA and visiting dignitaries. You can't have any.'[57]

Yet documentary records show Follows was correct about the mats being produced for FA Council members and foreign guests.[58] Phillips's original account also described Follows twice saying 'sorry' to Alf and dated the incident 18 months later than McKinstry's version; details that might not matter had McKinstry not labelled Follows 'an officious nobody',[59] based largely on this incident. Additionally, Phillips's testimony appears biased even in the light of evidence from his own voluminous autobiography. This described several disagreements, blamed by Phillips on Follows and the FA, but for which closer reading suggests he, and sometimes Alf, should perhaps share blame.[60] For example, the day after England lost their summer 1968 European Championship semi-final, Alf asked of Phillips a massive favour, namely 'to confirm my acceptance of the position of Honorary Team Physician to the Senior England team. He explained the position would be an honorary one. No payment was ever likely, in his opinion, from The Football Association.'[61] Despite Alf clearly warning 'no payment was ever likely', in successive chapters Phillips then berated Follows and the FA for not paying him a salary.[62] Other, minor disputes were also catalogued about travel claims,[63] the FA's storage of medical poisons,[64] and two of Phillips's free tickets for the coveted England v Scotland fixture at Wembley somehow ending up being used by the 'notorious ticket spiv Mr. S. Flashman'.[65]

There were obviously tensions, but perhaps sparked not by a ridiculous row over table mats, so much as Follows questioning Phillips over professional matters: particularly, his sheer capacity to doctor at all England's matches, advise regular London-based FA meetings, maintain being a full-time GP in Middlesbrough, and simultaneously juggle two other additional roles – those were 'Director and Medical Officer at Middlesborough [sic] Football Club', and 'part time medical officer at ICI' (Imperial Chemical Industries).[66] Given Phillips quickly used all his annual leave to fulfil those, then had to negotiate further unpaid absences with long-suffering GP partners, Follows's questioning seems professionally reasonable. Was Phillips logistically and physically capable of doing everything the FA needed, especially preparing for the Mexico 1970 World Cup, whilst working at all those other jobs, too?[67] Phillips himself admitted that Alf, in requesting his unpaid assistance, 'was asking me to achieve the impossible … to climb Everest!'[68] Yet he criticised Follows for scrutinising the arrangement, not Alf for requesting it. He also jealously recalled how, having already used his annual leave on England matters, in the summer of 1968 he had to watch as 'Alf departed with Denis Follows to Mexico observing the Olympic Games. I should have gone with them.'[69]

Certainly, Follows should gracefully have given Alf and Dr Phillips some table mats. In classic 1970s sitcom style, the FA subsequently over-ordered, and by 1974 most staff leavers 'got a set of these flipping mats … they were not locked up, just down in the basement because there was so many'.[70] Yet friction between Phillips and Follows arose from matters deeper than table mats. Phillips was patently envious of the capable, details-focused FA secretary, who had appointed Alf and then built a successful, close, working relationship with him. McKinstry quoted Phillips as claiming 'Alf's relationship with Denis Follows was awful from the start',[71] yet further evidence below shows that was untrue.

Ramsey and Follows: England's Winning Team

Given the English FA's centrality to football, and football's importance to many people's sense of Englishness, the FA has curated strikingly little documentary evidence from its own history. Desiccated committee summaries are publicly available, but practically none of the informal correspondence or discussion behind them. In such absence, personal testimony, and oral history, become historically significant. Pat Day, Denis Follows's 1970–73 secretary and later a senior FA figure, recalled that Alf and Denis:

> Got on quite well, I can't remember that they didn't … Alf was very much a person. I'm not saying Denis wasn't, but he was more of a strict administrator … slightly different kinds of characters … Alf, the people who worked with him liked him an awful lot.[72]

Margaret Fulljames was Alf's administrative FA secretary from 1967–74, but also knew Denis Follows well. Her perspective was simple, in that 'you would trust Denis Follows with your life'. Far from finding him the 'wishy-washy sort of person' described by McKinstry,[73] in some detail she recounted the opposite: a fair, strict, oddly charismatic leader with a 'little round red face and glasses … not a big man physically' but he had 'an aura'. His formality meant 'a lot of the men were quite scared of him', and Margaret recalled one FA middle manager 'literally shaking, terrified of him … most of the men were … it was very old school'. Alf 'would go into Dennis [sic] Follows office when they needed to meet' and in her experience 'Alf never said anything against him ever'.

Another witness who saw the two men together on several occasions, out of the FA offices, thought them markedly comfortable in each other's company. John Wood was Denis Follows's summertime office assistant and chauffeur in 1965 (for six weeks) and 1966 (for about ten weeks). He had just started a PhD at Bristol, was a family friend and played Sunday cricket with Follows. Because Wood:

> Saw and rubbed shoulders with Denis many times before and after the World Cup … there were a few occasions where I could watch them together … At the FA in Lancaster Gate in 1965 I saw him a couple of times in conversation with Alf. Then in 1966 we had a trip where Alf was in the car around Manchester, and particularly down at Wembley, when England was playing, Alf was around all the time, and they would brush into each other and chat.

Based on those observations, Wood described the two being:

Very easy and comfortable in each other's company … just used
to chat like two old friends. I did not hear the conversations
particularly, but they were very comfortable … Both were
extremely mild mannered, there were no histrionics and never
any shouting or raised voices … I never heard mutterings [about
Alf] … as about Thompson.[74]

Furthermore, in retrospect Wood testified how:

When Alf came up in conversation, glowing is a bit dramatic,
but Denis always spoke of Alf favourably … Denis regarded Alf
as a project that had succeeded for the FA … he was chuffed Alf
was the manager. He felt he had a lot of skin in the selection
of Alf … that Alf was his project and his baby … his preferred
nominee.

Denis's daughter Maggie echoed that: 'Alf coming from the background
he came from ticked my dad's boxes because Dad was always a great
believer in people achieving their ultimate potential, regardless of their
background, because that is what he did.'[75] Did Follows's knowledge of
'Alf's background' extend to GRT rumours about the Ramsey family?
Plausibly 'yes' given several different journalists from the 1960s onwards
knew and talked of those.[76]

Denis's and Alf's professional relationship also included regular co-
working. Here they are on 5 February 1963, in a committee selecting
the England team before Alf started the job full-time. Follows, literally,
is Alf's right-hand man.

More significantly, during his first calendar year (1963), Alf and Follows together attended, and would have prepared for and followed up, 21 FA committees on 18 different dates: 'International' (four), 'International Senior' (four), 'Under-23' (six), 'Youth' (five) and 'Selection Senior' (one).

Additionally, they would have met at most England matches, at key annual governance points like the FA Council, and events such as the FA's 1963 100th anniversary game and celebration. That pattern persisted in 1964, mutually attending most of 16 selection and planning committees, then continued into 1965 (17 committees) and 1966 (19 committees).

The 1966 balance shifted as World Cup tournament delivery intensified, with both men attending most of 11 'International Senior committee' meetings, and four of the 'International Committee'. It was, for example, the 4 April 1966 International (Senior) Committee, attended by Follows, Alf, an FA secretary and six FA Council and League representatives, that officially informed FIFA of England's 40 named squad players, then discussed this timetable of preparations:

(b) It was agreed that the clubs be informed that none of the above players would be available for their clubs after the 14th May except in respect of the following:—
    F.A. Cup Final—Replay
    European Champion Clubs' Cup Competition Final—Replay
    European Cup Winners' Cup Final—Replay
    Inter-Cities Fairs Cup Final—Ties and Replay.

(c) The following programme for the World Cup Squad was approved:—
    May 15th to June 5th—All players to have a complete rest.
    June 6th—Players to assemble at Lilleshall for special training until 17th June.
    June 20th—Players to re-assemble at the Hendon Hall Hotel, London, until 24th June when the Party will leave for its Continental Tour for the following matches:—
        June 26th—Finland v. England at Helsinki
        June 29th—Norway v. England at Oslo
        July 3rd—Denmark v. England at Copenhagen
        July 5th—Poland v. England at Warsaw.
    July 6th—Players be permitted to return to their homes.
    July 8th—Players re-assemble at the Hendon Hall Hotel, London.

Conclusion

The nature of England's 1966 World Cup win, and Alf Ramsey's place in it, are discussed in chapter 12. This chapter has shown how, in laying the foundations, he and Denis Follows were outsiders and underdogs, with their paths to power paved by sheer hard graft. Both were also essentially modest, moral characters; in Alf's case, so modest that he never applied for the England job, and moral because doing so would have entailed disloyalty to Ipswich.

On his FA accession, Denis Follows had been headlined the 'NEW MR SOCCER' (*Birmingham Sports Argus* 24 February 1962). Citing his trade union leadership, Birmingham FA Council member Edward 'Teddy' Eden, himself proposed for FA chairperson in 1963,[77] explained 'the idea in appointing him was clearly to have someone from the outside world'. Eden, 'one of football's progressives',[78] viewed Follows as a fellow moderniser (see also *Birmingham Post* 1 November 1958). In early 1963, another leading regional newspaper similarly noted how, within 12 months of Follows's appointment, the FA 'was taking a very different approach to some of their problems compared with ... their predecessors' (*Leicester Mercury* 16 February). Follows, like Alf, spoke modernising truth to old-fashioned power, whether within his own FA organisation or to the UK government. In February 1964, and timed for the imminent general election, Follows publicly argued to the Conservative government:

> Football in this country has not progressed as it has in most other countries ... stadia and facilities are completely out of date ... Not one stadium measures up to the requirements of this modern television age ... at national level the game is crying out for a medical and research centre.[79]

His positioning paid off. After the election and as seen previously, Follows quickly built a warm relationship with Labour's new minister for sport. That brought tangible results such as 'World Class Grounds For World Cup – Soccer's Future and Problems To Be Studied – SPORTS MINISTER PLEDGES HELP' (*Nottingham Journal* 10 February 1965).

During the 1960s, Follows was also personally closer to England's playing and management team than previously acknowledged. Harold Shepherdson, Alf's assistant manager and England's trainer from 1957–74, testified 'the original idea' for having a team doctor at all England games 'came from the fertile mind of Mr Denis Follows ... early in January 1963'.[80] Shepherdson describes Follows, when two players were injured at the England v Scotland match on 6 April 1963, personally applying cold compresses, then running around the pitch to fetch a knee bandage. Three months later, Follows negotiated the 31-strong England party through passport problems at the Czech border.[81] In 1965, Nobby Stiles lost his tour bag the day before England played Sweden. Follows phoned home, his daughter bought replacement lubricant for Stiles's contact lenses and dropped it at London Airport (*The Guardian* 10 April

2020). There it was 'handed to the pilot on the next flight to Sweden ... in time for Nobby to play a storming game'.[82]

Unfortunately, journalists have consistently sidelined Follows. McKinstry's slant on that incident, written 40 years later, claimed it was Alf who 'made arrangements for more fluid' yet only Follows, with multiple airline connections and a family living near Heathrow, could possibly have done so. Referring to Alf's 1974 sacking, which happened nearly a year after Follows had actually retired, McKinstry also unfairly painted Follows as 'not a man whom Alf liked or admired', and 'too weak to be able to challenge Alf seriously'.[83] Yet no evidence shows Follows ever wanting to challenge Alf Ramsey, the opposite being true. Follows eloquently empathised with the impossibility of the England manager's role, rebuking national over-expectation and using the FA's own national magazine as a platform for Alf's stout defence (*FA News* July 1972).

Other writers unfortunately followed McKinstry's hyper-critical route. Glanville (2008) traduced Follows as someone with 'no real background in football, scant authority and no innovative dynamism'.[84] Even Geoff Hurst believed Follows, on the day of the World Cup Final, had not known 'which full back was which' in England's own team,[85] a myth overlooking the inconvenient fact that Follows was partially blind in one eye (*The Guardian* 10 April 2020).

Perhaps Follows has become a sacrificial scapegoat in the crossfire of an unhistorical culture war? A popular struggle against the FA was for decades waged by journalists, and players, justifiably angry about how Alf was sacked and his closest colleagues mistreated. When Harold Shepherdson resigned in 1974, he returned the wristwatch Ted Croker's FA had bought him and asked for the money instead. He received a cheque for £39.50 and remained bitter until his death about his and Alf's appalling mistreatment.[86] Equally, Denis Follows had long gone before the FA bought Shepherdson an unwisely cheap wristwatch, and Follows had nothing to do with Alf's sacking. It was also FIFA's responsibility and decision, not the FA's, that Alf Ramsey, Shepherdson and the wider 1966 squad did not receive World Cup victory medals until 2009. If Alf 'had lived, we might have got them a bit sooner' commented Jimmy Greaves (*The Guardian* 10 June).

Sooner still, it might be thought now, had Denis Follows lived, too.

1 *Dictionary of National Biography* (2019)

2 Hayward, P. (2022) pp.65, 247

3 Ibid. pp.173-77

4 *Dictionary of National Biography* (2019); Hayward, P. (2022) p.144

5 E.g. *Portsmouth Evening News* 1 October 1934, *The Sphere* 29 February 1936, *Lincolnshire Echo* 7 February 1938

6 Edworthy, N. (2000) p.59

7 Morse, G. (2016) pp.33-4

8 Edworthy, N. (2000) pp.15-16

9 Glanville, B. (2008) p.19

10 Morse, G. (2016) pp.103-5

11 Ibid. p.108

12 Ibid. p.277

13 Glanville, B. (2008) p.18

14 McKinstry, L. (2007) pp.373-84

15 Hayward, P. (2022) p.128

16 Ibid. pp.128-9

17 Russell, D. (1997) pp.148-151

18 Hamilton, D. (2023) pp.25-27

19 Ramsey, A. (1952) p.36

20 Morse, G. (2016) pp.134-5

21 Ibid. p.229

22 Ibid. p.130

23 Ibid. pp.256-9

24 e.g. *Daily Herald* or *Newcastle Journal* 29 September 1961, *Scunthorpe Evening Telegraph* 17 February 1962, *Sunday Pictorial* or *The Observer* 18 February 1962, *Daily Mail* 19 February 1962

25 McKinstry, L. (2007) p.197

26 Marquis, M. (1970) p.65

27 See chapters 13-14

28 Morse, G. (2016) p.257

29 John Wood oral history interview 26 January 2023

30 Glanville, B. (2008) p.11

31 1950s FA minutes show Follows's varied voluntary FA roles: instructional committee, amateur international selection committee, managing the Universities Athletic Football Team, FA Council representative, Honorary Treasurer

32 Day, P. (2000)

33 Pat Day oral history interview 13 January 2023

34 E.g. *Nottingham Evening Post* 6 October 1930, *Yorkshire Post* 17 August 1934, *Nottingham Journal* 17 April 1938

35 I am indebted to Margaret Ferris, Denis Follows's daughter, for sharing BALPA (July 1962) *The Log* Volume 22 (7) and her oral history interview of 24 January 2023

36 *London Gazette* 2 June 1950 p.17

37 Margaret Ferris oral history interview 24 January 2023

38 Ibid.

39 e.g. *Birmingham Daily Post* 1 November 1958, 23 February 1960

40 Wrack, S. (2023) pp.83-85

41 History of the Women's Football Association website (no date) 'Charting the key developments in women's football from 1968 to 1993'

42 John Wood oral history interview 26 January 2023

43 E.g. Hutchinson, R. (1995) p.58, McKinstry, L. (2007) p.197, Glanville, B. (2008) p.30, Hayward, P. (2022) p.147

44 **FA Council minutes** 1 October 1962

45 Morse, G. (2016) pp.277-8

46 **FA Consultative Committee minutes** 8 August 1962 pp.98-99

47 Hamilton, D. (2023) p.102

48 Greaves, J. with Giller, N. (1993) p.29

49 Thomas, D. (2013) p.73

50 Morse, G. (2016) p.277

51 Butler, B. (1991) pp.135-6

52 Bowler, D. (1999) pp.149-50

53 Butler, B. (1991) pp.135-6

54 BBC News website (18 June 2018) 'World Cup winner Sir Alf Ramsey's England job letter fetches £3,400'

55 Phillips, N. (2007) pp.284-5, 534, 537-8

56 Hamilton, D. (2023) p.108

57 McKinstry, L. (2007) p.371

58 **FA Council minute** 26 September 1966

59 McKinstry, L. (2007) p.197

60 Phillips, N. (2007) pp.289-91

61 Ibid. p.289

62 Ibid. e.g. pp.278, 284, 297, 383, 473, 553-4

63 Ibid. p.324

64 Ibid. pp.324-6

65 Ibid. p.327

66 Ibid. p.291

67 Ibid. pp.289 and 290

68 Ibid. p.295

69 Ibid. p.296

70 Margaret Fulljames oral history interview 20 January 2023

71 McKinstry, L. (2007) pp.370-71

72 Pat Day oral history interview 13 January 2023

73 McKinstry, L. (2007) p.197

74 John Wood oral history interview 26 January 2023

75 Maggie Ferris oral history interview 23 January 2023

76 See chapters 1-4

77 **FA Council minutes** 29 June 1963

78 *Birmingham Sports Argus* 29 January 1966, also *Daily Mirror* 23 January 1959

79 **FA Minutes and Proceedings** 1966-67 'Report to be submitted to the Government Committee of Inquiry into the state of association football', Appendix C, February 1964

80 Shepherdson, H. (1968) pp.42-3

81 Ibid. pp.125, 128

82 Ibid. pp.148-9

83 McKinstry, L. (2007) pp.302 and 467

84 Glanville, B. (2008) p.33

85 Hurst, G. (2024) p.158

86 Phillips, N. (2007) p.554

CHAPTER 12

AN UNEXPECTED HERO

Alf's Unlikely World Triumph

Perpetual Jeopardy?

IF ENGLAND had failed in 1966, how might Alf Ramsey's story have changed? Alf the footballer had never acknowledged his racist nickname, and Alf the manager refused to discuss his family background. His silence muffled Fleet Street rumours, but history suggests failure would have changed that. For example, Brazil's unexpected home World Cup Final defeat, in 1950, signalled 'a recrudescence of racism' during which three Black Brazilian players became 'sacrificial lambs singled out'.[1] Seven decades later, 2021 England echoed 1950 Brazil, when three Black English players failed with penalties in the delayed Euro 2020 Final. All were targeted for online, racist abuse, despite 'the multi-racial make-up of the squad' having been 'hailed as reflecting a more diverse modern Britain'.[2] Why would 1966 have been any different, with England's manager offering the easiest target?

Modern England has conveniently forgotten how, until the 1966 tournament kicked off, Alf was 'the most abused man in England … public scapegoat number one' (*The Tatler* 14 May 1966). Because journalists knew of Alf's nickname and rumoured GRT background, in defeat those rumours would likely have leaked out. In March 1969, after even just a few poor games, Alf endured people throwing 'orange peel and apple cores at me' on a crowded train (*Sunday Mirror* 19 April 1970). When England's results worsened further, Alf experienced acidic 'bombardment from Fleet Street' and subsequent managers suffered increasingly 'ill-informed, vicious abuse'.[3] By 1992, 'total belittlement' had become mainstream, epitomised by 'Graham Taylor's head depicted as a turnip … a new level of ignominy' (*The Times* 13 January 2017). Previous chapters showed Alf's 'D****e' nickname as racist, that 1930s contemporaries used it, and how, from the 1950s, journalists knew of it, especially after its 1969 resurfacing on national television. In 1970, Alf's first biographer wrote, 'Maybe there is something behind the story of Ramsey looking so much like a Red Indian.'[4] England's 1966 captain, on a crowded team bus in 1973, mocked Alf as a Gypsy.

As a football obsessive, Alf rose above such undercurrents using meticulous professionalism and rigid control to 'ignore all the chatter ... soon ... you will be able to detach yourself sufficiently to be unaffected'.[5] All of which emphasises that Alf only ever took calculated risks. A good example is a September 1962 public statement that electrified the stalling England manager recruitment process. Alf predicted that, in 1966, easy travel and familiar food and climate would put things 'very much on our side'. If the Football League and FA could collaborate 'to give England proper time for preparation – I think we can win' (*Daily Mail* 14 September 1962). Alf's interviewer that day became one of the few journalists who agreed, despite almost universal press scepticism.[6] But in January 1963, now as England manager, Alf repeated his prediction on BBC television: 'I think with all sincerity ... England will win the World Cup in London in 1966' (*Sunday Mirror* 6 January 1963). That performance was recently described as 'uncharacteristically careless' and 'a bluff',[7] based partly on Alf himself later claiming that it was impromptu (*Sunday Mirror* 19 April 1970). But impromptu predictions cannot be made twice or more, as happened during Alf's first year.[8] Alternatively, it was just Alf doing what he always did and telling the truth as he saw it, a thread returned to towards the end of this chapter.

As England's new manager, Alf had inherited demoralised players and frustrated fans. One journalist recalled a 'curious anti-England feeling' at late 1950s international matches, with many spectators just 'waiting for an excuse to boo the national team'.[9] Another confessed, whilst interviewing Alf:

> When the chips are really down ... in all four post-war World Cups [England] never went beyond the quarter final and won only three ties ... out of 14 ... each time I returned in bitter disappointment because we fell so short.

He found Alf's persona puzzling. Superficially, Alf seemed 'formal, phlegmatic and shy to the point of aloofness' but 'put him in a track suit ... and he throws off 20 years. Get him talking football and you unearth a fierce and fervid creature' (*Leicester Mercury* 16 February 1963). Alf could communicate such fierceness to his players, and bind them together, by predicting England could win: 'If I showed confidence in them, they would have confidence in me and each other.'

Alf valued such mutual interdependence for practical reasons. His 'main objective' was always to retain the 'respect and confidence' of his players, and 'never let them down', because 'without their confidence we will not win matches and then I am unemployed' (*Sunday Mirror* 19 April 1970). Alf's management style to secure that had been developed and demonstrated at Ipswich: acute observation of matches, clinical feedback to players, detailed preparations and prioritising team dynamics over individual skills. His several confident 1962–63 statements about England should therefore be seen similarly, as an evidence-based strategy to prompt proper World Cup preparation, and force England's players and public to think differently. By 1966, the strategy was working, with much of the eventual 'confidence' around the tournament coming from 'Alf Ramsey's prediction that England would win'; his positivity prompted 'buoyancy of spirit'.[10] It increased the psychological pressure on England's players, but they were 'operating in a high-pressure situation anyway', which 'would only tighten the further England advanced'.[11] As one judged recently, 'Not for a second do I think Alf's forecast weighed on the players.'[12] Twelve months after Alf's first airing of England as potential winners, even the FA's newly elected chairperson chose to echo him: 'I am quite sure we can win the World Cup. Of course we can' (*Daily Herald* 1 October 1963).

Progress?

Alf started managing England on 31 December 1962 but also continued at Ipswich until April 1963. An FA committee therefore 'assisted' England team selection until he started full-time. His (and its) first game, in late February 1963, was a disastrous 5-2 loss to France that eliminated England from the European Championship. England's only competitive tournament before 1966 would now be the lop-sided British Home Championship. England then lost their next match to ten-man Scotland at Wembley, with one newspaper condemning England's players as a 'pathetic, groping bunch of individualists who will never make a first-class Soccer team' (*The People* 7 April 1963). Alf's only consolation was that FA committee involvement vindicated his sole control of future selection. Nevertheless, debutant Banks in goal, Moore in defence and Bobby Charlton in attack would become cornerstones in the 1966 and 1970 World Cups. In England's next match, a 1-1 home friendly with Brazil, Ramsey re-introduced a fourth 1966 victor, full-back Ray Wilson. Wilson, Charlton and Moore had all played during England's lacklustre 1962 World Cup, and its quarter-final loss to Brazil. Roger Hunt, ever-present in 1966, had also been in that 1962 squad. What was Alf doing differently in these opening months?

He picked new players, like Banks, but also demanded ultra-professionalism. Although that 1963 draw with Brazil was only Banks's second cap, Alf was stringently critical of him: 'Before the game we had studied the Brazilian team in close detail, and I discussed repeatedly … the free kick technique of their left winger.' When Brazil scored exactly the goal Banks had been coached against conceding, Alf was 'furious'. He stayed silent at half-time, wanting 'to calm the players down … but after the match I went for Gordon'. Such sharp feedback then helped Banks, he claimed, to become 'the greatest goalkeeper I've ever seen' (*Sunday Mirror* 3 May 1970). Alf's forensic coaching had outdone even the fanatically self-improving Banks.[13]

Alf had a simple mantra, preached bluntly and universally throughout his management reign: 'Skill WITHOUT detailed preparation foreshadows disaster' (*FA News* June 1971). He had said similar before it even started, in those mid-September 1962 newspaper interviews alluded to above. Whilst laying out what any new England manager needed, Alf used the terms 'rigid', 'set', 'method', 'plan' and 'system' 17 times. Perhaps incredulously, his interviewer remarked, 'You use the word rigid often. Do you believe it essential for really good players to have a set plan?' Alf's emphatic confirmation that he did harked back to his personal experience of England's disastrous 1950 World Cup debut: 'England's team was good then, but it would have been many times better' supported by 'a rigid plan' (*Daily Mail* 14 September 1962). Just as Gareth Southgate's England managerial career was characterised, in the 2023 drama 'Dear England', as shaped by his saved 1996 semi-final penalty,[14] so Alf's England management was steeped in his personal, 1950 playing calamity. Right from that 1962 interview, up to planning England's 1974 World Cup campaign, Alf never let go of his 1950 hurt: 'After all,' he asked, 'was I not a member of the England team which crashed 0-1 to the USA?' (*FA News* November 1970).

Reverting to Alf's England managerial beginnings in 1963, after drawing with Brazil he alone picked England teams. They won eight games before losing to Scotland on 11 April 1964. Four more straight wins followed but England were again humiliated when it mattered, in a three-match Brazil-based friendly tournament starting on 30 May 1964. The hosts thrashed them 5-1, Argentina beat them 1-0, and a 1-1 draw was scraped with Portugal. England would beat both Argentina and Portugal in the 1966 World Cup knockout stages. What underlay that turnaround?

Traumas and Turnarounds 1964–66

Alf's mindset always prioritised his players. Even when that 1966 World Cup Final whistle blew, he recalled, 'Everyone around me was going mad,' but 'I stayed watching from the Wembley touchline bench … My pleasure was looking at the players … getting so much enjoyment just out of watching them' (*Sunday Mirror* 3 April 1970). How had Alf honed his winners?

Progress zigzagged, but after that disastrous 1964 Brazil tour, England won five and drew five. May 1965 was particularly cheerful, with three wins and a draw against European opponents in just 11 days. England's World Cup prospects had previously been 'a write-off' and Brazil were still favourites, but bookmakers were now 'offering odds no longer than 5-1 … Pacesetters in this new Ramsey-built England are Nobby Stiles, Jackie Charlton and Moore' (*The People* 16 May 1965). Bobby Charlton had long played for England but brother Jack, a steely Leeds United centre-half, was aged nearly 30 before he and Stiles debuted on 10 April 1965. Their defensive strengths and ball-winning qualities would prove crucial platforms for stylish passing from the Bobbys, Moore and Charlton.[15] But a goalless draw with lowly Wales, on 2 October 1965, shredded media confidence. 'Alf Ramsey's dreams of world conquest look as far from realisation as ever' (*Liverpool Daily Post* 4 October 1965). Worse beckoned. After Austria won 3-2 at Wembley, overblown 21 October headlines screamed 'UNFORGIVABLE, ALF: Time to sharpen the axe' (*Manchester Evening News*), 'Heads must roll after this deplorable display' (*Birmingham Post*) and 'ENGLAND GET SLOW HANDCLAP AND JEERS' (*Belfast Newsletter*). Criticism frothed nationwide, sustained by television highlights. Fans proclaimed, 'we will not win the World Cup – that's a certainty', condemned Alf's 'collection of square pegs in round holes', and criticised 'the predictably apathetic London crowd, their vocal support conspicuous by its absence … a very sad night' (*Liverpool Echo* 27 October 1965). Six weeks later, Alf's team would brilliantly outplay Spain, the current European champions, winning 2-0 in Madrid. Why this rollercoaster?

Because his England tactics and team selection were still evolving. At Ipswich, Alf had blended aspects of Brazil's 1958 World Cup-winning 4-2-4, with a 4-3-3. This featured Jimmy Leadbetter, nominally a left-winger, spraying quick passes from deep midfield to fast, mobile forwards.[16] Alf's tactics always developed that way, prioritising the attributes of his players over theoretical formations. He had tried and failed with 4-2-4 during a 1964 English–Scottish interleague match, demonstrating that 'long hours of trial and error … are still needed'

(*Daily Herald* 19 March). Securing such safe experimental space was why Alf's England contract had demanded 'absolute control', without which 'tactical experimentation was impossible'.[17] Alf's discovery that 'although 4-2-4' could beat 'lesser sides' it then failed against 'stronger opponents', became part of a 'carefully controlled evolution towards winning the World Cup'.[18]

Craftily, Alf sometimes disguised such experimentation. Perhaps using 'high level discussions' about potential FIFA rule changes as cover, he feigned that a 1965 England training camp was preparing for a possible 'new offside rule'. As an aside he also admitted England were now practising 'a 4-3-3 system against the 4-2-4 they have been using'. Several different systems were 'being used in the world at the moment' so he wanted his 'players to understand them' (*Daily Mirror* 9 February). Because England used 4-3-3 to win the World Cup 18 months later, Alf's comments about it gain retrospective significance,[19] but he alternated formations and players right up to 1966's quarter-finals. Disciplined individuals, concerted teamwork and flexibility to respond to opponents were his hallmarks, not any single formation. When, in 1965, England beat Sweden, a Swedish observer purred that England 'are so fluid. All up in attack one moment, all back in defence the next. So elastic, so controlled' (*The People* 16 May). Seven of Alf's 11 eventual World Cup winners featured, with the now-settled defence of Banks, Wilson, Cohen, Moore and Jack Charlton, screened in midfield by Nobby Stiles and Alan Ball.

New attacking blends emerged six months later, when England played Spain on that freezing December evening, on a muddy Madrid pitch. Beforehand, one experienced journalist seriously questioned Alf's team selection, 'The most amazing England attack of his career … not one winger … Mystifying? Ridiculous? Take your choice' (*The Sun* 7 December 1965). But England's first-ever win in Spain stunned everyone and his match report dubbed Alf's 'revolutionary 4-3-3 line-up' as his 'wingless wonders … a thrilling victory, supreme in its tactical brilliance and mastery' (*The Sun* 9 December 1965). Ahead of a defensive back four 'the other six men all work in midfield as well as being the main goal scorers', an approach that depended upon high-calibre 'all-round footballers' like Bobby Charlton, Ball and Hunt (*Hull Daily Mail* 22 January 1966); but did England have enough of those? Star specialist goal-poacher Jimmy Greaves fell seriously ill with hepatitis for three months in the winter of 1965–66. Injured in England's final 1966 World Cup group game, he was replaced by the more versatile and disciplined Geoff Hurst,[20] a twist that takes this story back to Alf's upbringing.[21]

Remarkably, West Ham and England's trio of Hurst, Moore and Peters had been scouted as youngsters by another Becontree Heath local, like Alf, with a straw-dealing father and grandfather.[22] Wally St Pier, as a six-year-old, lived on Becontree Heath in 1911, later played for top amateur team Ilford, turned professional with West Ham (*Daily News* 23 April 1929) and never left. He became head scout, and Hurst's autobiography gave him 'much credit' for West Ham's 'youth scheme and culture'.[23] Hurst (aged 24) and Peters (aged 22) would score the four goals that clinched England's World Cup. Each had just eight previous caps, after late debuts in February and May 1966. Neither believed they would make England's World Cup squad.[24] Yet a year previously, Alf had publicly maintained, despite media criticism, he had 'to leave the door open for any new discovery or player who develops late' (*Sunday People* 16 May 1965). He probably had Hurst and Peters in mind, having from 1964 regularly picked both for England's youth and under-23 teams. Alf himself had been a late developer, his own 1930s talents having been missed by the same Wally St Pier who scouted Hurst, Peters and Moore.[25] Is that why Alf and Wally seem publicly never to have acknowledged each other, nor commented upon their shared Becontree Heath pasts? When the author asked Geoff Hurst directly whether either had ever talked about the other, he confessed to having 'no idea they lived closely in the same area, so this is all completely new to me'.[26] Was Alf resentful about his youthful talent being missed by the local league club or simply, as ever, obscuring his background?

Hurst and Peters were Alf's genius interventions, but not just for their crucial goals. A Peters cross created, and a Hurst header sealed, England's quarter-final win against Argentina. Two Bobby Charlton goals had secured a glittering semi-final win over Portugal, but the second came from a Hurst assist (*Manchester Evening News* 27 July 1966). A national newspaper described that game as 'the finest' at Wembley since West Ham's 1965 'European final against Munich' (*Daily Mirror* 27 July 1966). For Alf's England the omens looked good.

The Ultimate Contest?

As a brief byline, before visiting the World Cup Final an awkward question needs asking. Was 1966 a *whole World* Cup? FIFA had allocated 'just one' 1966 tournament place for 'Africa, Asia, and Oceania',[27] so in 1964 Africa as a continent, and numerous Asian countries, withdrew and boycotted it. They were protesting against FIFA's structural Euro-centric and quasi-imperial bias, amidst heightened tensions about FIFA's leniency towards apartheid South Africa. Arguably, Ghana's strong team would easily have qualified and could have triumphed[28] but ultimately, of 1966's 16 finalists, only diplomatically problematic North Korea lay outside of Europe (ten participants) and South America (five participants).[29] Because the Cold War had, since 1949, also divided Germany into East and West,[30] a pedant might argue that England's 1966 victory was gained not just over an incomplete world, but an incomplete Germany.

Even that victory stimulated controversies that will never die. Simple internet searches reveal various FIFA-approved films showcasing all the games.[31] Yet despite over 30 million UK television viewers watching England versus West Germany live,[32] and billions seeing it since, arguments persist to the present day. Should West Germany's last-minute equaliser have been disallowed for handball? Did England's third goal wholly cross the line? Thousands of blurry rewinds later, even some English players thought not.[33] In this book's quest to uncover the 'real' Alf Ramsey, of greater significance is his brief pitch-side team talk before extra time. The score stood at 2-2, England had conceded a last-minute equaliser, and some England players slumped on the soft Wembley turf, apparently exhausted and demoralised. Bobby Moore (number 6) and Jackie Charlton (number 5) are visible below.

The distinguished sportswriter Duncan Hamilton recently, elegiacally, related how rewatching films of the tournament nostalgically evoked 1960s England, but that 'myths and misconceptions' also surround it 'like a tangle of ivy'. Alf Ramsey's extra-time team talk, he argued, was one such myth. He questioned as 'fanciful' the long-accepted version of Alf telling his players, 'You've won it once. Now go and win it again.'[34]

His own interpretation starts with Geoff Hurst's stage-performed recollections, and Alf glancing at the scattered, white-shirted West German team before telling his players, 'Get off your arses. They'll think you're knackered … Look at them. They are knackered.'

But then, without evidence in support, Hamilton paints Alf more prosaically saying, 'You've let it slip once. Don't let it slip again,' rather than, 'You've won it once. Now go and win it again.' His reasoning? 'We should always be suspicious of smart remarks unless … from recognised speech-makers.'[35]

Strong evidence suggests otherwise. Interviewed four weeks later, Nobby Stiles recounted how Alf 'calmed us all down with one sentence … *You've won the game once. Now you've got to do it again*' (*Sunday Mirror* 28 August 1966). Alf's assistant manager, citing his 1966 handwritten diary,[36] described Alf's 'quiet controlled voice' saying, 'You have beaten them once, now go out and beat them again.'[37] Other players agreed: George Cohen on television in 1986 (*Sunday Mirror* 6 April) and in print in 2005,[38] Alan Ball in 1991 (*Daily Mirror* 30 July), and Geoff Hurst repeatedly,[39] including during a recent interview with this book's author. Of Hamilton's theory, he said, 'I don't think it's right. Not the way I remember it. It was *You've beaten the Germans once, go and beat them again*.[40]

Nevertheless, Hamilton's observation holds true that Alf was not naturally rhetorical.[41] So, what can unlock the puzzle of his team talk?

Previous chapters discussed Alf's obsessive approaches and potential neurodivergence, attributes illustrated by him lecturing Bobby Charlton, during the immediate post-victory mayhem, for losing possession during the game.[42] Building on that, an alternative hypothesis offers itself, incorporating Hamilton's observation. Alf's team talk was not rhetoric, just him doing what he always did: unimaginatively stating facts and football logic as he saw them. England had played better, West Germany's equaliser was lucky, so his 'you've won the game once' observation was as reasonable as the instruction 'now you've got to do it again'. It was others, retrospectively, who alchemised Alf's words into a rhetoric that then passed into football 'folklore'.[43]

That alchemy started with FA President Lord Harewood's brief foreword to the FA's 1967 'World Cup Report.' This aristocratic, socially liberal Leeds United fan (*The Guardian* 11 July 2011, Obituary) complained 'British press commentators' had consistently 'derided our chances.' Their scepticism switched only 'after the semi-final', when even 'the notoriously fickle Wembley crowd suddenly turned into a host of enthusiastic home supporters'. For Harewood, it was not them but 'team spirit' which 'won us the trophy', epitomised by 'Alf Ramsey's conviction':

> His remark to his players before extra time ... 'you've won it once and now you'll have to go out and win it again' – will go down to folk-lore history along with 'We'll hit Romell for six out of Africa.[44]

The confusion started here, by Harewood likening Alf to Field Marshal Montgomery in 1942,[45] and so layering on erroneous rhetoric. From its apex, the English FA was sowing seeds for Hamilton's 'tangle of ivy', promulgating 'myths and misconceptions' around 1966.[46]

A valid question nevertheless remains. Did ordinary people see Alf as 'heroic'? That has been tested through reading nearly 200 previously unpublished letters congratulating Alf, but written before his team talk publicly surfaced, in Nobby Stiles's *Sunday Mirror* interview (28 August 1966).

A People's Hero?

The collection consists of 196 different congratulatory communications written between 11 July and 22 August 1966,[47] 176 in English. Most were letters, from one to nine pages long and addressed to Alf personally, though there were also cards, postcards and drawings. Four in five were handwritten. Nearly all were date-stamped 'Acknowledged', suggesting replies had been made. For decades the box survived unnoticed at the FA's Wembley headquarters, before a senior staff member recognised its importance and secured safekeeping. Most have lain unread until now, apart from a few sentences in a 2004 academic article,[48] and one recent citation in an important book.[49]

The correspondence is personal, spontaneous and diverse. Seventeen letter writers (nine per cent) were children aged five to 16: 12 from England, three written in English from overseas (Fiji, Switzerland, Eire) and two in German. Most correspondents wanted nothing from Alf, with just 16 per cent requesting an autograph, photo, or souvenir. Only 20 (11 per cent) voiced commercial or organisational motives, generally FA-related, and just 22 writers knew Alf previously: 13 via football volunteering, or other shared personal history. These writings are mostly impromptu and personalised, and their authors more socially varied than 'traditional' 1960s football fans. One in five senders were definitely female, identifiable by personal names or letter content, and more may have been.

The overall age range was 31 per cent aged 18–39, 46 per cent 40–59, and 23 per cent 60 or over. The birthplace and perceived nationality of 41 were traceable. Unsurprisingly, of those 41, 32 (78 per cent) were English born, but by nationality three other writers were German, two Scottish, two Indian, one British Gibraltarian and one from Togo. Overall, 67 of the 196 communications (34 per cent) originated outside the UK, from 30 different countries or territories. Twenty were in languages other than English, most commonly German (ten). Of the 67 'overseas' correspondents, content suggests perhaps half were British people visiting, living, or working overseas.

Alf used some of this early fan mail mentally to prepare his team. 'On the day of the final' his players were 'given a time-killing chore by Ramsey … replying to the encouraging mail that had come into FA offices. It was basic psychology … team-building philosophy' (*The Independent* 7 June 2006). Six decades later, what does such correspondence say about wider public perceptions of Alf as an individual, and 1966 as an event?

Unexpectedly Emotional

Men and women of all ages, backgrounds and nationalities felt surprisingly emotional about England's success. Two days before the final, 28-year-old Thelma Biggs, from five miles west of Alf Ramsey's Becontree birthplace, wished him luck:

Without you we would never have made it. As a keen football fan everything has stopped in my house when a match has been televised and my poor husband has only had a dinner when there were no matches shown. I'm sure he has lost weight – when it is England's games I just go crazy with excitement.

That same day, from Kendal (in what is now Cumbria), 46-year-old Surjuram Kahojia Girdhari, who had migrated to England in 1955, congratulated Alf on 'your team's magnificent win in the semi-final. A great match worth keeping in memory forever ... I am myself Indian cricketer and my team I follow Manchester.' A day later, from Kent, the Ramsgate Branch of the Amalgamated Engineering Union, numbering 350 members, unanimously resolved to 'wholeheartedly congratulate the England team and all ... associated on the magnificent standard of skill and sportsmanship', alongside 'our thanks for the pride we feel at this moment, of being English'.

Similar feelings proliferated after the trophy was won. Derbyshire resident Marion Mellor, aged 32, and husband Peter found it just 'wonderful to see such happiness on all your faces. I really cannot explain how I feel ... it brought tears to my eyes. All the people in our village were just thrilled to bits ... God bless you all.' The 61-year-old Elizabeth Hughson, from Salford, 'never saw a match till this week' but found herself:

Seated in front of the television tears streaming down my face with Happiness. I could never explain what this win has meant to thousands but to me it is another great day for England. My husband is at work so I sat and cheered alone ... I said a Hail Mary for that last goal ... Thanks again for this wonderful moment.

Evereld Wilson, a Wiltshire woman of similar age, and a fan of Alf since Southampton days, had previously written after his first England cap (1948), Ipswich's promotion (1957), his England manager appointment (1962) and, 'Now, once again ... I nearly had heart failure Saturday afternoon, that last-second goal! Could hardly bear to watch the extra time.'

Scrawled in bright-red pen, from Northwich in Cheshire, came simply: 'Dear Mr. Ramsey and England Team. Congratulations on the wonderful games we are proud of you. A house full of supporters.' Ronald Stevens, a 29-year-old Oxfordshire amateur footballer, had won 'cups and medals galore' but when the final whistle blew it 'was the most touching moment … I just cried. I couldn't hold the tears back. Once again Mr Ramsey THANK YOU!' Frank Dobson, a language student lodging in West Germany recounted:

> Dear Mr. Ramsey … A great emotional experience. I was so overcome … I could not prevent myself from openly crying … To win as England did, deservedly, and in such an exhilarating final was more than I had dared to hope for … Words give an inadequate expression of my feelings.

From Lancashire 'Miss Marie Connor' praised Alf's:

> Wonderful job, tell the boys from me they were just great. I'm no football fan but I've really enjoyed watching all the games … I've mentally run up and down the pitch with [the] lads … helped to kick the goals in with them 'hee-hee.' I'm so very happy for you all.

Someone from Woking simply applauded, for their whole family, 'the magnificent victory of the great team which you have created. How we have suffered with them – despaired of them – but in the end how we have cheered them.'

Angles on Alf

Alf Ramsey's 1962–63 predictions that England would win suffused multiple letters. Neil Cliffe, aged 32, from Cheshire, thanked Alf for the 'wonderful feeling of pride … Saturday afternoon football supporters have in our hearts tonight … for England, for English football … You said from the beginning we could win the cup and I like many others doubted your wisdom.' Malta resident Charles Farrugia was:

> Overjoyed … I think I am dreaming … You achieved this in face of criticism from everybody. Last night at 11:45 PM I couldn't help but laugh when I heard Brian Saunders, of the BBC, praising you. I had in mind the words he said when he was in Malta: that England hadn't a chance for that World Cup.

Writers overwhelmingly sided with Alf against media criticism. Edward Milk, a 53-year-old Londoner, watched the World Cup whilst working in Moscow: 'So, in spite of the experts on the newspapers, radio and television, you've done it – many, many congratulations!' The 60-year-old Percy Pearson, from Tonbridge Wells, lauded Alf's 'patience and perseverance over the last three years' despite 'great criticism over your attitude and procedure ... But you have replied to ... Public critics by winning.' An Anglesey correspondent cited 'very unfair criticism in the newspapers for a long time' and Victor Newbury from Worcestershire lamented 'the silly, carping, and at times vicious criticism from the self-appointed and so-called "experts" ... How well and calmly you conducted yourself in the moment of triumph.' Czechoslovakian national and resident Dr Vladimir Mikula expressed 'admiration for the stubbornness with which you have realised your plans' despite the 'hard criticism of the press and experts ... just in these days I have admired you most'.

Mr Walsh from Kent was 'so pleased' because it 'upset all the knockers', and Mr Rogers from Cambridgeshire mocked 'the so-called experts both press and otherwise now trying to say, "I told you so" and finding it difficult because we ordinary chaps have long memories ... we get a laugh out of them.' Another self-labelled 'very ordinary bloke' from London candidly confessed: 'Whilst not really agreeing with the "England will win" pronouncements one must accept that this was part and parcel ... of instilling in the players the will to prevail, and how well it worked.'

Alf's leadership qualities featured regularly. Dorothy Wilson from Chichester thanked him 'for cleaning up football ... nothing is a success without discipline which you enforced'. A married couple's congratulations from Cumbria noted: 'We have always admired your quiet and sincere confidence in the 22 players under your control.' Middlesex resident Desmond Gleeson, aged 23, lauded Alf for bringing 'dignity to football and making ... the professional footballer a person to be respected in the world of sport.' Fellow Londoner Harry Lewis praised Alf's 'character and personality ... intellect ... sheer hard thinking ... and planning over such a long period', whilst honestly admitting how:

> In common with most English football supporters, I have roundly cursed you on many occasions during the past three years ... Having been privileged to watch every World Cup game at Wembley, I am only too delighted to eat my words and offer my sincere gratitude.

Pinpointing a fatal weakness, Lewis also lamented Alf being 'so reticent'. He had 'watched every TV programme' forlornly hoping for 'a lengthy interview … perhaps it is still not too late?' From New York, a 28-year-old 'exiled Englishman', and regular on Liverpool's Kop, praised Alf's 'courageous and inspiring management … I've only been out of England for a year' but 'our chances were being written off despite your confidence'. Wryly noting the fickleness of Wembley fans, he was 'thrilled to hear even the crowd for once really support their side'.

Communal pride permeated multiple letters, not just from England. The 'Newport County Supporters' Club' secretary wrote, 'Although many of us consider ourselves Welsh we have been 100% behind England … The trophy is at last in its rightful place.' From Liverpool, a Scottish Mrs Moss offered Alf: 'Thanks and congratulations … It has made us all very proud and happy … I am sure I am only one of the millions in Scotland who have been keenly supporting England.'

Many letters suggest ordinary football fans liked Alf, and he liked them. Regular correspondent Mr Thomas, 'writing once again', lavished paragraphs of praise: 'A real tonic, words fail me, I am more than overjoyed.' He thanked Alf's many previous 'lovely, interesting letters so kindly sent when I have written to you'. From Australia, recently emigrated 18-year-old Neil Ellis described being 'greatly thrilled' and sent luck for Saturday's final. Did Alf recall, when Ipswich manager, helping 'a young autograph hunter trapping his leg in a train door at Nottingham station?' He thanked Alf 'for the medical aid … kindly rendered'. Similarly, 40-year-old Suffolk woman Joan Czako cited how Alf Ramsey had:

> Helped Ipswich when it seemed all hope for them was lost. Now … England are the world's greatest football team. I did read in one paper that they might ask for a knighthood for you. Well Sir you deserve one as you have done a wonderful job for us all.

Sporting internationalism pervaded many other letters. From Hanover in West Germany, Ammi Hirschinkramer expressed: 'My heart wish for the future is that the co-operation [between] England and Germany will contribute to fasten the friendship of those two countries.' Indian citizen Hiralal Prasad, whose brother played football for India in the 1948 and 1952 Olympics, wrote lengthily from Calcutta recounting Alf's journey from 1950 World Cup disasters, through to 'your endeavour' and 'your prediction three years ago that England would win … I along with all my family members became very glad.' From Lomé, in French-speaking Togo, a telegram communicated: 'To Alf Ramsay [sic] and his undaunted players the sincere congratulations of members of Etoile

Filante football club for winning notably coveted World soccer gold cup STOP More grease to their elbows STOP AYEKU LAWSON.' Malaysian Chen Goke Lim, by airmail, congratulated Alf personally and applauded the 'English nation who so generously spur the North Koreans, despite being communists, to the quarter-finals ... the legendary sportsmanship of the English ... I am proud of the Koreans because I am an Asian.'

German national Eugen Henzler recalled meeting Alf when Ipswich Town played in Hamburg. He judged 'both teams were very fair (included friend Stiles) and correct ... as you know I'm German referee and pay attention to these things.' In social contrast, an English 25-year-old rock musician wrote from his resident nightclub in West Germany, where he played in The Hi-Fis:

> An English beat group ... today your team made us very proud thank you for the first-class football, good sportsmanship and great team selection. Incidentally we are playing soccer against a German beat group next month ... once again Mr Ramsey thanks a lot.

Patriotism versus Nationalism? The England–Argentina 1966 Quarter-Final

For Alf Ramsey, football was about professionalism and sporting patriotism, not nationalism or xenophobia. Similarly, only two of the 176 English language letters exhibited xenophobia. Yorkshire woman Freda Perrise recounted her 90-year-old mother enjoying 'every match on the TV' but then harked back to England's quarter-final with Argentina, by attaching a news story syndicated across several local newspapers.[50] Her gruesome cutting described an Argentinian rancher jealously killing 'his daughter's lover, roasting his dismembered body and forcing his family to eat it': evidence, Freda claimed, that Alf was correct 'about the Argentinians being animals' or 'even worse'. Only one other letter writer mentioned the Argentina game. Walter Cross, a self-described 'First world war veteran' in 'poor health' had already written from Canada, then a follow-up letter told Alf, 'You were quite right when you referred to that team as animals.'

Uncovering what lay behind those stories, and that match, starts with what has become 'one of the best-known photographs associated with the World Cup'.[51] It shows an angry Alf preventing England's Cohen from swapping shirts with an Argentinian, immediately after their World Cup quarter-final of 23 July, as shown on the next page.

Even more impactful was Alf's post-match interview, conducted at Wembley but reported across continents as him saying 'Argentinians were animals'. That fuelled genuine anger in Argentina,[52] brief diplomatic disquiet at the Foreign Office,[53] and became permanently entrenched even in British newspapers (e.g. *Daily Mirror* 29 June 1998, *Wales on Sunday* 28 June 1998, *Scotland on Sunday* 7 December 1997). Yet cooler analysis, and new evidence, reveals a more nuanced story.

Alf started that interview by lamenting 'that so much Argentine talent is wasted', before then saying, 'We have, still, to produce our best football. It will come against the right type of opposition, the team who come[s] out to play football, not act as animals.'[54] He neither named Argentina, nor criticised Argentinian nationality, nor cited Argentine individuals, nor directly said Argentine players *were* animals. The comments were rude and ill-considered, but ironically his oblique phraseology edged towards modern 'person first' approaches: verbal strategies, in caring professions, to separate specific or isolated actions from people's wider identities.[55] Yet having himself been nicknamed 'D****e' since childhood, Alf knew the dangers of careless labelling; he should never have implied England's opponents had 'acted as animals'.

Equally, evidence suggests poor on-field Argentinian conduct. BBC cameras apparently captured their players covertly committing numerous offences, footage never broadcast in an allegedly 'shameful act of self-censorship'. These unseen films featured 'kidney punches, ankle-taps, hair-pulling, treading on someone's foot, ear-twisting, pokes in the eye, elbows in the ribs' and 'pathetic, perpetual spitting'. Geoff Hurst in print recently described 'a brutal encounter' featuring 'the kind of foul play that most of us had never experienced before'.[56] He also confirmed it to the author, in person, as 'probably one of the nastiest and toughest games' England players had 'ever been involved in', despite all football then being 'tough and brutal'.

Alf and his assistants had forewarned England's players 'to expect' provocation but 'on no account' to retaliate. Their coaching worked, and Stiles, in particular, showed steely self-control.[57] In contrast, three Argentinians were booked, then, in the 37th minute, captain Antonio Rattín was sent off. Confusion followed when Rattín refused to leave the field for nearly ten minutes (e.g. *Scottish Sunday Post* or *Sunday Mirror* 24 July 1966). Even greater chaos ensued after the final whistle. What emerged in public from FIFA was that one Argentinian player had attacked the referee, and another spat in the face of a FIFA observer, bringing Argentina's future World Cup participation into question (*The Times* 25 July). But worse had been hidden from public view. An Argentinian player had urinated in the Wembley tunnel,[58] another threw a chair at the English dressing-room door, and for 15 minutes several more repeatedly kicked it, banged it and shouted to provoke a fight.[59]

In 1973 Brian Glanville, and in 1993 Jimmy Greaves, wrote about something that most British and Argentinian analysts have since ignored, or forgotten. Alf Ramsey's infamous 'act as animals' interview seems to have happened *after* he witnessed the highly provocative post-match behaviour described above.[60] Glanville implied it, Greaves stated it, and the possibility merits repeating. Alf's interview anger was less about the game, more about the indefensible post-match transgressions just witnessed. To test whether Alf had indeed experienced those first-hand, the author recently asked Geoff Hurst, the only English dressing-room witness still alive, whether Alf was in there with his players. Hurst thought hard, confessed to confessed to being unable specifically to remember, then added, 'I'd be very surprised if he was not, absolutely. I can't see him being anywhere else apart from in the dressing room.'[61]

Is it right that 'madness ran through Rattín that day'?[62] Perhaps, but media madness was internationally mutual. The British *Sunday People*'s headline inaccurately screamed 'ANIMALS! SAYS RAMSEY' (24 July 1966). The same day's Argentinian *Cronica* reproduced the infamous shirt-swap image above, headlined an Alf Ramsey photo 'THE TRAINER OF THIEVES', and devoted thousands of words to the story.[63] Such cocktails of myth and misunderstanding poisoned

Alf's popular historical image, and the 'belief he referred directly to the Argentinians as animals damaged Ramsey's reputation'[64] and 'endured for decades'. In Argentina, his remarks also provided an unintentional 'catalyst' for conversations about football to turn 'xenophobic', sometimes deploying 'metaphors of war and violence'.[65]

Yet this whole episode was politically manipulated. Four weeks previously a military coup had removed Argentina's democratic government, supposedly 'to restore social order, stamp out immorality and ... combat subversiveness'. The coup's leader, in rhetoric that echoed and encouraged the 'patriotic indignation' in newspapers, welcomed home Argentina's defeated team 'as heroes and representatives of the nation', and thanked them for 'putting Argentina's name where it belongs'. A mid-August 1966 photocall at the Presidential Palace pictured him shaking hands with the dismissed Rattín. Why? Because burnishing the national team's victim status was politically helpful to his new military regime.[66] Twelve years later, Argentina's hosting and winning of the 1978 World Cup assisted another set of dictators, but in a tournament mired in far deeper, darker allegations around the sportswashing of mass murder.[67]

In truth, British occupation of the Malvinas (Falkland Islands), not Alf Ramsey, was the 'real issue'[68] plaguing Anglo–Argentine relations. A day before the tournament opened, on 10 July, the *Sunday Express* had complained that a few weeks previously Argentinian 'impertinence' had decreed that Falkland Islands 'airmail ... must in future be addressed to the ... Islas Malvinas ... on which she has been casting an envious eye for some time'. Almost unnoticed, on 16 July 1966 the two governments had opened formal talks about the disputed islands at London's Foreign Office, talks that faltered within days (*The Times* 22 July 1966). Amid heightened tensions, the Malvinas featured in Argentinian newspapers before 1966's quarter-final,[69] were angrily aired in the Argentine team's changing room immediately after,[70] and brilliantly illustrated in this *Cronica* cartoon (27 July 1966):

The malign effects of the 'Alf–Argentina-animals' episode lingered for years, maintained and magnified by newspapers,[71] but why has responsibility rested mainly on Alf, and not been fairly shared? An incident resembling Rattín's dismissal had happened the week before, in a group game at Birmingham, when Argentina's manager persistently argued, on the pitch, against another player's dismissal (*Birmingham Daily Post* 25 July 1966). Even before kicking off against England, Rattín and 'several team-mates suggested a possible swindle by the referee', in an atmosphere described by an American researcher as 'nationalist fervour', spawning 'jingoism' and 'conspiracy theories'. Rattín later admitted this 'was an act of gamesmanship', echoing newspaper 'prebuttals' predicting a conspiracy. Nevertheless, more immediately afterwards, in an interview headlined 'PREMEDITATED EXPULSION', Rattín claimed: 'English football ... bought the referees' and Alf was a 'crazy ... charlatan' (*Cronica* 29 July).[72]

Undoubtedly, FIFA's 1966 tournament witnessed 'two different ethical codes ... Latin American and North European ... fighting for dominance in international football'. Indisputably, 'the triumph of the European code favoured England', as did '18 out of 23' tournament referees being European.[73] Nevertheless, the right-wing generals who had just seized power in Argentina ruthlessly exploited five million Argentinians having watched the game on television.[74] Alf's angry words were used to fan nationalism, bolster their regime, and embed the episode as a deliberate British 'insult for many Argentines'.[75] To that perceived attack some Argentinian reporters responded:

> That Ramsey, out of keeping with someone from England, was not 'a gentleman.' He was on the contrary 'a gypsy.' Suggestions had been made at home in the past that Ramsey, who had slightly darker skin colour ... was of Romany stock.[76]

Even internationally, would Alf Ramsey ever escape being born, to a family of dealers, next to that heath in Becontree? And how did his few ill-judged words after that quarter-final help sabotage not just Alf's career, but his historical reputation?

1 Filho, M. (2021) p.xi
2 Reuters website (12 July 2021) 'England's Black players face racial abuse after Euro 2020 defeat'
3 Scovell, B. (2006) pp.54, 7-8
4 Marquis, M. (1970) p.41
5 *Billy Wright's Football Album* (1954) pp.78-82
6 Sports Journalists' Association website (13 July 2017) 'Mail man James, who forecast England 1966 win, dies at 87'
7 Hamilton, D. (2023) pp.119, 120.
8 Hurst, G. (2024) pp.82-83
9 Hamilton, D. (2023) p.67
10 Hughson, J. (2016) pp.26-7, 66
11 Ibid. p.67
12 Hurst, G. (2024) p.85
13 Hurst, G. (2024) pp.164-65
14 James Graham's *Dear England* first performed at the National Theatre on 20 June 2023
15 Wilson, J. (2023) p.139
16 Wilson, J. (2009) p.144
17 Ibid. p.145
18 Ibid. p.147
19 Ibid. p.148
20 Rowlinson, J. (2016) pp.150-52, 202-3
21 See chapters 1-4
22 Walter John St Pier, 1911 census and George St Pier, 1871 census
23 Hurst, G. (2006) pp.46-47
24 Hurst, G. (2024) p.49
25 The 1939 census lists St Pier as West Ham's 'assistant trainer and scouting representative'
26 Geoff Hurst oral history interview 6 February 2025
27 Polley, M. (1998) p.3
28 BBC News website (11 July 2016) 'How Africa boycotted the 1966 World Cup'
29 Polley, M. (1998) pp.4-6
30 Thanks to the 'Turnstile Blues' collective for elucidating this
31 FIFA (30 July 2020) website 'England v West Germany 1966 FIFA World Cup Final | Final Replay '66'
32 Porter, D. (2009)
33 Ibid. pp.534-55
34 Hamilton, D. (2023) pp.242-43 and 379-80
35 Ibid. pp.242-43
36 *The Sun* 6 June 2020
37 Shepherdson, H. (1968) p.166
38 Cohen, G. (2005) p.250
39 Hurst, G. (2024) p.278

40 Geoff Hurst oral history interview 6 February 2025

41 Hamilton, D. (2023) pp.242-43

42 McKinstry, L. (2007) p.344

43 Carter, N. (2006) p.160

44 Mayes, H. (1967) p.5

45 The Tongue of Mars website (no date) 'General BL Montgomery's address to the officers and men of the Eighth Army, Cairo, 13 August 1942'

46 Hamilton, D. (2023) p.242

47 **FA Archive of 1966 Congratulatory Letters**

48 Chisari, F. (2004) p.108

49 Hayward, P. (2022) pp.245-46

50 e.g. *Reading Evening Post, Staffordshire Evening Sentinel* 4 August 1966

51 Hughson, J. (2016) p.69

52 Sibaja, R. (2013) pp.272-79

53 Hayward, P. (2022) pp.172-73

54 e.g. *La Prensa* 25 July 1966 in Sibaja, R. (2013) p.1 and *The Scotsman* 26 July 1966

55 Crocker, A. & Smith, S. (2019) p.126

56 Hamilton, D. (2023) pp.217-18; also Hurst, G. (2024) p.13

57 Hurst, G. (2024) pp.13, 94-96, 198; Geoff Hurst oral history interview 6 February 2025

58 Finn, R. (1970) p.27

59 Hurst, G. (2024) pp.96-97

60 Glanville, B. (1973) pp.197-98; Greaves J. with Giller, N. (1993) pp.41-42

61 Geoff Hurst oral history interview 6 February 2025

62 Hamilton, D. (2023) pp.220 and 218-20

63 'El Entrenador De Los Ladrones.' For this translation and others from other Argentinian newspapers many thanks to Jonny Brogden

64 Wikipedia website (3 April 2025) 'Alf Ramsey'

65 Sibaja, R. (2013) p.256

66 Ibid. pp.1, 257, 262-63, 277

67 Winner, D. 'A Dangerous Game': *Financial Times* 21 June 2008

68 Howell, D. (1990) p.173

69 Sibaja, R. (2013) pp.5, 93, 268 and 270

70 Ibid. p.275

71 Ibid. pp.256, 278-79, 291

72 Ibid. pp.267-68

73 Kuper, S. (2106) pp.273-74

74 Sibaja, R. (2013) pp.272-3

75 Ibid. p.273

76 Chapman, P. (2016) p.186. During correspondence with the author Chapman kindly recalled 'the word *gentleman* was in English, the Argentine source loading it with irony'

Part Four

SEEING WHAT WE WANT TO?

CHAPTER 13

FINE MARGINS

Sir Alf Starts to Slide

A Modern Knight

BY THE autumn of 1973, Alf Ramsey's managership would be doomed: unthinkable in 1966, when BBC viewers voted England's footballers their 'Team of the Year' and smiling Minister for Sport Denis Howell handed out the trophies on live TV (*Northamptonshire Evening Telegraph* December 1966). Labour had gained a narrow majority in 1964's general election, turned that into a landslide in March 1966, but in June 1970 were unexpectedly beaten by the Conservatives; a shock result that happened four days after England had lost a titanic, televised World Cup quarter-final. Historians are still arguing about whether the two upsets were related, the football defeat perhaps emboldening 'a particular political narrative',[1] but the summer of 1970 also proved slippery for Alf.

His popularity had peaked in 1966 when the image below, snapped hours after Wembley victory, was splashed across newspapers, then adorned the FA's official tournament history.[2] It shows from left to right Alf Ramsey, Denis Howell and Labour Prime Minister Harold Wilson.

In a metaphor for his media unease, a hand shields Alf's face. Moments later, Wilson took that arm and led Alf, the reluctant hero, on to a balcony to brandish the World Cup before thousands of adoring fans (*The Observer* 31 July 1966). What had Alf come to personify, that Wilson so basked in his presence? Put simply, popular modernisation. Alf's 1962 England job contract was signed by a new FA secretary, freshly elected from leading a trade union for airline pilots, who helped prise team selection away from FA committees of amateur volunteers.[3] In 1963, Wilson had similarly defined his political leadership as modernising, through a 'white heat of technology' annual conference speech pledging Labour to 're-defining and ... restating our Socialism in terms of the scientific revolution'. A Labour Britain, Wilson claimed, 'would break with old class barriers in a giant leap towards modernisation'. Wilson soon learned that delivering such modernisation was more problematic,[4] but using football to get himself noticed was simplicity itself; hence being photographed 'wearing a World Cup tie', newly arrived from Washington USA, before dashing to watch the 1966 final (*Sunday Mirror* 31 July 1966). The next day, his sports minister boasted, in an article headlined 'THE ALF RAMSEY REVOLUTION', that the World Cup represented 'the best half-million pounds the Government had ever spent' (*Birmingham Daily Post* 1 August).

Another easy way to symbolise Labour governments as popular, and modern, was rewarding national heroes in new ways. In January 1965, Wilson gave a first UK knighthood to an English professional footballer, Stanley Matthews. In January 1967, Alf Ramsey became England's first knighted football manager. Those were easy public pickings, but Labour's commitment to sport was real. Its 1966 election manifesto promised, then delivered, the creation of a Sports Council.[5] Wilson had recognised the modern truth that 'sport ... matters to British political leaders'.[6]

Culturally, too, it has been argued that Alf's new playing formations were to 1960s football what 'modernism' was to art, representing a type of 'modernist aesthetic ... parallel to other cultural happenings'.[7] That overstretches the evidence, but Ramsey's knighthood and transformation into 'Sir Alf' emphatically was not the British establishment rewarding 'one of its own'. Rather, it symbolised a left-leaning and modernising government's attempts to woo an electorate enraptured by Alf's and England's televised victory. For example, three days after the 1966 World Cup Final, a Cambridgeshire man, 'on behalf of my England-supporting mates', wrote to thank Alf for doing 'what few people in the football world thought you could do ... give us something to cheer about'. A knighthood would be 'just reward' but he, like ten other letter writers, also begged Alf to 'take our next team' to Mexico 1970.[8] Chronologically, though, another tournament came first, clues from which hint at Alf's later downfall.

The European Nations Cup 1967–68

Newspapers were the main platform for analysing 1960s and 1970s football, and print journalism moulded Alf's image. Piecemeal after 1966, and more widely after 1970, some journalists started caricaturing him as a chronic conservative or illiberal xenophobe. But might such representations have reflected the controversies newspapers needed, to stir reader interest, rather than what Alf actually 'did' or 'was'?

For example, of Wembley's 1967 England–Scotland game, a qualifying fixture for the 1968 'European Nations Cup', an English newspaper snidely attributed past Scottish failures to 'brilliant individualism' not being 'backed by modern thinking' (*Daily Mirror* 15 April 1967). Hours later, Scotland won 3-2, ending England's 19-game unbeaten run, and similarly crass Scottish reporting ensued. 'Scotland's Day Of Vindication As World Cup Form Proved False' trumpeted one headline, portraying Alf Ramsey's 'tattered World Cup champions' as 'subdued, tormented and outclassed'. Scotland's victory was hailed as 'exciting' for Argentina, Portugal, and the 'many who had not liked' England's 1966 methods. An adjacent column then veered outrageously into militarism. 'Now we know how Sir William Wallace felt after his success at Stirling. Victory over the English is especially intoxicating … they cannot field a team of old men against vigorous and talented young Scots' (*The Scotsman* 17 April). Alf, in courteous counterpoint, simply commented, 'Scotland always play well against England, and my word, they did on this occasion' (*Sunday People* 16 August 1967). Six months later, the Scotland versus England return match, before 134,000 spectators, would decide European qualification. A 1-1 draw saw England progress. The Scottish *Sunday Post* (25 February 1968) begrudgingly acknowledged England 'were just the better footballing side' but criticised their attitude with 'WHAT A WAY TO "WIN" A GAME!' Alf argued England had 'outclassed the Scots', but *The Scotsman* rather tortuously cited his previous 'use of words – animals for the Argentinians' to insinuate he was trying to insult Scotland through using 'outclassed'. Instead, the paper claimed Scotland 'had shattered method football with passion football' (26 February 1967).

Such language speaks for itself. Overblown nationalist rhetoric was a natural idiom for some newspapers and commentators, on both sides of the border, although not everywhere. In the European Nations quarter-final, England vanquished reigning champions Spain, winning 1-0 at home and 2-1 in Madrid. Spain's manager sportingly admitted England were 'physically and technically superior' (*Belfast Telegraph* 9 May 1968), and a delighted Alf claimed his players 'continue to amaze me' with apparently no 'limit to what they can be asked to do' (*Daily Mirror* 10 May 1968). Four weeks later, though, Alf was proved spectacularly wrong when Yugoslavia won an ugly semi-final 1-0. In the opening minutes, brutal fouls set the tone: one on Englishman Alan Ball, one by Englishman Norman Hunter that targeted Yugoslavia's 'principal creator'. Minutes from the end an England player was sent off, the thuggish game leaving a 'raw tang of basic disillusionment' in one journalist's mouth (*The Observer* 9 June 1968). Stifling intense personal disappointment, Alf still managed diplomatically to refute English suspicions that Yugoslavia's match-winning goal looked offside: 'The ball beat Bobby Moore in the air – Džajić did extremely well to take it' (*Coventry Evening Telegraph* 6 June). Yet three days later, Alf did *apparently* vent chauvinism. Why then?

England had just beaten Russia 2-0 in Rome to clinch third place, their 'best performance since winning the World Cup', but off-field matters had soured things for Alf. The moment Nobby Stiles's name 'appeared on the electric scoreboard … the crowd started their whistles and catcalls' (*Sunday Post* 9 June 1968). The backstory was that Stiles, in a 1966 group game, had so crudely tackled a French player that the FA's International Committee reputedly wanted him dropped, and Alf 'supposedly' threatened resignation.[9] Two years, later, Alf was still stoutly defending Stiles, claiming his treatment since 1966 had been:

> Horrible – booing from the terraces as soon as he stepped on the pitch, punches, kicks and insults from opponents … This is not football. These attacks have brainwashed people not only about Stiles, but about English football generally. I want to remind people that football started in England, the rules were formulated in England, and that in England we still play to those rules. (*News of the World* 9 June 1968)

Another English newspaper quoted Alf saying similar. 'Since the World Cup the people of Europe have been brainwashed about English football. We play to the rules always, and we go for the ball' (*Sunday Mirror* 9 June 1968). But a Scottish newspaper's version of the same press conference featured subtle differences, helping caricature Alf as blimpishly English. 'Since the World Cup the people of Europe have been bawling about English football. They should remember that we started the game' (*Sunday Post* 9 June 1968).

Did Alf really claim that 'the people of Europe have been bawling about English football'? No definitive audio recording exists, but analysis suggests that Alf's intended target at this press conference was not foreign countries, nor the 'people of Europe', but the English FA. FA chairperson Dr Andrew Stephen, the day after that 1968 Yugoslavia semi-final, had instantly criticised Alf Ramsey and his players, telling journalists that because England's 'reputation precedes us into matches – we ought to take a good look to see whether our way of playing is not too hard'. Correctly sensing discord, a leading English football correspondent then gleefully told the FA to '*Get off Alf's back!*' and stop unfairly repeating 'foreign accusations that Ramsey's professionals, who have sweated blood ... for five years ... are nothing more than butchers of innocent opponents' (*Sunday People* 9 June 1968). Such a furore had been prompted because, during that bruising European semi-final days before, for the first time a senior England international footballer had been dismissed. The player was Alan Mullery, who later claimed Yugoslavia were:

> Doing all the dirty stuff, going over the top into tackles and the referee ... was diabolical ... With one minute to go ... I'd had enough of them injuring people, so I kicked [Dobrivoje Trivić] in the bollocks. I regret it now ... we got beaten by a side that kicked us to death.

What happened in the dressing room afterwards was even more revealing. Mullery apologised but Alf just 'looked at me with a stern expression and said *I'm glad somebody retaliated against those bastards ...* He was very angry ... when I got back, he paid my £50 fine from the FA.'[10] Alf's payment of Mullery's fine illuminates the chasm between the English FA's volunteer committee members, and England's professional footballers. In this tempting space, one edge marked by Alf's clumsy media handling, the other by the FA's outdated amateurism, journalists could seek controversy and so write livelier news stories. Consequently, by the summer of 1970 and as explored below, some were sketching a public image of Alf that over the next three decades became deeply entrenched. Witness, how in 1997 a Scottish journalist could label Alf an 'unrepentant xenophobe' like Margaret Thatcher and assign him number one 'tit-irritant Englishman' for 'sheer superciliousness' (*Scotland on Sunday* 7 December).

Such rhetoric sounds closer to nationalist nonsense than anything Alf ever said, but the article also accused Alf, nicknamed 'D****e' from childhood, of 'racial intolerance'. In 1969–70, it claimed, Alf only just stopped 'short of calling the Mexicans sub-human dago incompetents'. Did that serious slur hold any truth?

England's Preparations for the 1970 Mexico World Cup

From the moment England lost that 1968 European semi-final, Alf became obsessed with retaining the 1970 World Cup. His eventual failure to do so was publicly attributed, even by FA secretary Denis Follows, to England's first-choice goalkeeper falling ill with 'Banksie's belly' just before their quarter-final defeat (*FA News* October 1970). Ironically, though, Alf and England's support staff had worked tirelessly to avoid that exact danger. A full two years earlier, Alf had challenged England's team doctor, an experienced GP but part-time volunteer, to provide 'the best medical support in the whole world'.[11] Then, Alf Ramsey and Denis Follows attended the 1968 Olympics to research Mexico City's summer heat and altitude, nearly two kilometres above sea level. That experience prompted Alf to compile 'a dossier' of fitness 'mishaps' involving European and Commonwealth athletes (*Birmingham Post* 16 October 1968). In 1969, England then tested the resultant research during a four-match tour of Mexico, Uruguay and Brazil.

Travelling with that touring England squad was Scottish journalist Alan Clifford. His was the 1968 article, cited above, that almost certainly misquoted Alf Ramsey claiming, 'the people of Europe have been bawling about English football'. Remarkably, 12 months later Clifford now lauded Alf's powers of football leadership. Whilst the Scottish FA were 'still waffling with basic problems', Clifford told Scottish readers, 'England are proving what world football is all about.' Alf's leadership 'gets through to you even as a non-playing member of the party ... you get the Ramsey-inspired mood of the players, a sort of quiet, confident belief in their own ability to take on anyone, anywhere, and beat them' (*Sunday Post* 8 June 1969). Even Alf's sternest English critic in 1970 similarly had to acknowledge his thoroughness in providing 'against every contingency ... [he] has done a magnificent job in his preparations'.[12]

Detailed logistical planning was crucial, because Mexico City's water-related health challenges were locally real and internationally known. A West German FIFA doctor, publicly reporting on the 1968 Olympic football (*Liverpool Echo* 26 October 1968), warned 'intestinal complaints, with diarrhoea, occur very often'. He advised 1970 World

Cup squads to take their own food, never drink tap water, not to eat salads washed in it, and to clean teeth only with distilled water.[13] The medically qualified British vice-consul in Mexico privately agreed, warning inefficient water purification meant local ice contained invisible 'raw sewage'.[14] The British Olympic Association's advice was stark: 'avoid salad, unpeeled fruit, and Mexican type food' (*FA News* March 1969).

England's squad, like other visiting teams, trialled various drugs to combat 'gastric troubles' (*Daily Mirror* 28 May 1969). They also, like Spain and West Germany during England's 1966 World Cup tournament,[15] and West Germany in Mexico 1970,[16] took their own food and water. Sponsor Findus Foods flew out 420 kilogrammes of meat, 45 kilogrammes of cheese, vast amounts of frozen vegetables and much else (*Sunday Mirror* 12 April 1970). A newspaper cookery page teased 'no nasty foreign rubbish for them', whilst conceding England's 'excuse for taking the food along … is reasonable enough' (*The Scotsman* 23 April). Such rational forward planning only failed when Mexican customs officers, citing food import regulations, unexpectedly embargoed then secretly burned the meat and dairy products (*Western Daily Press* 12 May). In response, a 'local Englishwoman' made sausage replacements (*Sunday Mirror* 9 May) and Findus Foods flew out vast quantities of fish (*Aberdeen Evening Express* 20 May). By England's first group game two weeks later, a 1-0 victory over Romania, the team doctor reported 'the Findus supply of food was working well'.[17]

Unfortunately, in the doldrum days before the tournament opened, this episode offered under-pressure reporters ripe imaginative opportunities. Under a banner headline 'They're Burning Alf's Bacon', one prominent English newspaper lamented Mexican newspapers now being able to present England as 'arrogant, difficult and intolerant of Mexican hotels, food, laws and climate'. Yet customs' contraventions were hardly Alf's responsibility, and the same report admitted that from Mexicans '*any* European success, would receive the coolest sporting acclaim' (*The People* 17 May). Martin Peters, after describing the tournament's 24-hour secret service security being 'trebled' amidst terrorist threats, similarly agreed that Mexican press 'hostility' and 'sarcasm' meant any eventual European success 'would be an outstanding achievement'.[18]

Yet contrary to most English accounts then, and interpretations that have prevailed until now, not all Mexican newspapers trumpeted negative comments by or about Alf. One quoted him saying 'Mexican food is naturally good' (*El Informador* 9 May 1970),[19] and plainly asserted he had 'not said anything against' England's Mexican accommodation. It then revealed that the people who *had* grumbled were 'special correspondents from English newspapers who have already begun to complain about everything'. It was the attitude of English journalists, their Mexican colleague reported, that most reflected imperialist English arrogance.

> They never thought a 'backward' country like ours could hold the best Olympic Games in history, and two years later ... the World Cup ... such frictions with the Europeans seem very natural ... not just English but many Europeans, who dominated the world years ago. (*El Informador* 8 May)

The same journalist then offered a fascinating description of an Alf Ramsey press conference, at which:

> [He] abandoned his Mister Hyde persona, and assuming that of Dr Jekyll, made a magnificent impression on the national and international press ... When he dedicates himself to the English team ... he works like a wise old man who does not allow any interference. At times he was not as nice as many would like. He did not try to appear as a celluloid star, but his desire for collaboration was clear. (*El Informador* 9 May)

The implication of such evidence is clear. How British and Mexican newspapers reported Alf Ramsey varied as widely within each nationality, as across both. When their stories contained simplistic nationalism, it stemmed less from Alf, and more from the reporting choices of both nations' individual journalists. For example, England's unpopularity in 1970 with some Mexicans was explained, to an English journalist, as them having:

> 'Never forgiven Ramsey for his remarks in 1966 about Latins being animals.' No amount of explanation on my part that Ramsey was referring to the Argentinians made any difference. 'This is the way the Press here reported it, and it has stuck', he said. (*Coventry Evening Telegraph* 24 June 1970)

Propaganda and Confusion: Alf Ramsey in Mexico

Alf's 1966 broadcast comments about Argentina's style of play had been damaging and insensitive, but in 1967/68 brutal club games between British (Celtic, Manchester United) and Argentinian clubs (Racing Club, Estudiantes) evidenced how 'Argentinian football became increasingly violent', with Estudiantes as the 'poster boys' for military dictator 'Ongania's new Argentina'.[20] Such savage matches also represented just one crack in the wider rift between Latin American and northern European football. In 1966, the 'triumph of the northern European code' of refereeing had undoubtedly favoured England (and West Germany),[21] hence many in Latin America genuinely believed 1966 had seen conspiratorial 'mistreatment of Brazil, Uruguay and Argentina'. The 'ultimate confrontation' was, therefore, not 'England versus the rest, but Europe against Latin America ... in Northern European countries the tackle from behind is part and parcel of the game, while in Latin America it is a strict no-no'.[22] Even Alf's most consistent 1970, Spanish-speaking critic observed 'two different worlds of behaviour' on the two continents, prompting on the pitch 'two different forms of reaction ... We become aggressive. They grow spiteful. The result is chaos.'[23]

Yet, when examined closely, Alf made no negative comments about other countries, whatever their continent, either before or during Mexico's 1970 World Cup. So why has his historical reputation been stained by accusations of xenophobia, often citing assumptions stemming from Mexico? For example, a beautiful book about England's 1966 victory recently claimed Mexican 'food wasn't good enough' for Ramsey, and 'nothing Mexico did or offered to Ramsey pleased him'.[24] This ignores that the England squad's rigorous dietary practices reflected neither Alf's personal taste, nor his 'apparent xenophobia',[25] but professional medical advice from FIFA, the British diplomatic service, and the FA's own doctor. English football's leading biographer similarly, recently observed that 'England's parochialism in Mexico [1970] will feel wince-inducing to today's serial international travellers'.[26] True, but Mexico *was* very different then.

Peripheral details about England's 1970 World Cup campaign have, it seems, been overinflated to bolster a wider narrative implying Alf as a bigot. But might Alf's controlling behaviours, over organisational details, have reflected neither nationalism, nor xenophobia, but professionally scientific attitudes to the health of his players? Alf's zeal for technical planning has, perhaps mistakenly, become identified with outdated imperialism. For example, another recent expert account accurately described how 'lingering bad feeling' in Mexico over FIFA's 1966 Eurocentric refereeing, and the England–Argentina quarter-final, encouraged some Mexican newspapers into 'baying for blood'. Yet it then accepted at face value confected 'fresh outrage' of the newspapers about the English FA's importation of food, and repeated the misleading conclusion that Alf was therefore 'a xenophobic, petty Little Englander'.[27]

On the pitch, a single June 1970 week saw England lose narrowly to eventual World Cup winners Brazil (1-0) and semi-finalists West Germany (3-2). Off the pitch, criticisms of Alf broadened to become cultural and have stuck to this day. He was losing an image war he did not understand, caught between forces he could not control. Yes, some Mexican newspapers possibly deployed 'lies and exaggerations' to run headlines like 'Odioso [hateful] Alf'. Equally, it now seems fair to question whether England had genuinely been lumbered with 'an arrogant image', through Alf's 'apparently incurable weaknesses in public relations' (*The People* 10 May 1970). Mainstream accounts of 1970 have long accepted that argument unexamined[28] but, that same day and unnoticed, a Mexican newspaper had described 'Sir Alfred' as:

> Tenacious ... and knowledgeable about his profession. He wants to have an excellent team and works to achieve it. He gets irritated when something, or someone, gets in his way and he says it clearly. But he is far from being the ogre that some opinions try to paint him as ... he even likes to socialise with Mexicans. (*El Informador* 10 May 1970)

Alf Ramsey perhaps became a fall guy for the media failures of others. The British Embassy in Mexico was meant to be handling 'the England squad's public relations',[29] but neither it nor FA staff seemed to help much. For example, a leading English football manager who attended the 1970 tournament observed 'there seemed no one around to do the necessary public relations work', and stoutly defended Alf: 'We have never had a more powerful or skilful World Cup squad.' When he asked Mexican 'taxi drivers and barmen' to explain England's unpopularity, they referenced the exaggerated controversies around England 'importing food', but also a further and entirely fictionalised insult. In the 'window of the England team coach under the word *Mexico*' it was claimed there had been an emblem that 'looked like a monkey ... locals claimed it meant that the Mexicans were monkeys. I tried to convince them otherwise, but they would not have it' (*Birmingham Sports Argus* 27 June 1970).

As with other Mexico 1970 stories, misunderstanding seems hardwired. England had brought their own air-conditioned bus, to justifiable Mexican annoyance,[30] but photos show no monkeys. What that bus did have, front and back, were small images of 1966's 'World Cup Willie' in a sombrero, perhaps later misinterpreted as a monkey.

Either way, Alf Ramsey was clearly not to blame. Closer examination suggests similar about other supposed controversies, this time from 1969. At a press conference that summer, just after England opened their 1969 South American tour in Mexico City, Alf *allegedly* made the following 'jagged and ill-chosen remarks' complaining about:

> A band [was] playing outside our bedroom at five o'clock in the morning ... we were promised a motor-cycle escort and didn't get one ... We were booed onto the pitch. I should have thought the Mexican crowd would have cheered us on ... then cheered their own side.

Why does this obscure story still matter? Because in 1999[31] and 2022[32] it was used, without its source being referenced, to support generalised judgements such as this in 2023, claiming Alf's 'diatribe was arrogant and patronising. The bad smell it left lingered in 1970.'[33]

Careful tracking now reveals that Marquis made those original allegations in 1970,[34] in his 'cruelly unfair' (*Birmingham Post* 2 May 1974) Alf biography. Marquis wrote occasional football reports for the *Sunday Times* but was primarily a scriptwriter and novelist.[35] As such, he was not on England's 1969 tour, unlike his *Sunday Times* colleague, leading football writer Brian Glanville. Glanville's own 1973 book seems to confirm he had been Marquis's source, because it describes an alleged 1969 Alf 'diatribe' as having been spoken 'outside the dressing rooms', during a 'short press conference', after he had been asked 'if he had anything to say to the Mexican press'.[36]

Yet, once again, fact-checking research raises important questions. Other reporters covering that same 1969 tour failed to mention Alf's supposed 'diatribe', and actually reported the opposite. This summary typified their consensus:

> A highly satisfactory trip. Not least, goodwill has been built up for the World Cup next year – a nice psychological touch that emphasises once again just how painstaking England's preparations are … this tour was a friendly in all senses of the word. (*The Guardian* 18 June, but see also *Daily Mirror* 5 June, *The Observer* 15 June, *The Times* 16 June)

Even more oddly, during the summer of 1969 Glanville's own reports made just one oblique mention of any possible Alf negativity, quoting him saying of the Mexico City crowd, 'The least they could have done was welcome England.' Yet Alf followed that slight criticism up, Glanville wrote, 'typically and immediately with a tribute to the Mexican people as a whole' (*Sunday Times* 8 June 1969).

These primary historical records are confusing and possibly flawed. If Glanville in 1970 thought Alf's 1969 comments significant enough to pass on to a *Sunday Times* colleague, or in 1973 to include them in his own book, why ignore them at the time? Then a full 30 years later Glanville further dented Alf Ramsey's reputation by describing how, two days after that 1969 'diatribe' of a Mexico City press conference, Alf showed similar animosity following a 'B-international' in Guadalajara. There, Glanville claimed, Alf had 'chased Mexican journalists' away 'like Christ chasing the money-changers from the temple'.[37] To support this portrayal, Glanville cited a local Mexican paper asking, 'What can you expect from a man who called the Argentines animals?'[38] Yet, once again, recent research suggests Guadalajara's leading newspaper, amidst extensive coverage of that 1969 match, appears neither to have mentioned those specific words nor that apparent incident. Its football columnist merely commented that after England's 'respectable victory over the Mexican team, Ramsey refused to make any statements to the Mexican public' (*El Informador* 4 June 1969).

If such reports are starting to seem contradictory, what soon becomes clear is that four days later Glanville disparaged Mexico with generalisations far more sweeping than any Alf Ramsey ever made or said. Ironically, he also did so in the same column containing the brief allusion cited above, of Alf's 'displeasure' at England being booed in Mexico City.

Yet it was Glanville, not Alf, who pitilessly pilloried the 1970 World Cup hosts:

> The truth about Mexican football is that it remains pitifully inept, a stunted plant which has resolutely refused to grow, after nearly 40 years of World Cup experience ... What the Mexican footballer lacks above all is confidence ... A reflection of Mexican character at large. (*Sunday Times* 8 June 1969)

Despite having made these blatantly Eurocentric generalisations Glanville, just four years later, devoted a page in his own best-selling book to Alf's 1970 World Cup communication weaknesses and alleged xenophobia:

> Whatever Ramsey's many solid qualities, diplomacy was scarcely one ... Apparent xenophobia was compounded by his well-known aversion to the Press, one which had by now been widely reciprocated ... England, indeed, had clearly become the team the Mexicans loved to hate.[39]

Yet, during the same tournament, Glanville himself generalised about Mexicans in ways Alf would never have dreamt of, telling readers that the 'behaviour of the Mexican crowds and Press towards England's team is essentially a study in self-hatred ... a curious, collective masochism'. To 'the Mexican', Glanville stereotypically claimed:

> The very essence of the fantasised, anachronistic figure which he takes to be the Englishman is a criticism of himself. These delusions, alas, have interacted with the guarded, outmoded public image displayed by Sir Alf Ramsey, itself based on models now defunct ... fantasies more to do with Mexico than England. (*Sunday Times* 7 June 1970)

A week after that, as a defeated England were catching the plane home, Glanville for the first time then explicitly quoted that 1969 press conference cited above, to support allegations of Alf's 'xenophobia':

> A year ago, when Ramsey swept through Latin America making enemies when he thought he was making friends, it should have become perfectly plain to the Football Association that ... conciliation couldn't be left to him. He is beyond doubt a

> great manager ... but his public relations even in England are disastrous, his xenophobia unquestioned ... Ramsey was entitled to expect help and has had none. (*Sunday Times* 14 June 1970)

Glanville covered 13 World Cups, resulting in uniquely well-informed football opinions, but had always disliked Alf's approach. Just hours after the 1966 World Cup Final, Glanville had confessed 'my reservations about England's team and its manager ... linger on' (*Sunday Times* 31 July 1966). Nearly 50 years later, in retrospect he claimed he 'didn't get on badly' with Alf but thought 'he should have gone two years before he did'.[40]

Whilst this book's next chapter agrees with that final statement, the wider narrative around 1970s Alf needs radical rebalancing. His public image, once resonant of 1960s sporting modernism, did slowly dull after 1968 when results on and off the field exposed his personal vulnerabilities; but something else was shifting, too. Alf's strong, uncomplicated sporting patriotism was becoming, in liberal discourse, associated with nationalism and even the 'xenophobia' Glanville claimed above. As the 1970s progressed, England's football, like the built environment of England's capital, suddenly seemed dingy when compared to the vibrant 1960s:

> During Wilson's first term, London had been a worldwide symbol of modernity and hedonism ... By 1974 all that was merely a faintly embarrassing memory ... London was not alone in presenting a remarkably shabby image ... the nation's great old cities seemed in sad decline.[41]

Mexico 1970: Actual Performances and Disastrous Post-Mortems

Of the four tournament games England played, from 2–14 June 1970, three finished 1-0. Two vital but dull group game victories, against Romania and Czechoslovakia, sandwiched a glorious 1-0 defeat to Brazil. England, therefore, finished second in Group Three, progressing to meet West Germany in the quarter-final, though only with the same goal tally as bottom team Czechoslovakia. The Romanians scored four but finished third, whilst the Brazilians totalled an entertaining 8-3 aggregate. These figures do not lie, and it was defensive qualities that underlay England's potency. Nevertheless, Italy scored just one goal in their group games and ended up as finalists.

England's 7 June game with Brazil was magnificent, even in defeat. Film fragments are easily available online, but even the best dims personally compared to the author's recollections of watching as a teenager. This was not just the first World Cup televised in colour but, when England played both Brazil and West Germany, the games kicked off at midday to maximise global TV audiences. Is it nostalgia making their memory pulse with such brightness, or was it searing Mexican sunlight?

To balance such sentimentality, the Brazil game is perhaps, therefore, best approached through the eyes of others. Ralph Finn had hated Alf Ramsey's football, even in 1966, but in 1970 admitted, 'We could have won this game ... England had far more of the play in the first half.'[42] Even 50 years later, a ninth-minute Banks stop was recently described as the 'save of the century', defying gravity to palm a Pelé header upwards and over the bar.[43] Overall England 'had at least six real chances to Brazil's two' (*Daily Record* 8 June 1970). After an hour Brazil scored, but England then missed two more clear chances and hit the bar. The Brazilian manager sportingly admitted it 'was in doubt up to the final whistle' (*The Times* 8 June). Mexico's 24 group games were condemned, at the time, as 'the poorest' in World Cup history, but the one 'classic contest' had been that 'Brazil against England' match (*The Guardian* 14 June). Nevertheless, defeat meant England now needed to win their last group match against Czechoslovakia. A disputed penalty redeemed so 'shocking' a performance 'It hurt to watch. England got the bird. They deserved the whole aviary.'[44] But three days later, after a bus trip to Leon, for 68 minutes England's game flew against West Germany.

Alf's detractors frequently criticised his perceived over-emphasis on defence, and under-deployment of speedily creative wingers. Finn wanted 'attacking football, Sir Alf, not the miserable apology for it that you made your team play'.[45] Glanville urged Alf, a week after Germany's substitute winger Jürgen Grabowski had helped eliminate England, to utter each night before bed, 'I do believe in wingers' (*Sunday Times* 21 June 1970). Yet England's two goals against West Germany, one in each half, were both assists by right-back Keith Newton, and overlapping full-backs underlay Alf's tactics. The first was a simple pass and return with Mullery, who right-footed the ball in about six yards from goal; the second a speedy Newton cross met at the far post by Peters, in the 49th minute. Surely England's iron defence could not concede three?

The first, in the 68th minute, was a Franz Beckenbauer shot from distance that ghosted under England's reserve goalkeeper Peter Bonetti. Perhaps it was an atmosphere-assisted 'altitude goal',[46] but even Bonetti's room-mate thought he 'should have had it'.[47] The 82nd-minute equaliser, an unusual backward flick that looped over England's goalkeeper, was 'a remarkable piece of heading' by Uwe Seeler, just 170cm tall. The third, in extra time, was a beautiful run and cross by Grabowski, volleyed goalwards in mid-air by Gerd Müller. Modern media pundits 'would have thrown their arms up in despair at the errors right across [England's] defensive line',[48] and in 1970 Finn also believed the Germans 'probably deserved to win it, just as England deserved to lose'. Caustically, he found it 'hard to be sympathetic to a side that betrayed itself or to a *manager whose insistence on being judged solely on results is legend*'.[49]

Finn's unsympathetic attitude was not widely shared, despite a growing consensus that the England squad's public relations needed improving. The *Daily Mirror* (17 June 1970) advocated that, and cited five other newspapers similarly arguing England should appoint a PR expert. FA secretary Denis Follows, in a private FA communication, agreed about 'improving our relationships with ... the media who influence the public'. England's team manager 'rightly' had 'complete control of the team' but in future 'some other spokesman' could communicate on matters 'not directly related to team tactics or selection'. Equally, Follows concluded, 'How this affected the players, if at all, is a moot point.' He said nothing directly criticising Alf, instead believing that England 'failed simply because the forwards were not good enough ... something we knew before we came to Mexico'.[50]

Alf Ramsey's own, confidential three-page FA report[51] ignored media relations, and focused solely on preparation and playing. Alf thought England were 'fortunate to win' against Czechoslovakia, although in physical fitness were 'equal at least' to all four teams played. Regarding 'individual skills techniques' and 'outstanding individual players ... the South American and Latin countries still lead'. Alf identified four such players from Brazil, two West Germans and one each from Peru, Czechoslovakia and Russia. By implication, Alf admitted England lacked equivalent individual talent so had to excel elsewhere to match South American countries' 'considerable improvement' in organisational teamwork. In a thought pattern fatal to his managership, Alf still insisted, though, that 'in utilising' combined 'skill, fitness, speed and strength into collective application *there is little to be learned from other countries*': a line unwisely pursued in public.

Despite defeat, hundreds of enthusiastic fans welcomed England's squad back to Heathrow. Alf promised a press conference, once rested, and only Jack Charlton said anything significant: 'The Mexican people seemed to hate us, and we didn't know why' (*Coventry Evening Telegraph* 17 June 1970). An English journalist, conveniently ignoring how newspapers fed on animosities, rather absurdly overclaimed that influential people had been 'appalled at the way England antagonised almost the whole of Latin America'. Despite that, he still argued it was 'bordering on lunacy' to criticise Alf:

> On every possible count ... Tactics, selection, public relations – nothing has been spared ... a ridiculous witch-hunt, which even his FA critics realise – for they are preparing for battle on one ground only. This is public relations, Ramsey's weakest point. (*The People* 21 June 1970)

Battle soon resumed on that precise ground, when Alf gave his promised press conference. Of this disaster *The Times* tactfully commented:

> Sir Alf is not at his best in these set pieces. He tends to lose his way in developing an argument ... But the essential honesty and integrity of the man show through. He may be hypersensitive, he certainly can be tactless, but he is a man of honour. He speaks his mind. (26 June)

Others were less forgiving. Accurately, Alf argued that Brazil had feared England, but he then made this ridiculous statement: 'I don't think that we can learn anything from Brazil.' Such a blatant contradiction of results and performances was a gift to critics. One described how Alf 'for almost two hours' whilst 'wearing his best Mona Lisa smile, parried question after question'. England, it seemed, were 'the real winners of the World Cup, but through some technical error the name of Brazil appears on the trophy!' (*The Scotsman* 26 June 1970).

In like fashion, Finn's critique of England's Mexico tournament, published later that year, parodied Alf by quoting 'I don't think we can learn a lot from Brazil' as the book's penultimate line.[52] Marquis's 1970 biography was equally critical, but shrewder at deciphering Alf's psychology: 'What he meant was *there is nothing to learn from Brazil that can be applied to the players we have at the moment.*'[53] A newspaper editorial agreed, noting 'Sir Alf likes to shock the press', and arguing this was just his 'way of saying England would not gain by adopting' Brazilian tactics, because Brazil were unique football 'geniuses' (*Newcastle Journal* 27 June 1970).

Alf had signalled his position in an interview five days before, accepting 'without recrimination' the 'severe and hard criticism ... directed at me personally'. Yet he would never 'deal out individual criticism. Criticise my players? It is impossible. It is not my way' (*Sunday Mirror* 20 June 1970). At the full press conference five days later, Alf then defended all his other decisions as stoutly and irrationally:

> If I had to do the job again, I would do it the same way. I would select the same team, make the same arrangements, and give the same instructions. On a different occasion, we would have got better results. (*Belfast Telegraph* 25 June 1970)

Stubborn defence of players was one thing, but these public self-justifications went a revealing step further. Marquis's biography ends with an epilogue entirely devoted to that disastrous press conference, offering numerous examples of Alf's 'unmatched talent for self-persuasion … fluent inarticulateness … and inability to express himself'.[54] Marquis found 'this complex man … so full of contradictions' that he was impossible to summarise. Alf's insistence that he would do 'exactly the same things again … indicates a staggering lack of self-criticism'.[55]

How can Alf's unusual behaviours be explained? Elsewhere he confessed that 'I seldom stop thinking about football' (*Daily Mirror* 8 November 1972), which helps contextualise his media performances. In Alf's mind ran an incessant internal monologue of football analysis that he seemed unable to switch off. Might responses to reporters have been answering those internal thoughts, as much as their external questions? When Alf foolishly claimed, 'We have nothing to learn from Brazil', it seems likely he was referencing his personal belief that had Gordon Banks not fallen ill, and England had reached the World Cup Final, they could have beaten Brazil. This may have been 'magical thinking'[56] but Alf sincerely, if privately, believed England would 'bring the pot back'.[57] Imprisoned in his own world view, Alf had always been unconcerned with how others saw him and, despite growing criticism a year later trumpeted exactly the same line. England may have lost in Mexico but 'in terms of individual skill and team ability, physical fitness and the will to win, the England team had no superior' (*FA News* August 1971).

Such fixed thinking may have reflected neurodivergence. Previous chapters explored that possibility using current UK NHS definitions of Autism Spectrum Condition (ASC). Similar recent Australian guidelines, italicised below, were likewise mirrored both in that June 1970 press conference, and Alf's lifelong awkwardness. They describe how adults with ASC are often told *'it is hard to know what you are thinking'* and frequently find *'small talk'* or *'joining in conversation difficult'*. Problems *'in using and responding to tone of voice'*, may make *'it easier to talk at people'* or sometimes to *'speak very formally'*. People with ASC can also often *'be blunt in their assessment of people'*, find *'building and maintaining close friendships difficult'*, and may prefer *'operating solo'*.[58]

Equally, if some of Alf's behaviours did originate in neurodivergence, they clearly helped his career. Marquis's final biographical page highlighted three qualities central to Alf Ramsey's success: 'prodigious memory of players and games', a 'deep analytical ability' and his players coming 'first and last, everyone else nowhere'.[59] Those 1970 observations echo the contemporary Australian guidance cited above, setting out four typical strengths of people with ASC: *'excelling in a chosen area of study'*, *'noticing details in the environment that others miss'*, having *'increased empathy or immense care for people'* and *'enjoying working independently'*. Alf's stubborn and distinctive approaches may have blighted his media relations but helped him significantly in managing professional footballers.

Alf's Historical Reputation Starts to Skew

Undeniably, though, suspicions of Alf were growing. Originating perhaps in his conservative dress code, inauthentic accent, open patriotism and clumsy communication, liberal opinion became increasingly critical. Success in 1966 had shielded Alf but, after England's 1970 Mexico exit, then the 1972 European Nations failure examined in the next chapter, scepticism escalated into parody. For example, the first, October 1972 issue of the student satirical football magazine *FOUL* openly scorned 'Ramseyism';[60] and in the autumn of 1973 *Private Eye* mocked a thinly disguised Alf for World Cup failure against Poland.[61] Alf's 1974 sacking halted such personal attacks, but something else soon clouded his historical reputation: culture wars during which his 1966 victory, and football in general, became political pawns in wider controversies. On one side was Conservative Prime Minister Margaret Thatcher, who held power from 1979–90. Along with various ideological allies she disliked all sport[62] but particularly despised football which, a BBC report claimed, 'came to reflect the social upheaval of the Thatcher years'.[63] Her attitudes to 1980s football hooliganism, and the 1984–85 miners' strike, were recently framed as 'part of the same attack ... presenting [football] supporters as an enemy of the state' just like 'the unions'. For example, in 1986 Thatcher personally condemned 'very ugly [football] scenes and very ugly trade union scenes', conveniently ignoring strong evidence linking 'football hooliganism with the far-right'.[64] Similarly, it was 'with the connivance of *The Sun* newspaper and Thatcher's press secretary' that the 1989 Hillsborough disaster, and its 97 deaths, were blamed by senior police officers on Liverpool's own fans, rather than police and local authority failings.[65]

'Thatcherism' created a polarised political atmosphere in which Alf also attracted scrutiny from left-leaning scholars. They positioned his World Cup victory as, for example, a 'recurring symbolic device, advantageously deployed by power elites to keep the public interested in an illusory national identity ... A *myth of 1966*.'[66] Alf's conservative public image superficially bolstered such claims of nationalistic 'mythologising',[67] but that argument only worked if a fundamental historical fact was ignored. Lifelong, Alf had lauded foreign footballers' superior skills.[68] Straight after the 1966 triumph, he publicly admitted that although his England side were the 'fastest and strongest ... I do not think we can ever match the individual techniques of the Latin Americans or Latin Europeans ... It has taken English football 100 years to realise that football can be played differently' (*Birmingham Daily Post* 1 August 1966). For Alf, England's footballing weaknesses were an English problem, soluble by learning from foreigners, a strategy anathema to any genuine xenophobe. Meanwhile, for Geoff Hurst, an undisputed English football hero, even the possibility of Alf Ramsey being xenophobic was, he confided in a recent conversation, just 'completely wrong ... seeing and talking to Alf ... I can't imagine that'.[69]

1 Kuper, S. (2011)

2 Mayes, H. (1967) p.235

3 See chapter 11

4 Edgerton, D. (2014) pp.12-13

5 Hughson, J. (2016) p.49

6 McMaster, A. and Bairner, A. (2012) p.215

7 Hughson, J. (2016) pp.102, 177

8 **FA Archive of 1966 Congratulatory Letters** 3 August 1966, Mr. Rogers

9 Hamilton, D. (2023) p.227

10 *The Athletic* (10 July 2021) 'England's 55 years of hurt – by the players who lived it'

11 Phillips, N. (2007) pp.320-21

12 Finn, R. (1970) p.37

13 Phillips, N. (2007. p.322

14 Dawson, J. (2001) p.60

15 See chapter 13

16 McKinstry, L. (2007) p.405

17 Phillips, N. (2007) p.425

18 Peters, M. and McNeill, T. (1970) pp.24-26

19 Grateful thanks to assistance from the Mexican National Newspaper Archive, see the 'Digital Newspaper Archive of *El Informador*' (2025) website

20 Wilson, J. (2009) pp.204, 208

21 Kuper, S. (2016) p.274

22 Dawson, J. (2001) p.124

23 Finn, R. (1970) p.34

24 Hamilton, D. (2023) p.299

25 Glanville, B. (1980) p.164

26 Hayward, P. (2022) p.219

27 Spurling, J. (2022) pp.38-39

28 For example, Dawson, J. (2001) pp.62-63, 66-67, Hamilton, D. (2023) p.300, Hayward, P. (2022) pp.216-17

29 McColl, G. (1998) p.56

30 Dawson, J. (2001) pp.37-38

31 Bowler, D. (1999) p.243

32 Spurling, J. (2022) p.38

33 Hamilton, D. (2023) p.299

34 Marquis, M. (1970) pp.125-26

35 See *The Stage* 2 January 1969

36 Glanville, B. (1973) p.219

37 Glanville, B. (2004) p.192

38 Ibid. p.192

39 Glanville, B. (1973) p.219
40 The Set Pieces website (2015) I. Macintosh 'Vox In The Box:
  Brian Glanville'
41 Sandbrook, D. (2012) pp.78-79
42 Finn, R. (1970) pp.71-72
43 Hayward, P. (2022) p.222
44 Finn, R. (1970) pp.76, 77
45 Ibid. p.162
46 Hayward, P. (2022) p.225
47 Peters, M. (1970) p.79
48 Hayward, P. (2022) p.226
49 Finn, R. (1970) op. cit. p.101
50 **Professional Papers of Sir Harold Warris Thompson**: D Follows
  15 June 1970
51 Ibid. 'WORLD CUP – MEXICO 1970 Report by Sir Alfred Ramsey'
52 Finn, R. (1970) p.164
53 Marquis, M. (1970) p.143
54 Ibid. p.142
55 Ibid. pp.143-44
56 Hamilton, D. (2023) p.310
57 Hurst, G. (2024) p.149
58 The Spectrum website (2025) 'Autism characteristics: checklist for adults'
59 Marquis, M. (1970) p.145
60 Spurling, J. (2022) p.50
61 Winner, M. (2006) pp.164, 149-50
62 BBC Sport website (9 April 2013) 'Margaret Thatcher's sporting legacy'
63 BBC Sport website (10 April 2013) 'Margaret Thatcher "never really
  understood sport"'
64 Campbell, T. (2023) pp.88 and 97
65 Baldwin, T. and Stears, M. (2024) p.182
66 Hughson, J. (2016) pp.132, 138
67 Ibid. pp.139-49
68 Ramsey, A. (1952)
69 Geoff Hurst oral history interview 7 February 2025

CHAPTER 14

FAILING MEN, ENDURING WOMEN

Alf Bullied and Dismissed

FA Cultures

ALF RAMSEY'S England leadership lasted 113 games; Gareth Southgate managed 102 matches. The 'points percentage' each gained was similar (Ramsey 73 per cent, Southgate 71.6 per cent),[1] though Southgate's eight years saw England's men tantalisingly reach, then lose, consecutive European Championship finals (2020 and 2024) and a World Cup semi-final (2018). England's agonising wait to win another World Cup may therefore end from a direction novel to Alf: female footballers. Until 1970, the English FA banned women from playing on FA-approved grounds or being refereed by FA-trained officials. In 2021, they appointed Sarina Wiegman as England women's manager; by 2023 she had already won a European Championship Final and lost a World Cup Final. England's national teams, at all age levels, now receive sustained FA funding and support in ways unimaginable to Alf. In contrast, this chapter tracks him being undermined and even bullied by a *voluntary* FA board member, then dismissed on 20 April 1974. Eleven days later, still in shock, Alf spent three hours at his home confiding to two vastly experienced football journalists. In their words, Alf's revelations 'made us realise he had worked miracles' overcoming FA committees-led 'petty officialdom'. Alf's muttered doorstep farewell said it all: 'The bloody amateurs are back in command.'[2]

Alf was referencing Harold Thompson, whose scientific career glittered with international publications and honours: Professor of Chemistry at Oxford, Fellow of the Royal Society and a 1968 knighthood.[3] Thompson started volunteering for the FA in the 1940s,[4] loved amateur football, and in 1948 helped found 'Pegasus', a new club drawn from Oxford and Cambridge undergraduates. In 1951 and 1953, Pegasus won the FA Amateur Cup before Wembley crowds of 100,000, but backstage Thompson caused 'continual upsets'. Some Pegasus officials resigned, in 1960 one punched him in exasperation, and 'Thompson's impact was almost entirely negative.'[5] Similarly, of his volunteering at the FA, male employees recollected, 'A bastard ... I could not stand him ... He treated the staff like shit. No one liked him. He would offend people so much.'[6] Even the diplomatic Geoff Hurst recently described Thompson as 'the ultimate amateur' and 'extremely rude' to England's players and staff.[7]

It was not just rudeness. Sir Stanley Rous told of 'a man who would force his attentions on women at any opportunity'.[8] Another unnamed FA source admitted 'Thompson had an appalling reputation for sexually harassing women', with one airline making 'a formal complaint about him trying to touch up a stewardess'.[9] Female former FA employees told me similar stories. One anonymously endorsed the published evidence, that 'ladies would not want to be in a room on their own with him ... very clever ... difficult to spot making a mistake ... could be a bully ... threatening'.[10] Another openly recalled 'a horrible man ... a bit of a lecher. Denis Follows you would have trusted with your life. You would not trust a dog to Sir Harold.'[11] Seemingly, Thompson, although 'a quite brilliant chemist' was a 'quite odious man;'[12] but when did he start to undermine Alf?

McKinstry's biography located the flashpoint to May 1973, drawing on an interview given just after Alf's 1974 sacking. In it Alf described Thompson smoking a cigar over breakfast with the England squad, at a Prague hotel, and 'politely' requesting he 'put it out or eat in another room', as Thompson's smoke 'was unpleasant' for England's players (*Sunday People* 12 May 1974). McKinstry speculated that Thompson 'had never been treated that way' so Alf's 'fate may have been sealed in that Czechoslovakian breakfast room'.[13] That influential story was then repeated in 2022[14] and 2023.[15] Yet previously overlooked evidence now suggests even worse bullying, because an identical incident had happened a decade earlier, when Alf's management was new. In April 1964, in a Scottish dining room, Alf had similarly to demand that 'Thompson either extinguish his cigar or leave the hotel dining room, when he presumed to join the England players for breakfast'.[16]

That significant, nine-year difference to the conventional version is supported by other evidence from the summer of 1963. After Alf's first overseas tour, and three England wins, a journalist present recalled that Alf's end-of-tour speech praised his players but sarcastically thanked accompanying FA committee members 'in particular for keeping out of our way' (*Daily Mirror* 7 November 1972). Alf's 1963 barb, the journalist argued, 'planted seeds of rancour' that grew into 'a major factor in his dismissal' (*Independent on Sunday* 2 May 1999). It also explains why

Thompson, in 1964, invited himself to an England team breakfast and rudely blew smoke over Alf's players. From the dawn of his England management, not its dusk, Alf was having to confront an eventual FA chairperson with fundamentally different values from his own. FA staff and volunteers found Thompson rude, domineering and sometimes sexually harassing; in contrast, Jimmy Greaves recalled Alf's kindness, in the mid-1960s, when discreetly assisting an aged FA dignitary who had fallen asleep during a foreign banquet.[17]

More significantly, Alf's young FA secretary from 1967–74, Margaret Fulljames, never heard him be chauvinistic to women: 'The perfect gent ... polite, respectful, never forgot a please or thank you ... all the secretaries liked Alf.' She 'never heard a bad word spoken about him' by other female FA employees,[18] and he 'treated everyone the same, never spoke badly of anybody'.[19] Similarly, 19-year-old office junior David Barber worked with Alf from 1970, and told the author 'there was never a cross word, even when I messed up ... he certainly wasn't posh in the office ... and smiling all the time. Whereas if he was interviewed he would be scowling.'[20] Alf's scowling at journalists was well known but, as one testified, an 'enormous majority' of his players 'DO like him. They refuse to criticise him, even for money' (*Daily Mirror* 6 November 1972). Despite lifelong immersion in what was then a single-sex professional sport, Alf also rarely displayed aggression. Evidence of just two physical confrontations have emerged from his entire adult life, neither resulting in violence, both involving journalists after what Alf considered unfair criticism.[21]

So why, after the 1970 World Cup, did Alf's England career have just 30 games and four years left to run? Beguilingly, the first ten games went well. Any lingering Mexico misery evaporated in November 1970, when 93,000 at Wembley welcomed a promising GDR (East Germany) side, boasting four recent wins. They succumbed 3-1 to England's 'imaginative and free-flowing forward play', leaving the 'usually most reserved' Alf 'patently bubbling with enthusiasm' (*The Times* 27 November 1970). A Scottish newspaper gracefully conceded that England had, apparently, learned much 'from Brazil' (*Daily Record* 26 November 1970). Nine more unbeaten games followed, over 18 months, before disaster struck. In brief, as the football of 1972–74 will be discussed shortly, at Wembley in April 1972, as in Mexico in June 1970, West Germany beat England in *the* game that mattered: winning the European Championship quarter-final first leg 3-1, then drawing the return.

Those 1970 and 1972 quarter-final defeats left England desperate to qualify for the 1974 World Cup, a hazardous process avoided in 1966 as hosts and in 1970 as holders. They also heightened Alf's vulnerability to his prime FA enemy, Professor Harold Thompson, who from 1967 was FA vice-chairperson and chairperson 1976–81.[22] Newspaper reports then,[23] and studies since,[24] agree Thompson was the 'driving force' behind Alf's sacking. Thanks to him, Alf's dismissal was 'handled with brutal insensitivity … kicked out after 11 years of unstinting service and unprecedented success with … a meagre annual pension of £1,200' (*The Guardian* 21 May 2009). Even at the time, a leading newspaper asked, 'What is it about those who administer sport which compels them so often to humiliate those who have served their game well?' (*Manchester Evening News* 2 May 1974).

FA Infighting

Alf confided he did not 'mix' with FA committee members, his sole concern being 'the players. I thought about them 24 hours a day.' He 'personally liked' FA employees, who 'were most efficient', but in a single damning sentence confessed that 'over the whole 11 years I never really enjoyed working for the FA' (*Sunday People* 12 May 1974). By 'the FA' he meant its controlling committees, in which Harold Thompson was prominent. In 1966, Thompson had sent a begrudging note congratulating 'Dear Ramsey … not only for what you have done, but for the way in which you did it. Many of us thank you.'[25] But just 22 months later, after England's 1968 European semi-final loss,[26] a newspaper warned the FA's 'interfering, criticising amateur officials' to 'stay off Alf's back and let him run England in his own way' (*Sunday People* 9 June). In 1969, Thompson publicly sided with Alf's stylistic critics, arguing 'football today needed … a spirit of enterprise and … attack' (*Rugby Advertiser* 16 May).

Six days after England's June 1970 World Cup quarter-final defeat, Thompson repeated that critique, privately and poisonously. A five-page typed letter to the FA chairperson threatened Thompson's resignation, commenting snidely on Alf: 'One would like to stand by a manager through bad times and good times alike', but the 'defensive style of play which has now been introduced, and is spreading all down the line, is doing damage to the game'. Thompson then raised six different criticisms of FA secretary Follows, alleging him to be 'in real difficulty with his staff, who may have lost confidence in him'.[27] That allegation was unfair, and probably untrue, but matters here because Follows was Alf's key FA ally.

Ten days later, Follows, apparently ignorant that Thompson was undermining him, sent the professor some innovative ideas for FA reform in a memo headed 'CONFIDENTIAL'. This suggested, two decades before similar changes eventually happened, that the voluntary chairperson be replaced by 'a full-time paid official',[28] and its 'Secretary' become a 'Chief Executive'.[29] Thompson delayed replying, then bluntly resisted. Follows's suggestions would make the FA 'a commercial affair and destroy any amateur part'. Outrageously, whilst acknowledging Follows's letter had been 'marked confidential', Thompson admitted to sending 'a copy ... to the FA Chairman'. Despite Mexico-related media criticism, Thompson also rebuffed Follows's proposal for an FA public relations officer. Rather, he argued, they should track 'which members of staff have not been doing their job properly'. Follows would be retiring in 1972, Thompson continued, and until then could 'handle ... public relations', but after that leadership should pass to voluntary FA Council members not yet 'given the chance to show what they can do'. Thompson was referring to himself, not other FA volunteers, who he labelled as too old or lacking 'experience, training or ability' in the 'worldly relationships of modern football'.[30]

Alf Ramsey evidently heard about this manoeuvring, as he later publicly revealed that Thompson had wanted to be 'England's Press liaison officer' for 1974's 'expected World Cup trip to West Germany'. England's players would stoutly 'have resisted', Alf observed, because they hated Thompson 'addressing them by their surnames'. In his view the professor could 'never' have been 'part of a team competing in a World Cup' (*Sunday People* 12 May 1974). Thompson's unpublished personal 1970 correspondence demonstrated his deep animosity towards Alf, a 'paid FA servant', who had a 'responsibility to the FA Council'. Alf's 'silent arrogance', fumed the professor, 'is as improper here as it was in Latin America'.[31]

Thompson harboured equally 'bitter hostility' towards Denis Follows (*Liverpool Daily Post* 20 December 1979), who on Alf's appointment had ceded selection powers away from FA committees.[32] The professor's 'perpetual, hectoring interference'[33] worsened Follows's chronic heart condition, which during 1971–72 needed major surgery.[34] Age-related retirement was then enforced, Follows's job was nationally advertised (*Daily Mirror* 20 September 1972), and nine months later the entrepreneur Ted Croker became FA secretary.[35] Alf was isolated, and the end was nigh. Croker's £10,000 annual salary dwarfed the manager's, newspapers noticed, and after losing 2-0 in Poland on 6 June 1973 Alf was 'under pressure now England are struggling to qualify for the World Cup' (*Sunday Mirror* 24 June 1973). Yet despite such acute anxieties, before that vital Poland game in Katowice, Alf still sent his habitual postcard back to junior office-based FA colleagues, sending 'Best wishes from Katowice from all of us here – Alf Ramsey'.[36]

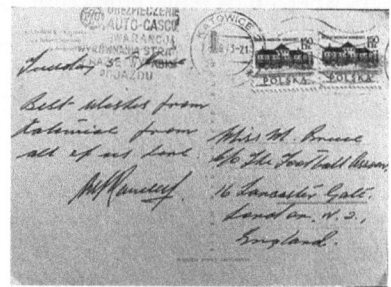

As FA chairperson from 1976, Thompson oversaw England's failure to qualify for the 1978 World Cup, too. FA councillors rebelled (*Daily Mirror* 12 October 1978) and in 1979 Thompson's poor decision-making legally lost the FA's winnable court case, around Don Revie's calamitous England managership (1974–77).[37] Equally, to catalogue his unpleasantness and failures is not to dispute that something managerially needed to change. It should have happened either in summer 1972, following Alf's European failure, or shortly after autumn 1973's World Cup exit. By then, even to close friends, Ramsey appeared 'too rigid … he did not understand how football was changing'.[38] The FA then made him hang on for another eight pointless months, with even Alf admitting 'the writing was on the wall … I was a dead duck' (*Sunday People* 12 May 1974).

Declining Football

The real villain was English football's organisational setup. Precipitous 1970s decline saw England failing to qualify for two World Cups, and one European Championship, after Alf's teams had reached quarter-finals in 1970 and 1972. Alf's 1974 departure also brought no quick fixes. After his 1968 European semi-final, it took 22 years, and four more managers, for England to reach that tournament stage again. Such serial under-achievement happened for cultural and structural reasons, far beyond Alf's or any other manager's personal control. For example, Alf's last contribution to *FA News* (May 1974) stringently criticised clubs for not releasing players to England, and the football authorities for not making them do so. Alf condemned as 'ludicrous that any international team manager should not have available a team of full strength … no other national activity – sport, art, political – would tolerate this state of affairs!'

Weeks later, he also cited the narrowing gap between the 'good and not-so-good nations'. England 'no longer' enjoyed 'any easy matches', so 'second-rate preparation' was fatal; more 'time must be found for matches and training'. Poignantly, Alf then admitted being England manager was 'a very lonely job', with 'no one to talk to at the FA'. Consequently, 'an assistant from professional football would have been a good thing'. Years previously, Alf claimed he had suggested 'the FA appoint a full-time professional manager for the England Youth team' but 'nothing was done' (*Sunday People* 19 May 1974).

On the pitch, between November 1970 and April 1972, England's results were statistically strong, with eight victories and two draws setting up a two-legged, European Championship quarter-final with West Germany. Yet those results had been against smaller countries with scant footballing success: an opening friendly with East Germany (the GDR); Northern Ireland, Wales and Scotland in the Home Championship; and Greece, Malta and Switzerland in the European Championship qualifying group, culminating on 1 December 1971 with a win in Athens. That unbeaten run also concealed other structural weaknesses. West Germany had battled through a tougher qualifying group including Poland, Turkey and Albania, and four weeks before travelling to Wembley had won a friendly in Hungary. England, meanwhile, had not played competitively for five months, nor even had the chance to train together. As the editor of the *FA News* lamented, two months before England even played their quarter-final 'What a way to run an international football team … without recent competitive practice or even the occasional get-together!' (February 1972).

This came about because, to West Germany's distinct advantage, the elite leagues of the two countries differed significantly. Its Bundesliga had 18 teams and 34 fixtures, while England's First Division had 22 teams, entailing 42. Both leagues kicked off on 14 August 1971 but by that 29 April 1972 Wembley showdown, West Germany's top clubs, after a mid-season break, had played just 29 league games. England's clubs had played 41. The English First Division's final game of the season featured fifth-placed Arsenal against sixth-placed Spurs, on Thursday evening, 11 May 1972,[39] just 48 hours before England played in Berlin. Meanwhile, the Bundesliga finished two and a half months later,[40] with no fixtures for six days on each side of both England–West Germany quarter-final games. Into the same calendar slot in England were crammed 15 fixtures, featuring the league's top eight clubs 11 times.

Shortly after England's 1972 quarter-final failures, Alf's main FA ally publicly aired English football's organisational problems. Secretary Denis Follows, his age-enforced retirement looming, railed against league and cup fixture congestion. England's squad mostly played in

Division One where fatigue entailed more frequent injuries, which heightened the reluctance of clubs to release England players. Follows wanted radical change, giving 'top priority' to 'preparation of the national team'. If not, England would become 'a third-rate footballing nation' just 'muddling along'. English Football's structural overloads, argued Follows, made being 'the England Team Manager virtually impossible' (*FA News* July 1972):

> [Alf's] every action, every expression is noted and analysed. His deepest thoughts are interpreted in accordance with the whims of the interpreter. He, more than the players, is subject to intense pressures. Mentally, he must have the hardest task ... to attempt to satisfy a nation, not a city or town. (*Hull Daily Press* 10 June 1972)

None of this excuses, though does lend perspective, to Alf's managerial mistakes in four pivotal games: the 1972 home and away encounters with West Germany, and a 1973 equivalent against Poland. For consistency's sake, the extracts below, from reports about those matches, all come from the vastly experienced chief football correspondent, Geoffrey Green of *The Times*.

Green catalogued Alf's team selection errors against West Germany at Wembley on 29 April 1972. England lost 3-1 because they 'were beaten in midfield. Without Mullery there to win the ball, Ball, Peters and Bell were a street behind Netzer, Hoeness and Wimmer as a creative productive force ... we fenced and parried sideways, they thrust swiftly.' West Germany's three glittering midfielders also supported 'the direct running of two probing wingers', with all five being skilfully fed by Beckenbauer. West Germany's captain, perched in front of his defence, strode 'majestically across the green stage sweeping up everything within sight at his own easy pace, a beautiful player' (*The Times* 1 May 1972). Half a century later, pundits still agree that Alf picked the wrong midfield. It was 'very creative' but 'there's no real hardman'. With Moore and Hunter in defence, 'two ball-playing centre backs',[41] that midfield imbalance defensively over-exposed 31-year-old Bobby Moore. As in Poland a year later, his misjudgements conceded two goals. It was 1-1 until the 84th minute but England lost 3-1.

Was Alf, too, having a confidence crisis? Bullishly, between the two games he reminded fans that since November 1970, 27 different players had represented England, 11 being 'new to senior international football'. At 2-0 down in Mexico, with less than 25 minutes left, West Germany had been 'in a worse position than we are now' (*Sunday Mirror* 7 May 1972). But his stringent critic and media maverick, Malcolm Allison,[42] privately described speaking 'deep into the night ... with an agonised Alf ... discussing possible tactics'.[43] Alf eventually selected more physical midfielders, hoping perhaps for an early goal, substitutions, then a platform for ambitious attack, but it ended goalless in torrential Berlin rain. Storey and Hunter fouled the opposition incessantly, one of whom, Günter Netzer, wryly vouched 'my legs were well autographed'. Ominously, Green's match report yearned for more youth and two 'real wingers'. Equally, before the next World Cup 'Sir Alf must receive more generous, honest help from the clubs. Too many are wearing parochial blinkers' (*The Times* 15 May 1972).

Little changed structurally over the next 12 months, but when the three-team World Cup qualifying group began, England beat Wales in Cardiff, drew with them at Wembley, then Wales beat Poland 2-0. If England drew their next game, in Poland on 6 June 1973, that would have left Poland needing to beat both Wales and England to qualify. Unsurprisingly, Alf's 4-4-2 tactics and team selection signalled 'in letters ten feet tall' that England went to Poland for a draw. But a deflected shot off Moore after seven minutes, and him losing the ball to Lubański early in the second half, handed Poland a two-goal victory. Journalist Green wrote that England were 'obsessed with the fear of defeat ... a state of mind – a tactical misapplication – that often gets what it deserves'. Mystifyingly, even after conceding two goals 'Ramsey's defensive attitude continued', with three alternative forwards sitting 'on the substitute's bench ... mute and ignored' (*The Times* 7 June 1973). Alf was losing his touch.

Even so, for the Wembley return on 17 October, England needed just a win to progress. During a 1-1 draw they hit the bar, the post, saw remarkable serial saves by Poland goalkeeper Jan Tomaszewski, and had '22 corners and a whole sheaf of shots' blocked or sail just wide. Yet, until two minutes from the end Alf, again inexplicably, substituted nobody and instead sat 'immobile ... what fires were burning inside him one will perhaps never know'. Green could 'find no excuse ... this England side basically was short of brain ... like a moth caught on a pin' (*The Times* 18 October 1973). Alf, unconvincingly, blamed his tardy substitution on mistakenly believing there was 'a little longer to go' (*Daily Mirror* 18 October), but Green argued he should have changed things 'half an hour' earlier. Worse, strategically he had 'allowed England's football to fall into a grey, predictable groove' and 'new thinking' was needed.

Yesterday Mr Ted Croker took over officially as the new secretary of the Football Association … It is a time for new brooms and there are four years ahead to sweep away the clouds for the next World Cup in Argentina. They should not be wasted again. (*The Times* 19 October 1973)

Alf's career had faltered against excellent teams. West Germany became 1972 European champions and 1974 World Cup winners, whilst Poland finished third in 1974. In contrast, Alf's elite career had just six months left to run and, when asked about his personal future, his stark reply crystallised his psychological and financial predicament. 'I have to work to live. My life is in football' (*The Times* 18 October).

Fans and Fractures

To journalists, Alf seemed frustratingly inaccessible. His interviews illuminated little, the rare sparks coming less from insightfulness, more from friction. Undeterred, the public often liked him, both established football fans and new ones attracted by 1966. For example, that year Margaret Humphreys, a Lancastrian living in London, wrote to Alf:

> As a mere woman who according to my husband doesn't know one end of a football pitch from the other … I've watched every one of England's World Cup matches, and I have been astonished to find myself actually enjoying them.

Hundreds of miles west, from holiday in Cornwall, 22-year-old Patricia Tustin similarly sent 'many thanks' for the enjoyment England's seven games gave her 'and my class of seven-year-olds in North Yorkshire … with the children you all achieved even greater popularity than Batman!' Meanwhile, in Somerset, in 1966, Norma Grist and her husband were 'very keen local supporters of Radstock town' and lived next to their ground. Norma wrote Alf a seven-page letter:

> This World Cup tournament has been a great tonic for English football … there must be many thousands like us … We have two small sons … it will be great fun and excitement to relate to them as they get older all the thrills and glory of this 1966 World Cup series.

Would Norma ever have imagined that England's next senior trophy, after 1966, would be won by women footballers in 2021? Perhaps she would, because apparently her daughter, unlike the two sons mentioned, did become interested in football.[44]

Alf's public image may have lacked warmth but, through regular travel on public transport, he remained personally accessible to fans in ways unimaginable now. One fan, during season 1970/71, later recalled being so excited he 'could barely speak' when on the London Underground:

> [Alf Ramsey] got on the train and stood next to me ... for several minutes we carried on a conversation about some of the players he was on his way to evaluate ... I will never forget his gentlemanly conduct, his genuine interest in a 'regular fan', and his charming manner.[45]

A 'Mexico 1970' competition winner, Elsie Hamlin, stayed at the England squad's hotel with her 13-year-old son. She found Sir Alf 'very easy to talk to once a conversation was underway. I don't think he deserved all the criticism' (*Reading Evening Post* 25 June 1970). Other ordinary fans agreed. Just after England had failed to qualify for the 1974 World Cup, a consistently critical national newspaper polled its readers. Most wanted Alf to remain as England manager: 44 per cent compared to just one per cent preferring his eventual temporary replacement (Joe Mercer) and six per cent for his permanent successor (Don Revie). Only Brian Clough, at 26 per cent, came close (*Sunday People* 28 October 1973).

Simultaneously, Alf sparked a comic local controversy in Tunbridge Wells. Should a newly built pub be called 'The Sir Alf Ramsey'? A property developer claimed such a name 'will attract all the wrong sort of people' and threatened to organise a protest march (*Sunday People* 4 November 1973). Meanwhile, the building workers [shown overleaf], encouraged by a newspaper, expressed exactly the opposite. The fuss rumbled on for weeks, with one embarrassed resident writing, 'This is 1973, not 1873 ... poor old Tunbridge Wells. No wonder comedians joke about it' (*Kent and Sussex Courier* 16 November 1973).

More significantly, Alf's splintering public image reflected national divisions. 'Establishment' dislike of him was nothing new but criticism from more liberal angles was starting to find fresh angles. One arch-critic dubbed Alf 'the Stanley Baldwin of England football ... inhibiting and soul-destroying of any elan and flair'.[46] This metaphor's politics were inaccurate, for if Alf's fortunes tracked any party, it was Labour. From 1970–74 especially, but also before and after, his most intimate

newspaper relationship was with the Labour-supporting *Daily Mirror*. Edward Heath's Conservatives may have benefitted from England's 1970 World Cup quarter-final exit, winning the election four days later in an atmosphere of 'pervasive gloom' (*The Times* 29 May 2020),[47] but, as with Alf Ramsey, the year 1974 saw their drawn-out dismissal. On 28 February, an indecisive election delivered a hung parliament,[48] culminating in Labour forming a minority government. A second election on 10 October secured Harold Wilson a 'majority of just three MPs'.[49] England, and the other UK countries, were nations struggling to define a future direction.

In football, a distinctive new voice echoed such political disquiet. *FOUL* proclaimed itself 'The Alternative Football Paper' but was actually penned in ancient Cambridge University. Some of its student contributors already wrote 'for the mainstream press', several more soon would, and all were male. *FOUL* debuted in October 1972, ceased publication in 1976, and within ten years even influential football fanzine writers didn't 'know of *FOUL*'s existence'.[50] Yet despite a tiny circulation, and just 18 editions published before Alf's 1974 sacking, *FOUL* has influenced how the 21st century views him.[51] 'Lady Ramsey's Diary', for example, has been claimed as having 'taunted the England manager'.[52] Its single appearance parodied Alf amusingly complaining to his wife, after England beat Scotland 5-0, about 'individuals playing so well' and therefore undermining 'the whole team effort'.[53]

By June 1974 (issue 19), *FOUL*'s editorial was positioning England's World Cup exit as 'an optimistic sign', offering 'a chance to start again'.

Another contributor amusingly mocked the hackneyed 1966 evocations of mainstream football journalists: 'Warm cups of tea as dive bombers screeched overhead, guts courage Nobby and Tiger, Jack the Giraffe, and Squadron Leader Sir God Alf leading the 11 brave and true to the highest pinnacle man has ever reached.' The myth of 1966, it continued, could 'at long last' now be buried. 'Ramsey grim faced and professional … ousted by a public-school putsch … Right thing, wrong way we all chorused.' Alf's problem, this *FOUL* writer unusually conceded, had not been 'picking the wrong players or … wrong tactics', but the underlying 'heretical fact that English football is not only not the best but not even in the top ten'.

Most other *FOUL* writers mercilessly scapegoated Alf. In June 1973 FOULMOUTH lamented 'the damage done in the 10 years of his reign', claiming the England manager had dictated 'the climate of English football, the attitudes of managers and young players'. Unfortunately, this was hyperbolic nonsense. Annually, Alf managed fewer than ten senior matches, whereas professionals might play 50 or more club games. Geoff Hurst gained all his 49 caps under Alf's management and became one of England's most famous international footballers. He told me recently, and categorically, that 'there wasn't time' for Alf fundamentally to change the styles of players, that 'the coaching and teaching is all done at club level', and, as England manager, Alf merely 'fitted them into his pattern'.[54] Moreover, perhaps a third of England's approximately 300 First Division professionals were Scots, Welsh or Irish. Of the 200 remaining English players only perhaps 70–80 were realistic international prospects (*Daily Mirror* 8 November 1972). Alf had merely sporadic contact with, and organisational authority over, a tiny proportion of England's professional footballers. That same *FOUL* editorial, similarly misleadingly, also invented for satirical purposes a 'whole underlying philosophy of Ramseyism'. Yet for England, as at Ipswich,[55] Alf the pragmatist persistently argued that players came before tactics 'every time'. Alf had 'no plan for Ipswich when I went there … I had to see how I could use whatever talents they had to the best advantage … That is where tactics must begin' (*Daily Mail* 13 September 1962). A decade later he still maintained 'tactics are designed to fit players' (*Daily Mirror* 8 November 1972), players who competed in English leagues. Of necessity, Alf's teams therefore reflected league playing styles. In Jimmy Greaves's opinion, Alf even introduced his revolutionary 4-3-3 trophy-winning formation merely 'as a means to an end'.[56]

Ridiculously, *FOUL*'s November 1973 editorial wanted Alf sacked because 'the whole idea of using illegal tactics as a defensive ploy …

to incapacitate the opposition … is sickening and a travesty of the way football should be played'. This pompous rhetoric inverted reality because it was English league football that moulded the players from whom Alf had to pick,[57] the same professionals who vigorously resisted stricter refereeing (*The Times* 9 September 1971). *FOUL*'s Cambridge undergraduate writers, ironically, wanted England to become more like 1950s 'Pegasus', Professor Harold Thompson's Oxbridge amateur footballers. Snobbery also imbued some of their student vitriol. Leading football journalist Mike Langley had 'limited powers of reasoning',[58] some England internationals were 'versatile work-horses', and Tesco wine 'the bitterest'.[59] *FOUL* raged, amusingly, against 1970s English football's greedy players, myopic clubs, insular managers, stupid administrators, cliché-ridden journalists and, above all, monotonous, muscular football, pretending to be better than it was.[60] But its lampooning of Alf, for good comedic ends, confused cause and effect by erroneously ascribing English football's systemic failings personally to him.

Public perceptions of the England manager's role were changing, and cultural tides were turning. Alf's patriotism and cautious playing style symbolised something *FOUL*'s fresh young writers could easily satirise as over-physical English football and unthinking nationalism. The magazine's October 1973 preview of England's pivotal World Cup game with Poland epitomised this mindset:

> It is said abroad that English teams do not let you beat them – they start fighting … The Polish players big problem is that they come from a socialist country, where the law of the jungle does not prevail … There are two certainties about the night of October 17 – the first is that it will be a thoroughly unpleasant evening, and the second is that England will win.

Both those predictions proved wildly inaccurate, offering an opportunity to ask: did *FOUL*'s stereotyping of English football as thuggish, and hyper-masculine, in any way reflect the actual character of the national manager?

Steadfast Women

On Saturday, 20 April 1974, Alf trekked to the FA's London offices to be sacked, by which he 'was shattered but not entirely surprised'. Returning that evening, he confirmed the bad news to his wife, then to others, including his daughter in the USA. His 78-year-old mother, 'to whom Alf is devoted, was called on personally at her cottage in

Dagenham' (*Sunday People* 12 May 1974). Mother, wife, daughter, the rollcall of Alf's emotional life. What do those relationships illuminate about him?

Florence Ramsey was his mainstay, 'the mother he adores – though he prefers to say admires' (*Daily Mirror* 9 November 1972). Born in 1895, married in 1915, dying in 1979, her whole life was lived in Alf's birthplace, mostly in a wooden building 'little more than a hut'[61] and eventually demolished in 1977.[62] That house is 'thought to be' the one photographed below, around Alf's birth year of 1920.[63] The rural setting looks superficially idyllic but careful examination, and evidence in previous chapters, suggests the Ramseys lived in a mere third, maximum half, of a building that during its time as a family home had no mains water, gas, or electricity. Despite that, Alf stipulated his 1949 transfer to Spurs rested on being allowed to move back there.[64]

In April 1950, when Spurs won League Division Two, 30-year-old Alf 'returned home full of enthusiasm to present to Mother' his first senior medal, which she immediately got engraved.[65] Alf lived there, apparently with three other siblings, until his December 1951 marriage prompted a two-mile move to a larger, newer end-of-terrace house in Westrow Drive Barking. In 1955, Alf, his wife and stepdaughter then moved to Ipswich, but he still regularly visited the parental family home. A neighbour recalled often seeing him 'waiting for a bus ... he used to walk across Five Elms, get a bus to Romford then a train to Ipswich' (*Barking and Dagenham Post* 29 July 2016).

Alf's mother was a guiding light, but his father barely featured in Alf's 1952 autobiography or later interviews; perhaps because he earned his living by collecting and sometimes recycling rubbish, using a horse and cart?[66] He died in January 1966 of lung cancer, the same day England's World Cup group was drawn. Alf's bereavement was 'not publicised', because to him it was 'private, separate, no one else's business' (*Daily Mirror* 9 November 1972). Later in 1966, Alf's mother briefly came to public attention, a letter writer mentioning her foregoing 'a VIP seat to watch it on telly. I can see now where you get your reservedness from.'[67] Public displays of feeling, Alf admitted, were alien. His mother was 'in many ways very like me … she doesn't show much emotion' (*Daily Mirror* 9 November 1972).

Cosmetically, Alf's marriage mimicked that maternal reserve. The 1966 full-back George Cohen knew the couple well, gave a moving eulogy at Alf's funeral, but affectionately admitted 'it is not easy to imagine Alf as a particularly romantic lover'.[68] Another close friend described never seeing the Ramseys 'touch … embrace or be tactile. They would shake hands when they saw each other.'[69] Yet several anecdotes in McKinstry's biography demonstrate how the pair's 'same serious temperament', and mutual desire for privacy, strengthened their marriage.[70] For example, despite regular opportunities, neither would place trivial stories about themselves with the *Daily Mail*.[71] In 1970, Mrs Ramsey, although staying in the same Mexico City hotel as the partners of four England players, 'kept herself so apart that they never actually spotted her'.[72]

Although gender roles in the marriage were traditional, Alf's wife held equal power.[73] Was it her that helped him establish a considerate, family-first environment that endeared Alf to his Ipswich Town players' partners and spouses?[74] Certainly, Alf's career came to rely on his wife's unstinting support. In 1952, months after their marriage, he claimed she was 'now interested in football and never misses a match'. After every game 'win, lose or draw', the couple would 'go off to tea, and a variety show'.[75] In August 1955, when Ipswich Town played a practice match for their incoming manager, Alf recalled Mrs Ramsey's shock at the low standards of his new players (*Daily Mail* 13 September 1963). Equally, her public faith in his judgement was unshakeable. A rare interview in late 1965, at home in Ipswich, endorsed her husband's World Cup confidence. 'I can't think of any reason why he shouldn't bring the Cup to England: He deserves it … He has a will like iron' (*The Sun* 11 December 1965).

The couple were also solicitous with fans. In 1952, Alf the player got 'about 150 letters a week', replying to which entailed a 'great deal of patience by my wife'.[76] After 1966's World Cup Final, the exhausted pair spent seven days at home answering hundreds of letters, punctuated only by an occasional walk.[77] Returning from Mexico in 1970, they were again dutiful. Alf 'stood for a long time, with Lady Ramsey at his side, patiently signing autographs until he was rescued by the airport authorities' (*The Times* 18 June 1970). After his 20 April 1974 dismissal, Alf requested secrecy for ten days from the FA so the couple could spend a 'week on the coast with close friends ... Vicky and I had 11 years of pressure, and we wanted time to think and plan.' Alf retained just one diary engagement that week, to present the 'Texaco Cup' trophy. He 'shook every player's hand', despite 'agonising' chatter about 'the future of England in which I [secretly] knew I wouldn't be playing a part' (*Sunday People* 12 May 1974).

Observant readers may have noticed how Mrs Ramsey's given names, in this chapter, have rarely been used. Why? Because at a point unknown, but associated with Alf, she informally changed her name to 'Victoria' from the 'Rita Phyllis' recorded on her 1921 Southampton birth certificate. That may have reflected personal preference, but as 'Rita' she had married Arthur Norris in 1941, then in March 1943 the couple adopted a baby girl. The 'Rita' whom Alf always called 'Vic' or 'Victoria' was married to another man when they met, and had a young child. Alf had finally found a woman to adore, other than his mother, but she seemed unobtainable.

Although in the late 1940s marriage breakdowns tended to be seen as scandalous, the couple overcame that, and their subsequent relationship seems marked by kindness and devotion. They had met during the 1940s, probably after the summer of 1946 when Alf left the army to play full-time for Southampton. A later close friend related to the author how 'Vic had always told him' they met 'in the dancehall slap bang next door' to Southampton's greyhound and speedway stadium.[78] Presumably, that was at some point between 1943 and 1947, when Victoria's marriage was disintegrating. According to Victoria's divorce documents, by November 1947 Arthur Norris had 'deserted the petitioner'.[79] Both parties remarried during 1951, and Alf became a dutiful stepfather to Victoria's adopted daughter, Tanya. Having more children was impossible, confided Victoria to a friend: 'I cannot have a family I am barren'. Equally, by then she seemed not to 'want a lot of children' being 'quite happy how she was'.[80]

From the 1970s Alf's stepdaughter lived in the USA, and he enjoyed meeting her extended American family (*Sunday People* 9 February 1975). In friendly emails to the author, Tanya always and touchingly called Alf 'my father', nevertheless declining to discuss him further because being 'a very quiet and private man ... my father would not be happy with me' (26 July 2022); a reluctance seemingly also related to 'comments made by my mother before her passing' (31 July 2023). Those comments may have been fuelled by Victoria Ramsey's anger about Alf's treatment, which in turn revolved around a familiar figure. Victoria, a friend confided, 'hated that Professor Sir Harold Thompson of the FA, she absolutely loathed that man ... she thought he was the main one against him'.[81]

The FA's 1970s financial meanness magnified and justified Victoria's anger. Alf's annual salary had peaked at £7,200, his meagre pension far less (*Sunday People* 19 May 1974), but just two months later his permanent successor was awarded £25,000 annually and a five-year contract.[82] Eventually, Alf shrugged off this insulting disparity but 'Vic used to rule the roost and ... she was very bitter ... the bitter one ... so bitter I sometimes could not understand it.'[83] Equally, during the last decade of her husband's life, Victoria was his prime carer, enduring multiple pressures. Alf's final years were in a care home where access was tightly controlled against invasive 1990s newspaper reporters. Their friend, a regular visitor, described her imposing:

> Strict rules that nobody should go and visit except myself ... I had to give my name at the door ... she did not want anybody else to go and see him ... because he had these sort of memory lapses.[84]

Alf's will left an estate worth approximately £200,000, mostly from the value of their modest family home. Its mortgage had been settled with post-tax proceeds from the FA's £6,000 World Cup-winner's bonus. The FA, a few years previously, had also 'voluntarily boosted his pension ... after hearing Sir Alf had fallen on hard times'. In 1995, they offered to pay for his 'medical bills and the nursing home' but 'his proud wife refused'. Instead, she described paying:

> For his nursing home bills out of my savings ... I don't care if I am left with nothing. I still have the memories of that wonderful man ... we may not have been well-off, but we had quality of life. (*Sunday Mirror* 29 August 1999)

Alf's career choices were also, apparently, made jointly with Victoria. After 1966, he regularly received lucrative club management offers, far exceeding his England manager's salary (*Sunday People* 12 May 1974). For a short period after his dismissal that continued and he declined attractive, well-paid job offers from England, Greece, Spain, the Netherlands and Saudi Arabia (*Sunday People* 12 May, 26 May 1974, 9 February 1975). Aged 54, Alf was tired and perhaps losing the energetic cutting edge necessary for football management. As Victoria admitted, ten months after his sacking 'we have been glad of this time to get to know each other again after years of Alf travelling and flying and driving off for the early train' (*Sunday People* 9 February 1975).

When Alf finally returned, it was all too late. Things started well as the temporary, unpaid manager at Birmingham City for eight weeks (*Daily Mirror* 3 November 1977), but football had changed. For example, 57-year-old World Cup winner Alf's Birmingham newspaper column shared the page equally with another by Trevor Francis, the club's star 20-year-old forward. Francis complained about spending Christmas Eve training with team-mates, but still declared without irony 'an international career is my burning ambition' (*Birmingham Sports Argus* 24 December 1977). Unsurprisingly, within two months national newspaper stories started appearing, whispering that Francis wanted out via a high-value transfer. Alf fined him and 'the split between' them 'widened into an agonising gulf' (*Birmingham Sports Argus* 18 February 1978). Three weeks later, two other players demanded transfers, Alf publicly lambasted the team's efforts after losing 4-0, and he resigned (*Birmingham Sports Mail* 6 March 1978).

Money and player-power had erased the football cultures in which Alf had excelled. A year later his mother would die, and the UK's post-war social and political consensus would be challenged, then shattered, by Margaret Thatcher's 1979, 1983 and 1987 election victories. Meanwhile, what endured, as Alf declined and English football struggled, was lifelong gratitude to his mother and the ongoing love of his wife: two women, one of whom remains silent to history, whose decades of supporting, shaping and advising Alf Ramsey had helped England win a World Cup.

1 England Football Online website (24 March 2025) 'England's Coaches/ Managers by Points Percentage in All Matches'

2 Greaves, J. with Giller, N. (1993) pp.45-46

3 Richards, R. (1985)

4 *Dictionary of National Biography* (2004) Sir Harold Warris Thompson

5 Porter, D. (2000) pp.21, 24

6 McKinstry, L. (2007) pp.451-52

7 Hurst, G. (2024) p.107

8 Morse, G. (2016) pp.261, 263

9 McKinstry, L. (2007) p.451

10 Oral history interview with 1960s FA junior female employee

11 Margaret Fulljames oral history interview 27 January 2023 – Margaret was Alf Ramsey's secretary 1967-74

12 Hamilton, D. (2023) p.311

13 McKinstry, L. (2007) p.453

14 Hayward, P. (2022) p.245

15 Hamilton, D. (2023) p.325

16 Frank Keating *The Guardian* 26 April 1999

17 Greaves, J. with Giller, N. (1973) p.42

18 Margaret Fulljames by email 22 July 2024

19 Margaret Fulljames oral history interview 20 January 2023

20 David Barber oral history interview 23 May 2022

21 *Daily Mirror* 6 November 1972; Greaves, J. with Giller, N. (1973) pp.36-37

22 *Dictionary of National Biography* (2004) Sir Harold Warris Thompson

23 *Daily Mirror* 2 May 1974, *The People* 12 May

24 E.g. McKinstry, L. (2007) pp. 466-73, Hamilton, D. (2023) pp.311-14, 323-35

25 **FA Archive of 1966 Congratulatory Letters** 2 August 1966

26 See chapter 13

27 **Professional Papers of Sir Harold Warris Thompson**: Letter to Andrew Stephen 20 June 1970 HWT/48/2/2

28 Butler, B. (1991) *The Official History of the Football Association* London: Queen Anne Press p.287

29 **Professional Papers of Sir Harold Warris Thompson**: Memorandum Denis Follows to Harold Thompson 29 June 1970 HWT/48/2/3

30 **Professional Papers of Sir Harold Warris Thompson**: Letter to Denis Follows 27 July 1970 HWT/48/2/3

31 Ibid. Also quoted in Hamilton, D. (2023) pp.312-13

32 See chapters 11-13

33 Glanville, B. (2004) p.130

34 Pat Day oral history interview (FA Deputy CEO 1993-97) 15 January 2023

35 Butler, B. (1991) p.185

36 Thanks to Margaret Fulljames for sharing this memory and postcard

37 Evans, C. (2021) pp.321-24

38 Ibid. p.457

39 *Rothmans Football Yearbook 1971-72* London: Queen Anne Press

40 World Football website (no date) 'Germany – Bundesliga 1971-72'

41 **It Was What It Was** podcast (2 July 2024) *The End of Sir Alf: The Fall of England's Greatest Manager* Part 1

42 Dawson, J. (2001) p.281

43 Glanville, B. (2008) p.89

44 Grateful thanks to the Grist family for email correspondence

45 BBC News website (1 May 1999) 'Your Tributes to Sir Alf Ramsey'

46 Finn, R. (1970) p.158

47 See chapter 13 and Kuper, S. (2011)

48 Bogdanor, V. (2015)

49 BBC News website (1997) 'Politics 97'

50 Brewster, B. (1993) p.14

51 Spurling, J. (2022) pp.49-50

52 Winner, D. (2006) p.164

53 *FOUL* (6) March 1973

54 Geoff Hurst oral history interview 6 February 2025

55 See chapters 10-12

56 Greaves, J. with Giller, N. (1993) p.31

57 Spurling, J (2022)

58 *FOUL* (19) June 1974

59 *FOUL* (9) June 1973

60 Ticher, M. editor (1987)

61 See chapter 3

62 Brilliantly discovered thanks to Teresa Trowers **Valence House Archive & Local Studies Centre**

63 'SB3157' courtesy of **Valence House Archive & Local Studies Centre**

64 Ramsey, A. (1952) p.49

65 Ibid. p.56

66 See chapter 3

67 **FA Archive of 1966 Congratulatory Letters** 31 July Henley-on-Thames, 1 August 1966 Malta

68 Cohen, G. (2005) pp.274-76, 178

69 McKinstry, L. (2007) p.77

70 Ibid. e.g. pp.71-79, 361-55

71 Margaret Fulljames by email 31 August 2024

72 Hurst, G. (2024) p.150

73 Cohen, G. (2005) p.176

74 Bowler, D. (1999) p.129

75 Ramsey, A. (1952) pp.62, 64
76 Ramsey, A. (1952) p.63
77 McKinstry, L. (2007) p.348
78 John Booth oral history interview 3 December 2022
79 McKinstry, L. (2007) p.73
80 John Booth oral history interview 3 December 2022
81 Ibid.
82 Evans, C. (2023) p.249
83 John Booth oral history interview 3 December 2022
84 Ibid.

CHAPTER 15

AN ENGLISHMAN OF HIS OWN INVENTION

Time to Challenge our Memories

How Alf's Voice Came to Matter to Me

AFTER YEARS of thinking more about Alf Ramsey than I dare admit, especially to my family, it is hard to imagine an inner life without Alf sitting there, staring back. So how did my life *now* get to be steeped in his life *then*? Alf's Portman Road statue was unveiled in 2000, as pictured overleaf with his proud widow. Like other Ipswich Town fans, I took to polishing its metal shoes for good luck before games.

Sixteen years later, I devoted a page to Alf in a children's book about football,[1] prompting my stepchildren's grandfather to share a 1954 photo of him in an East London league-winning amateur team.[2] Perched at the back was Alf, during a previously ignored coaching project. Although I felt intrigued life was too busy to pursue it further. Yet a decade later, here we are. What persisted?

A therapist might ask about losing my father, having in some ways just found him; about ending and starting different careers, moving house, marrying again, and ageing. Politics contributed: reading about Alf's racist childhood nickname in 2016, then England choosing Brexit that summer, despite a white supremacist assassinating a defenceless MP. Boris Johnson's baloney followed, then George Floyd's agonies and the white guilt involved in me understanding 'Black Lives Matter'. Meanwhile, English football's financial antics continued via hallucinogenic wages, fantastical transfers and English clubs bought up by overseas oligarchs, oil states and tax exiles. But nagging questions only pivoted into obsessive research on … my birthday. An imposed role change at work had killed off a beloved research project halfway through, so my wife suggested taking a day's birthday leave to cheer me up. What treat would I like?

Archives are beautiful places, staffed by special people, but they rarely host birthday parties. Nevertheless, an online catalogue of documents had suggested something that intrigued me. Might trundling through mid-December fog, on a chilly train to Ipswich, through my adored Suffolk countryside, offer a sad brain the tonic it needed?

That document was the 'Minute Book' recording meetings of Ipswich Town's directors, just after World War Two.[3] Excerpts have been threaded through previous chapters but on that day a single page leapt out, upended my birthday, then reshaped my research life over the next five years. What had grabbed me, on 'page 259', was a remarkable and coincidental storyline. The bottom paragraph described Alf Ramsey being formally interviewed for and offered the Ipswich Town manager's job, on 8 August 1955. At the top, beside the margin note 'Player Ted Phillips on Serious Charge at Court', a contrasting story unfolded. If Phillips pleaded guilty to or was convicted of a charge of 'Gross Indecency' his contract would end.

Was this really the same Ted Phillips, and legendary centre-forward, who I had heard so much about but never seen play? Scanning ahead and cross-checking soon confirmed this was indeed the same player whose 46 goals in season 1956/57 remain a club record. As the day closed, I sketched out a hypothesis. Ted Phillips's 161 Ipswich league goals had helped to win three divisional titles between 1955 and 1962, so underpinning Alf's management career.[4] Without Alf's support for Phillips, and Phillips's goals for Ipswich, would Alf ever have managed England, and would England have won the 1966 World Cup? That lightning-bolt electrified my birthday, and would make a fabulous film, but years more research beckoned. Ted Phillips's turnaround story called into question everything I *thought* I knew about Alf's stiflingly conservative public persona, but how did this remarkable episode relate to the rest of Alf's career?

I started to reflect on what I could personally remember. This book's introduction sketched our family huddled around a tiny Scottish television watching the 1966 World Cup Final. Days later, I was bought my first leather football with which to mimic Geoff Hurst's World Cup-winning hat-trick: physically and intellectually, I have been chasing footballs ever since. But looking back, the young 'me' never got beyond puzzlement about Alf sitting still, as his team won a World Cup, whilst everyone else leapt about. By his 1974 sacking, my carefree, nine-year-old self had become an angry adolescent, to whom Alf seemed as outdated as the other old men who ran Britain. As a brilliant 21st-century football scholar later summarised, Alf acted like a 'tight-wired, emotionally constipated man',[5] and as a 1970s teenager I did not mourn his dismissal.

During a recent conversation with Geoff Hurst, I admitted to that, and he agreed that Alf's popular public image was of a 'rather odd, very conservative, closed, uptight sort of guy'.[6] For me, that stereotype started fraying in 2019, on reading about Alf and Ted Phillips, then unravelled as I researched the multiple anomalies described in previous chapters. Young Alf's darker skin tone, his racist childhood nickname, a family rich in dealers, market traders, Gypsy-Travellers and greyhounds, his youthful career being saved by banned Sunday football, his likely neurodivergence, his previously ignored coaching experience at Eton Manor, and much more. Those unseen or underplayed storylines contradicted the conventional narrative entrenched in 50 years of books, media and my own psyche, positioning Alf personally, and 1966 nationally, as symbolising an outdated English establishment and its imperialist values.

Ironically, that simplistic caricature sprang from Alf's own mouth. His tortured, stifling speaking style cemented myth into history, demonstrated by an apocryphal allegation wheedling its way even into the *Dictionary of National Biography* (DNB): 'Before taking the manager's job at Ipswich, Ramsey took elocution lessons ... The lessons changed the way he spoke.' Yet no independent historical evidence supports the existence of such lessons and, as Alf was in southern Africa for two months prior to his August 1955 appointment, lessons seem highly unlikely. Until clear evidence surfaces otherwise, such a claim therefore feels unsafe. Equally, it established itself for understandable reasons. By the early 1960s Alf's accent did sound unnatural, he remained 'self-conscious of vowels and aitches', and his 'speaking voice became curiously strangulated'.[7] England players like Jimmy Greaves all 'believed Ramsey had taken elocution lessons' to 'iron out his broad Cockney accent',[8] recently echoed to the author by Geoff Hurst.[9] Yet as previously seen, Alf's 1950s accent had been rural.[10]

The elocution lesson myth first appeared in print, in 1970, when Alf's first biographer baldly asserted that he 'decided to take elocution lessons'.[11] By 1972, Alf was publicly refuting it, plausibly so, given any evidence would have been snapped up, for cash, by newspapers:

> One of the perpetuated inaccuracies that wearies him most is that he is supposed to have taken elocution lessons – the 'charge' is usually levelled with a sneering attempt to imitate his precise diction. Alf simply says: 'The truth is I have not had elocution

lessons. I wish I had. They might have been a help to me.' (*Daily Mirror* 6 November 1972)

In itself, this dispute is usefully illuminating. Both the allegations and Alf's denials can simultaneously *feel* true because although he changed little between 1955 and 1974, English society altered massively. In the 1950s, learning to 'improve' how you sounded, through manipulating voice and vocabulary, mattered as much to Alf as to members of my own family. When forced to leave school aged 14, reshaping how you spoke was a potent weapon for fighting inequality. My own father, once he had survived the brutal casualty rates for RAF bomber rear gunners in 1944–45, during three years of service edged himself up social echelons by becoming a flight lieutenant, and mimicking officer-class diction. Starting as an army private, Alf similarly ended his six-year military career as a respected colour sergeant and non-commissioned officer.[12] That learning journey then continued, as his 1952 autobiography proudly recounted, through further hard work to sharpen his public speaking and widen his reading.[13] Ramsey almost certainly never took elocution lessons, but in 1950 my own mother-in-law did, after failing to get into grammar school. By the late 1960s, things were different and, as Geoff Hurst recently admitted, fashions were shifting. Football players 'unlike Alf ... didn't have to change how we spoke to fit in'.[14]

Anyone who has viewed or heard an archival broadcast of Alf speaking will understand why, in 1973, Cambridge undergraduates mocked Alf's pronouncements for being 'enunciated so correctly',[15] as had Hurst's close friends Bobby Moore and Jimmy Greaves a decade earlier.[16] Bluntly, Alf's speaking style came to sound ridiculous. Yet for decades self-tutored speech modification, aping BBC English, had been widely accepted. In 1959, the middle year of Alf's Ipswich Town career, the newly founded commercial TV station for East Anglia proclaimed their 'three announcers will all have BBC accents'. When asked, 'why not East Anglian accents?', a spokesperson explained, 'Because we consider their BBC accents much safer.' The newspaper reporting the story used it to criticise social inequality, complaining that 'in this country, your accent betrays your origin and background' (*Daily Herald* 26 October 1959); and even in Bohemian cultural circles, speech modification was taken for granted. Alan Bates, a leading actor during the '*Angry Young Men* period in the early 1960s',[17] took elocution lessons in the late 1940s, a fact revealed in the same month Alf was appointed England manager (*Peterborough Evening Telegraph* 16 October 1962). Six months later, just as Alf started that job, two other actors from the innovative, sharply satirical BBC comedy show *That Was The Week That Was* similarly described having childhood elocution lessons.[18] In June 1962, a Labour-leaning national newspaper ran a story gathering young people's views on regional accents. Its final contributor, a 17-year-old female Mancunian, opined, 'It's the people without accents who get the best jobs.' In response, a male letter writer from Leeds agreed: 'An accent will keep you down. In this snob-ridden country if you want to get ahead ... talk like the BBC' (*Daily Herald* 12 and 15 June 1962). In 1967, the year Alf received his knighthood, another Labour-supporting newspaper scathingly reported a London employment agency advertising a clerical post stipulating, 'Must be English. Sorry, no regional accents either only best Oxford/BBC.' Just before Alf announced England's squad for the 1970 World Cup, that same paper reported a university psychologist surveying nearly 200 comprehensive-school adolescents and concluding that teenagers 'would rather have a BBC-type voice than a regional accent' (*Daily Mirror* 14 December 1967, 14 April 1970).

In other words, although Alf's accent always sounded slightly abnormal, for most of his career it spoke of mainstream social aspirations. Then, during the mid-1960s, fashionable currents started flowing in an opposite direction, by the mid-1970s leaving Alf beached high and dry. Backed by innovative educational research, people started arguing that the BBC should 'include in its panels of national newsreaders some with English regional flavour in their voices' (*Birmingham Daily Post* 15 April 1965). Two years later, a BBC documentary celebrated successful working-class celebrities who had retained local accents, with one London designer ironically commenting this had 'gone so far that I keep meeting people with Cockney accents and Etonian ties' (*Liverpool Echo* 26 April 1967). 'Sandie Shaw from Dagenham', Alf's home patch, featured on the programme, as did the 'Cockney comedy' TV writer Johnny Speight who in 1967 commanded '£1,000 a script' (*Daily Mirror* 10 May 1967). Speight devised the sensationally successful BBC sit-com *Till Death Us Do Part*, which from 1966 until 1975 parodied Alf Garnett as a white, working-class, racist, sexist, nationalistic and Conservative-voting football fan. Garnett's scriptwriting creator drew extensively on his own East End upbringing, and lifelong love of West Ham United, to create one of the most controversial characters of 20th-century BBC television. How does he relate to Alf Ramsey?

Bizarrely, in a connection unnoticed by previous biographers, when the pilot show broadcast in July 1965, it featured an 'ill-educated, tory-voting East End bigot' called 'Alf Ramsay'.[19] Speight promptly changed that 'because of the connection with the manager of the England football team' (*Daily Mirror* 3 June 1968), an obituary later confirming that 'to avoid embarrassing' Alf Ramsey 'the surname was changed to Garnett as the film crew were shooting in Garnett Street, Wapping' (*The Stage* 16 July 1998). Alf Ramsey and Speight had met as speakers and celebrity guests at various football functions (e.g. *Coventry Evening Telegraph* 11 April 1967, *Sunday Mirror* 21 May 1967). More significantly, the fictional Alf Garnett revelled in, but also complained about, the actual Alf Ramsey's 1966 World Cup win. A 1968 film version featured footage from the final and dialogue about it. Bemoaning England's shirts, Garnett complains 'that's a bleedin' cheek innit … Putting England out in red shirts. White, mate, that's England's colour.' Trumpeting his Conservative politics, Garnett claims:

> It's your bloody Labour Party's colours, red, innit? I see his plan … Harold bloody Wilson … he's putting England out in red hoping that if we win today everyone's gonna think it's the bloody Labour Party won the World Cup for us.[20]

Where Garnett became more complicated and controversial was in his explicit, brutal racism. To take but one of many examples, in that 1968 film he spouted, 'Too many foreigners. Old Enoch Powell, he's got the right idea. Chuck 'em all out. Especially the black ones.' The originators of the imaginary Alf Garnett had called into existence an uncontrollable character:

> Johnny Speight was a left-wing anti-racist writer. Warren Mitchell [Garnett's actor] was a left-wing anti-racist actor. Together they co-created a character beloved of right-wing racists … A project very sincerely intended to demonstrate the terminal futility of racism ended up helping to circulate racism.[21]

This relates to Alf Ramsey's image because Garnett's crude nationalism, and abhorrent racism, was sometimes illustrated using 1966 as a backdrop. In the 1968 film, against footage of the actual World Cup Final, Garnett aggressively taunts a West German supporter using World War Two insults.[22] The 1966 climax also adorned the front cover of a 1973 book of scripts from the programme. It shows royalty, seated by politicians and watching England play, but Garnett is grabbing Ted Heath, leader of the Conservative Party, shouting in his ear about England wearing red shirts 'SO'S WE'D ALL THINK LABOUR WON THE CUP!'

Later, poison from Alf Garnett leeched directly into Alf's reputation. In 1973, when England played in Russia, *The Guardian* (9 June) sneeringly reported that on the eve of the game England's squad would forego ballet at the Bolshoi Theatre to watch a *Till Death Us Do Part* film at the British Embassy. That snobbish comment conveniently ignored possible practical reasons behind the choice, but Alf's most recent biographer cited the incident to help label Alf an 'unabashed philistine' with an 'ingrained xenophobic streak'. He also quoted another undated *Sunday Times* report claiming that 'on his travels, the England manager is liable to seem more like Alf Garnett than Alf Ramsey'.[23] Two decades later, whilst reflecting on Alf's criticisms of Paul Gascoigne's behaviour during England's 1998 World Cup preparations, a different journalist wrote similarly that 'there will be those who sneer that this was Alf Ramsey sounding more like Alf Garnett'. Almost apologetically, he then confided that the actual Alf Ramsey was in 'the throes of some form of Alzheimers' (*The Observer* 7 June 1998).

What such innuendoes and associations ignored, perhaps because they contradicted already established Alf Ramsey myths, is that in 1972 the fictional Garnett viciously criticised Ramsey onscreen, during a fit of xenophobic rage. Broadcast on 20 September, four months after West Germany had beaten England in the 1972 European Championship quarter-final,[24] Garnett claimed to his astonished family that Alf had 'betrayed us to the Germans … Sir Bloody Alf … sold us out to the Germans for a handful of Deutschmarks … bloody Judas … they ought to put him in the bloody Tower an' shoot him'. When challenged to explain, Garnett insisted, 'Bloody fact, annit. It's international scandal … I got it from a good source … up the pub.'[25]

Why Alf Mattered to Football

This book's new evidence suggests radically revising popular understandings of Alf Ramsey, which in turn entails shifting some entrenched perspectives on what 1966 means to English identity.

In immediate, practical ways, Alf's World Cup victory boosted English league football by significantly increasing average attendances, especially in the higher divisions. 'England's success in the 1966 World Cup is generally held responsible for this rise, which saw attendances top 30 million in the 1967/68 season for the first time in almost a decade.' Totals continued over that mark during Alf's reign, fluctuated for a few seasons, then 'after 1977-78 the decline' became 'continuous'. By season 1985/86, total English league crowds had nearly halved to 16.5 million.[26] The fact that this attendance boom happened from

1966–74, whilst 'goal-scoring rates were relatively low',[27] fatally weakens arguments that Alf's tactics made football significantly less attractive to fans.

Ironically, too, given his communication deficiencies, the public profile of Alf Ramsey's England management compares favourably to the chaos caused by his permanent successor. Don Revie's July 1977 bombshell exit, from his job as England manager, kicked off English football's 'continuous' decline in paying spectators after season 1977/78. Public impressions of that tumultuous episode surface in two surviving letters, comparing Revie and Ramsey, from FA Council regional leaders to their chairperson in late July 1977. From Sussex, one wrote of 'a lingering dissatisfaction over the Ramsey sacking and the Revie appointment'. Another, from Hertfordshire FA, expressed wider disillusionment:

> We do not want another Revie type of man, one of the Alf Ramsey type could well be more appropriate ... some folk seemed to think the World Cup could be won with money. It was won before with far more meagre expenditure, but then perhaps there was some feeling of pride in playing for the Country and not for grasping money right, left, and centre.[28]

Although the 74-year-old writer, Percy Poulter, could be dismissed as an 'FA old man', that demographic mattered to football because elderly supporters 'were abandoning what had become a less pleasurable environment'.[29] Declining attendances reflected unease around hooliganism, and ramshackle stadiums, were worsened by unemployment and racism,[30] then exacerbated by the national team's deteriorating public image.

At the opposite age range, *FOUL* magazine's male Cambridge-undergraduate writers were as disillusioned by 1970s league football as they were by Alf's England tactics and teams.[31] More importantly, socially ordinary young fans and players praised his leadership. Malcolm Macdonald debuted for England aged 22 under Alf Ramsey, playing also for Mercer and Revie. Macdonald recalled how 'nobody had that all-embracing manner which Sir Alf managed. I thoroughly enjoyed playing under Alf and playing to his instructions ... he had huge respect for every one of his players and treated you as such.'[32] Similarly, 23-year-old London football fan, Desmond Gleeson, in 1966 eulogised how Alf's leadership style had brought 'dignity to football' by:

Making ... the professional footballer a person to be respected in the world of sport. When the joy of victory has faded into memory, the England team will have much more to remember you for ... that dignity, pride in their job, is of much more importance than sometimes winning.[33]

Eleven years later Alf's successor, Don Revie, acted very differently. He announced leaving England for Dubai on the *Daily Mail* front page, before the FA had even read his resignation letter. More significantly, greed had tempted him to abandon a national team still struggling to qualify for the 1978 World Cup. Revie's annual FA salary was £25,000 in 1977. In 1974 Ramsey's had been just £7,200. Yet Revie still dumped his players, his employer and English football's international standing to triple his salary to £85,000 annually, overseas and tax-free. Revie's professional frustrations with Sir Harold Thompson's FA management had been genuine, but money seduced him.[34] Ramsey's naive patriotism contrasts starkly with such cynicism.

Professor Harold Thompson's role in engineering Ramsey's 1974 exit, sparking Revie's 1977 resignation, then losing a court case about Revie's ban from English football, also damaged the FA in another way. The cruelty of Alf's sacking, and the chaos of his lacklustre successor, have historically and reputationally overshadowed both the FA's successful delivery of the 1966 tournament, and their strong support for Alf during two World Cups. Collective FA efforts, over many years, by a tiny staff, numerous unpaid volunteers, and multiple football 'others', were lost in the haze of Professor Thompson's vile smoke. Yes, there had been valid complaints in 1966 over tickets, training and media facilities, and genuine rage in South America over the FIFA-controlled Eurocentric refereeing. Nevertheless, squeamish liberal fears about parroting Alf Garnett-style nationalism, heightened by 1966 being heavily 'mythologised in England',[35] should not obscure that the tournament compared favourably to predecessors. In footballing terms, Sweden in 1958 'was not ... a distinguished competition' whereas 1966 was both 'passionate and controversial, with a 'glorious climax'.[36] In 1962, an earthquake-devastated Chile heroically hosted what Jonathan Wilson nevertheless has described as a 'hideously violent' tournament. Its opening eight games saw 'four sending-offs, three broken legs, a fractured ankle and a series of fractured ribs'. The Chile–Italy concluding Group Two contest has been termed 'football's dirtiest-ever game',[37] whilst towards the end of the Chile–Brazil semi-final two players were dismissed, Brazil's star Garrincha was cut on the head by a thrown bottle, and headlines afterwards told of prosecutions for ticket scandals.[38]

By comparison, 1966 had lower public levels of player and spectator disorder, encouraged perhaps by its groundbreaking TV coverage often being 'live' and pan-continental. Only the 1950 World Cup in Brazil had previously enjoyed bigger crowds than 1966's 50,400 average (*Hull Daily Mail* 24 May 1986). Cuddly 'World Cup Willie' became a successful first tournament mascot,[39] despite the incongruities of a shaggy-haired lion publicising an English tournament by wearing Union Jack colours. Even the embarrassing theft of the Jules Rimet trophy during March 1966, and some shady machinations for its recovery, were softened through its supposed recovery by a small scruffy dog called Pickles. Pickles attended the 30 July celebration dinner and was pictured there (see below) being held by Bobby Charlton whilst Alf Ramsey looks on.

The subsequent true story of Pickles is that he sadly strangled himself with his own lead, whilst barking up a tree;[40] a telling metaphor both for how 1966 came to be viewed by commentators hostile to football, and its current place in modern English consciousness. Crude 1966

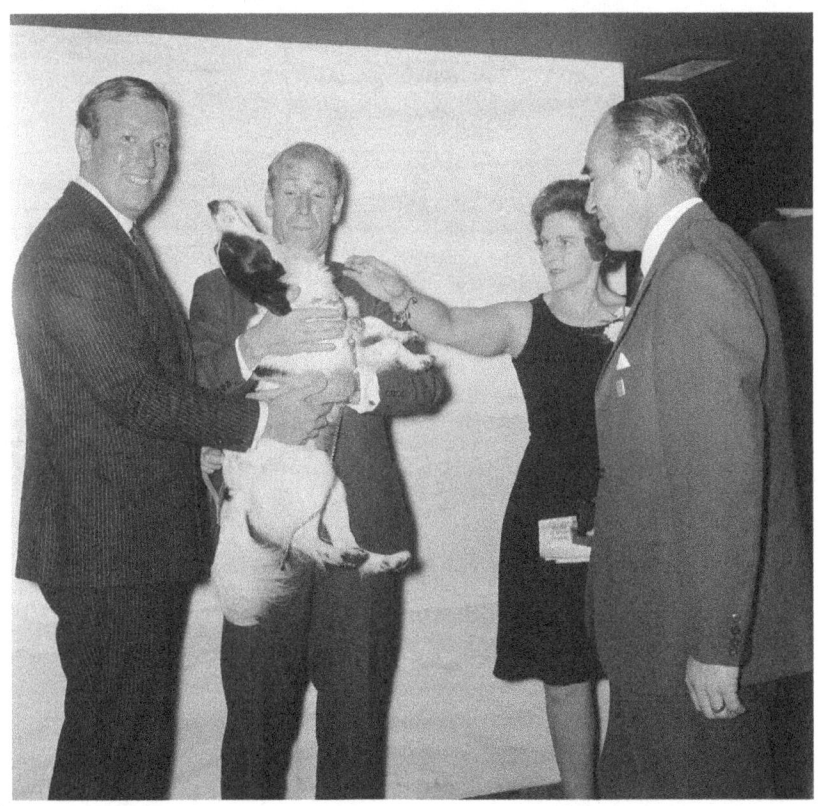

caricatures have pitched jingoistic conservatives, uncritically celebrating England's national football glory, against woke academics deriding not just the process by which England won the World Cup, but any remotely patriotic celebrations of it.[41]

Caught in the crossfire were Alf, living on a meagre FA pension and by 1993 suffering from dementia, and his entire 1966 squad. As Geoff Hurst has bluntly but eloquently stated, 'the fans have never forgotten us. The FA did … in the 1980s the FA found endless ways to make the 1966 team feel unappreciated.' Nowadays, Hurst's 'relations with the FA are good',[42] and a wider question can be asked. Might new perspectives on 1966 nudge English football followers, and football's place in English culture, away from Alf Garnett's old-fashioned nationalism, towards a modern and updated patriotism? In *Till Death Us Do Part* football was the sole shared interest of the middle-aged bigot and his young, socially liberal, Labour-voting Liverpudlian son-in-law.[43] In this image from the 1968 film, they are pictured happily watching football together in a racially diverse albeit stereotypically all-male crowd.

Could thinking differently about Alf Ramsey and 1966 help edge us, as modern English people, towards similar common ground? New and diverse stories about English football are needed because the Union Jack, as featured on World Cup Willie's ridiculous 1966 waistcoat, has airbrushed English history and does not foster civic unity. England's medieval empire grew from brutal military conquests of Ireland,

Scotland and Wales. By 1801, the long-standing territorial outcomes were being rebranded as 'The United Kingdom of Great Britain and Ireland', which also and conveniently helped repackage global ambitions as 'The British Empire'.[44] Such muddles of identity, not to mention morality, still manipulate England's contemporary inhabitants into believing ourselves subjects, not citizens. More importantly, the guilt associated with them psychologically hinders many liberal English people from patriotic expressions about anything very much, even something as popular as football.

Might Alf Ramsey help us? He appeared conventional, but as this book's true stories reveal, Alf was radically different in aspects unseen: coming from a poor family, with rumoured GRT heritage, having a darker skin tone and a racist nickname, his rural childhood bulldozed by centralised planning, working every Saturday so having to play football in banned 'Sunday leagues' – and those are just his childhood true stories. War, late development, probable neurodivergence, being paid by a charity to coach East End amateurs part-time – all were turned into learning and strengths by Alf's relentless hard work and sheer force of character. They offer powerful examples of battling adversity from within diversity. Waiting for years to marry the love of his life, a now-single mother undergoing divorce, whilst winning successive titles at Spurs, nudges Alf's plotline into personal and football romance. Moving with her to obscure Ipswich Town, then winning three different titles, clinched by – in those three seasons – 99 league goals from a player prosecuted for homosexual behaviour, stretches credulity. Yet less than four years later, and despite never applying for the job, as England manager Alf Ramsey won the World Cup. If this fantastical storyline was pitched as a fictional film it would be instantly rejected, as ridiculously over-romantic, but every single twist is true.

Which is why, especially for younger English people, Alf Ramsey could become a 21st-century hero. During the 1940s his life was delayed, and could have been ended, by six years of army service, rather like many young lives were frozen by the 2020s pandemic. Alf's experiences of being bullied, by a childhood racist nickname in the 1920s, through vicious criticisms as England manager, to his unceremonious sacking in 1974, will chime with anyone who has fallen victim to powerful others. We will never know with scientific certainty whether Alf was neurodivergent but his patterned behaviour and language, obsessive mastery of detail, and relentless learning about football strongly suggest he saw the world differently. Alf was always personally shy, and intensely private, but he conquered his nerves to play before vast crowds, and as a manager face a voracious media. Alf Ramsey's faults can readily be listed: insecurity, over-sensitivity, emotional and verbal clumsiness, terseness, irritability when challenged, a lack of imagination, impatience with poor performance, obsessional interests, narrowness and more. Yet what mitigated and easily outweighed such shortcomings were three simple loves: of family, especially his mother and wife, of football as a sport, and of England as his home. Alf was unfashionably patriotic about his homeland. Is there anything 'we', as modern English people, might learn from that now?

Why Alf's Story Still Matters to England

In the year Alf Ramsey died, the 20th-century closed, and this book's author was helping lead a project teaching children about English history through local-global stories; a version of Englishness and identity that grew upwards and outwards from where children lived, rather than top-down from government templates.[45] Drawing from inspirational other educators[46] storyteller Fiona Collins and I worked in Greenwich, London, the historical home to an imaginary global line known as 'longitude', and modern home to murdered local teenager Stephen Lawrence, and his racist killers. With community members we collected and created real stories, built from historical evidence, locally to represent English history and diversity. Why? Because we saw ourselves as 'celebrating the distinctive diversities of English society' and building a 'proud, multicultural and local English historical identity which … can counteract racism'.[47]

Alf Ramsey's biography sits within such traditions, not only because diversity ran through his life, but because he lived ultra-locally whilst working globally. For 70 of his 79 years, Alf's home lay in just two places: his birthplace of Becontree in south Essex, then from aged 35 in Ipswich in Suffolk. From those places he reached outwards, travelling all over England and to Palestine during six army years, then from aged 26 to 35 trekking across the UK, Europe, South America and southern Africa to play football. That globetrotting widened even further as England manager, and the boy who had never travelled anywhere until aged 20 achieved global fame. Yet despite all that, Alf is still often portrayed as a 'little Englander', his management style in the 1970 Mexico World Cup being recently sketched as 'neurotically risk-averse' and 'constantly agitated' like:

A reluctant tourist on one of the earliest package holidays, who doesn't speak the language, isn't brave enough to try a local dish, doesn't want to learn about the customs and culture, prefers not to drink the water and sits uncomfortably on the beach in socks and sandals, a white knotted handkerchief protecting his head.[48]

Such playful imagery pokes fun but reinforces assumptions of Alf as jingoistic, even bigoted. He was indeed a fiercely competitive England player and manager, but did competitiveness express jingoism? Probably not, since Alf displayed exactly that characteristic during schoolchild, Sunday league and army games,[49] and when coaching 1950s amateurs and Ipswich Town.[50] Alf's desire to beat foreigners at football stemmed not from disliking them, but from his obsessive, meticulous approach as England manager. His unquenchable desire to win expressed professionalism, not prejudice, and like those fabled elocution lessons, assumptions of jingoism and xenophobia have become heavily mythologised. Geoff Hurst, who in international settings was managed by Alf for eight years, recently and vehemently told the author that he denied any such possibility. 'No. Never, never at all. Not for a second' did accusations of xenophobia fit Alf 'as a character, as a person.'[51]

In reality, Alf's modernist methods contradicted a trait key to nationalistic 'little Englanders', namely that 'amateurish exceptionalism' can secure English victories. Caroline Lucas, an experienced political leader, critically cited such arrogance as still blighting England, tracking its significance in failures from the collapse of 'Test and Trace' during the 2020–22 pandemic, through the 2016 Brexit vote and fallout, back to military disasters such as Dunkirk in 1940. Such episodes, she argued, arose from notions that England 'was in some ways better off by isolating itself', citing as evidence speeches by the 2019–22 Conservative Prime Minister Boris Johnson. Exceptionalist complacency had, in her analysis, seduced politicians into believing 'that almost any policy or public service can be reframed' to fit the idea 'that England … has an innate moral or practical superiority'.[52]

Alf Ramsey knew, from intimate playing experience, that such amateurish ignorance led to sporting catastrophe. In 1950, England entered its first football World Cup, were eliminated at the group stage and lost 1-0 to the USA's part-timers. Alf played in all the games. Then, in 1953, his last international appearance, England were thrashed 6-3 by Hungary at Wembley, their first defeat on home soil to players from beyond the British Isles. Both matches left profound scars on Alf, wounds made all the more painful because warning signs had been ignored. In 1949, England had already lost three of eight matches, including a 2-0 defeat at Liverpool to the Republic of Ireland, heralded by England's 'exaggerated confidence that they would win comfortably' (*Dublin Evening Herald* 22 September 1949).

Those 1949–53 defeats and humiliations span precisely Alf Ramsey's England playing career and underline why, as England's manager, his desire burned so strongly. Alf's intense focus on enabling his players to win sprang not from the populist nationalism or ugly xenophobia widely associated with football, and sometimes mistakenly attributed to him, but from unstinting professionalism and genuine patriotism. Take for example Alf's red-hot footballing rivalry with Scotland, cited by various journalists as xenophobic or even racist. If he *genuinely* hated Scots people, why in 1973 would Scotland's recently appointed manager, Willie Ormond, have paid the following tribute just after England's disastrous draw with Poland?

> If ever a team deserved to win that team was England. We felt they did enough to take them through. Personally, I am very sorry that Sir Alf did not make it. Since I took over the Scotland job no one could have been more helpful or cooperative. (*The Times* 19 October 1973)

Alf's ambition was fuelled not by bitterness towards other nations, but by love of his job and his country. Those attributes are central to this book's retelling of his life story, but helpful also in making sense of our modern, muddled English national identities. For example, Caroline Lucas (cited earlier) does not identify as a football fan. From 2010–24 she was the Green Party's only MP in England, and sometimes its leader. Lucas recently identified 'trying to nail down a coherent version' of England's national story as a key national challenge, because current popular versions seemed 'almost a caricature ... a rich stew of myths ... nostalgia and outright misrepresentation'. She then identified 'the 1966 World Cup' as one of that stew's ten ingredients, alongside '*Dad's Army*, Rorke's Drift ... Maggie's handbag ... Vera Lynn, Dunkirk and the Falklands'.[53] But in admiration of ethnically diverse, socially aware contemporary English footballers, under the leadership of progressive managers, Lucas also argued football could help solve English identity crises. Others agree. Football's urban, working-class roots make it a 'significantly more effective platform for meaningful multiculturalism than any number of awareness training courses or diversity questionnaires', co-wrote Prime Minister Sir Keir Starmer's recent biographer, in the year Starmer came to power. Going further, he positioned England's national football team 'as one of the few clear expressions of England itself, that can still feel like it has a higher purpose'.[54]

Another progressive patriot who shares similar perspectives, to that and to my own, is the singer-songwriter Billy Bragg. He was born in Barking, the historically larger town of the now combined London Borough of 'Barking and Dagenham', home also to Alf Ramsey's Becontree birthplace. In 2006, Bragg wrote a book musing on his Barking childhood whilst gazing outwards to history, music, memories, landscape, ideas and politics; a defiant, reflective response to some shocking local election results.

In May 2006, the then 'British National Party' (BNP) won 12 seats on the borough council, and 'for the first time a fascist party had become the official opposition in an [English] council chamber'.[55] After several chapters undercutting BNP thinking through stories of diverse, local-global English identities, Bragg's book closed by sketching how England's 'flag of Saint George' remains a contentious, sometimes class-riven symbol of national identity.

England's red cross is present, but also overshadowed in the Union flag, 'the last cross' on which had been added in 1801 after the militarily enforced 'union' adding Ireland to England, Wales and Scotland.[56] As Bragg wryly observed, two centuries after that union English identity, too, has suffered from it. Of 'the 32 countries that competed for the 2006 World Cup ... only one didn't have its own parliament, passports or national anthem: England'.[57] The 'St. George flag' became popular when England hosted the 1996 European Championship,[58] perhaps helping it be 'shorn of its bigotry'. But Bragg also acknowledged an urgent need to find 'other signifiers' for 'the pride we feel in being English'.[59] Might such a mission be helped by this book's retelling of Alf Ramsey's life story?

Bragg and I talked that through during a video call whilst he was on tour in North America. As a lifelong football fan, Billy knew who Alf was, and 1966 had pivoted his childhood. 'Before the World Cup we never seemed to play football. After the World Cup, we only played football.' But despite Billy's mother growing up on the Beacontree Estate, Alf's rural background and racist childhood nickname were entirely new to him, and Bragg 'never realised he came from pre-Beacontree Estate days'. When I laid out some of the other diverse threads in Alf's life, Billy was quick to see how such a 'great story' might contribute to progressive English identities, and we have promised to keep chatting. As he told me, 'there are as many types of patriotism as there are of identity and we just have to keep battling away.'[60]

The fertile ground football offers for exploring identities featured in another recent book, rooted also in Essex and cataloguing *Stories of Modern England*. Its author, eminent political journalist and commentator Jason Cowley, opened by recalling the 2020 lockdown's neighbourly, doorstep thanksgivings for NHS heroism. Such events were whistling, saucepan-banging moments of 'magic mutuality and togetherness' seldom experienced 'outside of a World Cup or Euros summer when England are doing well and nearly everyone ... seems to be talking about the football'.[61] Racist rioting in the summer of 2024, weeks after a Labour UK landslide had ended 14 years of Conservative government, prompted Cowley to headline the magazine he then edited *'England Undone: Can a country traumatised by riots find a new national identity?'* The backdrop to those words was Britannia wielding a Union Jack shield, wearing a riot helmet, and for Cowley 'the question of what it means to be English and British in the age of market-driven globalisation has been as neglected as the local economies of the old northern mill towns' (*New Statesman* 16–22 August 2024).

Equally, football's simplicities should not seduce us into believing 'Englishness' is straightforward. As Bragg mentioned above, and a searing critique repeats below, England has not been an embodied, legal or independent state for over three hundred years:

> What, we might ask, does our modern, ethnically diverse population of 56 million really have in common with the 5 million or so white people who lived in England prior to its mutation into the United Kingdom in 1707? I would suggest very little ... Nationalism has a dubious history when it comes to progressive causes. (*The Guardian* 15 July 2020)

That first sentence above asks an important question, an answer to which has been touched on previously. Ever since the Roman invasion, England's population has never been uniformly white and from the early 16th century, migrants, including GRT people, visibly increased England's ethnic diversity.[62] More specifically for this book, Alf Ramsey's life is one more thread in the ongoing story of that diversity. Alf's unwanted, racially labelling nickname reflected his 1920s upbringing and 1930s adolescent skin tone. That nickname was published in 1952 during his playing career, broadcast in 1969 when he was England manager, and persisted from the 1970s onwards in the rumours and whispers of reporters. In 1973, even Bobby Moore had mocked Alf's supposed 'Gypsy' heritage before other players and journalists. That word 'Gypsy' is still used to bully people in contemporary England, and feels racist to some.[63] Its origins, as previous chapters mentioned, are in 16th century Romany people being inaccurately labelled as migrants from Egypt. Any white nationalist claims using 1966, or any other English footballing triumph, are made ludicrous by the simple fact that English football's only 20th-century global trophy was won by someone labelled with a racist nickname derived from a darker skin tone, and his family's assumed GRT background.

In 2020, the academic cited above had asked what modern England's 'ethnically diverse population of 56 million' had 'in common with the 5 million or so white people who lived in England' before 1707. In 2024, football helped him answer his own question. Just before England's men lost another European Championship Final, he argued that:

> The one national institution capable of embodying a coherent sense of what England is, or rather could be, is the national football team. At certain key moments in our post-imperial history (notably in 1966, 1990 and 1996), the England team has succeeded where countless politicians have failed.[64]

Despite England being an oddly 'ambiguous nation ... a sort of ghost realm which sacrificed its historic identity to become the dominant power in the United Kingdom and ... the British Empire', English senses of identity, he argued, were regularly redeemed by football. That begs a question on which to close this book. How can we as English people most constructively remember Alf Ramsey, the architect of England's 1966 victory?

One approach might be to coax Billy Bragg, or Ed Sheeran, or someone else who loves football into writing a song that celebrates Alf's place in English history. Something more locally tangible might be for councils at Barking, Dagenham, Southampton and Ipswich to commemorate, in Blue Plaques or equivalent, the places where Alf lived his personal and professional lives. A national equivalent would be for the FA to replicate for Alf Ramsey something done for Bobby Moore, and commission a statue to stand outside Wembley. Currently only a modest bust of Alf Ramsey stands inside, overseeing the final steps of players and managers as they emerge from dressing rooms into a corridor, then out on to Wembley's pitch.

That essentially hidden Wembley location of Alf's current sculpture is a metaphor, albeit unintentional, for how history has viewed him. Key elements in his life have lain secret or unseen far too long. Even the bust's 2009 unveiling, pictured below, became 'an event held to boost England's chances of hosting the World Cup in 2018',[65] rather than a public show of affection for Alf Ramsey.

An alternative to such cynicism is that England's football people, from fans to the FA, indeed *any* English people, could borrow from Alf by trying to stay optimistic. If optimism seems an odd quality to claim given his ultra-cautious personality, for nearly four years after his 1962 appointment Alf swam against defeatist flood tides in his insistence that England could, and probably would, win the 1966 World Cup. On the day that happened he was, according to the hat-trick hero who clinched it, 'as full of joy as anyone will ever see him'. But when congratulated later by that player's wife, Alf insisted in private, soon repeated in public, that it was the players who won it 'not me'.[66]

Commemorating 1966, 50 years later, another experienced observer optimistically remarked that the intervening 'years of hurt could be reconstructed instead as decades of healing … Englishness has a formidable relationship with football' because football, more than anything, 'has helped shape a modern national identity for England'.[67] Which is why knowing, and publicly celebrating, Alf Ramsey's formerly unseen storylines might help promote qualities and values he advocated all his life: community, co-operation, effort, equal opportunities, fairness, fitness, learning to improve, loyalty, patriotism, professionalism, purposeful work, resilience, sport of all types and, above all, playing football with enjoyment whilst always trying to win. Or, more succinctly and as the unfashionably patriotic Alf saw it, becoming as good as your talents allowed at the sometimes real, but also imagined best qualities of 'being English'.

1 Bage, G. (2016)
2 See chapter 8
3 **Ipswich Town Minute Book 1947-58**
4 See chapters 9-10
5 Goldblatt, D. (2007) pp.452, 453
6 Geoff Hurst oral history interview 7 February 2025
7 *Dictionary of National Biography* (2017) 'Ramsey, Sir Alfred Ernest'
8 Greaves, J. with Giller, N. (1993) p.31
9 Geoff Hurst oral history interview 6 February 2025
10 See chapter 2
11 Marquis, M. (1970) p.15
12 See chapter 5
13 Ramsey, A. (1952) pp.61-64, 79
14 Hurst, G. (2024) p.140
15 *FOUL* (12) November 1973: FOULMOUTH 'Farewell Without Tears'
16 Dickinson, M. (2014) pp.70-72
17 BBC News website (28 December 2003) 'Obituary Sir Alan Bates'
18 Kenneth Cope (*Crewe Chronicle* 27 April 1963), Roy Kinnear (*Fife Free Press* 18 May 1963)
19 *Dictionary of National Biography* (2004) 'Speight, John'
20 Movie Scripts website (no date) 'Till Death Us Do Part (1968)'
21 Conrad Brunstrom blog (2 June 2020) 'Thoughts of Chairman Alf. Johnny Speight would have been 100 years old today'
22 Hughson, J. (2016) pp.131-32
23 McKinstry, L. (2007) pp.xxx, 359
24 See chapter 14
25 Speight, J. (1973) p.28
26 Russell, D. (1997) p.182
27 Ibid. p.187
28 **Professional Papers of Sir Harold Warris Thompson** Letters received 25 and 27 July 1977 HWT/48/2/4
29 Russell, D. (1997) p.188
30 Ibid. pp.186-94
31 See chapter 14
32 Hetherington, C. and Hetherington J. (2024) p.124
33 **FA Archive of 1966 Congratulatory Letters** 1 August 1966
34 Evans, C. (2021) chapter 22 pp.305-27
35 See chapter 12 and Burnton, S. (2016) *Guardian Football Blog* 24 July 2016 'Why not everyone remembers the 1966 World Cup as fondly as England'
36 Glanville, B. (1980) pp.87, 132
37 **It Was What It Was** podcast (29 July 2024) *Football's Dirtiest Game Ever: The Battle of Santiago*
38 Glanville, B. (1980) pp.111, 126

39 Game of the People Blog (12 June 2016) Jensen, N. 'Last Hurrah: The meaning of 1966'

40 **Stealing Victory** podcast (2020) *The Untold Story of the 1966 World Cup heist* Pettifor, T. Auddy Limited

41 Hughson, J. (2016) pp.138-149

42 Hurst, G. (2024) pp.253-54, 8, 153

43 Speight, J. (1973) pp.60-101, episodes broadcast 8 December 1966, 14 January 1968

44 Lucas, C. (2024)

45 Bage, G. (2000a) chapters 1 and 4

46 E.g. teacher and researcher Sylvia Collicott in Collicott, S. (2007); storyteller Hugh Lupton in Bage, G. (2000b) pp.9-15

47 Bage, G. (2000a) p.75

48 Hamilton, D. (2023) p.298

49 See chapters 5-6

50 See chapter 9

51 Geoff Hurst oral history interview 6 February 2025

52 Lucas, C. (2024) pp.202, 47, 48

53 Lucas, C. (2024) p.20

54 Baldwin, T. and Stears, M. (2024) pp.162-63

55 Bragg, B. (2006) p.19

56 Schama, S. (2003) p.77

57 Bragg, B. (2006) p.275

58 Baldwin, T. and Stears, M. (2024) pp.185-86

59 Bragg, B. (2008) p.90

60 Interview with Billy Bragg, 8 October 2024

61 Cowley, J. (2022) p.1

62 Olusoga, D. (2021) pp.29-32, 57-76

63 Anti-Bullying Alliance and Friends, Families and Travellers (2020)

64 New Statesman website (13 July 2024) 'England After Gareth Southgate' Alex Niven

65 BBC Sport website (6 November 2009) 'Ramsey statue unveiled at Wembley'

66 Hurst, G. (2024) pp.282, 147

67 Perryman, M. (2016) pp.75-76

ACKNOWLEDGEMENTS

ONE OF the loveliest things about researching a book is visiting the places from which knowledge grows. This book has debts to many of those, but especially the archives, libraries, museums and record offices that collect and store historical evidence, and without which history would be impossible. I have had the pleasure of working in many such places, but three have felt as personally significant to me as they are to Alf Ramsey's story.

The first is the **Valence House Archive and Local Studies Centre** in the London Borough of Barking and Dagenham; an inspirational local archive, library and resource for anyone interested in vibrant, community history. I am indebted particularly to Teresa Trowers, its Local Studies Officer, but also to archivist Karen Rushton, other archive staff and its many volunteers. Your friendly, professional approach is a model for how history can be part of a locality's rich cultural heritage. A second archive that significantly helped my research, and also works ceaselessly to connect with its community, is **The Hold** at Ipswich, which safeguards the county of Suffolk's archives in a magnificent new building. The third location, dear also to Alf's heart and central to his life, needs no introduction. At **Wembley Stadium** the English FA's Jane Bateman has been patiently building a library of printed material, supplemented by important documentary evidence, illuminating the history of England's international and club football. Jane has regularly helped me access this growing collection, offered wise suggestions and useful contacts, and been a real source of encouragement.

It has also been an enormous pleasure, over five years and more, to work in many other libraries and archives, and to talk with their knowledgeable staff and volunteers. Notable amongst these excellent research facilities have been the Bishopsgate Institute in London, the British Library in London, the Cambridge University Library, the Essex Record Office in Chelmsford, the Museum of Freemasonry in London, the Imperial War Museum in London, the National Football Archive in

Preston, the National Archives in London, the Royal Society in London and the Schroders Historical Archive in London. To all the people who have so generously and skilfully helped me in those places, thank you. Other organisations have helped my research by sharing valuable resources digitally or online, especially Bodmin Keep (Cornwall's Army Museum), and the commercial online archives of Find*my*past, and Ancestry.

Numerous other experts have kindly shared their knowledge and enthusiasm. The specialisms touched on have been diverse, but especially important has been family history and genealogy, local and community history, and the history of football. It has been a privilege to get to know scholars in these fields, and sometimes to end up as friends. The following individuals have helped me significantly: Royston Jones has been an invaluable source of interesting evidence about Alf Ramsey's ancestry, and an inspiration in the complex field of family history; I really enjoyed our chats at Valence House and walks around Beacontree. I am grateful to John Grimme and Tony Benton for meeting with me and sharing local knowledge and photographs, some of which are in the book; to the Barking Historical Society for useful materials on their website; and to Valence House Museum and Steve Bolton for interesting displays and exhibitions featuring football's place in local history.

Many other people have been kind enough to chat online and share time, knowledge and resources: Sheila Herd about Ramsey family history, Phil Sammons about the games Alf played for Essex Schoolboys, Alex Alexandrou and James Inglis about his army days, and Duncan Holley and David Bull about key aspects of Alf Ramsey's Southampton playing career. It has been fascinating and important to talk with Maggie Ferris about her father, Denis Follows, and grateful thanks to her for sharing documents, images and memories.

Similarly, these people have graciously shared direct memories of Alf through oral history interviews during this book's research: David Barber, John Booth, Pat Day, Margaret Fulljames, Sir Geoff Hurst, Bill Turner and John Wood. Thanks also to Peter Chapman, Alan Maltpress and Denis Newell for friendly online or face-to-face sharing of other memories, to Jonny Brogden for helping with translations, to Neil Roskilly for taking photographs, and to Mark Chipperfield and Ed Hanson for crucial deadline assists. Conversations with Susan Gardiner over a decade ago helped confirm my interest in Alf, as have more recent events hosted by the Ipswich Town Heritage Society, ably led by Tim and Liz Edwards.

Most historical books draw on the different types of sources mentioned above, but to become history their evidence needs sharpening with questions, and the answers then shaped into narrative. Many people have helped me with that but I am especially grateful to: Phil Renshaw and David McComish for reading all or most of the proposed book, and to Gavin Barber, Anna Bage, Jane Bage, Tom Bage, Chloe Davies, David Luxton, Jennie McCluskey, Diane Rich and Ralph Turner for reviewing drafts of proposals, chapters and sections, long before publication.

Enthusiasm feeds research, and many people have helped sustain mine when the going has proved tough. At crucial moments Ed Davison made suggestions, Paul Hayward was generous, David Luxton was positive, and Billy Bragg was interested. Particular thanks go to everyone involved in the Turnstile Blues collective. Over the last decade and more you have kept alive the hope that football can be thoughtful as well as fun, and I am particularly grateful to Gavin Barber, Emma Corlett, Rob Freeman, Stuart Hellingsworth, Matt Makin, Steve Moore, Alasdair Ross and Stephen Skeet for their camaraderie in fandom, and personal encouragement of this book.

Other friends and family members have shown similar kind and shrewd interest during conversations over many years, including: Zina Bage, Jonny Brogden, Pete and Amanda Carpenter, John Dixon, Mary Jane Drummond, Luke Grisoni, Jeannie and Matthew Grisoni, Richard Hatfield, Marcus Kohler, Geoffrey Leigh, Carenza Lewis, Fiona Mannion, Michael McCluskey, David McComish, Chris and Jenny Neild, Peter D'Sena, Lisa and Dickon Turner, Andrea, Anna and David Turner, John Turner and Igor Wowk. At Pitch Publishing, Jane Camillin and Clive Hetherington have offered timely and wise editorial advice, fellow authors Matt Tiller and Jon Berry genuine encouragement, and I am grateful to Duncan Olner for the cover design, and Chris Eldergill, and Alex Daley for planning promotions.

The men's book group I belong to has lent convivial support for the processes of reading, thinking and chatting about books, which is a handy bedrock when you are trying to write one, and the Pembroke Ramblers have been consistently encouraging. Similarly, playing football with friends on Tuesdays and Fridays might confirm our mutual ageing, but it rekindles enthusiasm for the serious nonsense that is recreational football. Alf Ramsey would have approved, for he despised writers with no practical experience of just how hard it is to make a football obey orders.

Finally, I offer heartfelt thanks to my wife Jane, and the rest of our family, for your tolerance of being bombarded at random moments by unprompted anecdotes about Alf Ramsey, and observations about why his life still matters. Thank you for looking after me, whilst I was trying to look after him.

REFERENCES

Introducing the evidence referenced in
this book's endnotes

The purpose of endnotes is to share with readers, chapter by chapter, the evidence on which this book's arguments have been made. The purpose of this references section is then to enable anyone with a deeper interest to visit that evidence for themselves, when it is held in public places such as archives, articles, books, broadcasts, libraries, museums, publications or websites.

Newspapers, magazines and other publicly available publications are frequently referred to, especially in this book's main text, but also in endnotes. Whenever this happens their titles are italicised and a date provided, for example *Bury Free Press* (20 December 1926).

Four other types of publicly available key evidence are also regularly cited within the endnotes, signalled by four slightly different styles of font and presentation. In an approximate order of frequency, these four types of evidence are:

Types of evidence	*Abbreviated in endnotes as:*	*Cited fully in the 'References' section as:*
1. Books and articles	Hayward, P. (2022) p.252 *[shows author name, date and relevant page number]*	Hayward, P. (2022) *England Football The Biography 1872–2022* London: Simon & Schuster *[shows author name, date, title and publisher]*
2. Archive collections	**Valence House Archive and Local Studies Centre** *[shows location of archive and references for any document cited]*	**Valence House Archive & Local Studies Centre** Various documents, maps, oral history booklets and reminiscences *[shows location of archive and general guidance about the types of material drawn on in this book]*

3. Web-based material	The Spectrum website (2025) 'Autism characteristics: checklist for adults' *[shows website name, any date and title of section]*	The Spectrum website (2025) 'Autism characteristics: checklist for adults' https://thespectrum.org.au/autism-diagnosis/checklist-adults/ *[shows website name, any date, title of section and URL]*
4. Broadcast material	**Channel 4** (2002) *Sir Alf* Director Ken McGill *[shows series title, date, and episode]*	**Channel 4** (2002) *Sir Alf* Director Ken McGill https://licensing.screenocean.com/record/216437 *[shows series title, date, episode and other useful information, e.g. URL if accessible via web]*

BOOKS AND ARTICLES

Alldritt, K. (1997) *W.B. Yeats The Man And The Milieu* London: John Murray

Anti-Bullying Alliance and Friends, Families and Travellers (2020) *Bullied, Not Believed and Blamed: The Experiences of Gypsy, Roma and Traveller Pupils – Recommendations for Schools and Other Settings* London: National Children's Bureau

Badawi, Z. (2024) *An African History Of Africa* London: Penguin

Bage, G. (1999) *Narrative Matters: Teaching and Learning History Through Story* London: Routledge

Bage, G. (2000a) *Thinking History 4-14: Teaching, Learning, Curricula and Communities* London: Routledge

Bage, G. (2000b) 'Tales for millennial teaching?' *Education 3-13*, 28:1 pp.9-15

Bage, G. (2016) *The Story Of Football* London: HarperCollins

Baldwin, T. and Stears, M. (2024) *Seven Myths That Changed A Country – And How To Set Them Straight* London: Bloomsbury

Bartlett, D. (1910) 'Traces of Gypsy Settlements in England' in *Journal of the Gypsy Lore Society* January 1, 1910 (4)

Beales, D. (1980) 'History and Biography: an inaugural lecture' in *History and Biography – Essays in Honour of Derek Beales* Editors Blanning, T. and Cannadine, D. p.277

Belton, B. (2002) *When West Ham Went To The Dogs* Stroud: History Press

Benjamin, M. (2016) *Complete Communities or Dormitory Towns? Case Studies in Interwar Housing.* University of Hertfordshire: MA Research Thesis

THE UNSEEN SIR ALF

Binder, P. (1975) *The Pearlies: A Social Record* London: Jupiter Books

Bloch, M. (2015) *Closet Queens: Some 20th-century British Politicians*

Bogdanor, V. (2015) Gresham College 20 January Lecture 'The General Election: February 1974' https://www.gresham.ac.uk/watch-now/general-election-february-1974

Bogdashina, O. (2016 2nd edition) *Sensory Perceptual Issues in Autism and Asperger Syndrome* London: Jessica Kingsley

Bowers, J. (no date) *The Travellers Times Online FAQ Pack Gypsies and Travellers Lifestyle, History and Culture* https://www.travellerstimes.org.uk/sites/default/files/paragraphs/filelink/Gypsies%20and%20Travellers%20Lifestyle%20History%20and%20Culture%20FAQs_0.pdf

Bowler, D. (1999 edition, first published 1998) *Winning Isn't Everything: A Biography of Sir Alf Ramsey* London: Orion Books

Bowler, D. (2021) *The Prime Ministers of Football: Sir Alf Ramsey: England 1973* Self-published

Bradshaw, S. (2012) *Asperger's Syndrome – That Explains Everything* London: Jessica Kingsley

Bragg, B. (2006) *The Progressive Patriot* London: Transworld Press

Bragg, B. (2008) 'New Traditions For An Old Country' in *Imagined Nation: England After Britain* Edited by Mark Perryman London: Lawrence & Wishart

Breslow, M. (2020) 'Neurodiversity – The New Normal' in *Autism Spectrum News*, issue 1568, 1 January 2020

Brewster, B. (1993) *The Sports Historian* 'When Saturday Comes and other Football Fanzines' Volume 13 (1)

Brooks, M. (2011) *Ipswich Town: Champions 1961-62* Stroud: The History Press

Buckle, S. (2015) *The Way Out: A History of Homosexuality in Modern Britain* London: L.B. Tauris

Bull, D. (2004) *Dell Diamond* Bristol: Hagiology Publishing

Butler, B. (1991) *The Official History of the Football Association* London: MacDonald

Calvin, M. (2018) *State of Play* London: Century

Campbell, T. (2023) 'The enemy within': football hooliganism and the Miners' Strike, *Sport in History*, 43:1

Carter, N. (2006) *The Football Manager: A History* London: Taylor and Francis

Chapman, P. (2016) *Out Of Time: 1966 and the End of Old-Fashioned Britain* London: Bloomsbury

Chisari, F. (2004) 'Shouting Housewives!' The 1966 World Cup and British Television, *Sport in History*, 24:1

Cohen, G. (2005 edition) *My Autobiography* London: Headline

Collicott, S. (2007) 'The 200th Anniversary of the Slave Trade Abolition Act' in *Race Equality Teaching* Volume 26 (1)

Cook, M., Mills, R., Trumbach, R., Cocks, H. (2007) *A Gay History of Britain* Oxford: Greenwood World Publishing

Cooney, B. (2011) *Fingerprints of a Football Rascal* (Kindle edition)

Cowley, J. (2022) *Who Are We Now? Stories of Modern Englishness* London: Picador

Cressy, D. (2018) *Gypsies an English History* Oxford: Oxford University Press

Crocker, A. & Smith, S. (2019) 'Person-first language: are we practicing what we preach?' *Journal of Multidisciplinary Healthcare*

Crossley, A. (2007) editor *Taking it on the Chin* Chingford: Leyton & Leytonstone Historical Society

Darlow, M. (2000) *Terence Rattigan: The Man and his Work* London: Quarter Books

Dawson, J. (2001) *Back Home: England and the 1970 World Cup* London: Orion Books

Day, P. (2000) 'The administration of football in the twenty-first century', *Soccer & Society*, 1:1, pp.72-78

Diangelo, R. (2018) *White Fragility: Why It's So Hard For White People To Talk About Race* London: Penguin Random House

Dickie, J. (2020) *The Craft: How Freemasons Shaped The Modern World* London: Hodder & Stoughton

Dickinson, M. (2014) *Bobby Moore: The Man in Full* London: Yellow Jersey Press

Duke-Evans, J. (2023) *An English Tradition? The History and Significance of Fair Play* Oxford: University Press

Eastwood, J. and Moyse, T. (1986) *The Men Who Made The Town* Almeida Books: Sudbury

Edgerton, D. (2014) 'Doomed to Failure? Wilson's "white heat of the scientific revolution" and renewal of Britain' in *British Politics Review* 9 (3)

Edworthy, N. (2000 edition) *The Second Most Important Job In The Country* London: Virgin Publishing

Evans, C. (2021) *Don Revie: The Biography* London: Bloomsbury

Filho, M. (2021 edition) *The Black Man In Brazilian Soccer* translated by Jack Draper: University of North Carolina Press

Finn, R. (1951) *My Greatest Game* London: Saturn Press

Finn, R. (1970) *World Cup 1970* London: Robert Hale

Fisher, T. (2010) 'Football and Fascism' in *History Today*, Volume 60, Issue 6

Foster, R.F. (2003) *W.B. Yeats: A Life* Oxford: Oxford University Press Volume II

Fryer, P. (2018) *Staying Power: The History of Black People in Britain* London: Pluto Press

Garnett, T. (2002) *100 Greats Ipswich Town Football Club* Stroud: Tempus Publishing

Ghaziuddin, M. (2018) *Medical Aspects of Autism and Asperger Syndrome: A Guide for Parents and Professionals* London: Jessica Kingsley

Glanville, B. (1973) *The Sunday Times History Of The World Cup* London: Times Newspapers

Glanville, B. (1980 edition) *The History of the World Cup* London: Faber and Faber

Glanville, B. (2004 edition) *Football Memories* London: Robson Books

Glanville, B. (2008 edition) *England Managers: The Toughest Job In Football* London: Headline Publishing

Godfrey, G. and Goldsmith, R. (1966) *The History of the Duke of Cornwall's Light Infantry* London: The Regimental History Committee

Goldblatt, D. (2007) *The Ball Is Round* London: Penguin Books

Goldblatt, D. (2015 edition) *The Game of Our Lives* London: Random House

Greaves, J. with Giller, N. (1993 edition) *Don't Shoot The Manager* London: Boxtree Ltd.

Griffin, P. and Martin, H. (2021) 'The 1919 "race riots" – Within and beyond exceptional moments in South Shields and Glasgow' in *Political Geography* vol.88

Hadgraft, R. (2002) *Ipswich Town: Champions of England 1961-62* Westcliff-on-Sea: Desert Island Books

Hamill, J. and Prescott, A. (2006) 'The Masons' Candidate': New Welcome Lodge No. 5139 and the Parliamentary Labour Party in *Labour History Review* 71 (1)

Hamilton, D. (2023) *Answered Prayers: England and the 1966 World Cup* London: riverrun

Hayward, P. (2022) *England Football The Biography 1872–2022* London: Simon & Schuster

Heffer, S. (2022) editor *Diaries of Henry 'Chips' Channon*, Volume 3 1943–57 London: Penguin Books

Henderson, J. (2013) *The Wizard: The Life of Stanley Matthews* London: Yellow Jersey Press

Henderson, M. (2008) Larry Carberry in *Match of My Life: Ipswich Town* Studley: Know The Score Books

Henderson, M. (2009) *Mr John – John Cobbold: The Most Eccentric Man In Football Ever* Studley: Know The Score Books

Hetherington, C. and Hetherington, J. (2024) *Lions in the Wilderness: England's Decade of Decline* Chichester: Pitch Publishing

Higgins, P. (1996) *Heterosexual Dictatorship* London: Fourth Estate

Hodges, C. (2014) *Cobbold & Kin: Life Stories from an East Anglian Family* Woodbridge: The Boydell Press

Holley, D. (2022) *Fireworks, Flash-Lights And Football: Southampton FC's 1948 tour to Brazil* Southampton: awaiting Publication

Hopcraft, A. (1968) *The Football Man* London: Aurum Press (2006) edition

Howell, D. (1990) *Made in Birmingham* London McDonald: Queen Anne Press

Hoyland, J. (1816) *A Historical Survey of the Customs, Habits, & Present State of the Gypsies* York: Alexander

Hudson, W.H. (1909) *A Shepherd's Life: Impressions of the South Wiltshire Downs* London: Methuen

Hughson, J. (2016) *England and the 1966 World Cup: A Cultural History* Manchester: Manchester University Press

Hurst, G. (2006 edition) *My Autobiography: 1966 And All That* London: Headline Publishing

Hurst, G. (2024) *Geoff Hurst Last Boy of '66: My Story Of England's World Cup Winning Team* London: Penguin

Hutchinson, R. (1995) *The Real Story Of England's 1966 World Cup Triumph* London: Mainstream Publishing

Ipsos MORI (2021) *Public attitudes towards offensive language on TV and Radio: Quick Reference Guide.* Ipsos MORI research for Ofcom London: Ipsos MORI Public Affairs

Jablonski, J. and Chaplin, G. (2010) 'Human Skin Pigmentation as an Adaptation to UV Radiation', chapter nine in *In the Light of Evolution IV: The Human Condition* editors Avise, J. and Ayala, F. Washington: National Academies Press

Jacobs, C. (2022) editor *A New Formation: How Black Footballers Shaped The Modern Game* London: Penguin Random House

Jenkinson, J. (2008) *Black 1919: Riots, Racism and Resistance in Imperial Britain* Liverpool: Liverpool University Press

Jivani, A. (1997) *It's Not Unusual* London: Michael O'Mara Books

Kenney, J. (2016) *Brought to Light: Contemporary Freemasonry, Meaning, and Society* Wilfrid Laurier University Press

Kendrick, D. (2004) *The Romani World – A Historical Dictionary of the Gypsies* University of Hertfordshire Press.

Kent, G. (2007) *The Great White Hopes: The Quest to Defeat Jack Johnson* Cheltenham: The History Press

Kuper, S. (2011) 'Sports Populism' in *Americas Quarterly* 5 August: https://www.americasquarterly.org/sports-populism/

Kuper, S. (2016) 'Why England Won' in *1966 And All That* London: Repeater Books edited by Perryman, M.

Kynaston, D. (2009) *Family Britain 1951–57* New York: Walker Press

Lawrence, J. (2003) 'Forging a Peaceable Kingdom: War, Violence, and Fear of Brutalization in Post–First World War Britain' *The Journal of Modern History*, Vol. 75 (3) pp. 557-589

Laybourn, K. (2019) *Going To The Dogs: A History of Greyhound Racing in Britain* Manchester: Manchester University Press

Liew, J. (2021) 'The Yorkshire cricket scandal shows that racism remains entrenched and insidious' *New Statesman* Volume 150 no.5646 19-25 November 2021

Lucas, C. (2024) *Another England: How to Reclaim Our National Story* London: Penguin

Marquis, M. (1970) *Sir Alf Ramsey: Anatomy of a Football Manager* London: Arthur Barker

Matthews, S. (2000) *The Way It Was* London: Headline Publishing

Mayall, D. (1981) *Itinerant Minorities In England and Wales in the Nineteenth and Early Twentieth Centuries: A Study of Gypsies, Tinkers, Hawkers and Other Travellers* Sheffield University D.Phil. thesis

Mayall, D. (2009 edition) *Gypsy-travellers in nineteenth century society* Cambridge: CUP

Mayes, H. (1967) *The Football Association World Cup Report 1966* London: William Heinemann

McColl, G. (1998) *England: The Alf Ramsey Years* London: Andre Deutsch/The FA

McKinstry, L. (2003 edition) *Jack and Bobby* London: Collins Willow

McKinstry, L. (2007 edition, first published 2006) *Sir Alf* London: Harper Collins paperback edition

McMaster, A. and Bairner, A. (2012) 'Junior Ministers in the UK: The Role of the Minister for Sport' in *Parliamentary Affairs* 65

Mills, R. (2016) 'An Exception in War and Peace: Ipswich Town Football Club c. 1907–1945' *Sport in History* 36, 2, pp.214-241

Mitchell, A.M. (1999) *Fascism in East Anglia: the British Union of Fascists in Norfolk, Suffolk and Essex, 1933–1940*. PhD thesis, University of Sheffield https://etheses.whiterose.ac.uk/3071/

Morse, G. (2016) *Sir Walter Winterbottom* London: John Blake Publishing

Okwonga, M. (2022) 'Tomorrow Never Came' pp.46-7 in *A New Formation* ed. Jacobs, C. London: Penguin Random House

Olechnowicz, A. (1997) *Working Class Housing in England Between the Wars: the Becontree Estate* Oxford: Clarendon Press

Olusoga, D. (2021 edition) *Black and British: A Forgotten History* London: Picador

Orwell, G. (1945) 'The Sporting Spirit' in *Notes on Nationalism* London: Penguin (2018 edition)

Orwell, G. (1952) 'Such, Such Were The Joys' In *A Collection of Essays* Boston: Houghton Mifflin Harcourt (1981 edition)

Overy, R. (2010) *The Battle of Britain* London: Penguin

Oxbury, P. (2014) *The League of Forgotten Men* Norwich: Paul Oxbury Books Passingham, I. (2016) *66: The World Cup in Real Time* Brighton: Pitch Publishing

Perryman, M. (2016) 'They Thought It Was All Over' in *1966 And Not All That* Edited by Mark Perryman, London: Repeater Books

Peters, J. and Edmundson, J. (1955) *In The Long Run* London: Cassell

Peters, M. and McNeill, T. (1970) *Mexico 70* London: Cassell

Pethania, Y., Murray, H., Brown, D. (2018) 'Living A Life That Should Not Be Lived: A Qualitative Analysis of the Experience of Survivor Guilt' *Journal of Traumatic Stress Disorders & Treatment* 7 (1)

Petrolini, V., Jorba, M., Vicente, A. (2023) 'What does it take to be rigid? Reflections on the notion of rigidity in autism' in *Frontiers in Psychiatry*

Phillips, N. (2007) *Doctor To The World Champions* UK: Trafford Publishing

Polley, M. (1998) 'The Diplomatic Background to the 1966 Football World Cup', *Sports Historian*, 18:2

Porter, D. (2000) 'Amateur football in England, 1948–63: The Pegasus phenomenon', *Contemporary British History*, 14:2, 1-30

Porter, D. (2009) 'Egg and Chips with the Connellys: Remembering 1966', *Sport in History*, 29:3

Powell, H. (2021) 'Living It' in Holding, M. and Hawkins, E. (2021) *Why We Kneel, How We Rise* London: Simon and Schuster

Preston, P. (2011) 'A Catalan contribution to the myth of the contubernio Judeo-Masónico-Bolchevique' *Modern Italy*, 16:4

Ramsey, A. (1952) *Talking Football* London: Stanley Paul

Richards, R. (1985) *Biographical Memoirs of Fellows of the Royal Society* Volume 31 'Harold Warris Thompson'

Roberts, A, (2001) 'Prime Minister Halifax: Great Britain makes peace with Germany, 1940' in *The Collected What If? Eminent Historians Imagine What Might Have Been* (2001) Edited by Cowley, R. New York: Penguin

Robson, R. (2005) *Farewell But Not Goodbye* London: Hodder & Stoughton

Rowlinson, J. (2016) *Boys of 66* London: Random House

Russell, D. (1997) *Football and the English* Preston: Carnegie Publishing

Sandbrook, D. (2012) *Seasons In The Sun: The Battle For Britain 1974–79* London: Penguin

Schama, S. (2003 edition) *A History Of Britain 1776–2000* London: BBC Worldwide

Scott, W. (1817) *Rob Roy* Edinburgh: Archibald Constable: https://www.gutenberg.org/files/7025/7025-h/7025-h.htm 1893 classic edition Volume II, chapter 17

Scovell, B. (2005) *Football Gentry: The Cobbold Brothers* Gloucestershire: Tempus Publishing

Scovell, B. (2006) *The England Managers: The Impossible Job* Stroud: Tempus

Shaw-Kennedy, R. (1969) *Biography of Arthur Villiers* Privately published

Shawcross, J.P. (1904) *A History of Dagenham in the County of Essex* London: Skeffington

Shepherdson, H. (1968) *The Magic Sponge* London: Pelham Books

Sibaja, R. (2013) *Animales! Civility, Modernity, and Constructions of Identity in Argentine Soccer, 1955–1970* Dissertation for Doctor of Philosophy, George Mason University, North Carolina, USA

Smith, H. (2012) *A Study of Working-Class Men Who Desired Other Men in the North of England c. 1895–1957* University of Sheffield Ph.D. thesis

Smith, M.T. (2001) 'Estimates of cousin marriage and mean inbreeding in the United Kingdom from *birth briefs*', *Journal of Biosocial Science*, 33 (1)

Speight, J. (1973) *Alf Garnett Till Death Us Do Part: Scripts Written and Selected by Johnny Speight* London: Woburn Press

Spurling, J. (2022) *Get It On: How The 70s Rocked Football* London: Biteback Publishing

Tammet, D. (2024) *Nine Minds* London: Profile Books

Taverner, C. (2023) *Street Food: Hawkers And The History Of London* Oxford: OUP

Taylor, B. (2014) *Another Darkness Another Dawn: A History of Gypsies, Roma and Travellers* London: Reaktion Books

Taylor, B. & Hinks, J. (2021) 'What field? Where? Bringing Gypsy, Roma and Traveller history into view', *Cultural and Social History*, DOI: 10.1080/14780038.2021.1960552

Theodore, T. (2022) 'Life at the Vanguard, Again and Again' in Jacobs, C. editor *A New Formation: How Black Footballers Shaped The Modern Game* London: Penguin Random House

Thomas, D. (2013) *Jimmy Adamson: The Man Who Said 'No' To England* Durrington: Pitch Publishing

Thompson, T. (1926) 'Gypsy Marriage In England' in *Journal of the Gypsy Lore Society*

Ticher, M. editor (1987) *FOUL: Best of Football's Alternative Paper 1972–1976* London: Simon & Schuster

Tiller, M. (2023) *The Lion Who Never Roared: Jack Leslie* Chichester: Pitch Publishing

Turpin, N. (2023) *Arthur Push-And-Run Rowe* Manchester: Empire Publications

Venables, T., Nottage, J. and Montgomery, A. (2001) *Terry Venables' Football Heroes* London: Virgin Books

Wanga, J. (2022) 'The Accidental Trailblazer' p.119 in Jacobs, C. (2022) editor *A New Formation: How Black Footballers Shaped The Modern Game* London: Penguin Random House

Wansell, G. (2009) *Terence Rattigan: A Biography* London: Fourth Estate

West, J. (1993) *Personal Memories of Dagenham Village* Arthur Stockwell: Devon

Wilkerson, I. (2020) *CASTE: The Lies That Divide Us* London: Penguin Random House

Wilson, J. (2009 edition) *Inverting The Pyramid: The History of Football Tactics* London: Orion Books

Wilson, J. (2023 edition) *Two Brothers: The Life and Times of Bobby and Jack Charlton* Abacus: London

Winner, M. (2006 edition) *Those Feet: An Intimate History of English Football* London: Bloomsbury

Wolstenholme, K. (1996) *They Think It's All Over ... Memories Of The Greatest Day In English Football* London: Robson Books

Wrack, S. (2023) *A Woman's Game* London: Guardian Faber

Young, T. (1934) *Becontree and Dagenham: A Report Made For The Pilgrim Trust* London: Sidders and Son

ARCHIVE COLLECTIONS

The text draws on multiple commonly available archival and documentary sources. For the sake of brevity, most examples have not been individually referenced but they include: census returns and registers from 1841–1939, court and criminal records, birth, death, and marriage certificates, newspapers, directories and other printed information. Such records have been accessed through subscription or purchase from online archive collections, primarily **Find*my*past**, **Ancestry**, and the **General Record Office**.

Other key archival collections referenced in the text, currently unavailable online, but which can be visited in person include:

1st Battalion DCLI War Diary National Archives WO 166 and 169 (various) 1943–46

6th Battalion DCLI War Diary National Archives WO 166 (various) 1940–42

Blything Petty Sessions Court Register 1954 Suffolk Record Office BB2/1/3/1

Bodmin Keep – Cornwall's Army Museum

Dagenham Parish Council Minute Book 1894–1908 Valence House Archive & Local Studies Centre BD75/A/1/1

East Suffolk Petty Sessional Division of Blything Suffolk Record Office B105/2/127

East Suffolk Quarter Sessions 1950–62 Suffolk Record Office: B105/2/127

FA Archive of 1966 Congratulatory Letters FA Headquarters Library, Wembley Stadium

FA Consultative Committee minutes, FA Council minutes, FA Minutes And Proceedings as above, also National Football Museum Archive Preston

FOUL Cambridge University Library

Ipswich Town Minute Book 1947–58 Suffolk Record Office GC 426/2/2/2

Journal of the DCLI Imperial War Museum and Bodmin Keep – Cornwall's Army Museum

Minute Book Brentwood and District Elementary Schools Football League 1901–1935 Essex Record Office D/2 521/1

Museum of Freemasonry Freemasons Hall, London

Preston North End Minute Book National Football Museum Archive Preston

Professional Papers of Sir Harold Warris Thompson Royal Society Archive HWT 48 2 E7

Up The Manor Oral History Project Bishopsgate Institute London

Valence House Archive & Local Studies Centre Various documents, maps, oral history booklets and reminiscences

WEB-BASED MATERIAL (accessed April 2025)

Another View From The Tower website (1 July 2020) 'Blackpool's first ever black player' https://avftt.co.uk/index.php?threads/blackpool%E2%80%99s-first-ever-black-player.5888/

Anti-Capitalist Resistance website (10 July 2021) Kellaway, D. 'More Than Just A Game – What We Can Learn From The Euros' https://anticapitalistresistance.org/more-than-just-a-game-what-we-can-learn-from-the-euros/

Barking and District Historical Society website (9 October 2014) Robert Tanner 'Beacontree Simister Football League' http://www. barkinghistory.co.uk/beacontree-simister.html

Barking & Dagenham website (no date) 'Population and demographics' 2021 census https://www.lbbd.gov.uk/council-and-democracy/ statistics-and-data/population-and-demographics

Barking & Dagenham website (no date) 'About the Borough – About Becontree ward' https://www.lbbd.gov.uk/council-and-democracy/ statistics-and-data/about-borough

BBC2 (2022) 'Inside Our Autistic Minds' website https://www.bbc. co.uk/programmes/p0bbnh47

BBC Culture website (14 April 2021) 'The School That Rules Britain' John Self https://www.bbc.com/culture/article/20210413-the-school-that-rules-britain

BBC Home website (15 October 2014) 'WW2 People's War – A Quarryman's Tale' https://www.bbc.co.uk/history/ww2peopleswar/ stories/81/a6824081.shtml

BBC News website (1997) 'Politics 97' https://www.bbc.co.uk/news/ special/politics97/background/pastelec/ge74oct.shtml

BBC News website (1 May 1999) 'Your Tributes to Sir Alf Ramsey' http://news.bbc.co.uk/1/hi/uk/332698.stm

BBC News website (28 December 2003) 'Obituary Sir Alan Bates' http:// news.bbc.co.uk/1/hi/uk/3352149.stm

BBC News website (11 July 2016) 'How Africa boycotted the 1966 World Cup' https://www.bbc.co.uk/news/world-africa-36763036

BBC News website (18 June 2018) 'World Cup winner Sir Alf Ramsey's England job letter fetches £3,400' https://www.bbc.co.uk/news/uk-england-suffolk-44475075

BBC News website (17 August 2019) 'Tony Martin: Man who shot burglars knows he still divides opinion' https://www.bbc.co.uk/news/ uk-england-norfolk-49355814

BBC News website (12 July 2022) 'Gary Lineker stays top of BBC star pay list' https://www.bbc.co.uk/news/62122985

BBC Sport website (6 November 2009) 'Ramsey statue unveiled at Wembley' http://news.bbc.co.uk/sport1/hi/football/ internationals/8347830.stm

BBC Sport website (9 April 2013) 'Margaret Thatcher's sporting legacy' https://www.bbc.co.uk/sport/22085827

BBC Sport website (10 April 2013) 'Margaret Thatcher "never really understood sport"' https://www.bbc.co.uk/sport/football/22085707

BBC Sport website (18 October 2020) 'Eddie Parris: The forgotten story of the first black footballer to play for Wales': https://www.bbc.co.uk/sport/football/54526475

BBC Sport website (8 October 2022) 'Jack Leslie – the first black player to be picked for England' https://www.bbc.co.uk/sport/av/football/63185134

Conrad Brunstrom blog (2 June 2020) 'Thoughts of Chairman Alf. Johnny Speight would have been 100 years old today' https://conradbrunstrom.wordpress.com/2020/06/02/thoughts-of-chairman-alf-johnny-speight-would-have-been-100-years-old-today/

Daily Express website (22 June 2022) 'Lineker's "racist abuse" claims blasted by Daubney' https://www.express.co.uk/showbiz/tv-radio/1628894/Gary-Lineker-racist-abuse-claims-blasted-Martin-Daubney

Digital Newspaper Archive of *El Informador* website (2025) http://hemeroteca.informador.com.mx/#

England Football Online website (24 March 2025) 'England's Coaches/Managers by Points Percentage in All Matches' http://www.englandfootballonline.com/TeamMgr/MgrPtsAll.html

Eton College website (2025) 'Collections – Ventures in giving: the Eton Mission and Manor Boys' Club' https://collections.etoncollege.com/ventures-in-giving-the-eton-mission-and-manor-boys-club/

FA website (no date) 'The Story of Women's Football in England' https://www.thefa.com/womens-girls-football/heritage/kicking-down-barriers

Fan Banter website (no date) 'Gary Lineker receives backlash after speaking out on racist abuse aimed at him' https://fanbanter.co.uk/gary-lineker-receives-backlash-after-speaking-out-on-racist-abuse-aimed-at-him/

FIFA (30 July 2020) website 'England v West Germany 1966 FIFA World Cup Final | Final Replay '66' https://www.youtube.com/watch?v=y3bcX8NaYW0

Football Writers' Association website (10 August 2018) 'Brian Scovell becomes 1st Life Vice-President' https://footballwriters.co.uk/editorial/brian-scovell-becomes-1st-life-vice-president/

Game of the People blog (12 June 2016) Jensen, N. 'Last Hurrah: The meaning of 1966' https://gameofthepeople.com/2016/06/12/last-hurrah-the-meaning-of-1966/

History of the Women's Football Association website (no date) 'Charting the key developments in women's football from 1968 to 1993' https://wfahistory.wordpress.com/wfa-development/personalities-60s-70s/

Imperial War Museum website (2025) '10 Facts About Football in the Second World War' https://www.iwm.org.uk/history/10-facts-about-football-in-the-second-world-war

Imperial War Museum website (2025) '8 Things You Need To Know About The Battle of Britain' https://www.iwm.org.uk/history/8-things-you-need-to-know-about-the-battle-of-britain

Imperial War Museum website (2025) 'The Atomic Bombs That Ended the Second World War' https://www.iwm.org.uk/history/the-atomic-bombs-that-ended-the-second-world-war

Institute of Race Relations website (9 March 2021) Liz Fekete 'Who gets to define racism?' https://irr.org.uk/article/who-gets-to-define-racism/

Internet Archive Pride of Anglia website (2005) 'Alf Ramsey – Your comments' https://web.archive.org/web/20080304043352/http://www.tmwmtt.com/sql/managers/profile.phtml?&managerid=4

Johansen, M. (2013) Blog 'Adventures in the Wild East: the Story of the Eton Manor Boys' Club' https://mjohansenblog.files.wordpress.com/2013/05/adventures-in-the-wild-east_michelle-johansen_2013.pdf

London FA website (2025) 'History of London Football Association' https://www.londonfa.com/about/history

Metro website (23 June 2022) 'Gary Lineker proved that there is no such thing as whiteness' Opinion – Nels Abbey https://metro.co.uk/2022/06/23/gary-lineker-proved-that-there-is-no-such-thing-as-whiteness-16879324/

Movie Scripts website (no date) 'Till Death Us Do Part (1968)' https://stockq.org/moviescript/T/till-death-us-do-part.php

MyLondon website (26 June 2022) Christopher Baughurst 'I'm a Met police officer from the Romani community, I used to hide it but now I want to inspire others' https://www.mylondon.news/news/zone-1-news/im-met-police-officer-romani-24216658

National Anglo-Jewish Heritage Trail website (no date) 'Nat Shaw – the Waterloo Cup and Ipswich Town Football Club' memories from Mavis Sotnick (daughter) and Monica Bogen (niece) http://www.jtrails.co.uk/trails/bury-st.-edmunds/letters/c-706/nat-shaw-the-waterloo-cup-and-ipswich-town-football-club/

National Autistic Society website (14 August 2020) 'Obsessions and repetitive behaviour' https://www.autism.org.uk/advice-and-guidance/topics/behaviour/obsessions/all-audiences

National Autistic Society website (2025) 'What Is Autism?' https://www.autism.org.uk/advice-and-guidance/what-is-autism

National Football Museum website (no date) 'Hall of Fame – Alf Ramsey' https://www.nationalfootballmuseum.com/halloffame/sir-alf-ramsey/

New Statesman website (13 July 2024) 'England After Gareth Southgate' Alex Niven https://www.newstatesman.com/culture/sport/2024/07/england-after-gareth-southgate

NHS website (11 November 2022) 'Signs of autism in adults' https://www.nhs.uk/conditions/autism/signs/adults/ This document will be reviewed in November 2025

Open University website (no date) 'Making Britain: discover how South Asians shaped the Nation 1870–1950' https://www.open.ac.uk/researchprojects/makingbritain/content/1919-race-riots

Reuters website (12 July 2021) 'England's Black players face racial abuse after Euro 2020 defeat' https://www.reuters.com/world/uk/uk-pm-johnson-condemns-racist-abuse-england-soccer-team-2021-07-12/

Romany and Traveller Family History Society website (last updated April 2017) 'Was Your Ancestor A Gypsy?' https://rtfhs.org.uk/gypsy_identity/

Scots Football Worldwide (2025) 'Scott Duncan – and a certain other' https://www.scotsfootballworldwide.scot/scottduncan

Southampton FC Player Archive website (2025) https://www.saintsplayers.co.uk

Sports Journalists' Association website (4 May 2011) 'Fleet St's legendary sportswriter Peter Batt has died' https://www.sportsjournalists.co.uk/the-giller-memorandum/peter-batt-sportswriter-and-eastenders-scriptwriter-has-died/

Surrey County Council website (February 2025) 'Tracing Gypsy Romany and Traveller Ancestors at Surrey History Centre' https://www.surreycc.gov.uk/culture-and-leisure/history-centre/researchers/guides/tracing-gypsy-romany-and-traveller-ancestors

The Fighting Cock website (1 March 2012) 'A Very English Visionary' Cloake, M. https://thefightingcock.co.uk/forum/threads/arthur-rowe.22881/

The Hamlet Historian website (22 December 2014) Jack McKinroy 'Arise Sir Les' http://thehamlethistorian.blogspot.com/2014/12/arise-sir-les.html

The National WWI Museum and Memorial website (no date) 'Red Summer: The Race Riots of 1919' https://www.theworldwar.org/learn/wwi/red-summer

The Orwell Foundation website (20225) https://www.orwellfoundation.com/

The Players' Tribune website (8 June 2021) 'Dear England' Gareth Southgate https://www.theplayerstribune.com/posts/dear-england-gareth-southgate-euros-soccer

The Reclaim Party website (2021) 'Principles' https://reclaim-political-party.squarespace.com/#page-section-61939c936ad585014918b2f7

The Set Pieces website (2015) I. Macintosh 'Vox In The Box: Brian Glanville' https://thesetpieces.com/interviews/vox-box-brian-glanville/

The Spectator website (21 June 2022) Tom Goodenough 'Why won't Gary Lineker name those who racially abused him?' https://www.spectator.co.uk/article/why-won-t-gary-lineker-name-those-who-racially-abused-him-

The Spectator website (2025) 'Leo McKinstry' https://www.spectator.co.uk/writer/leo-mckinstry/

The Spectrum website (2025) 'Autism characteristics: checklist for adults' https://thespectrum.org.au/autism-diagnosis/checklist-adults/

The Tongue of Mars website (no date) 'General BL Montgomery's address to the officers and men of the Eighth Army, Cairo, 13 August 1942' http://www.fieldmarshalmontgomery.com/speech-to-8th-army-upon-assuming-command.html

The Traveller Movement website (2025) 'Romani (Gypsy), Roma and Irish Traveller History and Culture' https://travellermovement.org.uk/gypsy-roma-and-traveller-history-and-culture/

Those Were The Days website (28 April 2022) 'TWTD Replayed – John Elsworthy Interview' https://www.twtd.co.uk/ipswich-town-news/42626/twtd-replayed--john-elsworthy-interview

UK Government website (29 March 2022) 'Gypsy, Roma and Irish Traveller ethnicity summary' https://www.ethnicity-facts-figures.service.gov.uk/summaries/gypsy-roma-irish-traveller/

UK Government website (22 July 2021) 'The national strategy for autistic children, young people and adults: 2021 to 2026' https://www.gov.uk/government/publications/national-strategy-for-autistic-children-young-people-and-adults-2021-to-2026/the-national-strategy-for-autistic-children-young-people-and-adults-2021-to-2026

UK Government website (2025) 'When you can annul a marriage' https://www.gov.uk/how-to-annul-marriage

UK Parliament Committees Correspondence website (16 November 2021) 'Azeem Rafiq Witness Statement to the Leeds employment tribunal' 11 December 2020 p.17 https://committees.parliament.uk/committee/378/digital-culture-media-and-sport-committee/publications/3/correspondence/

UK Parliament website (2025) 'Regulating sex and sexuality: the 20th-century' https://www.parliament.uk/about/living-heritage/transformingsociety/private-lives/relationships/overview/

sexuality20thcentury/#:~:text=Sexual%20Offences%20Act%20
1967,for%20Northern%20Ireland%20until%201982

United Grand Lodge of England website (2025) 'What Is Freemasonry?'
https://www.ugle.org.uk/discover-freemasonry/what-is-freemasonry

Valence House Collections website (no date) 'Dagenham Bomb Map'
https://valencehousecollections.co.uk/browse/dagenham-bomb-map/

Wikipedia website (3 April 2025) 'Alf Ramsey' https://en.wikipedia.org/
wiki/Alf_Ramsey

World Football website (no date) 'Germany – Bundesliga 1971-72' https://
www.worldfootball.net/all_matches/bundesliga-1971-1972/

BROADCAST MATERIAL

BBC Radio 5 Live 'Replay' (released 31 December 2018) *1966 – England
win the World Cup Final* https://www.bbc.co.uk/sounds/play/p06qct94

Channel 4 (2002) *Sir Alf* Director Ken McGill https://licensing.
screenocean.com/record/216437

High Performance podcast (20 June 2022) *Gary Lineker* interviewers
Damian Hughes and Jake Humphrey

History of Football (2001) *Sir Bobby Charlton on Alf Ramsey* https://
www.youtube.com/watch?v=mMlVoWDXAk8

It Was What It Was podcast (2 July 2024) *The End of Sir Alf: The Fall
of England's Greatest Manager* Part 1

It Was What It Was podcast (29 July 2024) *Football's Dirtiest Game Ever:
The Battle of Santiago*

London Weekend Television (1969) *Sir Alf Ramsey – England Soccer Team
Manager* Producer Adrian Metcalfe BFI 74862 https://collections-
search.bfi.org.uk/web/Details/ChoiceFilmWorks/150073518

London Weekend Television (1991) *The Game* Episode 1 presenter Danny
Baker https://www.youtube.com/watch?v=2t1ECK9yWK4&t=267s

Stealing Victory podcast (2020) *The Untold Story of the 1966 World Cup
heist* Pettifor, T. Auddy Limited

INDEX